GALATIANS

THE NIV APPLICATION COMMENTARY

From biblical text . . . to contemporary life

GALATIANS

THE NIV APPLICATION COMMENTARY

From biblical text . . . to contemporary life

SCOT McKNIGHT

ZONDERVAN.com/
AUTHORTRACKER
follow your favorite authors

We want to hear from you. Please send your comments about this book to us in care of zreview@zondervan.com. Thank you.

ZONDERVAN

The NIV Application Commentary: Galatians
Copyright © 1995 by Scot McKnight

Requests for information should be addressed to:
Zondervan, *Grand Rapids, Michigan 49530*

Library of Congress Cataloging-in-Publication Data

McKnight, Scot.
     Galatians / by Scot McKnight.
        p. cm. — (NIV application commentary)
     Includes bibliographical references and index.
     ISBN 978-0-310-48470-7
     1. Bible. N.T. Galatians—Commentaries. I. Bible. N.T. Galatians. English. New International.
1995.   II. Title.   III. Series.
     BS2685.3.M34 1995
     227'.407—dc20   94-18276

Edited by Verlyn D. Verbrugge

Printed in the United States of America

09 10 11 12 13 14 15 16 • 37 36 35 34 32 31 30 29 28 27 26 25 24 23 22 21 20 19

Table of Contents

The NIV Application Commentary Series

When complete, the NIV Application Commentary
will include the following volumes:

To see which titles are available,
visit our web site at http://www.zondervan.com

NIV Application Commentary
Series Introduction

THE NIV APPLICATION COMMENTARY SERIES is unique. Most commentaries help us make the journey from the twentieth century back to the first century. They enable us to cross the barriers of time, culture, language, and geography that separate us from the biblical world. Yet they only offer a one-way ticket to the past and assume that we can somehow make the return journey on our own. Once they have explained the *original meaning* of a book or passage, these commentaries give us little or no help in exploring its *contemporary significance*. The information they offer is valuable, but the job is only half done.

Recently, a few commentaries have included some contemporary application as *one* of their goals. Yet that application is often sketchy or moralistic, and some volumes sound more like printed sermons than commentaries.

The primary goal of The NIV Application Commentary Series is to help you with the difficult but vital task of bringing an ancient message into a modern context. The series not only focuses on application as a finished product but also helps you think through the *process* of moving from the original meaning of a passage to its contemporary significance. These are commentaries, not popular expositions. They are works of reference, not devotional literature.

The format of the series is designed to achieve the goals of the series. Each passage is treated in three sections: *Original Meaning, Bridging Contexts,* and *Contemporary Significance.*

THIS SECTION HELPS you understand the meaning of the biblical text in its first-century context. All of the elements of traditional exegesis—in concise form—are discussed here. These include the historical, literary, and cultural context of the passage. The authors discuss matters related to grammar and syntax, and the meaning of biblical words. They also seek to explore the main ideas of the passage and how the biblical author develops those ideas.

After reading this section, you will understand the problems, questions, and concerns of the *original audience* and how the biblical author addressed those issues. This understanding is foundational to any legitimate application of the text today.

THIS SECTION BUILDS a bridge between the world of the Bible and the world of today, between the original context and the contemporary context, by focusing on both the timely and timeless aspects of the text.

God's Word is *timely*. The authors of Scripture spoke to specific situations, problems, and questions. Paul warned the Galatians about the consequences of circumcision and the dangers of trying to be justified by law (Gal. 5:2–5). The author of Hebrews tried to convince his readers that Christ is superior to Moses, the Aaronic priests, and the Old Testament sacrifices. John urged his readers to "test the spirits" of those who taught a form of incipient Gnosticism (1 John 4:1–6). In each of these cases, the timely nature of Scripture enables us to hear God's Word in situations that were *concrete* rather than abstract.

Yet the timely nature of Scripture also creates problems. Our situations, difficulties, and questions are not always directly related to those faced by the people in the Bible. Therefore, God's word to them does not always seem relevant to us. For example, when was the last time someone urged you to be circumcised, claiming that it was a necessary part of justification? How many people today care whether Christ is superior to the Aaronic priests? And how can a "test" designed to expose incipient Gnosticism be of any value in a modern culture?

Fortunately, Scripture is not only timely but *timeless*. Just as God spoke to the original audience, so he still speaks to us through the pages of Scripture. Because we share a common humanity with the people of the Bible, we discover a *universal dimension* in the problems they faced and the solutions God gave them. The timeless nature of Scripture enables it to speak with power in every time and in every culture.

Those who fail to recognize that Scripture is both timely and timeless run into a host of problems. For example, those who are intimidated by timely books such as Hebrews or Galatians might avoid reading them because they seem meaningless today. At the other extreme, those who are convinced of the timeless nature of Scripture, but who fail to discern its timely element, may "wax eloquent" about the Melchizedekian priesthood to a sleeping congregation.

The purpose of this section, therefore, is to help you discern what is timeless in the timely pages of the New Testament—and what is not. For example, if Paul's primary concern is not circumcision (as he tells us in Gal. 5:6), what *is* he concerned about? If discussions about the Aaronic priesthood or Melchizedek seem irrelevant today, what is of abiding value in these passages? If people try to "test the spirits" today with a test designed for a specific first-century heresy, what other biblical test might be more appropriate?

Yet this section does not merely uncover that which is timeless in a passage but also helps you to see *how* it is uncovered. The author of the commentary seeks to take what is implicit in the text and make it explicit, to take a process that normally is intuitive and explain it in a logical, orderly fashion. How do we know that circumcision is not Paul's primary concern? What clues in the text or its context help us realize that Paul's real concern is at a deeper level?

Of course, those passages in which the historical distance between us and the original readers is greatest require a longer treatment. Conversely, those passages in which the historical distance is smaller or seemingly nonexistent require less attention.

One final clarification. Because this section prepares the way for discussing the contemporary significance of the passage, there is not always a sharp distinction or a clear break between this section and the one that follows. Yet when both sections are read together, you should have a strong sense of moving from the world of the Bible to the world of today.

THIS SECTION ALLOWS the biblical message to speak with as much power today as it did when it was first written. How can you apply what you learned about Jerusalem, Ephesus, or Corinth to our present-day needs in Chicago, Los Angeles, or London? How can you take a message originally spoken in Greek and Aramaic and communicate it clearly in our own language? How can you take the eternal truths originally spoken in a different time and culture and apply them to the similar-yet-different needs of our culture?

In order to achieve these goals, this section gives you help in several key areas.

First, it helps you identify contemporary situations, problems, or questions that are truly comparable to those faced by the original audience. Because contemporary situations are seldom identical to those faced in the first century, you must seek situations that are analogous if your applications are to be relevant.

Second, this section explores a variety of contexts in which the passage might be applied today. You will look at personal applications, but you will also be encouraged to think beyond private concerns to the society and culture at large.

Third, this section will alert you to any problems or difficulties you might encounter in seeking to apply the passage. And if there are several legitimate ways to apply a passage (areas in which Christians disagree), the author will bring these to your attention and help you think through the issues involved.

In seeking to achieve these goals, the contributors to this series attempt to avoid two extremes. They avoid making such specific applications that the commentary might quickly become dated. They also avoid discussing the significance of the passage in such a general way that it fails to engage contemporary life and culture.

Above all, contributors to this series have made a diligent effort not to sound moralistic or preachy. The NIV Application Commentary Series does not seek to provide ready-made sermon materials but rather tools, ideas, and insights that will help you communicate God's Word with power. If we help you to achieve that goal, then we have fulfilled the purpose for this series.

— *The Editors*

General Editor's Preface

WHY SHOULD TWENTIETH-CENTURY Christians read Galatians? What application does it have to a church removed from its original audience by nearly two thousand years? That's the question I kept asking myself as I read Scot McKnight's excellent commentary on this letter of Paul. And I found myself coming back again and again to this answer: The book of Galatians speaks to a crucial issue facing the church today, the question of how to exercise visionary leadership. Let me explain.

As editor of *Christianity Today Magazine* and *Leadership Journal* for ten years, I visited hundreds of churches across the country and met thousands of pastors and lay leaders. Among the many things I learned, one issue stands out: how difficult it is to lead a church community today.

It is not difficult, mind you, to *grow* a church, to *manage* the day-to-day affairs of a church, or to *chair* committees and task forces. True leadership, however, is another matter. It's tough to lead primarily because people don't want to be led. If the people won't follow, what's a church leader to do?

Two approaches probably won't help. We can't turn church members into good followers overnight; it takes time to change behavior patterns so deeply entrenched. And it's questionable if more leadership skills or training programs will help. In our managerial age, we have booked, seminared, and tested church leaders to the point of exhaustion. So what can we do?

Enter Paul and Galatians.

One of the major issues facing Paul in dealing with the churches of Galatia was a faction in the church that questioned his authority. He struggled with a group of people who did not want to be led. In this situation, Paul did what most of us would do—he defended himself (see chaps. 1–2). Paul was human, after all. But it's instructive to note the *way* in which Paul defended himself.

Most of us would lash out angrily and then begin toting up our list of accomplishments and reasons why our authority should not be questioned. Paul lashed out too—but not angrily. Paul toted up a list of reasons about how his authority was valid—but what an odd list of reasons. Paul did list his "accomplishments"—sort of. He listed the things in his life that he was surely ashamed of, particularly his former persecution of Christians. His intent was to show the marvelous reversal that had come about when God touched his life. He used his own weakness to show God's strength.

Thus, when Paul defended his authority, he admitted he had none of his own. He claimed his standing came only from God, not from other human beings. And when he defended the content of his preaching, he did not cite its theological coherence and trustworthiness. In fact, Paul didn't talk about "doctrines" at all. He simply wrote: "My gospel is correct because of where it came from—from Jesus Christ."

Paul ended his defense by noting his call. He had not decided to become an apostle to the Gentiles. Rather, God called him to this task, and he could do nothing but obey.

In summary, Paul argued that his effectiveness came about because of his ineffectiveness, that his authority came about because of his submission to God, that the content of his preaching could be traced solely to his reliance on Jesus Christ, and that his biggest claim to fame was that he once was a sinner but now was saved.

It was this approach to visionary leadership that enabled Paul to confront the burning question of Galatians: the relationship of the Mosaic law to the gospel of Jesus Christ. As Scot McKnight so expertly details, Paul challenged the Galatians' mistaken understanding of the law. They were, in effect, creating a new gospel. Had Paul been content to focus on leadership technique and style and to list his leadership accomplishments in the standard way, he would have been implicitly using the same methodology as the "Judaizers." Instead, at every possible point, Paul pointed away from himself toward Jesus Christ. That is the essence of visionary leadership, and that is the essence of Scot McKnight's "new" approach to the book of Galatians.

—*Terry Muck*

Author's Preface

ON A COLD, RAINY NOVEMBER NIGHT in 1971, in Freeport, Illinois, I entered into our local Christian bookstore with my girlfriend to peruse the bookshelves. After a few minutes, I lit upon a yellow and black bound commentary on Galatians by William Hendriksen. I purchased it, not knowing that Galatians would become a fascination of mine for the next twenty years, climaxing in the book before you. That night I began to work through Galatians, verse by verse and passage by passage, until, about a year later, I finished my first inductive Bible study of an entire book. Since then I have preached on, taught, and read through many books on Galatians. It remains my favorite of the Pauline letters. I am thankful to Jack Kuhatschek and Terry Muck for giving me the opportunity of trying my hand at a commentary on this letter. I am thankful because I have stepped out of my area of expertise (Jesus and the Gospels) and have been trusted to walk my own way.

I also did not realize that night that the girlfriend who entered that bookstore with me would become my wife and that she, too, has been with me for over twenty years. From Kristen I have learned more than can be put into many books, but two items must be mentioned. Kris, more than any other human being, has taught me what it means to live both in Christ and through the Spirit, the two main themes of Galatians. As a token of my love for her and as a memorial of thanksgiving for what I have learned from her, I dedicate this book to her. Since the publication of my first book I have waited to dedicate a book to her—a book, I promised her, that would be as practical as it would be appropriate for one dedicated to her. I also hoped that this one would stay in print longer than my previous academic books.

Several others deserve mention for their help in various stages of the progress of this book. David Paul King, now since passed to his eternal reward, was our youth pastor when I began studying Galatians; he suggested Galatians as a suitable book for me to study. George Stiekes was my college pastor and he recommended that I work systematically through Galatians with a high school Sunday school class. That first struggle at trying to make sense of Galatians for others has influenced this book more than I shall ever know. My students at Trinity Evangelical Divinity School, particularly those in our NT 741 Galatians class, have provoked me to further reflection (especially on the relationship of my views of Galatians to Romans) and have frequently forced me to reconsider other options; to them I am deeply indebted. Two Sunday school classes at our current church, Libertyville Evangelical Free Church, have asked me questions and listened to my views in the last year, both with encouragement and queries that have sharpened the contours of my thinking. I am particularly thankful to Roger Scott and Bob Dudley for invitations to address their classes. Our good friend and neighbor, Willa Williams, read the manuscript and asked questions that have been answered in the revisions.

Two scholars deserve special mention for the way in which they have influenced my thinking over the last decade: Professor James D. G. Dunn and E. P. Sanders. The former was my dissertation supervisor, has himself written at length on Galatians in different academic publications, and deserves my heartfelt thanks for his stimulating studies and personal guidance on "matters Galatian." E. P. Sanders, with whom I have breakfasted but once, has influenced my work in massive ways through his major publications. I have followed the light that these two scholars have shed on Galatian problems and theology to the degree that they have become my mentors.

In the first writing up of this book I was also enjoying a marvelous summer with fourteen boys who comprised the Libertyville Little League (Majors Division) All-Star team (for twelve-year-olds). Hardly a practice went by without them asking me if I was done with my book. At one session I promised them that, if they qualified for the Illinois State Tournament in Taylorville, I would mention each of their names. Not only did they qualify, they finished third place. As a tribute to each of these courageous boys who fulfilled part of their dreams to go to the Little League World Series, and for "freeing" me from the computer on sunny afternoons, I mention each of their names: Justin Anderson, Jason Berngard, Scott Carberry, Brad Fiore, Matt Hansen, Mike Lowry, Lukas McKnight, Barth Morreale, Tim Nied, Jim Oboikowitch, John Paraszczak, George Poulos, Jamie Ronin, Mike Ronin, and Mike Ward. I like coaching these boys because of the company it allows me to keep.

Finally, I want to thank the editors of this series who have explored with me the tricky issues of moving from a first-century Diaspora world, struggling to figure out the difference between Christianity and Judaism, to a modern Western society which I struggle to keep up with. I thank Jack Kuhatschek, Marianne Meye Thompson, and Terry Muck, along with the encouragement I received from Eugene Peterson, Klyne Snodgrass, and Stan Gundry. Verlyn Verbrugge looked after the book carefully, from beginning to end, and his insights both as editor and theologian have improved my ideas. To him I am grateful.

Author's Preface

Looking back over the gestation and birth of this book makes me pause to give thanks to God for the gift of Christian community. Without these various people and the Christian communities mentioned, this book would never have been written.

— *Scot McKnight*
Deerfield, Illinois

Works Consulted

The following biblical studies proved helpful in the preparation of this commentary. Many more, of course, could be cited, but it is also my hope to provide for interested readers a brief bibliography, while standard reference works are cited only in the abbreviations that follow. Commentaries that are listed here are mentioned with a brief title in the text.

Selected Bibliography

Aquinas, T. *Commentary on Saint Paul's Epistle to the Galatians.* Albany, N.Y.: Magi Books, 1966.

Barclay, J. M. G. *Obeying the Truth: A Study of Paul's Ethics in Galatians.* Edinburgh: T & T Clark, 1988.

Barrett, C. K. *Freedom and Obligation: A Study of the Epistle to the Galatians.* Philadelphia: Westminster, 1985.

Betz, H. D. *Galatians.* Hermeneia. Philadelphia: Fortress, 1979.

Boice, J. M. "Galatians." In *The Expositor's Bible Commentary*, ed. F. E. Gaebelein. Volume 10. Grand Rapids: Zondervan, 1976, pp. 407-508.

Bruce, F. F. *The Epistle to the Galatians.* NIGTC. Grand Rapids: Eerdmans, 1982.

Burton, E. De Witt. *The Epistle to the Galatians.* ICC. Edinburgh: T & T Clark, 1921.

Dunn, J. D. G. *Jesus, Paul and the Law: Studies in Mark and Galatians.* Louisville, Kentucky: Westminster/John Knox, 1990.

Fung, R. Y. K. *The Epistle to the Galatians.* NIC. Grand Rapids: Eerdmans, 1988.

Guthrie, D. *Galatians.* NCB. Greenwood, South Carolina: Attic Press, 1974.

Hendriksen, W. *Exposition of Galatians.* Grand Rapids: Baker, 1968.

Lightfoot, J. B. *The Epistle of St. Paul to the Galatians.* Grand Rapids: Zondervan, 1971 (reprint of 1865 ed.).

Longenecker, R. N. *Galatians.* WBC 41. Dallas: Word, 1990.

Sanders, E. P. *Jewish Law from Jesus to the Mishnah. Five Studies.* Philadelphia: Trinity Press International, 1990.

Sanders, E. P. *Judaism: Practice and Belief. 63 BCE–66 CE.* Philadelphia: Trinity Press International, 1992.

Sanders, E. P. *Paul.* New York: Oxford University Press, 1991.

Sanders, E. P. *Paul and Palestinian Judaism: A Comparison of Patterns of Religion.* Philadelphia: Fortress, 1977.

Stott, J. R. W. *Only One Way: The Message of Galatians*. BST. Downers Grove, Illinois: InterVarsity, 1968.

Note: The commentary of J. D. G. Dunn (*Galatians;* Peabody, Mass.: Hendrickson, 1993) appeared too late to be of use in this study. I am delighted by the lines he draws in this commentary. Nor was I able to make use of the excellent new compendium of Paul (*Dictionary of Paul and His Churches;* ed. R. P. Martin, G. F. Hawthorne, and D. K. Reid; Downers Grove, Ill.: InterVarsity Press, 1993).

Abbreviations

ABD—*The Anchor Bible Dictionary*. Ed. David N. Freedman. 6 volumes. New York: Doubleday, 1992.

DJG—*Dictionary of Jesus and the Gospels*. Ed. J. B. Green, S. McKnight, and I. H. Marshall. Downers Grove, Ill.: InterVarsity Press, 1992.

EDNT—*Exegetical Dictionary of the New Testament*. Ed. H. Balz, G. Schneider. 3 volumes. Grand Rapids: Eerdmans, 1990–1993.

NIDNTT—*New International Dictionary of New Testament Theology*. Ed. Colin Brown. 3 volumes. Grand Rapids: Zondervan, 1975–1978.

NISBE—*The International Standard Bible Encyclopedia*, new edition. Ed. G. W. Bromiley, et al. 4 volumes. Grand Rapids: Eerdmans, 1979–1988.

TDNT—*Theological Dictionary of the New Testament*. Ed. G. Kittel, G. Friedrich; trans. G. W. Bromiley. 9 volumes. Grand Rapids: Eerdmans, 1964–1974.

Introduction
Legalism Then and Now

THE MODERN, WESTERN READER always collides with the cultural context of the Bible. This collision is routine experience for the one who wants not only to read the Bible well but, more importantly, who wants to make the message of the Bible relevant to our world. It will not do to think that we and the Bible inhabit the same cultural, intellectual, and social world. There are too many differences, too many years, too many miles, and too many social upheavals.

Listen to words of a modern pastor and world-renowned Christian who, perhaps more than any other contemporary, has been used by God to show Bible students everywhere how God speaks from his ancient Word to our modern world:

> Whenever we pick up the Bible and read it, even in a contemporary version like the Good News Bible, we are conscious of stepping back two millennia or (in the case of the Old Testament) even more. We travel backwards in time, behind the microchip revolution, the electronic revolution, the scientific revolution and the industrial revolution, until we find ourselves in an alien world which long ago ceased to exist. In consequence, the Bible feels odd, sounds archaic, looks obsolete and smells musty.[1]

These sane, and entirely accurate, remarks of John Stott express the foundation upon which this commentary is built: to interpret the Bible requires an ability to study two horizons—the ancient horizon and the modern horizon. Furthermore, it requires people who desire to bridge those contexts and make the ancient one speak forcibly to the modern one. This process is performed every time a Christian claims that God has spoken to him or her through his Word. And I believe this happens daily to anyone who listens to God's Word. But I also believe that such an event requires patient observations about the biblical texts and critical discernment of our age. I also know that this maneuver is made by Christians with rarely a reflection upon

---

1. J. R. W. Stott, *The Contemporary Christian: Applying God's Word to Today's World* (Downers Grove, Ill.: InterVarsity Press, 1992), 186.

what is actually going on. This process, both conscious and unconscious, will come to the fore in the pages that follow.

Earlier in the same book, Stott described the entire process in the following category:

> I believe we are called to the difficult and even painful task of "double listening." That is, we are to listen carefully (although of course with differing degrees of respect) both to the ancient Word and to the modern world, in order to relate the one to the other with a combination of fidelity and sensitivity . . . [and] only if we can develop our capacity for double listening, will we avoid the opposite pitfalls of unfaithfulness and irrelevance, and be able to speak God's Word to God's world with effectiveness today.[2]

There are at least three conversations going on simultaneously in this kind of double listening. First, we must be conversant with the ancient world, especially the Jewish world, to understand what God was saying at that time. Second, we must be conversant with our culture—with our economical world, with our political world, with our moral world, with our emotional-psychological world, with our intellectual world, etc. And third, we must be conversant with the changes in our culture. What God said to your parents and mine is probably different than what he is saying to you and me and to our offspring. I am not suggesting here that somehow the gospel has changed. No, the gospel of Jesus Christ is that God brings his love into our lives by his grace through Jesus Christ, and we need simply to respond to him to find that grace. However, the particular crystallizations of that gospel change from generation to generation because our social perceptions change from generation to generation.[3] And the sensitive interpreter of the Bible who wants to make God's Word relevant to our world will be engaged in this conversation of cultural change at the same time he or she interprets the ancient text and our modern world.

It has been said of Karl Barth that he believed the pastor was the one who held the Bible in one hand and the daily newspaper in the other—and it goes without saying that, while the Bible never changes, our newspapers do. This means we need to have cultural sensitivity as we seek to speak to our world today about the good news of Jesus Christ. In the pages that follow, then, I

---

2. Ibid., 13. For his further ideas, see 186–206.

3. A highly sophisticated book, but one that has been used with great profit by theologians and pastors for understanding the importance of culture and society in our perceptions of the world, is P. Berger and T. Luckmann, *The Social Construction of Reality* (New York: Doubleday, 1966).

shall consistently attempt to delineate the ancient context as well as the modern significance of the Word of God. In such a move, however, I shall also attempt to explain how we move from the one to the other. This introduction attempts to move the whole message of Galatians from ancient Turkey to modern society.

THE *ORIGIN* OF Paul's letter to the Galatians is well known: after Paul had evangelized the southern districts of Galatia[4] successfully and established some churches during his first missionary journey, he returned to Antioch (cf. Acts 13–14). While there he caught wind of some Jewish Christian teachers who infiltrated these Galatian churches with a polluted message that was, according to Paul, endangering the entire gospel. For two millennia we have referred to these intruders as the "Judaizers." This term will be used throughout this commentary to refer, not to Jews in general, but to a specific movement in earliest Christianity that believed conversion to Christ also involved a further conversion to their (Pharisaic) form of Judaism.

Before Paul could get off on his second missionary journey (cf. Acts 15:36–18:23), and just before the Apostolic Council of Acts 15, Paul sent this urgent and emotional missive to Galatia with the prayer and hope that it would straighten out the Galatian churches. What happened to the Galatians and how they received Paul's emotional letter, we simply do not know. What we do know is that this letter, penned probably in the late 40s of the first century, has given both life-transforming instruction and heartfelt admonition to the church for nearly two millennia.

The *problem* of the letter to the Galatians is also well known, at least in its general orientation. In a word, the problem was *Judaizing legalism*. But legalism is a tricky term that gives rise to many fashionable applications tailored no doubt to our contemporary churches, and it is here that we first encounter the need to be sensitive both to the ancient world and to our own world. To show the particular angle of this commentary, I will immediately dip into the problem of application. For example, for some people modern-day legalism is the institutional legislation of any specific Christian practice—say, manda-

---

4. More accurately, Paul ministered in the southern districts of the province of Galatia, most probably in and around the cities of Pisidian Antioch, Iconium, Lystra, and Derbe. Scholars have debated whether Galatians was originally written to the southern districts (south Galatian theory) or to the northern districts (north Galatian theory). A convenient and readable summary of the issues and evidence may be found in F. F. Bruce, *Galatians*, 3–18. See also "Original Meaning" at 2:1–10.

tory weekly (or biweekly!) church attendance, a total prohibition of smoking or alcohol consumption for pleasure, separation from ungodly people, overt affiliation with a particular political party, commitment to particular political activities, or the use of a specific translation of the Bible. While the New Testament clearly contains commandments for Christians, some believers think the legislation of anything is modern-day legalism; after all, it is argued, we (Christians) are to be led by the Holy Spirit.

For others, there is a perception that while some specific Christian mores are wholesome and worth legislating, others are left to the individual believer, with all the ambiguity such freedom may create. This so-called "Christian freedom" has given rise, particularly among the Protestant free churches in the United States, to a multitude of emphases and factional interpretations. One needs hardly mention the sad state of affairs produced by local factions in the church, factions that often seem to be rooted in the call to individual freedom as seen in the life and legacy of Martin Luther.

But we are getting ahead of ourselves, for before we can determine just what legalism is *today*, we must determine what legalism was *then*. Application must always follow exegesis and exposition of the Bible. Jumping the gun in Galatians—that is, finding applications of Judaizing legalism in our modern Christian framework before discovering what Paul had in mind—has led to a sad preoccupation of Christian leaders with the Roman Catholic church as the major application of Galatians.[5]

I will argue in what follows that this frequent Protestant interpretation and application is, almost always, a serious misunderstanding both of Galatians and how we should apply Galatians today. So here we must go through Galatians carefully to see what Paul has in mind when he is criticizing the Judaizers. As will be seen, the problem Paul sees in the Judaizers is more than legalism, and in this sense the term *legalism* is not totally satisfactory for describing the problem. However, in light of its widespread usage in the Church, I shall continue to use that term but try to provide a more accurate sketch of what Paul has in mind. What does Galatians teach us here?

Legalism Then—or, Was It Legalism?

TO INTERPRET A biblical book properly means investigating the text in its context. That is, if we want to understand the book of Galatians, we need to know

---

5. This misunderstanding of Galatians and Paul has been thoroughly exposed by E. P. Sanders in his scholarly *Paul and Palestinian Judaism: A Comparison of Patterns of Religion* (Philadelphia: Fortress, 1977). A more popular presentation can be seen in his *Paul* (Past Masters series; New York: Oxford University Press, 1991). See also "Contemporary Significance" at 6:11–18.

something about the course of Paul's life (cf. Acts; Gal. 1–2), about the nature of his opponents, and about the impact of his world (both Jewish and Gentile) on his own ideas and his expression of those ideas. Thus, it is good if we can learn something about Paul's religious, social, and cultural contexts, for everything about Paul is related to those realities. The same applies to us. If I were to say to someone "Jump in the creek," the context determines whether this is a slur (as you might say to someone you are arguing with) or a simple directive (as I might say to my son so he can fetch my golf ball). In other words, before we can understand Galatians we need to know what Paul is fighting against. In the past, Paul has been understood to be responding to a "works-righteousness" religion, much like the Roman Catholicism Martin Luther faced in the fifteenth and sixteenth centuries. "On this view, what is at issue between Paul and his opponents is a matter of pure theology and pure theory: they debate the merits of two rival answers to the question, How can man be accepted by God?"[6] This approach assumes that the issue is purely theoretical; it is a theological problem. Others, more numerous today, contend that the theological debate is only one dimension of a larger debate that involved both theological and social issues, both theory and practice, both religion and culture. We must emphasize that the only way to interpret the letter correctly is to understand it in its context. So we need to examine what Paul was criticizing before we start applying it to various groups today.

Before going through the evidence, I offer a definition of legalism according to what we find in Galatians: *Legalism, according to Galatians, was a religious system that combined Christianity with Mosaism in a way that demanded total commitment to Israel's law as the climax of one's conversion to Christ. This "deeper commitment to the law," according to Paul, was a subversion of the adequacy of Christ's work and an abandonment of the Holy Spirit as God's way of guiding Christian ethics. In other words, the legalism of the Judaizers is more than a problem: it has become a new message, a different gospel.* As I shall show below, it is this implication—that it is a different gospel—that forces Paul to action.

It takes little convincing to show that the concern of the Judaizers was primarily with the *law*. Thus, in a central passage of his argument, Paul asks: "Did you receive the Spirit [the sure sign of conversion] by observing the law, or by believing what you heard?" (3:2). The answer is clear: the Galatians knew they had received the Holy Spirit as a result of believing, not as a result of obeying the law. Further, Paul asks in the same section, "Does God give [notice the change to current experience] you his Spirit and work miracles among you because you observe the law, or because you believe what you

---

6. F. Watson, *Paul, Judaism and the Gentiles: A Sociological Approach* (SNTSMS 56; Cambridge: Cambridge University Press, 1986), 1.

heard?" (3:5). Again, the answer is clear: the Galatians know from their experience that God grants miracles as a result of faith, not as a result of some legal practices. But Paul goes further in describing the Judaizers' essential view: "You who are trying to be justified by law have been alienated from Christ; you have fallen away from grace" (5:4). In fact, "All who rely on observing the law are under a curse" (3:10). Clearly, the Judaizers were a law-centered movement in that the law was the central focus of their religious orientation.

We must also point out that the Judaizers Paul faced were not (or did not see themselves as) opponents of Christianity. By the use of a subtle term in Galatians 3:3 Paul says that the Judaizers were seeking to supplement Christianity—better yet, perfect or consummate Christianity—by adding the specific laws of Moses. Paul says, "After beginning with the Spirit, are you now *trying to attain your goal* by human effort?" (emphasis added). The Judaizers saw their message as Jesus Christ *plus Moses*, not just Moses, not just Jesus Christ. It is like telling a new convert from a Billy Graham Crusade today that he or she must also become Lutheran, Methodist, Presbyterian, etc., before the conversion process is truly complete and acceptable to God. When this sort of thing takes place, the message itself is changed; it is no longer "surrender to Christ" but "join our group." The focus of salvation shifts from Christ to movement.

But these concerns of the Judaizers about the law take on actual and specific form: they were concerned primarily with circumcision (2:3; 5:6; 6:12) and Jewish food laws regulating not only what was *kosher* but also with whom one was permitted to eat (2:11–14). These are the two major concerns of the Judaizers as presented in the evidence of Galatians.[7]

We also need to argue here that the Judaizers were not just law-centered but that their legal concerns had a definite nationalistic-racial basis; this underlay everything that was going on between Paul and the Judaizers. Their concerns were not just theoretical or ethical: Obey the law! Rather, their concerns were nationalistic, highly pragmatic, and social: Obey the special laws that mark off the Jew from the Gentile. In other words, we are looking at a form of cultural imperialism. In reading through Galatians we will see that whenever Paul gets specific about the law that the Judaizers were pushing, he does not do so theoretically. The Judaizers' concern was more than "you converts must submit to Moses." Instead, we find that their concerns were with specific Jewish laws: "You converts must be regulated by those spe-

---

7. It is possible that they were also concerned with the observance of Jewish calendars (cf. 4:10). However, this concern appears only once in the letter and so will not be discussed in detail. It should be noted that this concern was as much social as the other two concerns, since calendars regulate one's basic life and provide one a social identity.

cial concerns (we) Jews have that separate us from the Gentile world." It is true that Jews saw these very commandments as tantamount to the entire law, for it was through these social laws that Jews expressed their commitment to the law—similar to the way in which some Christians see their giving of a tithe to their local church as a vibrant witness to their total submission to God and so turn it into a commandment of massive consequences, to the point that those who do not tithe are seen as either spiritually inferior or even apostate.

Two of these well-known (to Gentiles) Jewish laws concerned circumcision and food purity, two religious regulations that have almost no bearing on contemporary Western society. True enough, we Westerners are intoxicated by dietary restrictions (low cholesterol and fatty percentages), but these are not what Jews had in mind. They were concerned with living according to Mosaic law in such a way as to live honorably before God. Contamination of food had nothing to do with diet; it had to do with one's general fitness before God. What we see as diet, they saw as piety. To be sure, circumcision is performed on the vast majority of boys born in the United States, but clearly this is not a religious rite: it is performed because it makes good sense for health. Thus, for us to understand Paul's directives we must understand both the religious dimension (these things are understood to be mandated by God) and the social dimension (these things reflect commitment to one's Jewish heritage) of these laws. The Judaizers saw their entire religion and society at threat in Paul's supposed "law-free" gospel because he was allowing people to find God's grace without becoming socially conformed to the law.

These observations have many implications for our interpretation of Galatians. For one, the argument of Paul gains a racial-social nuance and not just a theological one. In contesting the Judaizers, Paul is contesting not just theological variation but theology that serves social and racial interests. The Judaizers were not simply converting others; they were nationalizing others. This needs to be explored as we read through Galatians. Paul was also opposed to what we now call cultural imperialism (the view that one culture is superior to another), and this cultural imperialism had become enmeshed in a religious system.

In addition to the law, Paul states that the Judaizers' system was *human-oriented and fleshly*. Whether Paul has Moses in mind (which is possible) or simply the traditions of the Pharisees (which I think is more likely), he has something profound at the bottom of his argument: the religious system of the Judaizers is not from God, is not based in the revelation of Jesus Christ, and does not depend on the Holy Spirit. The letter itself begins on a polemical note in this connection: "Paul, an apostle—sent not from men nor by man, but by Jesus Christ" (1:1). He implies already here that the Judaizers are sent "by men"—undoubtedly the Jerusalem leaders. Further, Paul says he is not seeking the approval of humans (1:10) while he, we must suppose, thinks the Judaizers have the wrong source of approval (6:12). More radically, Paul lines up this human-centered message of the Judaizers with the *flesh*, a term that has no positive implications. "After beginning with the Spirit, are you now trying to attain perfection *through the flesh?*" (3:3; see also 6:8).[8] The return to Moses, i.e., to the Jewish laws, is not an addition; rather, it is a subtraction of all that is important: Christ and the Spirit. To live before God apart from Christ and without the Spirit is to live in the flesh. Thus, the Judaizers have a fleshly system. The system is one of "addition by subtraction"—adding to the gospel by subtracting the sufficiency of Christ and the Spirit.

It is commonly understood here that Paul is talking about effort, about "works righteousness." Put differently, when Paul asks, "Are you now trying to attain your goal through the flesh?" (3:3), he is talking about a persistent religious problem: the problem of humans trying to please God through their own efforts, sincerity, and works. Ernst Käsemann, a noted German scholar, asks this: "What does the Jewish nomism against which Paul fought really represent? And our answer must be: it represents the community of 'good' people which turns God's promises into their own privileges and God's commandments into the instruments of self-sanctification."[9]

This view has an entire set of assumptions about Judaism that have rarely been tested by the evidence of Judaism itself. These assumptions include: that Jews thought God's will was to be found in the law of Moses, that they had to follow it completely to be accepted by God, that the sacrificial system was not of much use when it came to the forgiveness of sins, that this created a crisis or burden of conscience before God, that this led to the development of a view of merit in which the good works would outweigh the sins and so provide acceptance before God, that this system did not make for healthy people emotionally and psychologically, and that therefore some of the Jews were thrilled when the message of salvation by grace was revealed in Jesus and Paul. In other words, these people think that God will accept them if their good works outweigh their sins. Furthermore, many who argue for this view of the problem Paul is facing are the first to argue that most of

---

8. The NIV translates *sarki* (lit., "by flesh") with "by human effort." While this translation may capture some of the idea, it focuses too much on effort (effort is involved in the system of Christ as well!) and misses the crucial ideas associated with "flesh." For Paul, the flesh is existence apart from dependence on the Spirit and trust in Christ. See notes on Galatians 2:15–21; 3:3; 5:19–21.

9. So E. Käsemann, "Justification and Salvation-History in the Epistle to the Romans," in *Perspectives on Paul* (Philadelphia: Fortress, 1971), 72.

these Judaizing legalists did not even know this is what they were arguing. The question we must ask is: Is this a fair description of either Judaism or the Judaizers?

I believe nearly every one of the assumptions in the previous paragraphs is wrong. I also think this is grossly inaccurate, and one notable scholar, E. P. Sanders, has argued persuasively that this view of Judaism and the Judaizers is more indebted to our perception of Martin Luther's personal struggles with the medieval Roman Catholic Church than to our knowledge of Judaism. I have read vast amounts of literature from Judaism, including most of the published material found at Qumran (the Dead Sea Scrolls), the Old Testament Apocrypha and Pseudepigrapha, hundreds of published papyri, and a multitude of sections from rabbinic writings. I am more than ever convinced that Judaism was not essentially a "works-righteousness religion" in the sense defined above. Christians can read Jewish literature with great profit, particularly the Babylonian Talmud. What we find there is that Jews throughout the ages have always been convinced that they are God's elect people, that they were "saved" because they are God's elect people, that they were to try to live by the law (and most did), that the atonement sacrifice set up by God through Moses remedied the presence of sin in their lives; furthermore, they believed that the final judgment was a judgment of works. Thus, they believed in salvation by covenant participation, knew that God had imposed upon them an obligation to keep his laws, and were convinced that God would judge them according to their deeds.[10] The simple reason why Jewish documents emphasize morality is that acceptance with God was for them not the issue; that was promised to the people of Israel from the days of Abraham on. What mattered to them was how to live *as the people of God*, and there was much debate over that.

Now what is important here is to realize that Jesus, Paul, and the writers of the New Testament teach nearly the same thing: (1) that salvation is by God's grace *(but in Christ)* and the result of his election, (2) that salvation implies an obligation to live according to God's will or in the Spirit or in submission to the commandments of Jesus (Matt. 28:20), and (3) that the final judgment will be a judgment of works (cf. Matt. 25:31–46; 2 Cor. 5:1–10; Rev. 20:11–15). The polemical language we use of Judaism as a "works righteousness" would be amazingly foreign to Paul. In Galatians, when Paul speaks of "through the flesh" he is not talking about "efforts to gain salvation" but about attempting to live before God without depending on the Spirit. Put

---

10. A scholarly defense of this view can be found in E. P. Sanders, *Paul and Palestinian Judaism*, 33–428; his famous summary is on 422–23. See now his further study, *Judaism: Practice and Belief. 63 BCE- 66 CE* (Philadelphia: Trinity Press International, 1992), 241–78.

differently, he is talking about how we are to (or not to) *live before God as Christians*, not how we *become* (or do not become) *acceptable before God as humans*. It is simply inaccurate, not to say religiously insensitive, to describe Judaism as a works religion.[11] Thus, the issue in Galatians was not works righteousness versus grace righteousness, but the relationship of Christianity to Judaism, the relationship of the larger world of believers to the narrower world of the Jewish nation. Francis Watson puts it well: "The essential issue in Galatians is thus whether the church should be a reform-movement within Judaism or a sect outside it."[12]

Our final point about legalism is that it becomes a *total system* (5:3) that ends up *nullifying the grace of God in Christ and the power of God in the Spirit* (2:21; 5:2, 4, 16–25). In effect, it becomes another gospel (1:6–9); but this "other gospel" is one that cannot save. By opting for Jesus plus Moses, the Judaizers, Paul argues, are destroying the need for Christ. Paul states clearly that "if righteousness could be gained through the law, Christ died for nothing" (2:21), and that "if you let yourselves be circumcised, Christ will be of no value to you at all" (5:2). With respect to denying the power of God in the Spirit, Paul says: "If you are led by the Spirit, you are not under law" (5:18). That is to say, those who opt for the Spirit choose against Moses; those who opt for Jesus choose against the law. One cannot have both. Paul's message is uncompromising: Christ alone.

We see, then, that the Judaizing legalism that Paul faced at Galatia was a religious system that combined Christianity with Mosaism in a way that demanded total commitment to the law, particularly as the climax of one's conversion to Christ. Paul shows that this "deeper commitment to the law" undermined the work of Christ and rejected the sufficiency of the Spirit for determining Christian practice. Accordingly, it is illegitimate for us to focus simply on the "legal" aspects of the Judaizers. These teachers had created a different gospel, the Christ-plus-something gospel. In our attempts, then, to move into our society with Paul's letter we may miss many applications if we restrict his message to the anti-legalism theme as frequently described and applied. What Paul was opposing was the perversion of the gospel expressed by the Judaizers in their Christ-plus-something gospel. The legal features happened to be the particular contributions the Judaizers added when they

---

11. I am not saying that Judaism never showed itself in particular authors or locations as a works-righteousness religion. But this is also true of Christianity. I have encountered numerous pockets of Christianity that are as much, if not more, works-righteousness oriented as anything I have ever read in Judaism, and that includes 4 Ezra, an unusual Jewish pseudepigraph.

12. F. Watson, *Paul, Judaism and the Gentiles*, 49.

altered the gospel; but it was the alteration of the gospel that Paul opposed, not the addition of legal elements.

Paul's Argument

HOW DID THE Jews see the law, and how does Paul respond to their view? This multifaceted question has been answered in three main ways in the discussions of the church. The first view, the *principle of salvation view*, contends that Jews and the Judaizers saw the law as the means of salvation and that Paul opposed it as a principle of salvation, because, so it is assumed, the Judaizers did not understand their inherent sinful nature. Thus, according to this view, the Judaizers were trying to get the converts at Galatia to embrace the law *so they could be accepted by God*. This view of the *Judaizers*, I believe, is only partly correct. Then it is argued that Paul responded to this by arguing that humans cannot, because they are sinful and weak in the flesh, obey the law. So, if they embrace the law as a principle of salvation, they are asking for big trouble: damnation. But this view of *Paul's response*, I believe, fundamentally confuses the points if it is given emphasis.

The problem here is that there is a list of assumptions implicit in the view that are neither Jewish nor taught by Paul (and if he does, he does so rarely that this view must be subsidiary to his argument). The primary assumptions (and false ones) are that Judaism thought one had to keep the law perfectly in order to be accepted by God and that the sacrificial system did not take care of the problem of sins. As a matter of fact, no Jew thought the law was impossible to keep because they knew it could be kept; and when not kept, atonement could be made so one could be restored back to the level of a law-abiding Jew. Paul is not lying in Philippians 3:6 when he says he kept the law: he kept it, and when he sinned, he went to the temple to take care of his transgression.

The biggest problem with the "principle of salvation" view is that Paul is not seen in Galatians attacking this kind of problem. The issues involved here are far more practical: they are social and they are theological. What we see is Paul squaring up against those who thought one had to become a Jew in order to become acceptable to God. For this reason, the Judaizers thought one had to submit to the law to be fully acceptable to God; but Paul's response is not along the lines that merit-seeking is the problem. Again, Paul is not fighting off the problem of motivation: he is not asking, "Do you do the law in order to be saved?" and then attacking those who arrogantly think they are good enough to please God.

To be sure, Paul did see the Judaizers as thinking the law was necessary for salvation, and he knew they were adding it to his message. But his argument is not, "You misunderstand human nature," but, "You misunderstand what the law is given for." Thus, Paul does not appeal to the biblical view of human nature to counter their views; instead, he appeals to the biblical view of the law. They misunderstood the purpose of the law, not the ability of humans. They were every bit as realistic about human nature as Christians have been through the ages: humans sin and need God's forgiveness. What are we to make of the temple if it is not the tacit confession that humans are incapable of perfect obedience to the law? If this is the orientation of the temple, then Paul would never win his argument if he pursued the idea that the Judaizers should see that no one could be sinless.

A second view, the *salvation-historical view*, contends that Jews saw the law as an abiding revelation of God's will, which Paul saw as now eclipsed in the coming of Christ. This view is solidly taught in 3:19–25, where Paul shows that the law had a limited purpose (to reveal sin) for a limited time (until Christ came). Thus, Paul argues against the Judaizers that they should not be foisting the law on these converts because the era of God's will being revealed through the law is over. The time under which we now live is guided by the Spirit of God. I believe this view is correct but is not completely correct. Thus, the Jews thought the law was God's will (which Paul would agree with—tongue in cheek) but Paul thought that the "law as God's will" was now an era that was eclipsed by God through Christ and in the Spirit. This second view needs, however, to be supplemented with the third view.

The third view sees the Law *as a social and nationalistic boundary marker*. This view contends that the Judaizers saw the law as God's gift to the Jews (which it was), that God has always worked through Jews (which he had), and that this means God was still working only through the Jewish nation (which he was not). Thus, they argue, one must embrace the law as necessary if one wants to be acceptable to God. And the laws that they focus on are the major social boundaries between Jews and Gentiles: circumcision and food laws. This view of what is going on in Galatians is also partly correct and helps us as we proceed through Galatians. For these Jews, the law was essentially a special contract between God and Israel, and this meant Jews were special; to be acceptable to God, they would have argued, means one has to become a Jew.

So, what is going on in Galatians is that the Judaizers did not change with the times; they failed to see that when Christ came, the era of the law ended. They could not accept this because they thought God worked through the Jewish nation to dispense the promises of Abraham (the third view). Paul's argument is salvation-historical (the second view): in God's plan of history the law has now served its purposes, and therefore it is wrong to follow it and to demand that Gentiles accept it. That leads to his sociological argument: it is wrong to think God still works in nationalistic ways. God's people now comprise individuals of all sorts from all nations.

Paul's letter to the Galatians is a polemical letter, designed from front to back to be both a rebuttal of the Judaizers and a positive statement of the apostolic gospel. His argument moves on three levels: an autobiographical account of the origin of his call and gospel (1:10–2:21), a theological argument of the finality of the law in Christ and the adequacy of the gospel of grace in Christ (3:1–4:31), and the practical application of his letter to show that God's new life is to be found in living in the Spirit (5:1–6:10).

What Paul found wrong with the Judaizers, then, was (1) they did not understand the sufficiency and universality of Christ's work, (2) they did not understand what Christ and the Spirit have done to the Mosaic law and its national character, and (3) they did not perceive that God has granted the Holy Spirit to all believers (Jew and Gentile), with the result that Christians do not need to be guided by the law and do not have to live in the flesh; instead, they have the Spirit to guide them in ways that conform to, fulfill, and transform the law.

There are two options: one can choose either Christ or one can choose Moses.[13] A chart illustrates the options:

Christ	Moses
Spirit	Law
Spirit	Flesh
Faith	Works of the Law
Promise	Law
Blessing	Curse
Freedom	Slavery
Mature Sonship	Slavery; Infancy
New Creation	Circumcision/ Non-circumcision
Grace	Law
Christian Church	Jewish Nation

---

13. F. Watson, *Paul, Judaism and the Gentiles*, 46, says (in sociological categories): "The function of these antithetical contrasts is to express the ineradicable distinction between the sect (in which salvation is to be found) and the parent religious community (where there is only condemnation)." On the same page he gives a fuller listing of the antitheses in Paul's letters.

Introduction

Outline

I. Introduction (1:1–9)
   A. Salutation (1:1–5)
   B. Occasion of Letter (1:6–9)
II. Paul's Personal Vindication of His Message (1:10–2:21)
   A. The Declaration of His Independence (1:10–12)
   B. The Demonstration of His Independence (1:13–2:21)
      1. From Human Teaching (1:13–17)
      2. From the Major Churches (1:18–24)
      3. From the Jerusalem Pillars (2:1–10)
      4. From the Apostle Peter (2:11–21)
III. Paul's Theological Vindication of His Message (3:1–4:31)
   A. The Thesis Stated (3:1–5)
   B. The Evidence Given (3:6–4:31)
      1. From the Old Testament (3:6–14)
      2. From Covenants (3:15–18; excursus 3:19–25)
      3. From Sonship (3:26–4:20)
      4. From the Law (4:21–31)
IV. Practical Application of His Message (5:1–6:10)
   A. Thesis (5:1)
   B. Applications (5:2–6:10)
V. Conclusion (6:11–18)

Before discussing how we should move forward to our day with Paul's message, it might be helpful to the reader if I provided a brief sketch of the social context of Galatians.

Historical Reconstruction

In Jerusalem there were several currents of Christianity, the two major parties being the progressive Hellenistic wing (out of which Paul came) and the conservative Hebrew wing (out of which the Judaizers came). There can be no doubt that the conservative wing put pressure on the progressive wing to conform to the Jewish law, and this pressure was exerted because of a common Jewish context. And conversely, the progressive Hellenistic wing no doubt had its vocal proponents for a more liberalized form of Jewish Christianity where the temple cult and purity laws were not seen as crucial.

As I said, Paul came from the progressives. As Paul began his mission in the Diaspora, he immediately found that the gospel was powerful and that scores of Jews and Gentiles were converting to Jesus as the Messiah. In addition, these Jews were less socially conventional than the Hebrew Christians and typical Jews of Jerusalem. This different social context allowed the new converts to accept and work out a gospel lifestyle that was less law-centered. And so they did—in ways quite unacceptable to the Jews of Jerusalem. Here is where the tension began: the law-abiding Jews of Jerusalem heard about the "lawless" Jewish and Gentile Christian converts of the Diaspora and began to put pressure on the conservative wing of the Jerusalem Christians. We must understand that the concern of the Jerusalem Jews was probably not with the law per se but with the boundary markers that these new converts were willing to abandon. They came to the conclusion that the new converts to Christianity were not Jews at all if they were not willing to live according to the basic Jewish distinctives. Their conclusion: pressure the conservative party to engage in an active proselytization of these new converts to get them to conform to the law. And so the conservative party (called "men . . . from James" at 2:12) sent out some Judaizers to "follow-up" the evangelism of Paul.

It is also possible that the Galatian converts were feeling a little insecure about Paul's moral guideline: live in the Spirit, live in freedom, etc. Their conversion was a conversion (in most instances) from pagan lawlessness to what was perceived to be a Christian lawlessness. It is likely, I think, that they began to feel the need for laws and regulations, particularly if some of their members were beginning to drift a little in the direction of indulging the flesh. The Judaizers, thus, had a perfect "in" with the Galatian converts.[14] The efforts of the Judaizers were no doubt partly successful. We are probably justified in seeing Paul's concerns with divisions (5:15, 20–21, 26; 6:12–13) in the churches as related to the Judaizer's efforts. Some of the converts were converting to Judaism now and others weren't; there would have been lots of rhetoric, heated rhetoric, in such a context. Paul feared the creation of two denominations: Jewish Christianity and Gentile Christianity.

Paul, who was already more progressive to begin with, reacted with strong emotion to the mission of these Judaizers because he saw in their attempts: (1) an attack on the adequacy of Christ (2:21), (2) a misunderstanding of God's plan for the law (3:19–25), and (3) a capturing of the gospel by a national and racial message (a rejudaization of the gospel; see above). From Acts 15:36–41, I infer that Paul's letter had some success.[15]

---

14. See J. M. G. Barclay, *Obeying the Truth*, 68–72.
15. See F. F. Bruce, *Galatians*, 277–78.

Bridging Contexts

I INDICATED ABOVE that moving immediately from the word *legalism* to modern Christian practices is a potentially misleading application of Paul's message. While legalism may express itself normally in moral rules, it is not moral rules as such that Paul opposes. It is the transformation of the gospel into something more than Christ alone.

The specific legal issues that were apparent in Galatia must be left to the side if we wish to make progress in applications. That is, it goes without saying that there are probably no Christian groups, churches, or movements that explicitly demand circumcision as necessary for conversion or that restrict table fellowship on the basis of interpretations of Old Testament levitical instructions. This means we are seeking to apply Galatians only to analogous situations today. But in moving to these applications we must be sure that they perform the same functions that legalistic practices played at Galatia.

It must be remembered that in the very letter in which Paul hotly contests legalism, he also says that "in Christ Jesus neither circumcision nor uncircumcision has any value" (5:6). Paul did not simply deny the value of circumcision here; instead, he denied the inherent value of both statuses. We must also remember that it was this same Paul who had Timothy circumcised when Paul needed him for ministry among the Jews (Acts 16:3). Apparently, Paul thought that at times circumcision would be valuable for ministry; at other times it would be detrimental to ministry. But what Paul is against is *the necessity of circumcision for conversion and social identity*. So before application takes place, we must reflect on the role circumcision and food laws played at Galatia. And here we find the foundation for our applications.

Paul was not against good things; he thought the law was good, he thought circumcision was good, and he probably thought eating kosher food was a good idea. From the New Testament itself we learn that Paul himself lived according to the Jewish calendar (cf. Acts 20:16) and occasionally took on himself Jewish vows (see Acts 18:18). If these things could be performed without causing offense or if these things needed to be done in order to reach Jews, Paul was for them. But, if these things were done as a necessary supplement to faith in Christ, then Paul was diametrically opposed to their practice. He was against the legalism of the Judaizers *because it usurped the work of Christ and the power of the Holy Spirit and forced all converts to become Jews.* It was not what was done that rankled Paul; it was *why these things were done* that produced his quick reaction.

Here is Paul's principal argument against Judaizing legalism: whatever practices detract from the all-sufficiency of Christ and the enabling ministries of the Spirit must be opposed; whatever practices build walls between people who believe in Jesus Christ must be torn down; whatever practices seek to supplement trust in Christ and dependence on the Holy Spirit must be cleared away; whoever seeks to demand any such things must be countered. In effect, whatever message that is not Christ and the Spirit alone is a perversion and must be radically denounced.

In addition, our point must be stated positively, for Paul goes on to state his views in positive form as well (5:1). Paul is for any practice that encourages the freedom of the Spirit to operate among Christians (5:13). Paul is for an ethic that is characterized by love: "The only thing that counts is faith expressing itself through love" (5:6; cf. 5:14). If asked about the essence of Christian living Paul would say: "So I say, live by the Spirit, and you will not gratify the desires of the sinful nature" (5:16). Paul's solution to Christian holiness was not self-mortification (though he believed in that, too) or more reading of sacred books: he knew that holiness came only through God's *Holy* Spirit. And here is the essence of Christian living to Paul: living in Christ in the power of the Holy Spirit. When a person lives in the Spirit (i.e., under the total guidance of God's Spirit), that person does everything God wants, and so the law cannot condemn that person. When a person lives according to the leading of the Spirit, that person will always do the fullness of God's will, of which the law of Moses was but a preliminary glimpse.[16]

The essence of Christianity, then, is straightforward: it is not living by the law; it is living in trust in Christ and depending on the Holy Spirit. The Judaizers were wrong because they sacrificed Christ and the Spirit on the altar of Judaizing legalism.

To FIND CONTEMPORARY analogies to the legalism of the Judaizers we need to find more than identical features (circumcision, food restrictions, calendars) of regulated behavior among Christians. We must be in search of practices and features of modern Christianity that debunk the sufficiency of Christ and relegate the Holy Spirit to a nonessential feature of Christian living. We must become systems analysts, examining what we teach to see if it roots everything in Christ or whether it has traits of the Christ-plus-something system.

I begin by poking around among mainline Protestant ideas that, while not written down in creedal form, do seem to be typical of what passes off as Christian for many groups. I recently had a friend tell me about her unfortunate

---

16. This viewpoint on the relation of the Christian to the law will be explained more completely at 3:19–25.

experience in such a church. She was, in her own words, a "mild evangelical with fundamentalist roots." She began to worship in a mainline denominational church and found immediate acceptance. She liked the social climate, the educational level, and the warmth of the people. She eventually was asked to teach an adult Bible class that met weekly, and it was in this setting that she began to feel uncomfortable. She found, as a result of pressure from the pastor—who did not attend the classes but heard about her biblical teaching from others—that she "did not belong" in their church. She found that there were two themes in her pastor's gospel: (1) love, defined ambiguously as "God loves all," but without reference to the cross of Christ; and (2) American fundamentalists are wrong, dangerous, and to be avoided. Because she was quite sincere about the Bible (and knowing her, I know she was sensitive and diplomatic about how and what she said) and because she was challenging her class members to take the message of the Bible with utter seriousness, she was branded as a "fundamentalist" by her pastor.

What she experienced over the next couple of years was social ostracism and a refusal to allow her gifts to be exercised in a setting that needed her and her ministries. She came to the conclusion that even in liberal Protestantism, there was a "fundamentalism of liberalism" and that fundamentalism was charged with peer pressure against any Christian who took seriously the biblical teachings of Christ and Paul. She found that to be a member of that church in a functioning way, she also had to agree to all kinds of political, economic, and ideological themes—themes with which, while she respected them, she had some problems. Put differently, she felt that to be a genuine Christian in their eyes she had to become like them—regardless of whether or not that image was in conformity to Christ or the Scriptures. What struck her, upon further reflection, was this church's neglect of teaching about Jesus Christ and an almost complete void of believing that the Christian life was life in the Spirit. Jesus was for them a profound person and the Spirit was a mystical oddity. I suggest this example is not dissimilar to the Judaizing controversy at Galatia, where conformity to one's group was more important than any revelation from God about Jesus Christ or the Holy Spirit. In criticizing this mainline denomination, I am not suggesting that all mainline Protestant churches are of the same weakness; nor am I suggesting that evangelicals ought not to be worshiping in liberal churches. What I am pointing out is that it is not just fundamentalism or evangelicalism that is susceptible to the same sins as found by the Judaizing legalists of Galatia. What we are looking for in applying Galatians are strands of Christianity where the adequacy of Christ and the sufficiency of the Spirit are held in check by other ideas and social movements.

We might continue by observing that the evangelical church in the entire Western world is now in a post-legalistic era.[17] Since the late sixties and early seventies it is not only our society that has changed; along with this change, the moral makeup of the evangelical movement has been dramatically altered. Prior to this time the church lived comfortably in a fairly settled and uniform society that had (at least) an externally Christian ethic as its moral guideline. After the social revolts of the sixties and seventies biblical morality and social norms have separated themselves significantly. Prior to these revolts the evangelical movement was still largely expressed in Protestant fundamentalism, and that movement was a reaction to the growth of liberalism in American society, culture, and mainline denominations. Furthermore, the ethic of large portions of Protestant fundamentalism was admittedly legalistic, rigorous, socially restricting, and self-conscious. This ethic has been significantly changed by social changes and by some serious reflections on the nature of the Christian life. The evangelical movement itself is an attempt to cut loose from the legalistic and antagonistic moorings of fundamentalism.

My own spiritual biography reflects this very movement. I was reared in a Protestant fundamentalist home and church, both of which emphasized the ethic of legalism. For whatever reasons (and I cannot detail but one of them here), my own convictions about how Christians are to live changed along with the development of the evangelical movement. I am persuaded that the leading voice in my own development is the letter of Paul to the Galatians. This change in the church from a legalistic to a post-legalistic era makes the

---

17. This chapter depends indirectly on the depiction of the history of the Protestant fundamentalist movement in the United States as presented by G. M. Marsden, *Fundamentalism and American Culture: The Shaping of Twentieth-Century Evangelicalism, 1870–1925* (New York: Oxford, 1980), and the description of the modern state of affairs presented in J. D. Hunter, *Evangelicalism: The Coming Generation* (Chicago: University of Chicago, 1987). As normally defined, legalism has not been as integral a part of the mainline Protestant churches of the U.S. or the state churches of Europe as it has been of the fundamentalist-evangelical churches of the U.S. and Europe. For an example of a critique of why legalism is not found as frequently in the German Lutheran Church, see H. Thielicke, "The Freedom of Decision: The Impossibility of Casuistry in Ethical Christianity," in his *The Freedom of the Christian Man*, trans. J. W. Doberstein (Grand Rapids: Baker, 1975), 148–66. For a survey of the rift of conservative and liberal evangelicals in Britain, see D. Bebbington, *Evangelicalism in Modern Britain* (Grand Rapids: Baker, 1989), 181–228, who teases out of British church history some clear examples of legalism in the evangelical movement. It has become clear to many that the Keswick Conventions of Britain, with their variety of evangelical influences, beginning in 1875, have been extremely influential on Protestant fundamentalism and its sometimes legalistic ethic (on this see Bebbington, 151–80). But just as crucial to the development of the legalistic ethic, as Marsden has pointed out, has been social changes in the U.S., against which legalistic practices were devised as a battering ram.

---

interpretation and application of Galatians more difficult today. It is simply no longer adequate to talk about smoking cigarettes, attending movie theaters, and drinking alcohol, and to think that in talking of these things one is talking about how to deal with legalism. These features are no longer seen as central to the identification of the evangelical movement (formerly they were), and we are left now with questions on how to apply Galatians. In fact, the modern evangelical movement is caught up so much in Christian liberty, a lack of accountability, and individualism that any talk about legalism can sound like a foreign language.

However, if our perception of Paul's essential points is correct, namely, that Judaizing legalism was wrong because of its weakening of the centrality and sufficiency of Christ and the Spirit, we are left with all kinds of applications—in all contexts of the church in the Western world. Christ has been pushed to the side and the Spirit has been neglected as much in evangelicalism as they have been in the German state church, the Anglican communion of Great Britain, and the mainline denominations of the United States.

In addition to a revision of how we have looked at the so–called legalism of Galatians, we are also dealing with massive changes in society. Before we can apply Galatians we must grapple both with the text of Galatians in its historical context so we can understand God's message, and with our modern culture and church so we will know how to apply that message of Paul. Before we proceed to the commentary we need to sketch just what "Judaizing legalism" is in its essential manifestations today. I am concerned here, then, with the basics of application.

First, in attempting to apply Galatians we are primarily looking for practices, attitudes, and theological views that *add to the gospel in such a manner that* (1) *the sufficiency of Christ is compromised, and* (2) *the centrality that the Holy Spirit plays in spiritual freedom is jeopardized.* As already stated, we are not looking in our churches simply for chafing rules or binding regulations. Rules may in fact be good for spiritual development. The rub at Galatia was that the addition of required obedience of Moses to conversion made the sacrifice of Christ unnecessary or at least insufficient. In other words, the legalism at Galatia was more "heresy" than it was the addition of binding rules. This form of legalism was a contamination of the gospel. And our quest today must be for contaminating influences and perversions of the sufficiency of the gospel. "Legalism" will be manifested in such distortions of the gospel.

A word of emphasis needs to be given to the value of rules, regulations, and disciplines in spiritual development. These rules are pronounced by some to be the telltale signs of "Judaizing legalism." There are few Christians who will contest the view that consistent prayer, Bible reading, meditation, and regular fellowship with other Christians are fundamentally important disciplines for spiritual growth. One of my greatest blessings as a seminary teacher is the contact I have with students who were InterVarsity campus leaders at American colleges and universities. In my regular conversations with these students I have heard a frequent chord: we struggle with newly converted college students in getting them to develop consistent spiritual habits. And local pastors will be the first to affirm the need for Christians, young and old, to practice spiritual disciplines. What I am saying, then, is not that disciplines, rules, or regulations are wrong. Rather, I am saying that when we seek to apply Galatians we need to find perversions of the gospel, and that sometimes these will be evident (as they were at Galatia) in rules and regulations.

So what are we talking about in these "additions"? What are some "rules and regulations" that might become similar to the Judaizing legalism of Galatia? Of what could be a long list, I mention four. (1) At times *laws and regulations* are added in such a way that they distort the gospel as they relegate Christ and the Spirit to the periphery. When, for example, because of a hectic schedule as a result of a busy family, one finds it impossible to read the Bible in the morning (or evening, or both!), and as a result one feels unloved by God, distant from him, or in need of forgiveness, one has distorted the gospel. We *are* loved by God in Christ, we have been brought near to God in Christ, and we have been forgiven in Christ; Bible reading does not make us relationally closer to God. However important the discipline of Bible reading may be, that discipline does not make us acceptable to God. We have compromised Christ and sacrificed the power of the Spirit on the altar of a discipline if we think we cannot live spiritually without reading the Bible every day. Other such "laws" easily develop in Christian circles.

(2) At times *experiences* become the essence of a relationship to God, rather than trust in Christ and life in the Spirit. For some it is an experience of speaking in tongues, for others it is a vision, and for others it is simply mystical prayer or the rapture of the soul with God in prayer; and for still others it may be protest against a nuclear storage site or a commitment to a particular political agenda. Again, while each of these experiences has played an important role in the history of the church, and while each may be spiritually transforming for some, when these experiences become the very center of one's relationship to God—without which the person feels distant from God or out of sync with his will—we are compromising Christ and the Spirit of God. We dare not preach, teach, or even insinuate that we are more acceptable to God if we have certain spiritual experiences. Dale Bruner, in his large study of the Holy Spirit, speaks of Pentecostalism too often lean-

ing in this direction of an experience being the "fullness" of the Christian gospel, a fullness that ends up supplanting Christ. He states:

> It is one of the ironies of nomenclature among those going by the name "full gospel" (and even, at times, "evangelical") that the evangel or gospel itself is not considered full enough to cover and enable the whole of the Christian's life but must be joined with other means, conditions, steps, or laws of the spiritual life in order to be full.[18]

(3) At times one's *education* is seen as fundamentally important to acceptance with God, and these displace Christ and the Spirit as the crucial identifying markers. Here we are not talking simply about degrees, whether from colleges, technical schools, or seminaries. We are talking about the message given at times in Christian circles of the necessity of education and intellect in order to be really in tune with God's will. I once heard a pastor say that "the dumbest farmer grows the best potatoes." While I doubt this principle can be proven to be true in each case, this quote does illustrate our point here, namely, that education is not the necessary route to success or to living God's will. How does this "legalism" manifest itself? Frequently our graduates are accused of attempting to turn churches into seminary classrooms. While we may applaud the effort of a young minister to pass on his or her enthusiasm for study and theology, we also have to point to what is often enough a grievous error here: theology may be important but education is not the only path to living before God with integrity. A local church, while it educates, is more than an educational institution, and when education becomes a necessary ingredient for true spirituality, then acceptance with God on the basis of Christ and life in the Spirit is compromised.

Again I emphasize, various disciplines, experiences, and education are not wrong. But when these things usurp the roles of Christ and the Spirit, then they are fundamentally wrong because they distort the gospel.

(4) Sometimes it is *cultural imperialism* that finds its way into the hearts, eyes, and ears of the listener of our message. Whether it is racism (especially in places like the U.S. and South Africa), or simply cultural snobbery, sometimes people sense that what is being preached is not Christ, not life in the Spirit, but life according to our customs and according to our heritage. Rarely is this the reflected view of the preacher or evangelist; much more often, however, it is the perception of the one being evangelized. At times, however, what comes across is that one must become white or an American or a European in order to be fully acceptable to God.

---

18. F. D. Bruner, *A Theology of the Holy Spirit: The Pentecostal Experience and the New Testament Witness* (Grand Rapids: Eerdmans, 1970), 240.

As a result of these four major ideas that creep into our gospel presentation and end up being "additions"—and therefore legalism, because they supplant Christ and the Spirit—it is no wonder that Roman Catholicism is not the primary focus of our attention. That movement within the Christian church is only one possibility. There are so many other areas for our exploration of applications. To be sure, at times the Roman Catholics have added to the gospel, but so have Protestants, in other ways. It is unfair to our Roman Catholic brothers and sisters to pin the whole book on them. A closer reading of the letter shows that the issues are far more normal and far more complex than this one application.

A second manifestation of Galatian legalism needs to be brought in here. I believe that these kinds of additions inevitably lead to an *overemphasis on performance* as the means of acceptance with God and how we maintain our relationship with God. I am not talking now about "works righteousness" in the form presented above. Rather, I am speaking of the things added to the gospel becoming the central things because they distinguish themselves socially and personally. If a group focuses, say, on experiences, then that group quickly becomes defined by those experiences, and individuals wanting membership in that group seek those experiences. The result is inevitably an overemphasis on those things. More often than not, these experiences are associated with performances. Soon it is performance that becomes the means of acceptance with the group and therefore with God. This means that life in Christ and in the Spirit are no longer the means of acceptance with God or the community; when this happens, we see a "Judaizing legalism" in our world. The leading (and socially defining) question for this kind of group is this: "Have you ever done this?" or, "Has this ever happened to you?" However important performance is in our relationship to God, it is *not* the means of God's acceptance of us. Christ has done all we ever need. The emphasis upon these performances, I suggest, blurs our vision of God's work on our behalf in Christ through the Spirit.

I have seen such "group dynamics" take place in the church for various performances. I have seen such take place for the political activity of stubbornly boycotting an abortion clinic by conservative evangelicals or for the political agitation of protesting places for military registration; and I have been in small groups where, if one had never spoken in tongues, one did not feel like one was "fully up to snuff." This kind of pressure on people will make them want to "perform" such things in order to be accepted to the group because such acceptance is perceived as what God wants one to do to be acceptable to him. Thus, we find in current examples of Judaizing legalism an inevitable emphasis on performance and a corresponding lack of trust in Christ and dependence on the Spirit.

....

Third, a Galatian legalism usually develops *barriers between people groups, races, denominations, and opinions.* These barriers are not simply "Christian options" but true barriers to mutual fellowship. They are human constructions that particularize what one group believes is God's ordained will for human beings. They become social rules regulating behavior for all in the group. At Galatia, the Judaizers believed (I'm sure with full integrity) that God wanted these new converts to socialize into Judaism—and in so doing they would relieve the pressure at Jerusalem on the conservative party. But Paul saw these social rules (table fellowship, circumcision, etc.) as barriers to fellowship and as human constructions contrary to God's will. We must remember that the social rules we create are not simply options. We give off a message by our social conventions, namely, that this is God's will for all. What happens in this manifestation of legalism is that the essential message becomes "join our group" and not "live in Christ." The necessary requirement for full conversion becomes "join our church" rather than "surrender to Christ." The current fracturing and splintering of the church is abundant evidence of the presence of an unnecessary group mentality in segments of the church. While at Galatia it was the age-old (to us) distinction between Jew and Gentile, this same group mentality manifests itself today in lines drawn between races (e.g., blacks and whites), sexes (women and men), and denominations (e.g., Methodists and Southern Baptists).

....

Fourth, contemporary Galatian legalism inevitably develops a *judging mentality* based upon its own concerns. While the intention may have been originally sound (circumcision will offend few people; Wednesday evening church attendance is good for spiritual development; protesting nuclear sites shows one's commitment to the gospel of Jesus, the King of Peace), inevitably others will be judged on the basis of one's performance of these social rules now understood to be God's will for a particular group (and if for us, why not others?). Judgmentalism is a sure indicator of Judaizing legalism and seems to grow naturally in its dark corners. But judging others without regard to Christ and the Spirit leads to serious errors and a distortion of the gospel. Our first question might instead be: "Can we share the Lord's Supper together?" If so, perhaps we can erase some of our lines.

....

Fifth—and this must be emphasized both for Paul and us—current displays of Galatian *legalism's concerns are almost never wrong and never bad*. What is inherently wrong with circumcision? Nothing, Paul says (5:6). What is wrong with eating only kosher food? Nothing. After all, God prescribes it especially for the priests, and it can't be wrong for all to seek to live in that degree of purity. What is wrong with limiting or prohibiting alcohol consumption? Nothing. Surely, the world would be a better place if alcoholism would end and if drunk drivers would cease to end the lives of innocent victims. Furthermore, there are precedents of commitment in the Bible that suggest that total abstinence of alcohol is at least one of God's wise ways. Thus, it must be kept to the fore that the concerns of Judaizing legalism are not bad. Christians must be the first to see this: legalism's concerns are almost always with practices that, neutrally seen, are not at all harmful and can be a positive good. The problem, however, is that these "good (but quite neutral) concerns" supplant the greatest concern: life in Christ and the joy of the Spirit.

Sixth, a regular feature of Judaizing legalism is that it *goes beyond Biblical prescriptions*. Let us take the issue of table purity that so concerned the Galatian Judaizers. Clearly table purity,[19] at some level, is taught in the Old Testament. After detailing the items that may not be eaten by the covenant people, God tells the Israelites that they may not eat these things for a reason: "I am the LORD who brought you up out of Egypt to be your God; therefore be holy, because I am holy" (Lev. 11:45). The purity demanded of the priests is even more intense (Lev. 21–22). Some first-century observant Jews obeyed not only the Old Testament laws but also the development and applications of these laws as taught especially by the Pharisees. In general, Jews did not eat unclean foods (Acts 10:14) and refused to eat at table with Gentiles (Acts 10:28). In fact, biblical scholars today agree that the Pharisee movement was a purity movement at some level: a group of zealous Israelites who sought to apply some of the Old Testament priestly laws and other extensions of the law to the everyday world of normal people in Judaism in order that the people of Israel would be holy before God.[20]

---

19. Table purity refers to the practice of eating permissible food and not eating impermissible food and doing so according to certain purity practices, like washing one's hands in a ceremonial fashion (so Mark 7:3).

20. For an excellent discussion of purity, see S. Westerholm, "Clean and Unclean," in *DJG*, 125–32, esp. 125–28. That purity, especially priestly purity, is the central feature of Pharisaism that has been successfully contested by E. P. Sanders, *Jewish Law from Jesus to the Mishnah* (Philadelphia: Trinity Press International, 1990), esp. 131–308; see also the shorter survey in his *Judaism: Practice and Belief. 63 BCE–66 CE*, 431–40.

It is this zeal that gets us back to our point: in their zeal to obey the law, these Pharisees often went beyond the law. In fact, *in going beyond the law these Pharisees thought they were protecting the law from being broken*. There developed the notion of "building a hedge around the law": if the law says, "Eat in the temple precincts in total purity," then the hedge would be constructed away from that by saying, "Always eat in purity." In saying this, the following becomes operative: If you always eat in purity (the hedge), you will not break the law of temple purity. That is, if one obeyed the interpretation, one could never break the law.

It is precisely here that legalism becomes apparent: in going beyond the law, legalism develops other laws that become just as binding—all in an attempt to protect the law from being broken and to provide for the covenant member a certain ease of obedience. But if God's law is "temple purity," then we are wrong if we construct a law more rigorous. If we take the Bible to be God's Word, then we can trust that God knew what he was doing. His moderation must become our moderation. While in a previous point I argued that legalism's concerns are almost never bad, here I am arguing that legalism's concerns become instinctually wrong-headed (though not necessarily bad in concern) when they go beyond the law in attempting to protect the law. If God in his infinite wisdom did not think total separation from unbelievers was proper, then it is wrong for us to think total separation is God's will—as has been unfortunately done in sectarian movements. What happens here is a serious distortion: the love of God for people is held at bay by a desire to perform certain kinds of behavior.

Finally, I describe something I label as *reverse legalism*. For many legalists it is implied that in not breaking the law one has necessarily obeyed the law. One hears such things as: "I did not break the rules, so I must have obeyed the rules." As love of my wife is more than "not divorcing her" or "not hating her," so obeying God's will is much more than "not breaking his laws." Obeying God is a matter of the heart and involves a total orientation of one's self; not breaking the law can be done accidentally, it can be done out of a bitter heart, and it may be done without any desire for God's glory. But legalism develops far too frequently the tacit assumption that not breaking a law is being a law-abiding person.

In applying this to our day, I make only a few observations. Let us take a fairly rigorous movement (and perhaps one that hardly exists anymore), one with a singularly authoritarian pastor and a set of rules that includes: tithing one-tenth of gross income, no movie attendance (developed in the direction of no R-rated movies for the home VCR), no consumption of alcohol, regular attendance at all services of the church, reading the Bible only in a prescribed version, active involvement in the pro-life movement, religious and theological separation from the mainline denominations in the community, and no divorce for leaders in the church (including Sunday school teachers and choir members). What we need to see here is that one could be actively committed to each of these practices (none of which is bad in its essential concerns) and one could, at the end of the year, take stock and conclude that one has not broken any of the "social laws" of the church. I am personally persuaded that the person who so evaluates himself (or herself) will inevitably also think that he or she has been God-fearing and obedient to the will of God for the entire year. What I am contending is against this: a person could live life according to these practices and *miss the will of God entirely* because one can live a life of not breaking these rules but never live a life in the freedom of the Spirit. I am also more than convinced that a person could live according to these rules and also live within God's will,[21] although that person may need at times to flex on these rules because of the leading of the Lord. My point is simple: not breaking laws is not identical to obeying God's will.

Applying Galatians to our world today is the heartfelt need of this book. Applying it properly is the thrust. It is my contention that Paul is against practices performed by Christians that detract from the work of Christ, that neglect the absolute need for the Holy Spirit, and that erect social boundaries between people that don't need such boundaries. Paul is opposed to ideas that threaten the purity of the gospel. The commentary that follows will seek to apply that concern of Paul to our day. May God in his grace guide us in the ministry of his Word.

Now Read This

IN THIS SURVEY of the message of Galatians and areas for its application in our modern world, I have introduced several new ideas, and I wish to lay them before the reader in a more concise (definition-type) form. I will look at three such terms or expressions.

Legalism. Legalism here is taken to be Judaizing legalism, and Judaizing legalism is adherence to the law of Moses as a necessary step in being pleasing to God. But legalism is not simply adherence to, and insistence upon, certain rules. Rather, what is wrong with Judaizing legalism is that it supplants

---

21. Without getting into all the issues here, however, I am of the view that such rules should not be constructed by local churches. Such rules tend to harden and become archaic (but binding) when they should be abandoned as social mores change. As society changes, Christians need to adapt their strategies and concerns.

Christ and the Spirit. Judaizing legalism is wrong because (1) it does not understand that Christ and the Spirit are the fulfillment of Mosaic law and, therefore, the law of Moses now belongs to the former era, and (2) the Judaizers who are pushing this legalism are forcing Gentiles to be Jews. These two arguments form the basics of Paul's argument against the Judaizers. They neither understand the Bible nor the universality of the gospel. In defining legalism, and Paul's countering of legalism, in this manner, I need to make it clear that Paul is not countering the simple addition of rules to the gospel as being motivated by a human's propensity to justify oneself before God. Paul is not attacking motives (merit-seeking or self-centeredness, etc.); rather, he is attacking an unbiblical perception of the role the law played in history and the nationalistic impulses of these Judaizers.

Works of the law. Again, we are dealing here with practices performed by the Judaizers that are in conformity to the law of Moses; what makes them wrong is that they are done in such a way that the practitioners are claiming that Christ's work and the Spirit's guidance are insufficient for daily life. But with the coming of Christ and the gift of the Spirit, the revelation to Moses has been fulfilled and is no longer the primary revelation of God to his people. "Works of the law" is an expression that emphasizes the word *law*, not *works*—especially if by works one wants to emphasize merit-seeking and self-centeredness. One thing that makes "works of the law" wrong, then, is that they are actions dictated by a law that has now been supplanted by Christ and the Spirit. Thus, they are "old-fashioned ethics." Furthermore, "works of the law" is a description of particular Jewish practices that erect boundaries between Jews and non-Jews; it is a description of "nationalistic righteousness." What makes them also wrong, then, is that they are social instruments for separation, not a revelation of God's will for all people, Jew or Gentile.

Flesh. Flesh is frequently understood in conjunction with works of the law as the "self-motivated expression of a person who wants to be justified before God on the basis of performance." But this is not as accurate as we need. What Paul means by "flesh" is a life lived before God without dependence on the Spirit. Thus, it is "un-Spiritual" living rather than "merit-seeking life" as such. Flesh, then, naturally aligns itself with the law because the one who wants to be governed by the law is the one who refuses to live in the Spirit and without dependence on Christ.

Galatians 1:1–9

P AUL, AN APOSTLE—SENT not from men nor by man, but
by Jesus Christ and God the Father, who raised him
from the dead—²and all the brothers with me,
To the churches in Galatia:

³Grace and peace to you from God our Father and the
Lord Jesus Christ, ⁴who gave himself for our sins to rescue us
from the present evil age, according to the will of our God
and Father, ⁵to whom be glory for ever and ever. Amen.

⁶I am astonished that you are so quickly deserting the one
who called you by the grace of Christ and are turning to a different gospel—⁷which is really no gospel at all. Evidently
some people are throwing you into confusion and are trying
to pervert the gospel of Christ. ⁸But even if we or an angel
from heaven should preach a gospel other than the one we
preached to you, let him be eternally condemned! ⁹As we have
already said, so now I say again: If anybody is preaching to
you a gospel other than what you accepted, let him be eternally condemned!

WHILE THIS LETTER appears to begin as typical
ancient letters began (Writer . . . Addressee . . .
Greetings . . .),¹ the careful reader observes not
only variations, but also the themes that moti-
vate the letter. In general, Paul's introductions are longer, just as his letters are
longer than the average ancient letter. Furthermore, Paul's greetings emphasize his own apostolic status (cf. Rom. 1:1; 1 Cor. 1:1; 2 Cor. 1:1; Eph. 1:1)
and the divine origin of salvation. More importantly, Paul's introductory
greetings are truly introductions: in each of them he begins to express his concerns for the entire letter. In this letter Paul begins to speak of his unques-
tionable apostleship (v. 1: "sent not from men nor by man" is an early

---

1. A nice collection of ancient letters may be found in J. L. White, *Light From Ancient Letters* (Philadelphia: Fortress, 1986). See also S. K. Stowers, *Letter Writing in Greco-Roman Antiquity* (Library of Early Christianity 5; Philadelphia: Westminster, 1986); W. G. Doty, *Letters
in Primitive Christianity* (Philadelphia: Fortress, 1973); I wrote a popular introduction to Paul's
letters: "More Than Mere Mail," *Moody Monthly* 88/9 (May 1988): 36–38.

criticism of the status of the Judaizers) and of salvation by grace (1:4); both of these themes, of course, dominate the letter.

This introduction comprises two sections: (1) the salutation (vv. 1–5) and (2) the occasion of the letter (vv. 6–9). The salutation includes Paul's particular status (v. 1), the addressees (v. 1), those who are with Paul (v. 2), and the greeting of grace and peace (v. 3). Paul greatly expands the greeting by speaking of the true origin of grace and peace (vv. 4–5). The occasion of the letter begins with a statement expressing Paul's befuddlement at the fickleness of the Galatian churches (v. 6). This Paul clarifies in verse 7 when he states that, in fact, the message to which the Galatians were being attracted was not the gospel at all. Paul's convictions are so strong about their departure from the pure gospel that he invokes an eternal curse on those who distort the gospel of Christ that he received and preached to them (vv. 8–9).

Paul's *salutation* has some interesting features that we need to examine, including the significance of the title "apostle" (v. 1) and the meaning of "the present evil age" (v. 4). To use the title "apostle" as the second word of the letter is to claim authority and to expect agreement on the part of the churches of Galatia. While our age may be essentially dialogical in its orientation, Paul's world was more hierarchical and authoritarian. To understand this we must sketch what an apostle was in the Jewish and early Christian world.[2] The Greek term for "apostle" (*apostolos*) is parallel to the Hebrew word *shaliach*. This Hebrew term was used to describe a personal agent, representative, or ambassador. In fact, a post-first-century definition has become standard for how we understand what an apostle was, even in the first century. I quote from the third-century Jewish Mishnah: "One who prays and errs—it is a bad sign for him. And if he is a communal *agent* [who prays on behalf of the whole congregation], it is a bad sign for them that appointed him. [This is on the principle that] a man's *agent* is like [the man] himself" (Mishnah Berakhot 5:5).[3] Notice in this definition that others make inferences about a given authority on the basis of his agents. (The term "agent" is a translation of the Hebrew *shaliach*.) That is to say, one's agents become the very representations of the person who sent them, much as international ambassadors are official representatives of the national leader himself. With this in

---

2. On *apostle*, see K. Rengstorf, "ἀπόστολος," *TDNT* 1:401–7; E. von Eicken, et al., "Apostle," in *NIDNTT* 1:126–37; J.-A. Bühner, "ἀπόστολος," *EDNT* 1:142–46; N. Turner, *Christian Words*, 23–25; H. D. Betz, "Apostle," *ABD* 1:309–11.

3. All quotations from the Mishnah are from the translation of Jacob Neusner. See *The Mishnah: A New Translation* (New Haven and London: Yale University Press, 1988). Words in brackets are implied. A similar definition can be found in Origen, *John* 32.17 (Migne, 14.785C).

mind, we can clearly see that Paul saw himself as *an official representative of Jesus Christ*. He knew he had been called by Jesus Christ and been appointed an official apostle of Jesus Christ, and he knew the implication of being called an apostle.

Paul worked this out in several directions. While he knew there was a special class of apostles, the Twelve (cf. 1 Cor. 15:7; Gal. 1:17, 19), he knew he was also an apostle in a parallel sense, even if he was "last of all" (1 Cor. 15:8; cf. Rom 1:1; Gal. 1:1; etc.).[4] While it is clear that Paul at times had to struggle with others over his status (e.g., at Galatia and Corinth), his own convictions were firm. Paul knew he had been called by the risen Jesus (1 Cor. 9:1; 15:7–8; Gal. 1:15–16) and that the Lord had revealed to him in that call the specifics of his ministry: Paul was to go to the Gentiles (Gal. 1:16; 2:7). This call was confirmed in Paul's missionary successes and in his miracles (cf. Rom. 1:5; 11:13–16; 15:19; 1 Cor 3:5–6; 4:15). In fact, Paul tells the Corinthians: "you are the seal of my apostleship" (1 Cor. 9:2). We should also observe that Paul, along with the testimony of the church, saw the role of the apostles to be a special one in history; he knew that they performed a crucial function in the period just after the resurrection of Christ (1 Cor. 4:9; Eph. 2:20; 3:5—6; Col. 1:24–27).

Paul, then, writes as an apostle—as one who has been called personally by Jesus Christ, who therefore represents Jesus Christ, and who has a crucial role in the history of the church. He claims at least that much in the second word of this letter. He expects the Galatians to listen; he knows that disagreement is no longer dialogue; disagreement is heresy when it comes to the essentials of the gospel as made known through the apostles and prophets. Even Paul himself must submit to his own gospel (1:8, 10).

Paul's greeting is the typical early Christian mixing of the Greek and Jewish greetings ("grace and peace"). However, Paul's greeting is not simply from one mortal person to another; the grace and peace Paul invokes upon the Galatians is the grace and peace "from God our Father and the Lord Jesus Christ." Paul, in adding the origins of his greetings, distances his greetings from the secular world and makes them sacred and religious. This greeting is one shared only by Christians.

In describing the origin of the greetings, Paul goes on to comment on Jesus, saying that Jesus Christ "gave himself for our sins to rescue us from the present evil age" (v. 4). Forgiveness of sins is important for Galatians but it plays a mediating role there. For this letter forgiveness implies that work of Christ is sufficient (2:21). To bring up forgiveness, then, implies that the

---

4. Besides for himself, Paul uses the term *apostle* also for those outside the circle of the Twelve: see Rom. 16:7; 2 Cor. 8:23; Gal. 1:19 (see notes); Phil. 2:25; 1 Thess. 2:7.

Galatians have not yet grappled enough with how potent the work of Christ was. To put this another way, while the Galatians may have thought they were forgiven by Christ (2:15–21; 3:10–14), they did not realize that this forgiveness was also sufficient to rescue them from "the present evil age." It was the present evil age that concerned Paul because he believed that those who consistently lived in Christ would not succumb to it.

What is "the present evil age"[5] from which one is rescued through the cross (cf. 3:13)? How is one rescued from a "time period"? While it may be correct to say that in comparison, the present for Paul is evil and the future is good (cf. 2 Cor. 5:1–10), this is not nuanced enough for what Paul is getting at. Judaism frequently distinguished "this age" from the "age to come," the latter a description of the establishment of God's justice and peace. But the revolution that took place in Paul's understanding of history when he encountered Jesus Christ adds a new dimension to "this age." It is probably best to regard this expression as describing "life dictated by the law." Because Christ has eclipsed the age of the law and brought history to a new era (see notes at 3:19–25), life under the law, whether lived now or in the past, is considered "an evil age" (cf. 4:3, 9; 5:1; see also 5:16–26). One who trusts in Christ is rescued from the present evil age: "he gave himself for our sins to rescue *us*" (1:4). This expression, then, probably reflects the polemical situation of Galatians: the present evil age is the age in which the Galatians are being seduced to live, and life in Christ is a life of freedom (5:1–12).

Paul's introduction moves next to a description of the *occasion* for the letter (vv. 6–9). It has often been observed that this is the only surviving letter of Paul's that does not contain a thanksgiving for the church to whom he is writing. It is then usually inferred that since Paul does not give thanks, he is either not thankful to God for them or he is so angry with what has taken place he cannot express his thanks. These observations, in some form, are probably accurate. However, we should also observe that many hold this letter to be the first canonical letter Paul wrote and that, in light of this, it is hard to argue a departure from his typical practice since that practice had not yet begun. It is just possible that Paul's practice of expressing thanksgiving in his letters developed later or that such a practice developed out of his harsh experience at Galatia.

The reason why Paul wrote this letter, and the reason we have it, is because the Galatians had "changed positions" on a crucial subject: the means of acceptance with God and the role Christ played in that acceptance.

---

5. For further discussion, see R. N. Longenecker, *Galatians*, 8–9; F. F. Bruce, *Galatians*, 76–77; W. D. Davies, *Paul and Rabbinic Judaism* (4th ed.; Philadelphia: Fortress, 1980), 285–320; E. P. Sanders, *Judaism: Practice and Belief*, 279–303.

Paul is amazed that their change took place "so quickly" (v. 6). At 5:4 Paul states that this change was opting for a system in which grace was not crucial and in which Christ's work was not sufficient. Paul states here that they were "deserting the one who called you" (v. 6); that is to say, their move was not just an intellectual one. Rather, it was a desertion of God as made known in Christ; it was abandoning of their personal relationship with God. If we use the categories of 3:19–25 (see notes there), their departure was a decision to live in B.C. days when the A.D. days had arrived. It was a decision to recede back in time into the days of Moses and to reject the epoch-altering revelation in Christ. While Paul suggests this was a move to a "different gospel," he goes on in verse 7 to clarify this by saying that this is "really no gospel at all."[6] The move of the Galatians was not one of those views of legitimate Christian differences; it was total and devastating. Paul counters here any suggestion of simple Christian differences. When the gospel of grace in Christ is supplemented with the system of Moses, the result is not a perfected, fully mature gospel; rather, it is a gross perversion and a totally different message.

Gross perversions of the gospel are heresies. Paul's final words here are potent. He invokes a curse on anyone (including himself!) who distorts the gospel. Paul's sentences in verses 8–9 are largely parallel and synonymous with one interesting variation. The expression "the one we preached to you" in verse 8 has its parallel in verse 9 in "than what you accepted." The latter expression is related to his apostolic calling. Paul uses here the technical language of passing on sacred traditions ("what you accepted"; Gk. *parelabete*) in such a way as to guarantee authenticity and heredity. It is the same language used by rabbis for handing on their sacred traditions, and it is the same term Paul uses for the tradition of the Lord's Supper (1 Cor. 11:23). The message Paul preached is the message that ultimately derives from the Lord because it is has been transmitted to others through his apostles.

Those who distort this message are rejecting the authority of Christ and are therefore cursed (*anathema*). This word is used in the Old Testament for something consecrated to God for his destruction (cf. Deut. 7:26; Josh. 6:17–18). Paul is not talking here about church discipline; his language is far too strong for that. He is invoking God's final damnation and wrath on people who distort the gospel of grace in Christ and substitute, in effect, Moses' law as the preeminent form of revelation. They are like those who reject the message of the prophets (1 Kings 11:30–31) or apostles (Matt. 10:14).

---

6. Some scholars see an intentional word-play by Paul in "turning to a different [*heteron*] gospel—which is really no gospel at all [*allo*]." The first word is said to mean "a different kind" and the second "(not) another of the same kind." See the discussion in Burton, *Galatians*, 22–24, 420–22.

Paul's introduction encompasses much: it moves from wishing God's grace and peace on believers to cursing those who refuse that grace; it moves from Paul's titled status (apostle) to the severest form of that status (cursing). It introduces us to the heart of the Galatian problem: a gospel of grace at war with a gospel that minimizes Christ.

ANY BIBLE READER knows that reflection and meditation upon even the smallest of words and sentences of God's Word can produce applications for life. Because of the scope of this commentary we cannot suggest applications for everything Paul says in these first nine verses. We have to examine the land and find the more significant contours. This is usually done by finding the more logically important words, the most theologically significant ideas, and the more practically relevant issues. Even then we will omit some important things. For example, the resurrection of Christ is crucial both for Christian life and for apologetics.[7] Paul mentions the resurrection in verse 1, but the resurrection does not play a critical role in the theology of Galatians. Since this is not a word-by-word commentary, we will not be able to trace out the applications of every expression. In this particular section (1:1–9), we point out three elements of "bridging the context."

(1) It is clear to any reader of this letter that Paul faced different problems than we face. He was a Diaspora Jew, probably raised in Jerusalem, and he encountered traveling missionaries who distorted the apostolic gospel of Christ by adding Moses to it in such a way so as to make life in Jerusalem (and elsewhere) more socially comfortable. I have rarely heard of Christians converting to Judaism in such a way that they thought they were bringing Christianity to its fullest form. I have heard, sadly, of some who have rejected Christ and opted for Judaism (or some other faith). Put differently, when we apply even this introduction, we must be aware of the differences as well as the similarities. We must be aware of the social context of the Judaizers as a potential clue for application. Perhaps we will find groups of Christians who are deeply influenced by leaders who themselves are seeking acceptance with some social group. Perhaps they, like the Judaizers, are imposing a message on others to avoid persecution of some sort.

What is needed is an ability to understand both what Paul meant by "which is really no gospel at all" (v. 7) and what currents and ideas today have altered the gospel itself. This is the burden of the letter to the Galatians. We fail to understand this letter if we become absorbed with legalism as the main

---

7. E.g., see J. R. W. Stott, *Contemporary Christian*, 70–85.

application. Legalism was wrong not because laws are somehow wrong, but because legalism supplanted Jesus Christ and the Holy Spirit. As we pointed out in the introduction, we need God's grace to discern when Christ has been minimized or decentralized and when the important role the Spirit has in our Christian life has been eliminated. The thrust of the entire letter of Galatians makes this clear. If we simply move from Paul's context to ours, we might think only in terms of heresies that distort the gospel of grace by supplementing it with Mosaic law. We might even broaden this to include any form of supplementing the gospel with legalism. But this misses the heart of Galatians. Paul urges on us here the centrality of Christ and the cruciality of the Holy Spirit. The specific kind of distortion is much less important than what happens to Christ and the Spirit in that distortion. As we seek to apply Galatians we must be looking for ideas, practices, and people who supplant the sufficiency of Christ and the power the Spirit plays in our life.

Again, we must be on guard against the idea that every rule or regulation in Christian living is a necessary form of Galatian legalism. In fact, we are persuaded that rules can be educationally useful for Christian development. What we are looking for in applying the message of Galatians are rules or regulations that *distort* the gospel. We are looking for systems analysis, an ability to discern the workings of various messages so that we can see each part in the light of the whole.

Heresies are transformations of the real thing. In seeking for parallels in our current world we need to see what happens when the gospel is supplemented, augmented, altered, or changed. What happens when we emphasize, for instance, that salvation is solely by grace? Do people develop a complacency? Do Christians begin to sense that Christian holiness is an option? Then we need to ask if this is consistent with the gospel of grace. Of course, it is not. In other words, we must explore where our gospel is giving off such an impression and to alter our original statements. What happens when we emphasize the demand of the gospel? Do Christians begin to develop a lack of confidence in the sufficiency of Christ? Do they begin to sense that the gospel is a burden? What happens when we emphasize the disciplines of the Christian life? Do Christians, especially young Christians, begin to neglect the dynamic the Spirit brings into our life? What we need, in all of this, is a balance that comes only as a result of God's grace, a balanced appreciation of both God's grace and the demand that grace has upon our lives. We must preach both God's grace and the transforming powers of the gospel. Perhaps we can move at our problems from the other end: if we see people who are complacent, who are independent of the Holy Spirit, or who do not seem to live in total dependence on Christ, then we need to examine our gospel to see if it is leading people astray from these centralities.

(2) It is not unusual for me to receive letters at my office from prospective students whose letters begin with a near-Pauline salutation. Imitation of Paul is not wrong, but I am not persuaded that Paul is teaching us here how to write letters. He is not instituting a form of Christian communication. Our form of letter writing is different: "Dear David, etc." Letters that begin "Scot McKnight, a preacher and teacher of the Bible, etc.," sound stilted and peculiar today. Rather, what I must emphasize here is that the integral connection between Paul and his churches at Galatia remains the same: we are greeted, like the Galatians, because we are, like the Galatians, also ones who have been rescued from the present evil age (with its perversions of the gospel) by trusting in Christ. While we learn something here about the relationship Christians have with one another (and indirectly how those with more authority need at times to relate to those in their charge), the enduring lesson does not revolve around the nature of letter writing. It revolves around our spiritual unity as a result of Christ and how we can approach one another in that unity.

(3) What does it mean for us that Paul was an apostle? Anything? Are we to have apostles today? For most of us (and I include myself) it should be said that we do not have apostles around who can direct our minds authoritatively toward theological orthodoxy and point out heresies that confront the church today. How do we relate to apostles like Paul, and how does our relationship to Paul affect our relationships to other authorities in the church today? While we who believe in the Bible, and in particular in the letter of Paul to the Galatians, are the first to admit that we want to submit to Paul's authority enshrined in his letters, we want to do this as a result of reflection. Such reflection demands both the investigation of the ancient text and its meaning then and the investigation of our contemporary society and churches.

But surely our approach today is to recognize that we still have apostolic guidance in this letter and that this letter can lead us in a way that is consistent with the gospel. While we may need, at times, Christian pastors and teachers who can point us in our modern society more decisively, we are persuaded that this letter, when read properly and applied discerningly, can guide us in our times of heretical deviations and doctrinal distortions.

HAVING BRIEFLY STUDIED the text in its ancient context and also having mentioned some of the steps taken when a reader moves the ancient text to our modern world, we need now to arouse the reader's attention by highlighting some potential applications. Sometimes the material presented in this section might be useful for those who are involved in teaching or preaching the gospel, but our design is to make each application useful for the life of all Christians.

First, our response to Paul's letter is an indication of our attitude toward Christ. Jesus said: "He who receives you receives me, and he who receives me receives the one who sent me" (Matt. 10:40). If it is true that an apostle is a personal agent of Jesus Christ, and if it is true that an agent is a personal representative, then it follows that Paul's message is a message from Jesus Christ. Acknowledging this implies that every Christian must accept apostolic letters as authoritative, for their message is a message from Jesus Christ. Of course, this works out in various ways. For instance, we may be inclined to add to the gospel ourselves; encountering Galatians will challenge us to drop any such additions. We may be charmed by radical pluralism today with its attractive suggestion that all will eventually be saved. But if we accept the earliest definitions of an apostle, then we must also accept the message of Paul that states that additions to the gospel bring the wrath, not the acceptance, of God.

Submission to the apostolic message because it is a message from Christ is why believers today are concerned with studying the Bible and anchoring their views in the Bible. Whether we read about "Home Bible Studies" in South America, Europe, Romania, or the United States, we are reading about a central affirmation necessary for the Christian: submission to the Bible. A quick glance at almost every published picture of Billy Graham's preaching shows Billy holding the Bible and preaching from the Bible. Church architecture confirms the authority that the Bible plays in the church: in most churches there is a podium (lectern, etc.) in the front, either in the middle or to the side, and this placement of the pulpit symbolizes the front place the Bible has for the church's ministry.

Yet another example of this may be taken from the life of Dietrich Bonhoeffer who, as part of the Confessing Church, was the sole teacher of an underground seminary (in Finkenwalde). Students here were taught the authority of the Word of God and the fundamental importance of meditating and praying over it. It has even been said that Bonhoeffer did not permit his students to critique other sermons because the proclaimed Word was to be heard and heeded, not evaluated and debated.[8] John Stott says it well:

> This, then, is our dilemma. Are we to accept Paul's account of the origin of his message, supported as it is by solid historical evidence? Or shall we prefer our own theory, although supported by no historical

---

8. See E. Bethge, *Dietrich Bonhoeffer: Man of Vision, Man of Courage* (New York: Harper & Row, 1970), 361–63; E. Robertson, *The Shame and the Sacrifice: The Life and Martyrdom of Dietrich Bonhoeffer* (New York: Collier, 1988), 123–26.

evidence? If Paul was right in asserting that his gospel was not man's but God's (cf. Rom. 1:1), then to reject Paul is to reject God.[9]

However, we must also urge that such a submission involves interpretation of the text. While some may say that this is the slippery escape from full submission to the text, I am persuaded that all readings of a text are interpretations and that it is the Christian's responsibility to interpret a text as accurately as possible. Our stance is submission to whatever the text says, regardless of what that means for our thinking and lifestyle. We are using a slippery escape when we distort the interpretation so that it fits our predispositions; we are not finding a slippery escape when we accept the text as it stands, regardless of its implications for life. Every honest interpreter can give countless examples of finding himself or herself to be simply wrong and in need of God's grace as a result of reading the Bible with the purpose of hearing God's word.

Second, a crucial note is sounded by Paul in verse 1: "sent not from men nor by man." An application from this verse is both simple and penetrating. Put simply, we need to guard our ideas and scope our practices to see if they are constructed in order to please people or if they have been constructed by people. We need to be constantly reforming our theology and our practices by checking each against the revelation of God in Christ and in his written Word. Paul knew that the Galatian heresy of legalism was constructed by a group bent on gaining the approval of others. He also knew that the notion of perfecting Jesus by adding Moses was not from God; rather, it was a human-oriented and human-based system of religion. How we track our interpretation of God's Word is both difficult and simple: it is difficult because of the complexity of Christian systems today and simple because ultimately we need only to check our ideas and our practices against the biblical revelation and, I believe, against the historically significant creeds and confessions of the church that have withstood the tests of time. Ultimately, however, the final check of all things is the Word of God.

In my own lifetime I have experienced pressure from different groups that I now realize was almost certainly a reflection of a human-oriented message. I have gone through the period when the only permissible translation was the KJV. I once had a youth pastor tell me that while I could read the NASB at home, I was never to bring it to church. I now believe this was social pressure from higher authorities who did not want to see their cherished translation give way to newer (and better) translations. I have heard preachers rant and rave about going to movies, social dancing, television, nuclear warfare,

---

9. J. R. W. Stott, *Only One Way*, 37.

and the like. I am also certain that, while the motivations were usually a desire to be consistently Christian, there was much more social and peer pressure than any of these leaders would ever admit. I have seen the same from other leaders who refuse to associate with Christians of a differing political stripe. On the one side we have those who believe in more government involvement in the moral and economic issues that face us, and on the other those who believe in less government involvement. I have seen Christians on both sides who severely curtail their involvement with those on the other side less they lose face in their own crowd. This, sadly, is too often motivated by a "fear of people" and not a "fear of God."

Another area for consideration is that our unity as Christians transforms our approach to one another. We can perhaps learn a lesson from Paul's greetings. While the world around Paul greeted one another with "graces" and "peaces," Paul greets the churches of Galatia with the grace and peace that come from God the Father and from the Lord Jesus Christ. Our connection with other Christians transcends our social relationships; our connection owes its origins to God's gracious work for us in Christ and his workings of the Holy Spirit. Perhaps it would be better if Christians of all persuasions learned to greet one another with: "May the peace and grace of the Lord be with you." This may be uncomfortable for some outside of a liturgical context, but it may also be much more effective and a source of spiritual dynamic in our lives.

Like the situation facing the Galatians, the age of grace can become an age of rescue, but it can also become "a present evil age" if we distort the gospel. According to Paul, God's grace in the cross of Christ has rescued us from this present evil age. As we will see in chapters 5 and 6, this rescue brings forgiveness, love, and the freedom that come from the Spirit. This is the typical Christian life. However, I argued above that this present evil age in Galatians describes a life under the law after Christ has come to deliver us from that law. And what Paul says is that if we distort the gospel in minimizing the centrality of Christ or the Spirit, we slip back into an age when Christ is not the rescuer and where the Spirit is not the one who brings us a life of freedom and love.[10] Paul urges us to watch our gospel lest it be transformed into a "different gospel" that prevents acceptance with God.

Let us be careful to understand that tampering with the gospel is not Christian experimentation with new ideas. The gospel is a sacred trust that remains, like Jesus Christ, the same yesterday, today, and tomorrow. Society and culture change; applications change; Christian lifestyle and even specific doctrinal formulations change; but the gospel of Jesus Christ does not

---

10. On whether this means "loss of salvation," see the notes on 5:1—12.

change. We are given every freedom to explore the vast domains of life and reality that are still unknown frontiers to us.[11] We are given every freedom to explore the implications of the gospel for our world today. But we are never given any freedom to alter the original gospel of the grace of God in Christ.

The outcome of perverting the gospel is God's wrath, and this truth we need to keep in front of us as we discern our message and the message of others. This is perhaps the most distasteful dimension of the gospel as revealed throughout the pages of the New Testament. Our society is inherently pluralistic and finds its ability to cope with the massive diversity of our world by appealing to pluralism. In the United States, the constitution makes freedom of religion a cardinal virtue. But Christians, while they may believe that freedom of religion is a necessary law for a diverse society to live in peace, cannot at the same time infer that all religions are true just because tolerance is needed in a diverse society. Here our current Christianity has gone astray; here we have succumbed to the forces of our age. While we may defend the rights of others to worship in the manner they choose, we do not at the same time minimize the truth of the gospel by suggesting that these other faiths are also *the* truth.[12] What Paul teaches—and here again we touch upon his apostolic authority—is that distortions of the gospel, whether they are protected by constitutional rights or not, are contrary to God's will and subject to God's final displeasure.

Examples in our culture abound.[13] The following example is, of course, extreme, but its extremity forces the issue upon us. As a college student I was involved in the Billy Graham Crusade in Brussels (Belgium); along with a large number of other American students I had spent the early part of the summer assisting different Greater Europe Mission missionaries. Our routine was a morning worship time—led by such notables as John Stott, Festo Kivengere, and Luis Palau, followed by small group Bible study. In our small group were two young women who were part of what they called "The Children of

---

11. A book that has been helpful to me in this regard is A. F. Holmes, *All Truth Is God's Truth* (Grand Rapids: Eerdmans, 1977).

12. I am not, however, assuming that everything in every other religion is false. See on this, Sir N. Anderson, *The World's Religions* (4th ed.; Downers Grove, Ill.: InterVarsity Press, 1975) and *Christianity and Comparative Religions* (Downers Grove, Ill.: InterVarsity Press, 1970). A recent provocative book in this regard is C. H. Pinnock's *A Wideness in God's Mercy: The Finality of Jesus Christ in a World of Religions* (Grand Rapids: Zondervan, 1992); this author distinguishes helpfully between "exclusivism," "inclusivism," and "pluralism."

13. A lucid survey has been done by Ruth A. Tucker, whose title comes from our text, *Another Gospel: Alternative Religions and the New Age Movement* (Grand Rapids: Zondervan, 1989); see esp. pp. 15–48 for the fundamental definitions and categories used in analyzing "heretical movements."

God." I had never heard of such a group, but one of the missionaries in Austria pointed out to me that they were a "borderline cult group." Both appeared to us to be sincere in their attempts to follow the Lord, and both seemed to know the Bible quite well; their prayers were rather typical, and nothing about them gave away that they had more than a few strange ideas. While I did not know much about them at the time, I have since learned much more.[14] Tucker says the Children of God "is a graphic illustration of how a religious movement can move from orthodoxy to aberrant beliefs and practices—beliefs and practices that sometimes defy the imagination."[15] David "Moses" Berg, the founder of this movement, began his evangelistic ministries in Huntington Beach, California, attempting to reach the Hippie generation; but, as is often the case with cultic leaders,[16] he moved more and more on his own until he virtually formed a cult group around himself. Berg himself degenerated into a polygamist and occultist and was eventually chased from the United States; he settled in England in 1972 (and it was in 1975 that we were in Brussels for Eurofest 75). To make a long, and tragic, story short, Berg eventually combined religious prostitution with evangelism in what is called "flirty fishing" and moved on to Tenerife (an island off Africa), changing the name of his group to the Family of Love. While the movement still exists (under various names), Berg's attraction has declined significantly.

Here is a classic example of a heresy, even to the point of being ludicrous in its final, essential orientation, but a heresy that started as little more than an evangelistic ministry that sought to reach out to a modern generation with methods that would speak to that very generation. Those young women who were part of our Bible study group may or may not have been involved in Berg's perversity, but they were nonetheless lured into his tent of operations and became part of a tragic cult. Distortions of the gospel, no matter how slight at first, can eventually degenerate into an obnoxious perversion of the gospel.

But how do we talk about such perversions? Do we use the same kind of harsh rhetoric that Paul used? Again, our culture is different from Paul's. What was seen as an acceptable form of disagreement then may not be seen as

---

14. A survey can be found in ibid., 231–43; I am deeply dependent on her survey in what follows.

15. Ibid., 231.

16. David Koresh, the cult leader of the Branch Davidians in Waco, Texas, is a recent such figure. As this chapter is being edited, the fires of the compound he dominated have still not calmed down. It is important for us to realize that Koresh's beginnings were dramatically unlike the endings of his leadership. While it is hard for us to understand how anyone could be connected to such a lunatic-type leader, had we seen him in the beginning of his movement we might better understand how it all can be explained.

acceptable today. In reading ancient literature I have seen this difference. The ancient world simply loved inflammatory language for expressing its differences. I can document a great deal of such language in their literature, but I have not been able to document any who thought such language was personally biased and out of line. The ancients delighted in overstatement, and overstatements were effectively countered with similar overstatements. Today, however, we have become, if anything, over-sensitized to offending special interest groups. So today we have editors who, admirably, reread our texts to see if they will offend racial, religious, and gender-sensitive groups. Ours is not the ancient world. For this reason alone I believe we need to state our decisions more carefully and in a less inflammatory manner than Paul did in Galatians 1.[17]

From Galatians, then, I believe we can learn some things about how to speak about the severe consequences of distorting the gospel. Paul speaks about the damnation of the heretics by clarifying that they were disagreeing not so much with him as with the gospel (v. 8). In other words, Paul made it clear that he was as subject to that gospel as they were and that he was in as much danger as they were if he distorted it. In our own warnings about heresies we should perhaps make it third person ("this is the case for this expression . . . ") rather than second person ("you will be damned if you distort the gospel"). Furthermore, Paul makes it quite clear what was wrong; he did not simply erupt into a dogmatic tirade against some people. The letter of Galatians is a carefully laid-out argument, both against the distortion of the Judaizers and for the expression of the gospel of grace. What we need today is less tirade, less emotional outburst, and much more carefully constructed arguments that vindicate the truthfulness of the gospel of Jesus Christ. Finally, Paul's entire letter focuses on the freedom and love that come from the Spirit. If in our preaching, teaching, and apologetics we express ourselves in such a way that obscures the glorious freedom of the gospel or in a manner that hides God's love for these people, then we fail from the outset to convey what the gospel itself is. Yes, we must be willing to confront; but we need to confront in such a way that is consistent with the gospel itself. Clearly and compassionately the Christian advocates the gospel of Christ, and in doing so in that manner his gospel is seen.

---

17. A technical study analyzing the acceptability of inflammatory ancient rhetoric is L. T. Johnson, "The New Testament's Anti-Jewish Slander and the Conventions of Ancient Polemic," *Journal of Biblical Literature* 108 (1989): 419–41.

Galatians 1:10–12

A M I NOW trying to win the approval of men, or of God? Or am I trying to please men? If I were still trying to please men, I would not be a servant of Christ.

[11]I want you to know, brothers, that the gospel I preached is not something that man made up. [12]I did not receive it from any man, nor was I taught it; rather, I received it by revelation from Jesus Christ.

Original Meaning

PAUL'S LETTERS MOVE from an introduction to the body of the letter. The body of Galatians begins at 1:10 and extends technically to 6:10. Galatians 1:10–2:21 is concerned with demonstrating the independence of Paul's gospel. In this large section, sometimes called the "Autobiographical Section," Paul argues that his gospel is independent of human teaching (1:13–17), of the major churches in Judea (1:18–24), of the Jerusalem "pillars" (2:1–10), and especially of the apostle Peter (2:11–21). By eliminating all these as the sources of his gospel, Paul accomplishes at least two things: (1) he creates the likelihood that his gospel is a direct revelation from Jesus Christ, and (2) he shatters the arguments of his opponents who contended that Paul's gospel was not independent but was from Jerusalem or at least from those connected with Jerusalem. Therefore, they had argued (we infer) that these new converts to Christianity would also have to be full converts to Judaism.

By "mirror reading"[1] we can legitimately infer from Paul's focus and tone in 1:10–2:21 that the opponents of Paul were bent on demonstrating that

---

1. "Mirror reading" here is a process of inferring from a negative statement by Paul (e.g., "My gospel is not from the Jerusalem leaders") to what the positive statement was made by the opponents ("Paul's gospel must come from Jerusalem because all good things come from Jerusalem"). This process is normal in exegesis and simply assumes that an author's tone and focus are directly related to the context to which he is writing. In this case we assume that Paul's need to state his independence became necessary because it was being denied. On this, see J. M. G. Barclay, *Obeying the Truth*, 40–41. Barclay finds four criteria that aid the reader in mirror-reading: (1) The tone of the remarks; (2) the frequency of the remarks; (3) the clarity of the remarks; or (4) the unfamiliarity of the remarks. Barclay has a fuller study of this in "Mirror-Reading a Polemical Letter: Galatians as a Test Case," *JSNT* 31 (1987): 73–93. The use of these criteria across the whole of Galatians, when done properly, will enable the reader to find a consistent picture of the Judaizers. Such a procedure can be done in one's own Bible study or in a Bible study group.

Paul's gospel ultimately derived from Jerusalem and from the early Jewish apostles who operated out of Jerusalem. By proving that each presentation of the gospel derived from Jerusalem, including Paul's, the Judaizers could then argue that they, too, represented Jerusalem. Perhaps they even argued that they represented the latest expression of the gospel from Jerusalem. Thus they could correct, modify, and supplement Paul's gospel with what they would argue to be the correct tradition. In fact, they may have argued that Paul's gospel was an abbreviated form of the true gospel; they would then have continued their argument that Paul abbreviated the authentic gospel in order to make it more attractive to the Gentiles in Galatia.[2]

While all of this may seem irrelevant to each of us, what we have once again is a sociological crisis. Washington, D.C., is crucial to American politics (what comes from Washington is final); there is no place like that for Western Christianity (though Wheaton, Illinois; Grand Rapids, Michigan; Nashville, Tennessee; and Fort Worth, Texas, have each made their cases). For earliest first-century Christianity, Jerusalem was home, and from it all good things were supposed to come. We are surely aware of the critical role Jerusalem played in ancient Judaism; the same holds true for earliest Christianity. There resided all the authorities and knowledge needed for the development of Christian thinking. The apostles were centered there for much of the time, and the knowledge of the Bible was explored there. The crisis was simple: Was Jerusalem the mother church or not? Were the Jerusalem leaders the authorities or not? Who would set the agenda for the Christian movement—Diaspora Gentile Christians or the traditional leaders in the homeland? Would the gospel of Jesus Christ eliminate its heritage in Judaism or would it stay true to the covenant established with Abraham?

The crisis was whether or not Israel would have a privileged existence and status in the new movement. The issue then became Jewish distinctives as opposed to the heterogeneous and, often enough, non-Jewish life of the Diaspora. Paul countered this by demonstrating that his gospel was not simply Jewish; rather, it came from Jesus Christ and comprised all people. Therefore, it did not demand the nationalization of Gentiles. What Paul opposed was a cultural imperialism that presented itself exclusively in religious attire.

The first part of 1:10–2:21 states this explicitly. Paul argues that his gospel is not in fact dependent on Jerusalem and its leaders. Instead, it is an independent expression. He does this first through a series of questions (1:10), each of which implies that he is not seeking to please human beings but God. He then states his independence negatively (vv. 11–12a: it is not

---

2. See further at J. C. Beker, *Paul the Apostle: The Triumph of God in Life and Thought* (Philadelphia: Fortress, 1980), 43–44.

from human beings) and follows this with a positive declaration (v. 12b: it is from Jesus Christ).

Paul's questions are important here. It is reasonable to argue that his questions contain their own answers. "Am I now trying to win the approval of men?" His answer: "No, in seeking to demonstrate that the Judaizers are wrong and that the gospel of grace is not nationalistic in its center, I [Paul] am merely seeking to remain faithful to God." The second question then is: "Am I now trying to win the approval of God?" His answer here may be one of two things: "Yes, I do everything in order to live with approval before God." Or, "No, neither am I seeking to gain God's approval; I have that in Jesus Christ." The former answer seems preferable here. Paul's next question is: "Or am I trying to please men?" The answer: "No, I am trying to please God."[3] If this is the case, it can be inferred that the Judaizers had tried to convince the Galatians that Paul had trimmed his gospel to the bare essentials in order to court their approval—much like a computer salesperson who cuts all the "bells and whistles" so as to make the system affordable to a penny-pinching customer. Paul counters: "I am not trying to win your approval; I am preaching what God has revealed to me." They respond back: "Paul is preaching cheap grace, grace without law, acceptance by God without submission to God. Paul preaches a gospel that does not include the cost of Judaism and the law."

For Paul there is a radical difference between "trying to please men" and being a "servant of Christ." For him, to accept the mantle of being a servant of Christ (similar to the term "apostle" in 1:1) was to eliminate once-and-for-all the desire to please people. His authority was now different.

What is "the gospel I preached" (v. 11)?[4] There are at least three dimensions to "Paul's" gospel: (1) that salvation is in Jesus Christ alone, in fulfillment of the revelation given through Moses in millennia past; (2) that one becomes accepted by God solely by faith, apart from living in accordance with the law of Moses; and (3) that this acceptance and church participation is open as much to Gentiles as it is to Jews. While the first two have been the focus of theologians since the Reformation, the center of attention in Paul's day was the third. It was Gentile inclusion into justification by faith in Christ apart from the law that was the bone of contention between Paul and the Jerusalem Judaizers. Justification in Christ was acceptable to the Judaizers

---

3. F. F. Bruce contends that the issue is the verbs of the two questions: "win the approval" and "please." He then argues that the answer to the first question is "humans" (Paul is seeking to persuade humans) and the second question is "God" (Paul is seeking the approval of God). See *Galatians*, 84–86.

4. On Paul's gospel, see G. E. Ladd, *A Theology of the New Testament* (Grand Rapids: Eerdmans, 1974), 359–568.

(after all, they claimed to be Christians). Justification for Gentiles was tolerable as well (Jews had plenty of precedent for conversion to Judaism by Gentiles). But it was justification before God *without obedience to the law of Moses* that became intolerable. This view threatened the very existence of Judaism and created the social crisis behind the letter.

As mentioned above, Paul makes his case by asserting two negatives: (1) his gospel is "not something that man made up,"[5] and (2) he "did not receive it from any man,"[6] as an apprentice learns a trade, nor was he taught it. Rather, in his positive statement: "I received it by revelation from Jesus Christ." Surely Paul is describing here his Damascus road encounter with the risen Lord, in which experience he was both converted and received his call to evangelize the Gentile world (cf. Acts 9:1–19). Paul's gospel derives, then, from a revelation *from* Jesus Christ. "Paul's claim . . . is this. His gospel, which was being called in question by the Judaizers and deserted by the Galatians, was neither an invention (as if his own brain had fabricated it), nor a tradition (as if the church had handed it down to him), but a revelation (for God had made it known to him)."[7]

The term *revelation* describes something made known by God to humans, in this case to Paul, that would otherwise not be known or accessible.[8] Revelation thus stands in glaring contrast to passing on sacred traditions. In fact, we must surely see here a criticism of the Judaizers, whose basis of knowledge was sacred tradition. Paul contends that while their gospel may represent some of the leaders in Jerusalem, his gospel is a direct revelation from Jesus Christ.

Bridging Contexts

THAT PAUL'S GOSPEL was independent of Jerusalem seems to matter little to most Christians today. Christians readily accept Paul's apostolic message as God's living Word. However, before we can apply the truthfulness of Paul's gospel, we must first understand why Paul needed to assert and demonstrate his independence. That is, before

---

5. The Greek expression is *kata anthropon*: "according to humans," "consistent with the way humans do things," "human-ish," "derived from humans." It stands in direct contrast to the divine and the revealed (1:12). See also Gal. 3:15, 29; 4:23, 28–29; Col. 2:8.

6. The expression "receive" (*parelabon*) is identical to the one in v. 9; Paul says he did not get his gospel as a result of the sacred process of handing on holy traditions.

7. Stott, *Only One Way*, 30.

8. See T. Holtz, "ἀποκάλυψις," *EDNT* 1:130–32; W. Mundle, et al., "Revelation," *NIDNTT* 3:309–40, esp. 314–16.

applications can be made, we must ponder what lies behind the quest of Paul to demonstrate the independence of his gospel.

We need to assert up front that *independence* is not the most important description of Paul's gospel and is not the issue on which we should set our focus. Our attention moves easily to independence because of our own Western political ideologies where freedom of speech and other freedoms are central to personal happiness. Rather, the most important description of Paul's gospel is that it is *a direct revelation from Jesus Christ* and, therefore, not an indirect gospel that had come to him through the Jerusalem authorities. If Paul's gospel were indirect (from Jerusalem), it could still be correct but it would need to be confirmed by Jerusalem. But since Paul's gospel is a direct revelation, it does not need to be confirmed by Jerusalem. In fact, the gospel emanating from Jerusalem could be wrong and, to reverse the trend, in need of being confirmed by the Pauline expression. Only after arguing that the gospel is a direct revelation from Jesus Christ does Paul argue that his gospel is independent.

Through this process of uncovering what was going on in Paul's argument we gain our first insight for application: the preached gospel, when faithful to the Pauline gospel, is a direct revelation from Jesus Christ. This means that we should be less concerned with churches and leaders being "independent" than with them being faithful to the direct revelation to Paul. Accordingly, we must then focus our applications on the foundation of Paul's thought (direct revelation from Jesus Christ).

In applying texts from the Bible, it is always helpful to glean as much as we possibly can from the historical context before we apply them to our world. In this case, it is fundamentally important for us to discern the social nature of the crisis at Galatia. We must learn what we can about the opponents of Paul (and not treat them as necessarily self-serving, evil, insecure merit-seeking Judaizers) and what motivated them. Our own contexts teach us the important lesson that when oppositions arise, disagreements are rarely simplistic matters. Rather, they are usually complex entanglements of theological issues, personal prejudices, and perceived significant implications for each social group involved.

I am sure we would be much kinder to the Judaizers (and less stereotyping of them) if we would take time to unravel their arguments in light of their situations. It was probably difficult for God-fearing Jewish Christians, who had grown up honorably in Judea in Judaism, who had then converted to the fulfillment of Jewish hopes as climaxed in Jesus Christ, and who had then fought with might and mane for the conversion of Jerusalem to this Messiah—it was probably difficult, I say, for such people even to imagine, let alone accept, a form of Messianic Judaism that was apparently running a course directly away from Judaism and the law of Moses. This we should not doubt, and we should also let such observations become fundamental to our thinking. Our first response to first-century (non-Christian) Jews should not be, "How could they have remained as they were?" but, "How can I understand why they remained as they were?"

To use a modern analogy, it is difficult for Christian parents to see their children, who have been raised in God-fearing Christian homes, go off to college and join some separatistic, fundamentalistic-type church. Such young people can become vibrantly enthusiastic about their new-found community. The parents of these children are shocked, not to say unnerved. They are aware of what happens to such young people: they mature into such a separatistic group, align all their friendships with such a group, raise "their" grandchildren to be like them, and, in effect, snap all connections with their childhood faith. So also the Jerusalem Christians were afraid: these Gentile Christians, they feared, would lose all contact with the fountain of their belief (Judaism, the Torah, Israel, the Land, one God)[9] and might collapse the faith they were seeking to express; they would become a small group with no future.

On the other hand, while we may be more sympathetic with the Judaizers by understanding their predicaments, we must also continue the force of Paul's argument if we seek to maintain apostolic authority and integrity. As far as Paul was concerned, however much the Judaizers' arguments were tied to their social setting and personal issues, the product they were marketing was damaged. Paul knew their gospel was incompatible with his and too socially restrictive. It did not permit the full expression of a "race-less" gospel and therefore was incompatible with salvation by grace through faith in Jesus Christ.

Finally, we need to reflect briefly on whether our expression of the gospel is "our gospel" in the same way Paul's was "his." I think not. Paul was an apostle and was given a direct revelation of the gospel through a personal encounter with Jesus Christ. He was a founder of the church. We are not apostles, and there is no apostolic succession today that has infallible author-

---

9. For readers who want to see a fresh and stimulating presentation of the relationship of earliest Christianity to Judaism, with special attention to the inner conflicts of the two movements, I recommend J. D. G. Dunn's book, *The Partings of the Ways: Between Christianity and Judaism and Their Significance for the Character of Christianity* (Philadelphia: Trinity Press International, 1991); a Jewish perspective is found in S. J. D. Cohen, *From the Maccabees to the Mishnah* (Library of Early Christianity; Philadelphia: Westminster, 1987). For a more popular survey of the history of the period, see P. Barnett, *Behind the Scences of the New Testament* (Downers Grove, Ill.: InterVarsity Press, 1990).

ity in matters of doctrine and practice. Thus, while we may be intent on conforming our gospel as closely as possible to the apostolic expressions, we must
not form a new gospel for our generation. The "I" in the "I received it by revelation from Jesus Christ" (1:12) is not an "I" that is interchangeable with our
own "I." Even if we may have been called to a specific ministry (as Paul was),
we are not given an independent revelation of the gospel in that calling.

 AGAIN, I MUST stress that independence is not the
main issue here; rather, it is the direct revelation
of the gospel to Paul through Jesus Christ. I suspect that the fundamental touchstone for our day
is whether or not we are willing to listen to those whom God has entrusted
with the sacred task of handing down the gospel from Jesus to the growing,
emerging, and diverse early Christian churches (i.e., the apostles).

We begin, then, with the observation that because Paul's gospel is a
direct revelation from Jesus Christ, it ought to bolster our confidence in the
message Paul proclaims and teaches. In the history of the church, it has been
the Roman Catholic Church that has emphasized apostolic authority. Protestant polemics against the Roman Catholics have led the former not only to
downplay the role of the original apostles, but also to weaken the biblical
message itself. The apostles, Paul says, are part of the foundation of the
church (Eph. 2:20); for this reason alone they retain authority and deserve
our respect.[10] Even though personal apostolic succession is denied, apostolic
authority must be retained; and it is retained when the writings of the apostles are held as authoritative and canonical. We can therefore be confident
that the message they teach is the message sent from God for his people.

As we read Galatians, we are reading a letter from a personal representative of Jesus Christ, the apostle Paul, whose message for us is the message of
God. He received this message from Jesus Christ. Thus the implications of
the gospel he spelled out are binding on us: the gospel cannot be restricted
to one nation (whether to Israel or to America). It means too that the gospel
spells freedom in the Spirit for all who call upon Jesus Christ.

A second significant area of application for us is that, along with Paul, we
need to examine ourselves to see if we are "seeking to gain the approval of
men" or succumbing to social and peer pressure (v. 10). Probably no feature
of life is more difficult than this: discerning where our own line of approval

---

10. A useful survey of the biblical message about the authority of the church and the
apostles can be found in Book IV, chapter 8, of John Calvin's *Institutes of the Christian Religion*
(Philadelphia: Westminster, 1960), 2:1149–66.

is actually going. Is it going in the direction of God or is it being rerouted through the approval of human leaders, spouses, and friends? Are we doing what we think is right or are we trying to be diplomatic or political? This rerouting can be subtle indeed: from the glance of a spouse during a conversation to a letter to a Christian friend. When the conviction of our own faithfulness to truth and the apostolic gospel gives way to the desire of approval from a friend, we have joined the ranks of those whom Paul attacks.

It must also be said that approval from friends, spouse, and leaders is not a bad thing. We have records throughout the pages of the Bible where people approve others and such approval is perceived positively (cf. e.g., Prov. 3:3–4; Luke 2:52; Rom. 14:18; Gal. 2:1–10). There is a fine line between being approved by others and having such approval as our motivation. Our motivation must always be to please God and him alone; if others disapprove of us when we know God approves of us, we must disregard their disapprovals. Our fear must be of God, not of humans. To be sure, at times the disapproval of others (parents, for example) may be disregarded at a later time if we discover that what we thought was God's will turned out not to be his will for a particular situation. We can learn from such decisions, either to be more attentive to the Spirit of God or to listen to the wisdom of others; but nonetheless it is important that each Christian learn to live in the light of what God's will is. Even when such hard lessons are found, the principle of seeking God's approval remains. The opposition endured by multitudes of Christians throughout the history of the church, including our own time, is a living example of the fundamental orientation of the Christian's life: living to please God.

Martin Luther, the leading voice of the Reformation, discovered in his monk's cell that God's grace had been so clouded by the darkness of church dogma and human works that there was no sun to be seen. When he announced his discoveries and their implications, he was called before the Roman Catholic authorities to see if he would willingly recant his ideas and so save his relationship to the Catholic Church (and the unity of the Roman Catholic world). The story is well known, and I quote from his famous words:

> Your Imperial Majesty and Your Lordships demand a simple answer. Here it is, plain and unvarnished. Unless I am convicted of error by the testimony of Scripture or (since I put no trust in the supported authority of pope or of councils, since it is plain that they have often erred and often contradicted themselves) by manifest reasoning I stand convicted by the Scriptures to which I have appealed, and my conscience is taken captive by God's word, I cannot and will not

recant anything. For to act against our conscience is neither safe for us, nor open to us. On this I take my stand. I can do no other. God help me. Amen.[11]

Luther is one, and his number is large, who willingly denounced human authority, peer pressure, and social stress and followed his conscience as God led him. The results have been a gift from God.

Third, we need constantly to examine our expressions of the gospel to see if they are consistent with the apostolic testimony. This is the principle of the Reformation, the revival of the church under Luther, Zwingli, and Calvin, when the church sought to straighten itself out by radically committing itself to the apostolic gospel and biblical writings. It must also be the principle of our day. And not only do we need to examine our expressions of the gospel, we need also to examine how people are hearing and living out those expressions. Both gospel and lifestyle need to be examined to see if the gospel is being heard correctly.

Let me give an example of this latter point. In my youth I was once told by a well-meaning Sunday school teacher that it did not matter how I lived morally. If I was a Christian (defined as someone who had accepted Jesus Christ as Savior by performing a certain prayer), then I was eternally secure and could live any way I chose. Now this teacher, a godly person, was quick to add that living a morally bankrupt life was not God's will and would certainly bring my life into chaos and ruin. However, it is this teacher's initial idea that I want to challenge. I maintain that the implication (the possibility of a morally bankrupt life for a Christian without endangering eternal status) is both inconsistent with the gospel and with the way the New Testament describes the effects of salvation. The gospel brings transformation (see 5:16–26). In other words, the original statement of the gospel may have been accurate: salvation is by grace through faith, not by works. But the implications drawn from it were nonapostolic: live the way you want. The apostles never drew the conclusion that some Christians do today, namely, that lifestyle is totally disconnected from faith and salvation.

A further point is that Paul's statements of independence need to be explained in such a way that they do not conflict with his other statements

---

11. My quotation comes from James Atkinson's wonderful survey of this period in the history of the church in *Eerdman's Handbook to the History of Christianity*, ed. T. Dowley (Grand Rapids: Eerdmans, 1977), 364; see the whole section on the Reformation at pp. 360–403, where other important Reformers are surveyed, including William Tyndale, John Calvin, Huldreich Zwingli, the Puritans, Thomas Cranmer, John Bunyan, and the Anabaptists. For more on Luther, see O. Chadwick, *The Reformation* (Baltimore: Penguin Books, 1968), 40–75.

of dependence (1 Cor. 11:23–26; 15:3–11) or confirmation (Gal. 2:9). In our own study of the Bible we must always examine our conclusions of particular passages to see if they are consistent with our conclusions drawn from other passages. Here in Galatians 1 it is clear that Paul asserts his independence. But we read in the first letter to the Corinthians that Paul saw some kind of dependence in his gospel. Rather than finding a blatant contradiction, which few authors commit, it is best to seek some kind of synthesis of the two positions in light of differing circumstances and purposes. The most appealing solution is straightforward: at Galatia, where Paul was being accused of being an abbreviator of the Jerusalem gospel (and therefore wrong), Paul asserts that his gospel did not come from Jerusalem but from Jesus Christ. In other words, Paul is talking about the *source* of his gospel to the Galatians. On the other hand, at Corinth Paul is seeking to demonstrate the essential *continuity* of his gospel with other apostolic expressions of the gospel and the *heritage* his gospel has. However much Paul wanted to assert that his gospel was independent in source, he did not shrink at the same time from observing that the Jerusalem leaders "gave him the right hand of fellowship" (see comments at 2:9); in other words, they approved of his independently derived gospel. The gospel Paul preached was consistent with the gospel of his predecessors; but the gospel Paul preached was not from them, since Paul got it by direct revelation.

Galatians 1:13–24

❦

FOR YOU HAVE heard of my previous way of life in Judaism, how intensely I persecuted the church of God and tried to destroy it. ¹⁴I was advancing in Judaism beyond many Jews of my own age and was extremely zealous for the traditions of my fathers. ¹⁵But when God, who set me apart from birth and called me by his grace, was pleased ¹⁶to reveal his Son in me so that I might preach him among the Gentiles, I did not consult any man, ¹⁷nor did I go up to Jerusalem to see those who were apostles before I was, but I went immediately into Arabia and later returned to Damascus.

¹⁸Then after three years, I went up to Jerusalem to get acquainted with Peter and stayed with him fifteen days. ¹⁹I saw none of the other apostles—only James, the Lord's brother. ²⁰I assure you before God that what I am writing you is no lie. ²¹Later I went to Syria and Cilicia. ²²I was personally unknown to the churches of Judea that are in Christ. ²³They only heard the report: "The man who formerly persecuted us is now preaching the faith he once tried to destroy." ²⁴And they praised God because of me.

PAUL IS PROVIDING his readers with a quick overview of his life, a mini-autobiography. But this life story is more than a family recollection of events in the past. As we have been arguing, the first section of Galatians is Paul's vindication of his gospel and its origins, validity, and authority. This narrative section is arranged around temporal adverbs: "when" (v. 15), "then" (v. 18), "later" (v. 21), "fourteen years later" (2:1), and "when" (2:11). These are the chronological pegs on which he hangs each of his arguments. He stops at each juncture to demonstrate his point.

In 1:13–24, the argument of Paul for independence from human authorities is developed in two directions: (1) he is independent of human teaching (vv. 13–17), and (2) he is independent of the major churches in Judea (vv. 18–24). The second chapter will develop Paul's independence from the leading authorities in Jerusalem itself, the so-called "pillar apostles" (2:1–10) and Peter himself (2:11–21). Paul's argument thus spins tighter and smaller as it gets toward Jerusalem: it moves from human teaching to the churches in Judea to the pillar apostles and finally to Peter, who is probably to be seen at this time as the most distinguished apostle in Jerusalem (though James eventually assumed this position).

The first argument in our section (vv. 13–17) concerns Paul's independence from human teaching. God's call came to Paul directly; he says that he "did not consult any man" (v. 16). His pre-Christian history in no way prepared him to be an apostle. Rather, his past was marked by two features: (1) he was a persecutor (cf. Acts 9:1–2; 1 Cor. 15:9), and (2) he was extremely zealous for the law and its national distinctives (1:13–14; cf. Acts 22:3; 26:4; 2 Cor. 11:22; Phil. 3:4–6). Paul's description of his past focuses on the sacred traditions that were passed on in Judaism ("zealous for the traditions of my fathers"),[1] the very element Paul is arguing against in this chapter.

His persecution of the church and his advancements in Judaism came to a screeching halt when God chose to make himself known to Paul in Christ.[2] So when God's call came upon him, he had two options: either to go to Jerusalem to gain an authoritative interpretation of his visionary call[3] or to be instructed elsewhere. Paul chose elsewhere, going immediately to Arabia and Damascus (v. 17). Thus, in his pre- and post-conversion experiences he was not prepared for the gospel of grace to go to the Gentiles,[4] nor was he simply another Jerusalem-based apostle. Paul often focuses on the Gentile target of his apostleship (Rom. 15:14–21; Eph. 3:1–13; Col. 1:24–2:3), and he knows that it was only by the grace of a sovereign God that he was given such a glorious ministry (Jer. 1:5; 1 Cor. 15:9–11; Eph. 3:7–13).

The second argument is the same in essence but concerns a different set of authorities. Paul now moves from human teaching to the churches of Judea (vv. 18–24). The significance of the Judean churches was brought to attention in our commentary section on verses 10–12 and need not be repeated here. We simply need to repeat that Judea, especially Jerusalem itself, was the mother of earliest Christianity. However central Galilee was during the

---

1. An excellent, though technical, book on Paul's past is M. Hengel, *The Pre-Christian Paul* (Philadelphia: Trinity Press International, 1991). For a more popular reading, see R. N. Longenecker, *The Ministry and Message of Paul* (Grand Rapids: Zondervan, 1976), 21–30.

2. This is seen in the tenses of the Greek verbs: whereas the three verbs of vv. 13–14 are imperfects (describing remote incomplete action), the verbs of vv. 15–17, describing the abrupt change in Paul's life, are aorist (describing the action as a whole).

3. The Greek word used by Paul is *prosanatithemi* ("consult"); it is frequently used for consulting a trained expert for interpretation of some dream or vision. Paul knew that the encounter with Christ, an experience "in me" (v. 16), carried with it an infallible interpretation so that he did not need consultation or advice to perceive its significance. On the verb, see J. D. G. Dunn, *Jesus, Paul, and the Law*, 109–10.

4. It is possible that the expressions of v. 14 are to be understood with an anti-Gentile force: "I was advancing in Judaism [not universalism]" and I "was extremely zealous for the traditions of my ancestors [in their protection of Jewish privilege and national distinctives]."

actual life of Jesus, Judea and Jerusalem almost immediately eclipsed Galilee as the seat of earliest Christianity.

Paul learned something[5] from Peter, but he spent only a few days with him—and, he adds, only "after three years" (v. 18). The other apostles were not present and so Paul got nothing from them; he did, he says, make contact with James the brother of Jesus. His non-contact with apostles is so crucial that Paul makes a declaration: "I assure you before God that what I am writing [about my non-contact with apostles] is no lie" (v. 20). We must infer from the seriousness of Paul's tone here that the Judaizers were arguing that Paul's first visit to Jerusalem was one designed for his instruction in the rudiments of the gospel. Paul counters: it was three years after my conversion, it was brief, and it was virtually nonapostolic! Hardly sufficient grounds, he argues, to be considered a Jerusalem apostle!

After this brief visit he went back to his home area (Syria and Cilicia), where he was no doubt busy debating Jews about the Messiah (v. 21). He claims, importantly for his argument, that at this time he was still "personally unknown to the churches of Judea" (v. 22). All they knew of Paul was that he had formerly been a persecutor but was now a preacher of the gospel. This generated praise on their part (v. 23–24).

Paul thus argues, in context, that his gospel came from Jesus Christ directly and that it was derived neither from human teaching nor from the Jerusalem-Judean churches. His argument thus for the need to listen to him and not to be corrected by the Judaizers holds up. Before we proceed to see further developments in his argument in chapter 2, we need to reflect on how we can apply this passage to our contemporary society.

Bridging Contexts

WHENEVER AN AUTHOR of the New Testament reflects on his own call or conversion to Christ, it is natural for us, since we are each sinners in need of God's grace and calling, to see a reflection of our own biographies in that person's biography. This seems entirely

---

5. The verb Paul uses is *historesai* (NIV: "to get acquainted with"). This verb is normally used to describe the attempt to obtain information and most likely means this here. Thus, the NIV could be improved to read, "to learn something [from Peter]." But would this then conflict with the thrust of Paul's argument here? We can assume it would not, or Paul would either have changed his mind or not mentioned it. Instead, we can assume that Paul thinks gaining information from Peter is compatible with the independence of the source of Paul's gospel. While Paul argues strenuously for the independence of his gospel as to source, he also argues that it is compatible with the gospel of the Jerusalem apostles. Thus, he had a full three years before he learned from Peter some of the facts about Jesus or the beginnings of the church. See further J. D. G. Dunn, *Jesus, Paul, and the Law,* 110–13.

reasonable to me and makes application relatively easy—even far-ranging at times. Biographies are an unusually fine way of educating and illustrating truths. A brief visit to a Christian bookstore will provide any visitor with ample selections of biographies of Christians.

But we must not forget, in our rush to get to applications, what Paul is aiming at here. He is not simply giving us his "life story." Rather, he is telling his life story with a slant and definite angle: he is emphasizing his early independence from Jerusalem. This same story could be covered from a different angle: how his past in Judaism had prepared him for his Christian ministry. He could then single out such things as his knowledge of the law, his fear of God, and his fierce sense of commitment, not to mention his education that prepared him for his polemics with Jewish and Gentile opponents. Biographies usually have angles, and this brief narrative of Paul's past has an angle that we must respect. It is not the whole story of his life. (For another angle, see Luke's portraits in Acts 9; 22; 26.)

In order to apply this biography of Paul we must first discern its essential purpose—and if that purpose is Paul's independence from Jerusalem and his direct revelation from Jesus Christ, then his biography is not as directly relevant as we might have initially thought. In fact, we should admit that we frequently apply secondary meanings of a text rather than its primary meaning. From this text, for example, our tendency in the Western world is to focus on the essence of a call from God or the nature of conversion. However legitimate such applications may be (and I do think they are valid, as we will see below), it is the interpreter's first responsibility to find the primary meaning of the text and seek to apply that meaning. In this case, the meaning is the independence of Paul's gospel from Jerusalem and its significance for (1) the justification of Gentiles and (2) a Christian life lived under the direction of the Holy Spirit.

Nonetheless we have here a description of Paul's conversion and calling that provides categories for perceptions of our conversion and call. What we need to realize is that this is simply one person's conversion; there is no justification for the notion that everyone's conversion or calling must take place as Paul's did. I know of few people that have had similar visions at their conversion or calling. Not everyone who senses that he or she has been called by God to some ministry has the same kind of blinding, sense-shattering experience. And not everyone's conversion or call is as sudden as Paul's. Some people are converted, like Peter, over a number of years and through various experiences. Just when was Peter converted? Luke 5? Mark 8? John 21? Acts 2? Some people are called, unlike Paul, as a result of a series of events and educational experiences. Others have had conversions and calls for which they cannot even find a beginning.

Some of my students, for instance, have come to Trinity with no sense of a calling to ministry, while others have had a sense of a specific calling from their earliest years. And yet, after a number of years at Trinity and after seriously searching out God's call on their lives, most of these students leave seminary with a clear perception of what God wants them to do. What I am saying is this: not everyone's experience is Paul's. Consequently, in applying this text we must be careful not to impose this Pauline conversion-call on all people. In fact, I have known few students preparing for ministry who have said that they received their specific calling to ministry at the time of their conversion.[6] For most, it has been growth in the grace of God, in his Word, and in discernment of their gifts that led them to a fuller appreciation of God's direction in their life.

And we should perhaps even say here that Paul does not teach that every Christian must have a call before that Christian begins to serve Christ or in the church. One may or may not have believed that, but such is not the concern here. What Paul is talking about is *his own* experience of God's grace—and that experience involved a dramatic conversion and a specific calling. What I would want to maintain is that we can see hues and colors about callings and conversions through the lens of Paul's narrative. I would not want to maintain that we can learn about all such conversions or callings.

AS MENTIONED IN the previous section (vv. 10–12), this passage's primary concern is the independence of Paul's gospel from the Jerusalem authorities. Since we focused on this topic in that section, we will bypass consideration of similar applications here. I suggest that the student of the Bible reread that section of application before moving to secondary applications. What I will do here is reflect on Paul's "biography," how he relates his conversion and call to his readers, and how his story can be helpful for us.

We can begin by observing how Paul has rewritten his own biography. The preeminent sign of conversion, according to sociologists (and anyone

---

6. Some scholars have, in fact, argued that the records of Paul's Damascus Road experience provide information only about Paul's *call*, not about his conversion. I am persuaded, however, that the information of the text is best understood when it is seen as a description of both a conversion and a call. A fascinating book in this regard, written from a Jewish and sociological perspective on Paul, can be found in A. F. Segal, *Paul the Convert* (New Haven: Yale University Press, 1990), esp. pp. 3–33, 72–114.

who reads Scripture attentively), is *biographical reconstruction*. The first thing a convert does is tell his or her own biography in a new way.[7] A basic reorientation is like this: what mattered most before no longer matters; what did not matter before is now central. As Paul himself later says, "But whatever was to my profit I now consider loss for the sake of Christ" (Phil. 3:7). Paul's perspective on his life is now entirely shaped around his encounter with Christ. In fact, he reconstructed his perception of himself. He knew that he was different. Thus, there was a self-transformation as well. This is what happens to all converts to Jesus Christ.[8]

The convert to Jesus Christ now perceives himself or herself entirely within the categories of a relationship to Jesus Christ. It is not unusual for students of mine, a small group of whom I meet with regularly on Thursdays, to refer to their "B.C. days," meaning their "Before Christ days." It might be profitable for readers of Galatians to write out a brief account of their own biographies in which they seek to orient their account around their conversion to Christ. Perhaps they could have three sections: (1) "Previous Way of Life," (2) "Conversion," and (3) "Present Calling." This is how Paul reconstructed his life, and it is a typical paradigm since conversion is the decisive change in every Christian's life. (However, in speaking of a "decisive change," I need to add that I do not think all conversions are alike, as I discussed above. Nonetheless, the Bible teaches that all Christians are converts, whether that conversion was sudden or progressive.)

But you can explore your past from more than one angle. You can also write your biography from the angle of how your past, whatever it was, prepared you for your present ministry and life; from the angle of your own spiritual development; from the angle of your encounters with the Holy Spirit; or from the angle of decisive changes that have made significant impacts upon your life. In each of these angles, you need to focus the story in such a way that your encounter with Christ is preeminent. This discipline, however time-consuming it may become, forces each of us to decentralize our own ego and centralize Christ. It teaches us to see our lives as God sees them, as lives that have been transformed by Jesus Christ and the Holy Spirit. It teaches us to shape our lives according to biblical categories.

---

7. Two important pieces of bibliography, coming from the world of sociology, are D. A. Snow and R. Machalek, "The Convert as a Social Type," in *Sociological Theory 1983* (ed. R. Collins; San Francisco: Jossey-Bass, 1983), 259–89; C. L. Staples and A. L. Mauss, "Conversion or Commitment? A Reassessment of the Snow and Machalek Approach to the Study of Conversion," *Journal for the Scientific Study of Religion* 26 (1987): 133–47.

8. My favorite Christian autobiography is that of C. S. Lewis, *Surprised by Joy: The Shape of My Early Life* (New York: Harcourt, Brace and Co., 1956), who clearly reorients his entire life around the life he found in Christ.

One sure result of this discipline will be a quicker facility in giving our testimony. When I was a child, I had a pastor who frequently asked people in our Wednesday evening service to give a "testimony" of something that happened during the week. He also expected (but so far as I know did not demand) all new converts to give their "reconstructed biography" in such a setting. I can remember the joy this generated in the entire church as people declared their allegiance to Jesus Christ and explained their conversion. Perhaps a focus on learning to tell our own story can lead the churches once again into such services.[9]

In addition, notice how Paul's conversion is a *complete* reordering of his life. Observe how arduously Paul persecuted the church: "how intensely I persecuted the church of God" (v. 13). Observe how zealously Paul pursued a pious reputation in Judaism: "I was advancing in Judaism beyond many Jews of my own age and was extremely zealous for the traditions of my fathers" (v. 14). And observe how complete his conversion was: "so that I might preach him [Christ] among the Gentiles" (v. 16). Paul moved from a strenuous commitment to Judaism to an even more strenuous commitment to Christ and the apostolic calling he gave Paul. Paul's commitments were complete.

> Such was the state of Saul of Tarsus before his conversion. He was a bigot and a fanatic, whole-hearted in his devotion to Judaism and in his persecution of Christ and the church. Now a man in that mental and emotional state is in no mood to change his mind, or even to have it changed for him by men. No conditioned reflex or other psychological device could convert a man in that state. Only God could reach him—and God did![10]

This man's conversion can become a standard by which we can evaluate our own commitments. Are we as committed to Christ, his claim on our lives, and his calling in our lives as we were to our pre-Christian vocation and pursuits?

While it is clear that Paul is not the one we are to follow (we follow Christ), it is also clear that Paul was an obedient apostle whose life was a shining example of piety. In fact, Paul frequently challenged his churches to follow him as he followed Christ (Gal. 4:12; 1 Cor. 4:16; 11:1; Phil. 3:17; 4:8–9). We can learn from Paul's commitment how we ought to be committed. The one mark that stands out in his life is that his commitment was complete.

---

9. To be sure, the natural setting for such a "story" is baptismal services. Besides the obvious division in churches over adult vs. infant baptism, few services can provide the time needed for such biographies. See also my comments at 3:1–5 ("Contemporary Significance" section).

10. J. R. W. Stott, *Only One Way*, 31–32.

It is a sad commentary on the Christian church today that so many of those who claim to be Christians have a commitment to Christ, to his gospel, and to his lifestyle that is far less than complete. We have Christians whose commitment is not much deeper than the perception they had of Christ and the Christian life when they made some kind of decision as children. We have Christian leaders who teach that obedience is not an inevitable result of true faith and who therefore lead their followers into thinking that commitment does not have to be complete. We have other Christians who think that eternal security is some sort of doctrine that protects them even if they live a life of sin. What, we are compelled to ask, do the martyrs of the faith (from James to Bonhoeffer, from Stephen to modern missionaries in Latin America) think of our "demand-less gospel"? And how can we look these martyrs in the eye and contend that our lives must not be laid on the line for God? And so, contrary to this entire (even if not dominant) orientation in the Western church, we have the example of Paul. He provides for us a stiff challenge: let us give our lives wholly to Christ and his calling in our lives. As in the days of Paul, the churches will praise God as a result of such a life (v. 24).

Yet a further implication of our passage is that Paul's calling in life was *specific*. It is not infrequent to hear of people who claim that God has called them to some specific task. Paul had the same clear sense of God's direction in his life: "so that I might preach him among the Gentiles" (v. 16). We have been taught that if we aim at nothing we will hit nothing. The same applies in Christian living: if we drift aimlessly in the Christian life, we will simply drift like a bottle in the ocean. We will accomplish nothing although we may bob around in many areas.

It is fundamentally important for Christians to discern their gifts and to use those gifts. It is just as vital for the same Christians not to allow themselves to become entangled in every good pursuit in life. Some Christians may get involved in such good things as political issues, social problems, and cultural developments, but these activities are not for everyone. Other Christians may become influential through sports, the various media, or public education. Still others may develop their Christian life along other avenues, such as Christian schools, local parish ministries, or missionary efforts. Whatever areas we are called to, it is important for each of us to discern what God has called us to do and to do that without trying to do everything else. What I am getting at is that when we sense the call of God on our lives, we need to stick to that calling and not let distractions prevent us from fulfilling God's will for us.

How do we discern God's will in our lives? Perhaps many readers of this book will be aware that there has recently been considerable discussion of how Christians can know God's will.[11] It is not my intent to debate these ideas and come to a final conclusion. I am of the view that God's will encompasses a broad range of options for a Christian, but I think that for some people God's will may involve a specific vocation. I recently met a man who thought God's will for his life was working with teen-age drug addicts through an ocean entertainment sailing business. That seemed quite specific to me—in fact, I was quite surprised that he could know so much about God's will! Others do not find God's will for them so specifically. We dare not impose any one model on all Christians. For some, God's will is not so specifically defined: living obediently as a spouse, serving in various capacities in the local church, and striving for justice in the local community through various opportunities. For others it may simply be being a Christian in a large corporation while enveloping such a vocation with an obedient, God-fearing life at home and church. For still others it may be something specific, like teaching health to Haitian refugees.

But how do we discern such a calling?[12] I believe there are three dimensions to discerning God's will. (1) We need an inner conviction that such a pursuit is what God wants for us. We see this in Paul, who says that God revealed his Son "in me" (v. 16). (2) We need the wisdom of our church leaders and elders. It is being a maverick, not a responsible Christian, to think we can simply announce that we have been given a special ministry without passing this by our Christian leaders and mentors. Not infrequently such leaders will be encouraging; other times they may offer some challenges, warnings, and advice that will enable a person to pursue such a calling in a more responsible way. (3) We need the feedback and evaluation of experts who observe us in the ministries to which we think we have been called. At least once a year I have to ask a student to come into my office while I share my concerns over his or her perception of a future direction in ministry. This has been one of the hardest tasks in my ministry; but it is, I believe, nonethe-

---

11. A major spark in this fire was G. Friesen, with J. R. Maxson, *Decision Making and the Will of God: A Biblical Alternative to Traditional View* (Portland: Multnomah, 1980). Friesen properly inveighs against the view that God has some specific will for each person for all aspects of life and it is that person's responsibility to find that will ("hit the bull's eye," or "the dot") or be forever "out of God's will."

12. Again, see J. R. W. Stott, *The Contemporary Christian*, 128–45, who helpfully distinguishes the general and specific senses of guidance, vocation, and ministry, and who offers wise advice about our topic. Stott suggests that Christians, in order to discern God's will, need to yield, pray, talk (to others in the community and to our parents), think, and wait (pp. 130–31).

less an important one. It is irresponsible for Christian leaders to permit others to pursue ministries for which they are not prepared or gifted. It is not unusual for faculty members at our seminary to have to share with some young person that he or she has not been granted the gifts of preaching and teaching. It is also my experience that such students are more than appreciative that someone was willing to spend time with them in prayer over their future plans. To learn now that we have not been called to something saves us a future of grief. (I also know that at times our perceptions of a student's future ministry may be inaccurate and, in spite of our advice, such students go on to fruitful ministries!)

Finally, Paul's description of his own life is honest and even potentially damaging. Paul knew that the Judaizers would get to read this letter and that they would scrutinize every detail about his description of his relationship to Jerusalem. If Paul distorted the facts, they would pounce on them and pronounce him a liar; and that distortion would forever jeopardize the integrity of Paul's gospel. Paul knew he had to be honest. And that is why he brings up the matter of having been in Jerusalem and having consulted with Peter and James. We can imagine that at that very point in his letter the Judaizers would have jumped up and said, "That is the information we need. Paul was in Jerusalem and at that point he got his gospel from the leaders." It would have been best for Paul if he had never even been to Jerusalem and if he had never met any of the apostles. But Paul will tell the story truthfully, even if he has to work hard to get the Galatians to realize that, though he did visit Jerusalem, he did not get his gospel from the leaders there.

How often are we tempted, when narrating any description of some facts or some story, to shape the facts in such a way that we border on not telling the whole truth? Paul eschewed dishonesty and told the truth about his relationship to Jerusalem. We can learn a lot from him in this regard about how we tell our own biographies and about how we narrate stories. We need to be as honest as we can.

This "angular biography" of Paul, then, can set the agenda for us as we contemplate our own conversions and our own callings to various vocations and ministries in our world. There are, of course, other applications of this passage. But it is our sincere concern to highlight the importance that Paul's conversion made in his own estimation of his life as he sought to serve God.

Galatians 2:1–10

FOURTEEN YEARS LATER I went up again to Jerusalem, this time with Barnabas. I took Titus along also. ²I went in response to a revelation and set before them the gospel that I preach among the Gentiles. But I did this privately to those who seemed to be leaders, for fear that I was running or had run my race in vain. ³Yet not even Titus, who was with me, was compelled to be circumcised, even though he was a Greek. ⁴[This matter arose] because some false brothers had infiltrated our ranks to spy on the freedom we have in Christ Jesus and to make us slaves. ⁵We did not give in to them for a moment, so that the truth of the gospel might remain with you.

⁶As for those who seemed to be important—whatever they were makes no difference to me; God does not judge by external appearance—those men added nothing to my message. ⁷On the contrary, they saw that I had been entrusted with the task of preaching the gospel to the Gentiles, just as Peter had been to the Jews. ⁸For God, who was at work in the ministry of Peter as an apostle to the Jews, was also at work in my ministry as an apostle to the Gentiles. ⁹James, Peter and John, those reputed to be pillars, gave me and Barnabas the right hand of fellowship when they recognized the grace given to me. They agreed that we should go to the Gentiles, and they to the Jews. ¹⁰All they asked was that we should continue to remember the poor, the very thing I was eager to do.

Original Meaning

IN ORDER TO demonstrate that his gospel was a direct revelation from Jesus Christ, Paul has tried to show that his gospel was not dependent on human teaching (1:13–17) or on the Judean churches (1:18–24). The next link in his argument (2:1–10) is his demonstration that his gospel was independent even of the Jerusalem pillars. He proceeds in 2:11–21 to clinch the argument for independence by showing that he did not get his gospel from Peter, the arch-apostle.

In Paul's autobiography the next important link with Jerusalem came "fourteen years later" (2:1).[1] This visit produced a major interchange between a more Jewish-nationalistic gospel and a more Jewish-and-Gentile-universalistic gospel. Paul spearheaded the latter and (apparently) the pillar apostles the former. The sides came, according to Paul, to a consensus: that Paul was called to preach what he preached and was called to do so to the Gentiles, and that Peter was called to preach what he preached and was called to do so to the Jews. However, by all appearances "what" each preached was the same; the differences came over "to whom."

The first unit in our section is concerned with *Paul's presentation of his message* (vv. 1–3). Fourteen years after his conversion Paul made a second trip to the holy city;[2] he took two of his friends with him: Barnabas and Titus. Barnabas, originally named Joseph, was a Levite who grew up in Cyprus. As a result of his ministries the apostles named him "Son of Encouragement,"[3] i.e., Barnabas (Acts 4:36). We later learn that he was the "cousin" of John Mark (Col. 4:10). His obedience (Acts 4:36–37), reconciling manner, and encouraging temperament (9:26–30), along with his dependence on the Holy Spirit, earned him a prominent ministry alongside Paul (cf. 11:22–26). If the order of names says something, it seems likely that Barnabas held the early lead in his ministry with Paul, but that leadership was eventually surrendered to Paul's apostolic gifts (cf. 13:1–15:41; but see also 14:14; 15:12, 25). Paul had two known disagreements with Barnabas: (1) over Peter at Antioch (Gal. 2:11–21) and (2) over John Mark at the beginning of his second missionary journey (Acts 15:39–40). It is more than likely that their breach was healed since later Paul ranks Barnabas as an equal minister (1 Cor. 9:6). Barnabas accompanied Paul to Jerusalem in Galatians 2:1 because he was a significant and respected person with the Jerusalem churches. His track record of healing discord and arbitrating between factions made him a suitable companion.

---

1. It is likely that this is fourteen years after his conversion (1:13–17). It is possible that it could refer to fourteen years after his first visit mentioned at 1:18, or fourteen years after his visit to Syria and Cilicia (1:21). If we date his conversion at A.D. 33, then this visit to Jerusalem, his second such visit, would have taken place probably in A.D. 46. For more information on the historical situation, see below at the end of the "Original Meaning" section (pp. 87–90).

2. This second visit came about because of a "revelation" (v. 2). Acts 11:27–30 describes a prophetic direction given through Agabus; Gal 2:2 may well be describing such a prophetic word as a revelation. See R. N. Longenecker, *Galatians,* 47.

3. Technically, the Aramaic name means "son of prophecy"; "prophecy" has at least two dimensions: (1) prediction and (2) consolation/encouragement.

The second travel companion of Paul was Titus. While we may be unsure why Titus accompanied Paul and Barnabas, his distinctive trait (and the reason he is mentioned at all) is that he was a Gentile. It is possible that Paul brought Titus, likely one of his early converts (cf. Titus 1:4) and a continual friend (2 Cor. 2:13), as a "test case," in which case Titus would have had unmistakable and unimpeachable Christian character while at the same time being a Gentile.[4] This would force the Jewish believers of Jerusalem to admit that God was as much at work among, and through, Gentiles as Jews. Furthermore, that he was clearly chosen of God would force the situation of his not being circumcised to arise. Paul's argument could not be clearer: if God had chosen and was using this uncircumcised Gentile, then certainly circumcision was not required to join the people of God.[5] Two verses later we learn that even though Titus was Greek, he was not "compelled"[6] to be circumcised. The import of Titus then is obvious: on Paul's second visit to Jerusalem the leaders had every opportunity to press the issue of circumcision if such were required for membership in the people of God. But they did not. Paul's argument has a decisive factor: since the "pillars" of Jerusalem did not demand Titus's circumcision, it can be assumed that they did not think circumcision was necessary for salvation. It can also be assumed that they did not think joining Judaism was necessary; Gentiles could simply turn to Jesus for their salvation by trusting in him.

Paul's argument against the Judaizers from this incident has a further proof: when he was in Jerusalem he met "privately" with the leaders (probably the pillars of vv. 6, 9) and "set before them the gospel" that he preached to the Gentiles. This gospel was surely the salvation of people through the work of Christ by simply trusting in God's grace in Christ. His gospel did not demand adopting the Jewish way of life and did not include submission to the law. Paul even states that he did this humbly: "for fear that I was running or had run my race in vain" (v. 3). This was a grand concession on Paul's part. However confident he was in the revelation that he thought was from Jesus Christ, he was still willing to submit his revelation to the evaluation of the leaders of Jerusalem. I believe Paul was being honest here and not playing rhetorical games. Furthermore, this gave Paul an even deeper argument (essentially the argument of vv. 1–10): his gospel was both independent of,

---

4. It is possible that the significance of Titus's Gentile status during this visit dawned on Paul after further reflection. But this is less likely, in my opinion, simply because first-century pious Jews immediately knew who was Jewish and who was Gentile. I think, therefore, that Paul took Titus along as a test case.

5. For other details about Titus, see G. F. Hawthorne, "Titus," *NISBE*, 4:864–65.

6. This is a strong term. See further the notes at 2:14.

and confirmed by, Jerusalem. This gave the Judaizers and the Galatians no way out.[7]

The second unit is concerned with *the opposition to Paul's message* (vv. 4–5). "This matter [i.e., the matter pertaining to circumcision] arose" because some of the Judaizers, whom Paul here calls "false brothers," were seeking to infiltrate the ranks of those who were free in order to spread their Moses-based gospel. Their intent was "to make us slaves." This must be understood as living under the law of Moses alongside the grace in Christ and without the freedom of the Spirit (3:10–14, 23–25), with grace and freedom thus being effectively eliminated. It is adolescence in comparison to liberating sonship and maturity, as Paul describes it at 3:26–4:7. Paul argues that the experience he and the Galatians were presently having with the Judaizers was identical to the one he had either in Jerusalem during his second visit to the city or in Antioch at an earlier date.[8] A gospel combining Jesus with Moses was being imposed on those who had converted to a simple faith in Jesus Christ. In light of Paul's comments in 1:6–9, we should not be surprised that Paul calls them "false brothers." This is the heresy Paul confronts: a "gospel" that minimizes the work of Christ and undermines the ministry of the Spirit.

Paul's response to the infiltrators is the theme of the entire letter: "We did not give in to them for a moment, so that the truth of the gospel might remain with you" (v. 5). At 5:1 he chooses different words: "Stand firm, then, and do not let yourselves be burdened again by a yoke of slavery." After encountering Christ, and in contrast to the liberation found in the Spirit of Christ, Paul describes life under the law (apart from Christ) as a life of slavery.

Paul's intent was "so that the truth of the gospel might remain with you." His motivation was not personal and individualistic, though he undoubtedly benefited personally from the gospel of Christ. He was not seeking to preserve some maverick status or some rebel reputation. Rather, he knew the implication of imposing the law on the new converts and he wanted to dis-

---

7. Some scholars have argued that Paul's submission did not pertain to the validity or truthfulness of his message but to its practicability and effectiveness (see F. F. Bruce, *Galatians*, 111). Bruce states: "His commission was not derived from Jerusalem, but it could not be executed effectively except in fellowship with Jerusalem." I tend to think this is drawing too fine a line of distinction. It can be easily imagined that Paul, however confident, could have submitted his ideas to them for consideration. Since they agreed with Paul, Paul had a deeper argument. I believe that, had they disagreed with Paul, he would probably have parted company with them.

8. F. F. Bruce has offered an ingenious suggestion as to the time of this infiltration, contending that it occurred after Paul and Barnabas left Antioch and that it occurred at Antioch not Jerusalem. This, he then argues, helps account for the silence on the issue of circumcision in Acts 11:30; 12:25 (see his *Galatians*, 115–17).

tance his gospel from Moses. He wanted to be sure that these new converts enjoyed the joy (and thrill) of the fullness of times (4:4). Paul himself could live in both worlds, sometimes assuming the law and other times not. But he knew that any drift on his part toward a gospel linked *inevitably* with the law would mean death to the new churches. It would mean nationalization. It would mean joining Judaism as any other convert to Judaism had done. It would not mean life in Christ. And so Paul continues the narrative with the important evidence for his case.

The third unit is concerned with *the unity expressed by the Jerusalem pillars and Paul over Paul's message* (vv. 6–10). Paul's contacts with Jerusalem may have been few and his interchanges brief. But, one thing is clear: the leaders of Jerusalem endorsed his gospel. Here we get to the nub of a problem: if Paul was so intent in chapter 1 to argue for the independence of his gospel, why is he so intent here on showing that his gospel was endorsed? Does this not undermine his earlier argument? Does this not make him vulnerable once again to the charge that his gospel, after all, did come from Jerusalem?

I think not. Rather, what we are seeing here is Paul's willingness to use both sides of an argument for his own case. In chapter 1 Paul argued that the *source* of his gospel was independent of Jerusalem. He got his gospel directly from Jesus Christ. Therefore, the Judaizers could not argue that he had to submit everything to Jerusalem. In chapter 2, however, he argues that while his gospel was independent in source, it was also *endorsed* by the Jerusalem pillars. That endorsement, for Paul, was not necessary, but as long as it worked out that way, he decides to use that endorsement as part of his case against the Judaizers.

As we seek to unravel the meaning of verses 6–10, it is important for us to figure out who the primary leaders were. Paul describes the leaders, and he is probably not referring to more than one group, as "those who seemed to be important" (v. 6), "those reputed to be pillars" (v. 9), and "James, Peter and John" (v. 9). It is most likely that this group is the same as the group in verse 2 ("those who seemed to be leaders").[9] Paul's gospel was now facing a crucial test: how did those whom everyone respected as authoritative in Jerusalem respond to it?

---

9. Paul uses the Greek verb *dokeo* ("to seem") in each instance. The "seemingness" of this group is surely Paul's perception of how others treated them: people of honor. Paul, however, treats them as of equal status and therefore no more than "apparently honorable." Because of his calling, Paul is willing to part company from this noble group. It is possible that Paul has himself changed his mind (he formerly thought they were to be highly regarded authorities and therefore obeyed) or that the new age of the Spirit had rendered the distinctions operating during the earthly life of Jesus no longer important.

First, they "added nothing to my message" (v. 6). The "added nothing" clearly means they did not think Paul's message was an abbreviated one, one designed to make the gospel more attractive to Gentiles. They did not think that Moses needed to be studied and obeyed in order to be a "full member" of the church, and they did not think such things as boundary markers needed to be imposed (like circumcision and food laws). They must then have thought that the message of Paul was the message of Peter and the other leaders, for his message had been accepted as Christ's message. Later in this chapter Paul describes an event during which he may well have used the logic of the agreement described here: if you earlier agreed with my message (vv. 6–9), you must now also agree (so do not demand table laws; vv. 11–21). To be sure, the leaders at Jerusalem probably had some hesitations about some of the ways the message was applying out in the Diaspora. Some of the major leaders no doubt would have preferred a more Jewish-looking community. However much they had some (social) hesitations, they were confident enough in the power of the gospel and the Holy Spirit to permit Paul's gospel to work itself out as it made an impact in the Gentile world.

Second, they officially recognized Paul's special calling (vv. 8–10). What these pillars perceived was that God had separate callings for Paul and Peter. They did not contend that each had a separate gospel but that each had a separate target for ministry: Paul with the uncomfortable, potentially disturbing, ministry of opening the rest of the world to the message of Christ and Peter with the more comfortable, home-missions ministry with all its social problems. Crucial in this decision was the conviction that "God . . . was also at work in my [Paul's] ministry" (v. 8).

To make it official, "James,[10] Peter and John . . . gave me and Barnabas the right hand of fellowship when they recognized the grace given to me" (v. 9). This is more than a Western "handshake." The "right hand of fellowship" was an official agreement between Paul (and his companions) and the Jerusalem pillars (James, Peter, and John).[11] They verbally, theologically, and now publicly agreed with Paul's message (it was pure and truthful) and his sphere of ministry (the Gentile world). They publicly announced that they thought

---

10. This is James, the Lord's brother, probable author of the book of James. Early Christian traditions inform us both about the preeminent role he played in Jerusalem Christianity (Acts 12:17; 15:13; 21:17–26; note here the order of names) and about his noteworthy piety. Paul's first visit to Jerusalem involved getting acquainted with Peter; that James is listed first at 2:9 may reveal the growing authority of James and the lessening of authority for Peter. On James, see the especially full discussion of R. P. Martin, *James* (WBC 48; Waco, Tex.: Word, 1988), xxxi–lxi.

11. A full citation of the evidence from the ancient world can be found in R. N. Longenecker, *Galatians*, 58.

God had called Paul to this very task. It could be profitably compared today to an ordination committee's endorsement of a candidate after lengthy questioning and discussion. Astute committees (then and now) can quickly get to the heart of the issues to determine whether a given candidate is orthodox or not. The endorsement by the "pillars" was genuine, and Paul was introduced as one who preached the gospel of Jesus Christ faithfully and accurately.

Third, "the pillars" simply encouraged Paul to remember his roots by working strenuously for the relief of the poor (v. 10). In giving Paul their endorsement, they also encouraged him to keep the communication lines with Jerusalem open by spending energies on behalf of the poor saints in Jerusalem. This additional item is the *only* thing they asked of Paul. Just as Paul had remembered the poor already,[12] so he would spend a great portion of his ministry collecting gifts from the Diaspora for the mother church in Jerusalem (cf. 1 Cor. 16:1–4; 2 Cor. 8–9; Rom. 15:27–29; Acts 20:16, 22; 24:17). The causes of poverty in Judea were probably numerous and mixed: overburden at the hands of increasing widows (cf. Acts 6:1–7), the early community's experiment with a community of goods (perhaps bringing with it some excesses), bad harvests, and persecutions that entailed financial stress. In any case, there was poverty, and Paul saw it as part of his ministry to help bring relief. To be sure, part of Paul's motivations were compassion, but we may also suggest that his drive is partly to be explained by his desire to demonstrate to Judea that his gospel and his churches were one with the gospel and churches of Judea. In other words, his apostolic calling was tied into his collection for the poor.

To summarize: Paul's second visit to Jerusalem resulted in an authoritative endorsement of both his message and his calling to the Gentiles. What at first sight appears to be largely arcane to us, on more careful inspection generates several applications for our world today.

··

A Note on the Relationship of Acts to Galatians and Paul's Visits to Jerusalem. The issue of the relationship of Galatians 2:1–10 to Acts 15 is of significance for (1) reconstructing earliest Christian history, (2) interpreting both Galatians 2 and Acts 15 (with respect to having finer details for our interpretations),

---

12. Cf. Acts 11:30; 12:25. The use of the aorist verb (*espoudasa*) suggests to most commentators that Paul had already begun the practice of collecting funds for the poor in Judea (see F. F. Bruce, *Galatians*, 126). However, the aorist may indicate here no more than *that* he was eager to remember the poor (rather than when he was eager). On the collection of Paul, see the especially fine discussion of R. P. Martin, *2 Corinthians* (WBC 40; Waco, Tex.: 1986), 256–58, upon which I draw deeply here.

and (3) assessing the historical reliability of each of the books. While by no means a necessary conclusion, many of those who have adopted a direct parallel between Acts 15 and Galatians 2 also contend that the book of Acts is not always reliable in its presentation of history.[13] In other words, even if the conclusions we draw are not directly relevant for applying the Bible, they become fundamentally significant for the authority of the Bible and for reconstructing earliest Christian history. The issue then is worthy of serious reflection by readers of the Bible.

According to a widely adopted hypothesis, assumed in this commentary, there are five recorded visits of Paul to Jerusalem after his conversion. A table presents this clearly.[14] I suggest that readers go through each of the references carefully and then fill in even more details from the passages until a full appreciation of the evidence is achieved.

Point of Departure	Date	Acts References	Parallels	Purposes
Damascus	35	9:22–30	Gal. 1:18–24	Interview Peter
Antioch of Syria	46	11:30; 12:25	Gal 2:1–3, 6-10	Relief for poor, Gentile issues
Antioch of Syria	49	14:26–15:29		Gentile conversion
Corinth	52	18:1, 18, 22		Attend Passover, Relief for poor
Greece	57	20:2–3; 21:17ff.; Rom 15:25–31		Deliver relief

That Galatians 2:1–10 corresponds, not to Acts 15, but to Acts 11:30; 12:25 deserves some explanation. We can chart the characters involved, the events, and the purpose of each visit to facilitate comparison. Again, I recommend that Bible students read through each passage to gain a fuller understanding of the issues and solutions.

While there are clearly resemblances between Acts 15 and Galatians 2:1–10, there are some noticeable differences between this two passages. (1) Acts 15 is a *public* gathering, whereas Galatians 2 is *private* in nature and Acts 11:30; 12:25 mentions nothing public. (2) The *chronology* of Galatians 2:1 fits more with Acts 11:30; 12:25 than with Acts 15 in that Galatians 2:1

---

13. An example of such an interpretation can be found in the widely used introduction of W. G. Kümmel, *Introduction to the New Testament*, trans. H. C. Kee (Nashville: Abingdon, 1975), 301–4.

14. This chart originated in a handout I received from my teacher, M. J. Harris, and is used here with his permission.

	Gal 2:1–10	Acts 9:26–30	Acts 11:30; 12:25	Acts 15
CHARACTERS	Paul	Paul	Paul	Paul
	Barnabas	Barnabas	Barnabas	Barnabas
	Judaizers			Judaizers
	Pillars	?	?	Pillars-Elders
	Titus			
EVENTS	Revelation		(Revelation?)[15]	Sent [by revelation?][16]
	Circumcision			Circumcision
	Opposition			Opposition
	Relief for poor	Barnabas persuades	Relief for poor	
	Paul confirmed			
	Return to Antioch	Paul off to Tarsus	Return to Antioch	Council's decision
PURPOSE	Explain message	Fellowship	Relief for poor	Circumsision issue
	Relief for poor			

mentions "fourteen years later"; Acts 15 would seem to be sixteen or seventeen years after Paul's conversion. (3) The *omission of the council's decision* (Acts 15:22–29) is surely significant for understanding Galatians. It is far more likely that Paul does not mention it because it had not yet taken place than to suppose that Paul deliberately suppressed what would have been a major supporting argument! (4) If Galatians 2 corresponds to Acts 15, Paul would have had to have *deliberately omitted a visit to Jerusalem*—not only making his argument false, but putting his entire apologetic with the Judaizers at stake. It is far easier to believe that Paul mentioned every conceivable visit to Jerusalem than to think he deliberately omitted one. (5) The *issue* is the same in Galatians 2 and Acts 11:30; 12:25 (the relief for the poor) while the focus of Acts 15 is a theological debate on the manner of including Gentiles in the church. Finally, as for omissions in Acts 11:30; 12:25 of items mentioned in Galatians 2:1–10, we need simply to note that the Acts narrative at this point is extremely brief while Galatians 2 is considerably more complete; this makes

---

15. As mentioned previously (footnote 2), I think this is the prophetic utterance of Agabus recorded in Acts 11:27–30.

16. It is possible to argue that the appointment mentioned in Acts 15:2 is revelatory.

omissions in Acts more than likely. So, even if the coincidences between Acts 15 and Galatians 2 are distinctive (and have led some scholars to opt for two descriptions of the same event), it is our considered judgment that Galatians 2 most likely corresponds to the visit mentioned by Luke in Acts 11:30 and 12:25. It was the second visit of Paul to Jerusalem and its purpose was the relief of the poor saints in Jerusalem.[17]

REPETITION IS CRITICAL for communication, and Paul's point here is the same as in chapter 1. When it comes to applications, therefore, we need not repeat our comments on the significance of Paul's independence for our lives today. The reader may consult our "Bridging Contexts" and "Contemporary Significance" sections on 1:1–9 and 1:10–12. Once again, the key issue for application in this passage is the truthfulness of Paul's gospel: justification is by faith in Christ, through the grace of God, for all—regardless of social standing, race, or economic status. Further direct applications are not hard to find here either, because some statements in texts lend themselves to simple and helpful applications. It is not difficult to apply Paul's statement, "All that they asked was that we should continue to remember the poor . . ." (2:10)—regardless of whether Paul had primarily the Christian poor or the poor in general in mind. But there are other avenues for application here, and I shall suggest two.

A natural form of application presents itself here: even though the characters and precise events are different from ours (rarely do Christians today have problems with some group that seeks to impose circumcision!), what we do see is a typical sociological and theological crisis working itself out exclusively in religious dress. A group of Judaizing "Christians" were intent on sneaking in to spy out all the latest trends of the Pauline churches to find out if they were living according to the law of Moses. Their goal, of course, was to get these Gentile converts "fully converted" to a Judaistic and nationalistic perception of the gospel.

On our part, we can find simple (and sometimes disturbing) analogies to this sort of pattern in the Christian church today. Thus, it is wise for the teacher of this passage to analyze his or her church to see if there are social crises behind theological agendas and debates. An important issue, but one

---

17. For readers who have gone through the texts and the evidence as suggested, I recommend that they now read carefully through the introduction of one of the commentaries listed on the "Works Consulted" page (pp. 17–18).

often surrounded by social and psychological reactions, is the final judgment. On the one hand, we have a crisis of truth in our world, and there is a consistent form of universalism or pluralism implicit in much of our culture. The concept of a final judgment over truth and over how one has lived in light of it seems impossible; thus, this doctrine is either toned down or denied. Furthermore, there are those who have had their best friends, their parents, and their children die without ever surrendering to Christ and who, because of these tragedies, refuse to accept the concept of a final judgment at face value.

Another issue concerns the Rapture (which we pretend to know much more about than we really can know). I have heard people over and over say that others can go through the Tribulation but not them (because they are "pre-tribbers"). Behind this little statement, often said in jest, may be a lurking fear of persecution—which hardly justifies a theological viewpoint. What I am saying is this: sometimes our own theological agendas are shaped as much by personal and social factors as they are by a concern for the truth. The keen Christian is alert to the social world shaping the positions in vogue at any given time.

On the other hand, it is wise not to press the social element too hard, as if all debates were simply social stress. Otherwise, before long, we have done nothing but explain everything religious in social terms; religion becomes nothing but a projection, an ideology, or a myth that helps humans to cope with distressing realities. There was, of course, a social problem behind the Judaizers. But I do not want to suggest for a moment that there was no religious problem involved. Some, unfortunately, have argued in this way for the issues discussed in Galatians.[18] But to explain earliest Jerusalem Christianity as an economical experiment in which the poor revolted against the wealthy and did so in religious categories simply won't do.

Furthermore, to explain the Judaizers as the religious establishment and the churches of Paul as nothing but sectaries who find theology to legitimate their own existence will not do either. What we need is balance, and that balance is found when the reader notices social factors that are working in and through religious factors. The balanced interpreter learns quickly that, in reality, theology and social factors cannot be separated: all theology expresses itself socially and social factors influence our theology.[19]

---

18. An example is F. Watson, *Paul, Judaism and the Gentiles*. I believe he explains far too much as nothing more than social factors. What we ought to learn to see is that while everything has a social context, other factors, like theological ones, are just as real and just as influential.

19. See esp. P. Berger and T. Luckmann, *The Social Construction of Reality* (New York: Doubleday, 1966); see also P. Berger's *The Sacred Canopy* (New York: Doubleday, 1967).

We also need to remember that analogies between the social crises behind Galatians and the social crises behind our theological problems eventually break down. What we need to do is find similarities at the central core and then find theological variations that have some social motivations. We also need to be careful in applying this text not to think that the difference was simply social. Social it was, but the social imposition by the Judaizers had so transformed the gospel itself that it was heresy. We are not seeking then simply social variations. We want to find social variations that are corrupting the gospel.

In the same vein, we can learn from the conflict in this situation and understand how it was that the early Christians were able to avoid a major rift within Christianity. What was at stake in this earliest of Christian debates was "denominationalism"—that is, the splitting of the church into two (socially and theologically based) segments, Jewish nationalistic and universalistic Christianity. How was this factionalism avoided? (1) The foundational churches in Jerusalem were not ignored or defaced by settling the matter out in the Diaspora. It was wise of the leaders of the churches in Antioch to send leaders to Jerusalem to get their perspective and wisdom on the issues. (2) Paul presented what he preached before the leaders to inform them and to gain their evaluation. Here we find the important principle of all conflicts: acquire the evidence before making judgments. (3) The evaluation of the Jerusalem pillars was based on the gospel of Christ, not on their own social conventions. (4) The leaders were able to agree because they recognized the work of God in each of the respective callings of Peter and Paul. (5) The leaders simply urged Paul (partly no doubt for social and political reasons) to remember the poor in Jerusalem as part of his ministry. In summary, therefore: recognize conflicts, acquire all the evidence, discern the matter theologically and socially, and come to a solution.

Does this procedure end all conflicts? Did it end the conflict in the early church? Certainly not. Read Acts 15 for the second chapter in the debate. But disagreements go a long way toward resolution if both sides live according to its wisdom. Unity in Christ and around the gospel, when recognized and lived out, can erase a lot of church conflicts.

I add, as a caution, that the procedure followed here is not a "cure-all" for all conflicts in our churches. We can learn from this conflict and its resolution, but that is all. To have a completely biblical view of "conflict management," about which the Bible speaks mainly in indirect ways, we would need to analyze every conflict situation in the Bible and discern its resolution in its historical context. Far too frequently, in our hurry to apply the Bible, we take the principles we learn from one passage and then turn those principles into rigid rules that do not always work the way we want. It is better to retain a certain humility about our principles and applications. Some conflicts are better handled with direct confrontation (cf. 2:11–14) than with "private meetings" (2:1–5); others are best handled by public councils (Acts 15).

ONE COULD EASILY find matters that are as much social as they are theological. Of course, whether the issue is primarily social or theological will depend on the case and, most likely, will be perceived by one group more theologically than the other (depending on which person or side you ask!). When we try to find an analogy between the Judaizers at Antioch and some imposing group in our world, we could easily discuss such analogies at length.

We take here one example: one's choice of Christian music. I have heard over and over in the last ten years all kinds of discussions about "contemporary worship" styles. Is the "Willow Creek" model, the "high church" model, the Southern Baptist model, or the traditional evangelical model to be preferred? Voices have been raised for each, and the discussions that follow are interesting. I heard one esteemed gentleman recently say that he did not like "contemporary worship" because, in consuming all the time in church services with that sort of music, he was afraid his children would not learn the "old hymns." I have heard some of the youth in our church (my daughter and son included) say they think "old hymns" are boring and slow and sound like funeral dirges. I have heard some Christians say that "Christian rock" is a contradiction in terms; yet I have heard others say that they became Christians because they became attracted to Christ through Christian rock music. I have heard others contend that Gregorian chants are the purest form of Christian music. Personally, I like the folk guitar and singing of Franciscan John Michael Talbot.

Is this debate simply theological and biblical? Certainly not. The issue here is partly social and partly theological. It is probably not to the point of what we see in the Galatian Judaizers. I do hope, however, that we can make applications in such a way that we see improvement before disaster takes place. I hope we do not have to let things get to the point of heresy before we see them as problems. What we find in the worship style and music issue of today is that at times one group imposes its desire on another group, in the name of theology, and the result is social and theological: social division and theological justification.

Socially speaking, we all love the familiar and we have learned to love it because that was what we were taught. If we have grown up on the "old hymns" (as I did), we probably have learned to love them. We have learned their tunes, tones, and words. We have been shaped theologically (and not always correctly) by their teachings. We learned to express our faith through singing these songs, and we learned to do so heartily. And it is also true, especially for our youth today and for those who have become Christians in the last decade or so, that many have not been reared on the "old hymns." They do not know the old classics by heart, but they do know the songs in contemporary worship handbooks and the lyrics of songs on the many Christian music stations. They know Amy Grant and Michael W. Smith (my daughter's favorites), not Isaac Watts, Fanny Crosby, and Charles Wesley (my generation's favorites). Therefore, it is important for all of us to recognize that this fight over worship styles is partly sociological. At times I have peered around in our local church during the singing of what I think is a great old hymn, only to be disappointed with many who do not know the words, do not know the tune, do not like the tune, or do not like the song at all. What was deeply moving to me was a bore to them. How can this be? In part, I believe, it is social.

On the other hand, the issue is also partly theological. True enough, not all hymns are theologically sound. However, I would maintain that the vast majority of traditional Christian hymns[20] are. And I am the first to say that much of contemporary singing is rooted in experience ("How happy I am") rather than praise to God ("Holy, holy, holy is the Lord God Almighty").

It is when a major shift takes place, as we are seeing today, and when that shift moves away from praise and adoration, that we find social stresses in churches. This is not to say that all hymns are praiseworthy and that contemporary worship should thus be greatly reduced. Perhaps it is because I have a home with two kids who like contemporary (even Christian!) music that I have come to appreciate that music as well. What we need is discernment of this debate in contemporary Christianity. What we need to see is that some of the arguments for each are good: old hymns are, on average, more theologically penetrating than contemporary songs, while contemporary music is more musically satisfying to most of the people today. Contemporary music tends to focus too much on experiences, while old hymns tend to have tunes that are out of touch emotionally with many people today. I should note too that some of the arguments are not worthy of serious consideration: old hymns are useless because I cannot understand the words; old hymns have inferior music; contemporary songs are leading our youth astray; and contemporary musicians are unconverted rockers.

---

20. Sadly, it must be added that some of the newer hymnbooks found in pew racks seem not to have been edited by those with theological acumen.

Like the Judaizers at Galatia, we may have in our churches, on this music debate, people who are trying to impose what they like (for both sociological and theological reasons) on others. We need to see how the churches at Galatia worked out such a problem to help us explore how to gain peace in this matter today. My suggestion is that the lesson at Galatia can be useful today: as they recognized separate callings but one gospel, we need to recognize that there are different kinds of praiseworthy music for different dimensions of our churches, but that there is one gospel that must be the heart of our singing and one God to whom we sing. We sing to God, through Christ, and in the Spirit — regardless of what and how we sing. Music that fosters those dimensions deserves respect.

What we need then is a social toleration of different styles (we can even call it "callings"), while we remain steadfast in our commitment to music that is theologically sound. I am suggesting that we need to see analogies in our churches to the situation at Galatia. Clearly, there was a situation there in which social differences (Jews versus Gentiles) were becoming theological agendas. And the theological agenda had become heretical in its attempt to impose one set of social conventions on another group of people. This kind of "analogy discernment" in our churches today, which I have tried to work out for one issue, can be a fruitful form of applying the Bible.

Fundamental to *Christian unity* is the recognition of different callings and movements in the church of Christ. The "penguin impulse" (better known as "peer pressure") is too observable in various segments of the church. What is the "penguin impulse"? Inasmuch as all penguins look and act alike, so also many Christians expect all Christians to be alike—from the clothes they wear to the translations they carry, from the schools they attend to the stores they patronize, from the political views they embrace to the kinds of cars they buy. But this can only go on for so long; eventually we find differences.

While we may poke fun at teenagers who think they are thinking for themselves but all dress similarly, we find the same features in adults and in adult Christian experience. My travels have impressed me with one observation: in whatever local church you find yourself, the majority of people in that church offer public prayers in highly similar language. Whether it is the ending or the beginning, the "our heavenly Father" or the "in Jesus' name" patterns emerge in local churches. Too often this is social conformity and not personal piety, and we can attribute it to the penguin impulse. This, however, is not true Christian unity. I once prayed with a young man who had not yet been influenced by the prayers of others; he ended his prayer with "I'm done, God. Thanks." My son once asked me what "Amen" meant; I told him it meant "So be it" or "I agree." The next night he wanted to pray before supper, and he ended his tidy, little grace with "So be it." It sounded strange (and it was funny), but it meant nothing more than our more socially familiar "Amen" (which is an Aramaic word anyway). What we need is genuine Christian unity.

The most profound experience I ever had in this regard, one that drew me out of a cloistered perception of the evangelical-fundamentalist movement, was a summer of missionary work and evangelism in Austria, in the summers of 1973 and 1975. There I encountered genuine Christians who were: (1) not from my denomination, which was Baptist at that time; (2) unable to read the King James Version of the Bible; (3) happy to use guitars and drums in church services; (4) charismatic; (5) non-American and even anti-American; (6) unconcerned about issues that I thought were important, like drinking, dress codes, and hair length; and (7) profoundly godly and spiritual. My world was partly shattered because I came to realize that what I thought was Christian was no more (if even that!) than a reflection of intertribal debates that were occurring in the United States. The consequence of these two summers changed my perceptions of the entire church. I recognized through this that *God works in different ways with different people in different parts of the world*. Not only was my world enlarged, but my perception of God increased and my realization of the church was magnified in quantum leaps. I no longer thought all Christians had to be alike; I learned from this that God is much larger than my perceptions of him and his ways. This realization was the liberating work of the Spirit of God. When we experience such "largeness" in God's work, we are liberated from our social conventions. We become "biblical universalists," and we experience what Paul wanted: freedom (see 5:1–12).

We do not need to travel to Europe to gain this perception, though it was there I realized it. We need simply to open our eyes and our ears. We need to see how varied the church is and hear how vibrantly different it is in different parts of the world. It is not unwise for Christians to visit other churches in their local communities to find out what God is doing in various churches. True enough, sometimes we may be disappointed with what we see, but frequently we will be encouraged by finding the faith of others expressed in slightly (but just as valid) different ways.

Those who minister to inner-city blacks will emphasize different themes than those who serve the wealthy in well-to-do suburbs. In the summer of 1990 our family began our weeklong vacation on a Sunday morning. I was scheduled to preach at an inner-city church that morning, so we decided to depart from there. The experience captivated us and generated several hours of conversation in our traveling later that day. There we found an old church building with a fresh re-arrangement of society. The church was racially mixed, unlike our current suburban church; the church's music was lively and loud, sometimes unlike our suburban church; the dress of the people was considerably less conspicuous than our suburban church; and the issues of concern on the bulletin board (which I make a habit of reading) were completely different than those on our suburban church's bulletin board. But they were people like those of the suburban church, people who wanted to know God, to follow Jesus, and to make an impact on their neighborhood. The Bible was the same, though its applications were different. The message was the same, but its calling was different. We were enthralled with our morning of worshiping with that inner-city church. We also grew from it. The work of God is much broader than our suburban, well-to-do, mostly white churches.

Along this same line we need to learn that *different callings are not mutually exclusive*. Local InterVarsity Fellowships and Navigator Bible studies are not in competition with local churches for people. What each is called to do needs to be acknowledged, accepted, built upon, and mixed together. Local churches should not see themselves in competition with each other and proselytize members away from other churches. Nor should we be competing with other churches for evangelizing the unchurched. If what another church is doing is biblical, we in our church need to support and pray for that church in its ministry. Attendance boards are largely irrelevant; impact on our community, personal godliness, and praise to God are all that really matter. When one church takes up a ministry (e.g., public political issues), another church might take up another ministry (e.g., evangelizing an unreached area). In my view, God is not pleased to see one four-way stop neatly dotted with four churches when each of those four churches have almost identical statements of faith and largely the same "clientele." Worse yet is when one of those four churches spends too much of its time criticizing the other three. Different callings in the world are not mutually exclusive.

Paul's quick response to the Judaizers needs to be seen in perspective. He was not simply justifying himself. He knew the future implications of a present heresy. He knew that if he did not get this matter clarified, it would jeopardize the "truth of the gospel" for the Gentiles (v. 5). And we need also to see that present deviations from the truth of the gospel produce tomorrow's heretics and heresies. This is why we need to be constantly guarding our confessions of faith and the content of our teaching in classes and pulpits. Strange ideas, no matter how innocent at first, can generate years of dry ministries. Because this is a frequently observed factor in the history of the church, it is fundamentally important for churches to have theological quality control of its teaching ministries. Sad to say, this is all too often

surrendered to denominational boards (who are usually too distant to understand what is going on) or to seminary professors (who are also too distant).
Local churches need to have a theologically astute leadership in order to protect themselves from devious ideas.[21] We need to listen and to learn; we need
to grow and to change; but the essentials of the gospel are constant, and in
these there is no change and no growth. To these we are to commit ourselves
with unreserved trust and faithfulness.

---

21. The finest book on heresies is H. O. J. Brown, *Heresies: The Image of Christ in the Mirror
of Heresy and Orthodoxy from the Apostles to the Present* (Garden City, N.Y.: Doubleday, 1984).
This book needs to be in every church library, and leaders of churches need to be familiar
with its contents.

Galatians 2:11–14

PETER CAME TO Antioch, I opposed him to his face, because he was in the wrong. ¹²Before certain men came from James, he used to eat with the Gentiles. But when they arrived, he began to draw back and separate himself from the Gentiles because he was afraid of those who belonged to the circumcision group. ¹³The other Jews joined him in his hypocrisy, so that by their hypocrisy even Barnabas was led astray.

¹⁴When I saw that they were not acting in line with the truth of the gospel, I said to Peter in front of them all, "You are a Jew, yet you live like a Gentile and not like a Jew. How is it, then, that you force Gentiles to follow Jewish customs?"

THE FINAL EVENT Paul musters for his case is one of the strongest confrontations presented in the Bible: the confrontation of Peter by Paul in Antioch. Paul has demonstrated that he received his gospel independently of human teaching (1:13–17), of the major Judean churches (1:18–24), and of the Jerusalem "pillars" (2:1–10). He now seeks to show that yet one more incident in his relationship with the leaders from Jerusalem reveals both his independence and the truthfulness of his gospel. That incident concerns Peter, the first apostle (Matt. 10:2). In its essentials, the event reveals a Peter who, in the normal course of affairs, was willing to shed the identifying markers of Judaism (food and table restrictions), perhaps even circumcision and Sabbath observance, to enjoy a new-found fellowship with Gentile Christians, but who also abandoned such a stance when "certain men came from James" (2:12). The sharing of a common meal was a visible and socially powerful symbol of the new slogan Paul was teaching his young churches: "there is neither Jew nor Greek, slave nor free, male nor female, for you are all one in Christ Jesus" (3:28).¹ But this symbol was publicly damaged by Peter's behavior.

Paul finds this behavioral change not only "hypocritical" (in the sense of contradictory) but also theologically wrong and dangerous. This latter point

---

1. On table fellowship as a social and religious occasion, see esp. S. S. Bartchy, "Table Fellowship," *DJG*, 796–800; D. E. Smith, "Table Fellowship," *ABD* 6:302–4. For a more extensive study, see J. Jeremias, *The Eucharistic Words of Jesus* (Philadelphia: Fortress, 1977).

is important: Paul was more than concerned with the "contradictory behavior" of Peter. True, he changed his color, like a chameleon, but changing colors may be necessary at times (see 1 Cor. 9:19–23). But Paul sees something more in Peter's behavior: he sees theological danger. It is proper, when with Jews, to live like a Jew in order to reach such people. But, *when with Gentiles, living like a Jew is wrong.* Furthermore, making Gentiles live like Jews (especially when that very person has himself lived like a Gentile) is abominable behavior. Peter was demonstrating a different gospel by his reversed behavior: a gospel that mixed conversion to Christ with conversion to nationalistic Judaism. That is why Paul needed to confront Peter.

The confrontation (v. 11). Verses 11 and 14 begin and end this section with the same content (in rhetorical terms, this style is called an "inclusio"). The first statement (v. 11) is a report of the confrontation, while the second statement (v. 14) is a direct quotation of the charge of the confrontation. Verses 12 and 13 explain what Paul means by "he [Peter] was in the wrong" (v. 11).

It is not completely clear when Peter "came to Antioch," but Acts 12:17 is as much evidence as we have. Luke tells us there that after Peter's miraculous deliverance from prison, he "left for another place." He knew he had to vacate Jerusalem temporarily because of the persecution (cf. 12:18–19). If we remember the narrative line of Acts properly, we will recall that Paul and Barnabas were in Jerusalem at this time delivering relief for the poor (11:30; 12:25). Following this, Paul and Barnabas returned to Antioch, only to be sent out for the first missionary journey (12:25–13:3). It is as likely as anything else that Peter departed from Jerusalem not long after he had given Paul the "right hand of fellowship" (Gal. 2:9). It seems likely that Paul and Barnabas then arrived in Antioch, some time elapsed, the "men from James" arrived, and the behavior of Peter became known to Paul. Verse 11 sounds like Paul was in Antioch when the behavior of Peter occurred, though we cannot be certain about the details.

What we do know from Paul is that he "opposed him [Peter] to his face" (2:11). This expression describes a public rebuke (because, I suppose, it was a public problem), and "because he was in the wrong" is a severe comment. Some commentators now agree that Paul was saying more than "you are wrong"; Paul was saying "you stand condemned by God."[2] As I said above, Paul is arguing more than that Peter was simply wrong or inconsistent; Peter had actually perverted the gospel itself with his behavior. Thus the meaning of "because he was wrong" is severe: that is, "because he stood con-

---

2. R. N. Longenecker, *Galatians*, 72.

demned before God."[3] Whenever it occurred, Paul publicly rebuked Peter for his hypocritical behavior because what he was doing was clearly contrary to God's will, that is, contrary to life through Christ and in the Spirit.

The explanation (vv. 12–13). Paul now pauses to explain precisely what Peter had done (and even why). Peter, in his life in the Diaspora, had become accustomed to eating with Gentiles, significant progress since the days prior to a divine revelation (Acts 10–11). At the time of that revelation, Peter had said, "I have never eaten anything impure or unclean" (10:14), implying that he has also perhaps never eaten with people who could make food unclean. It is important to remember that Jewish food laws functioned to separate Jews from Gentiles and to give them a sacred identity.

....

Note on Jewish Food Laws. To understand this text aright it is important to know what Jews thought about certain foods.[4] Basically, the Bible (Lev. 11; Deut. 14) prohibits the consumption of (1) all four-footed animals except sheep, goats, cattle, and a few kinds of deer,[5] the most notable prohibition being pork; (2) shellfish and molluscs;[6] (3) birds of prey;[7] (4) most insects (except locusts, crickets, and grasshoppers);[8] (5) swarming land creatures (like lizards, crocodiles, chameleons, and weasels);[9] and (6) dead animals (which should be obvious). Furthermore, for food that was permissible there was a further restriction: no food could be consumed that had either fat or blood (Lev. 3:17). In the passage of history, Jews added other prohibitions, like Gentile meat and wine (cf. Dan. 1:12–16), because both could have been cont-

---

3. Paul uses a periphrastic expression to convey his meaning here: *hoti kategnosmenos en* ("because he was condemned"). The imperfect verb with the perfect participle emphasizes the state of Peter and fullness of the sin (i.e., he was clearly behaving in the wrong manner). This Greek expression stands in contrast to the simple aorist "I opposed"; the aorist is used here to denote the fact that Paul opposed him.

4. On this, see the specialized studies of E. P. Sanders, *Jewish Law from Jesus to the Mishnah*, 23–28, 134–51, 272–83. The first two sets of pages describe practice in Palestine; the last set the Diaspora. I am deeply indebted to Sanders for my observations on Jewish food laws. See also G. Schramm and D. E. Smith, "Meal Customs," *ABD* 4:648–55.

5. What is noticeable here is that easily domesticated animals are permissible (with a few others) while the "wild animals" are prohibited (with a few exceptions: wild sheep and goats, since they are like the domesticated ones; deer and antelope).

6. What is permitted here is fish that have scales and fins.

7. These are prohibited because of their contact with corpses; corpses were a main source of impurity for Jewish regulations.

8. I am unsure about the distinctions among insects; one would naturally think of certain insects being more susceptible to corpse-impurity than others.

9. The reason seems to be because they creep and crawl on the ground (and are, therefore, more susceptible to impurities?).

aminated through idolatry. One other prohibition was the eating of food that was not properly tithed, though Pharisees debated this point quite heatedly. These rules were not rules governing only the behavior of priests; they were rules for all of Israel. While there were variations, it does appear that most Jews kept most of these laws: it was too easy for their neighbors to "rat on" them, and most Jews wanted to maintain good standing in the community. But more importantly, most Jews wanted to live before God in obedience. Sanders, speaking of the value of food laws for the Jews, infers: "the food laws stood out, along with the observance of the sabbath, as being a central and defining aspect of Judaism."[10]

When they did become unclean as a result of contact with one of these forbidden foods, the observant Jew did what the Bible said: he washed himself and waited until evening (Lev. 11:24–28). These rules seemed to vary only a little in the Diaspora, differing no doubt according to availability and the animal's perception in that part of the world. Thus, the precise animals listed in Leviticus 11:4–8 and Deuteronomy 14:4–5 were supplemented at times with the water buffalo and the giraffe. Gentile oil was also apparently prohibited in certain locations.[11]

It should also be said that there were variations among Jews about what constituted permissible food. Some Jews (like the Pharisees) were more radical in their applications of biblical laws than others and extended such laws to degrees that others thought were fanatical. It goes without saying that such a radicalism would have been found more often in Palestine than in the Diaspora. I am persuaded that the party that came from Jerusalem was more along the line of the radicals than along the line of the "strict, but accommodating" group. Some Jews would eat no food that came from Gentiles, but Diaspora Jews were forced to do this; some radicals, therefore, could have seen almost all food in the Diaspora as unclean (but I know of no evidence that suggests this); at any rate, some would have seen lots of danger in the food laws in the Diaspora. What we do find is that Jews frequently had to agitate in their Diaspora communities in order to acquire "pure food" because much of it had been previously offered to idols.

---

10. Sanders, *Jewish Law from Jesus to the Mishnah*, 27.

11. A significant discussion took place in ancient Judaism over oil. The Bible prohibits the consumption of liquids that were found to have a flying insect in them or on them (cf. Lev. 11:31–38 with 11:20–23). The issue became big: how were Jews to keep all their liquids free from flies and gnats? The rabbis made decisions that anything smaller than a lentil (about the size of a pea) did not defile liquids. (Thus, gnats did not defile but flies did.) Since water, wine, and oil were liquids and were often exposed to air, special rules were made to keep them clean. See ibid., 32–33, 200–205.

What, then, was Peter doing in Antioch?[12] My guess is one of five things: (1) he was eating food that had not been checked regarding its religious state (most red meats in a Diaspora market had already been offered to idols), that is, eating Gentile meat and drinking Gentile wine; (2) he was eating foods that were expressly prohibited in Leviticus or Deuteronomy; (3) less likely, he was eating meat that still contained blood or fat because it had not been properly slaughtered; (4) he was eating food that had not been properly tithed; (5) it is indeed possible that he was simply eating too frequently with Gentiles and the real issue was not *what* he was eating but *with whom* he was eating.[13] While we may never know—and there may have been several factors at work—it is important for us to try to understand what was going on (if not just so we can find analogies in our world).

My first guess is that the issue was the second one: Peter was probably eating "baby back" barbecued spare ribs or shrimp scampi, and the more conservative Jews took issue with his cavalier violation of the law—remember that this was the issue for Peter in Acts 10–11. It was later clear that unintentional violation of food laws was acceptable; intentional and flagrant violation was unacceptable. But, I grant, it is hard to imagine Jews, many of whom had become Christians, sitting down for pork meals or eating things expressly prohibited in the Bible. However, some have argued that Peter was simply eating things that would have been unacceptable only to the radical wing, which had a much stricter sense of food laws. Thus, he may have been eating food that (1) had been sacrificed to idols, or (2) that had been put to death improperly, or (3) that had not been tithed properly. In this case, what we find is a group of zealous Judaizers attempting not only to get full conversion to Judaism but also to their particular variety of Judaism (probably Pharisaism; cf. Matt. 23:15).

As already mentioned, Peter had grown accustomed to going against the rules and doing so with Gentiles. But when a party from Jerusalem arrived ("certain men from James"), he felt the pressure of their presence and their potential condemnation. Feeling their displeasure (and no doubt hearing about it from them), he "began to draw back and separate himself from the Gentiles." The table that had functioned wonderfully as a symbol of unity had become a table of separation once again for Peter.

Who are these "men from James"? Are they identical to the "circumcision group"? While many readers of Galatians have simply assumed that the two

---

12. A scholarly study of this point can be found in J. D. G. Dunn, "The Incident at Antioch (Galatians 2:11–18)," in *Jesus, Paul and the Law: Studies in Mark and Galatians*, 129–82.

13. This is the view of E. P. Sanders, "Jewish Association with Gentiles and Galatians 2:11–14," in *The Conversation Continues: Studies in Paul & John in Honour of J. Louis Martyn* (Nashville: Abingdon, 1990), 170–88.

are identical, a few modern scholars have suggested otherwise.[14] It is true that this term, "those who circumcise," could refer to Christian Judaizers (Acts 11:2), to Jewish Christians (10:45), and to non-Christian Jews (Rom. 4:12). The "circumcision group" is almost certainly not the same as the Jewish Christians at Antioch, since Peter had already enjoyed his "liberation" in their presence without criticism (Gal. 2:13). It is also questionable that Peter would be afraid of the "men from James" since he was previously on good terms with the Christians in Jerusalem where James was the leader (Acts 12). This makes it possible that the "circumcision group" is a party of non-Christian Jews who were physically persecuting those who were becoming associated with Christianity (which the circumcisers thought was an incomplete form of Judaism) and that their primary target in Antioch was Peter, a respected, and perhaps somewhat indecisive, leader. Such a reading of "circumcision group" makes Paul's use of the term "circumcision" in Galatians 2 consistent (cf. 2:7, 8; see notes at 6:12). In other words, this party was a group of law-abiding Jewish zealots bent on "forcing" Gentile converts, to either Christianity or Judaism, to convert fully if such converts wanted to be under the umbrella of Judaism. The other group, then, the "men from James," may have been either Jewish Christians from Jerusalem who were either honestly or falsely representing the position of James, or they may be identical to the circumcision party, in which case they were not Christians. I suspect they were truly from James, though they may not have been representing James with full integrity.

In order to understand the theological and social tensions working into this situation, it is best to chart out the "players involved" in our chapter. Because of its Western import, I have decided to display the "players" according to whether they were to the "left" (progressives) or to the "right" (conservatives). Without judging which is wrong or right, we see Paul as "leftist" because his efforts consistently stretched the outer boundaries of Judaism, and we see James as "rightist" because his form of Christianity was much more comfortable within the confines of Jerusalem. Peter, for convenience, is depicted here as a "moderate," because he sought to live within the two spectrums. His "moderation" in this instance, however, was hypocritical and not a genuine instance of moderation. "Jewish Christians," of course, could be either moderate or rightist, depending on the individual and the amount of liberation discovered in Christ and the Spirit.[15]

---

14. So F. F. Bruce, *Galatians*, 131; R. N. Longenecker, *Galatians*, 73–75.

15. A recent study has challenged this "leftist" versus "rightist" scheme of understanding the tensions of earliest Christianity; see C. C. Hill, *Hellenists and Hebrews: Reappraising Division Within the Earliest Church* (Minneapolis: Fortress, 1992).

The "Players" in Galatia		
Left	**Moderate**	**Right**
Paul	<— Peter —>	Circumcisers
		"James'" Party
Gentile Christians	Jewish Christians	
Barnabas —>		"Christian" Judaizers

To continue our story line, Peter's habits changed when the "men from James" arrived. Why? Paul says, "because he was afraid of those who belonged to the circumcision group." We have defined this latter group as a group of ardent Jewish nationalists, based in Jerusalem, who urged all groups in Jerusalem and Judaism to live faithfully according to the law. Peter, perhaps still smarting from his time in prison (Acts 12), thought one struggle with persecution was enough (cf. also 4:21; 5:40). Perhaps he even remembered the words of the "pillars" that he was called to the Jews and reasoned that he did not need to give up on his Jewish nationalism (Paul could do that). The presence of the "men from James" and their words that the nationalists were upset were enough for Peter to change directions and do an "about face" on eating with Gentiles.

Peter's change was perhaps acceptable, especially for one who needed to protect his Jewish image for his primary calling to evangelize the Jews. But "the other Jews joined him, . . . even Barnabas." When the others got involved, there developed a social rift in the churches in Galatia: a Gentile group and a Jewish group. This was intolerable for one who believed that in Christ "there is neither Jew nor Greek" (Gal. 3:28). There was now, in effect, two churches: a kosher church and a Gentile church. The symbolic rupture of dissociating from fellowship with the Gentiles by not eating with them was severe, too severe for Paul, and he set out to correct those in the wrong.

Paul charged Peter with "hypocrisy" (explained in v. 14). What is "hypocrisy"? A standard definition of "hypocrisy" is "intentional (and even unintentional) contradiction of belief and practice." Frequently, the term is used for those who "fake religious confessions" or who live in a manner in complete contrast to their religious persuasions. This is supposedly based on the historical origins of the word: *hypocrite* (Gk. *hypocrites*) was a theatrical term for the person who wore a mask on stage and who often interpreted the scene for the audience. In time, the term was used for the person who "play acted" a role, this usage naturally leading to a moral description of someone who was insincere or fake (our term "hypocrite"). However, as many have noted, *hypocrites* as used in the New Testament has Jewish (not simply Greek) roots and is in fact stronger than our term. It is fundamentally important to derive meanings from ancient texts, not from modern English dictionaries. The term carries with it the senses of wickedness, opposition to God and his truth, and even heresy.[16] In other words, Peter was not simply "acting" here; he was not simply "deceiving through pretense." Instead, he was *morally* wrong because he was *theologically* wrong (v. 11); not surprisingly, Paul would say next that Peter had jettisoned the "truth of the gospel" (v. 14). Peter had become heretical here. Why? The next verse answers this.

The charge (v. 14). Paul charges Peter indirectly and directly in this verse. Indirectly, Paul sums up Peter's behavior as "not acting in line with the truth of the gospel." As we mentioned in the previous paragraph, hypocrisy was a charge against one's conformity to truth. So, Paul says, Peter's behavior was essentially a failure to live in line with the truth of the gospel. The gospel Paul is talking about is clear: justification is for all who surrender in trust to Christ. Furthermore, justification implies a life of obedience to God's will and a life of freedom in the Spirit. Peter claimed justification by faith and the Holy Spirit but lived in contradiction to this when he held "faith" in one hand and "joining Judaism" in the other as the two requirements for acceptance with God. By his behavior Peter's gospel had shifted from "salvation for all without social restrictions" to "salvation for Jews alone" (and those who convert to Judaism). Peter had erected the old social barriers.

Directly, Paul accuses Peter in the following words: "You are a Jew, yet you live like a Gentile and not like a Jew. How is it, then, that you force Gentiles to follow Jewish customs?" Paul's first sentence is not without its own problems. It was not wrong for Jewish missionaries to the Gentiles to be Jews who lived like Gentiles and not like Jews. I do not think we find Paul's severest criticism in this first sentence. This behavior was tolerable for Paul. But it became problematical when those same missionaries (including Peter) then "force[d] Gentiles to follow Jewish customs." This word *force* is the most important word in this verse, for it tips us off as to what Peter was doing.

For some reason, commentaries have been prone to overlook this word in their explanations. More often than not, many scholars see this term as *moral* force, in the sense that Peter, through the power of his example, was pressuring the Gentiles then to act like Jews.[17] I find this explanation short of full persuasion. The term Paul uses is a strong one: "force" (Gk. *anankazo*) denotes

---

16. See further in N. Turner, *Christian Words* (Edinburgh: T & T Clark, 1980), 219–20. The finest history of the term is found in C. Spicq, *Lexique Théologique du Nouveau Testament* (Fribourg, Switzerland: Editions Universitaires de Fribourg, 1991), 1546–53; see also U. Wilckens, "ὑποκρίνομαι,κτλ.," *TDNT* 8:559–71.

17. So J. B. Lightfoot, *Galatians*, 114; R. N. Longenecker, *Galatians*, 78.

"physical force" against one's will. Two examples in Galatians are important. At Galatians 2:3 we read that not "even Titus . . . was compelled to be circumcised," and at 6:12 that Paul's opponents "are trying to compel you to be circumcised." Paul's earlier life of forceful actions against Christians is also telling in this regard. He demanded that these new Christians either be circumcised and adopt the whole law or face death (cf. Acts 9). We read at Acts 26:11 that "I [Paul] tried *to force* them to blaspheme" (emphasis added); here we can only think of the long line in history of those who have persecuted the Jews, torturing them until they either recanted or died. I am not, of course, eliminating the sense of moral persuasion in this term, but I am seeking to restore the physical dimension that was no doubt originally present.[18]

So what was Peter doing? He had previously enjoyed unrestricted social fellowship with the Gentiles, speaking their language, eating their food, drinking their wine, touching their children, and sitting in their homes. When the Jewish nationalists arrived, Peter, perhaps remembering his narrow escape in Jerusalem, reversed his behavior and withdrew from the Gentiles. His behavior and speech got others to go along with him. But, in addition, he then began to *force Gentile Christians to be circumcised (and to follow Jewish social laws),*[19] *to reduce the threat of persecution he was beginning to feel from these ardent Jewish nationalists.* Peter, in effect, was destroying the gospel of Jesus Christ by demanding that the converts at Galatia become Jews. In such a situation, there was no gospel because the work of Christ had been eliminated (v. 21).

Bridging Contexts

APPLYING EXAMPLES, AS I have said before, is relatively easy. In our search for modern applications of Paul's confrontation with Peter, we may want to find other instances of leaders leading others astray, either by way of example or outright physical force (which I suspect is quite rare). What comes immediately to mind is the responsibility of leaders. Their examples and teachings are followed by those whom they lead. We can think of the good example of Paul, who here fought valiantly for the freedoms found in the gospel; we can also think of the bad example of Peter, who

---

18. This physical demand of circumcision for converts has several chapters in its Jewish history. On this and the larger question of conversion to Judaism, see S. McKnight, *A Light Among the Gentiles: Jewish Missionary Activity During the Second Temple Period* (Minneapolis: Fortress, 1991), esp. 68, 79–82.

19. The term "to follow Jewish customs" (*ioudaizein*) may mean no more than to live like a Jew. However, I tend to agree with those who understand the term as "converting to Judaism" in the fullest sense. See H. D. Betz, *Galatians*, 112; see also J. D. G. Dunn, *Jesus, Paul, and the Law*, 149–50.

here succumbed to the pressure and threat of persecution. Both characters can be catalysts for applications.

Furthermore, we can think of the other characters in our quests for applications. Who today can be (or has been) like the "men from James" (and we need not restrict the applications to males)? like Gentiles? Jewish Christians? Barnabas? In our search for analogies in our world, it is best for us to stick as tightly as possible to situations that are similar to Paul's context. We are dealing here with a large church situation (not a work-place problem) that involves both several groups (not just a one-on-one disagreement) and the integrity of the gospel (not some squabble over how much bass should be in church music).

Each of these groups or individuals can be explored for applications, and I suggest we follow some of the ideas presented here. "Men from James" are conservative people who stand zealously for the faith but whose faith is erroneously restricted to one social group. Before one can find contemporary analogies to this group, one must also decide if they are identical to the circumcision party or not. Since I tend to think they are not identical, I would want to find analogies in people whose faith is sub-Christian (say, radical denominationalism) and who zealously present it as the final truth, as we find in such groups as the Mormons. If one contends that the "men from James" are in fact not Christians, then one would want to explore groups who seek to convert Christians to their religious persuasions.

The "Gentile Christian" versus "Jewish Christian" groups are not hard to explore either. What we need to find is some form of faction in our churches or in the church at large. This form, for purposes of application, need not be racial or social (though I would prefer to remain as directly in tune with the actual situation as possible); it need only be some form of a potential faction. Gentile Christians and Jewish Christians, we may be sure, sometimes got along and sometimes did not. Their differences were as much religious as social. The points of contention, we can imagine, were usually expressed in theological terms and were no doubt blown out of proportion by each side. Sound familiar? What we have, then, is a new group of Christians, united by a common faith in Christ and carrying a history of social conflicts. Their union will be hard to maintain and will take strenuous activity and difficult bending by both sides.

Barnabas is interesting. This man was a Jewish Christian with exemplary pastoral gifts in handling conflicts. But even great leaders fail; Barnabas is an example of a noble Christian collapsing under peer pressure and threats of persecution. The construction of Galatians 2:13 suggests that Barnabas was persuaded by the others and did not himself desire the separation.[20] Nonetheless, he was also wrong.

Paul and Peter are the easiest to interpret and apply: Paul was in the right and Peter in the wrong. Now in the nature of human conflict, it is predictable that each side will think it has its Paul and will see Peter in the other side. For our purposes, only the grace of God and insight into his Word and our world can enable us to perceive who is Paul and who is Peter in our conflicts. We must be careful to discern our gospel: Is our message the true gospel of grace and freedom, the gospel that has come to us through Jesus Christ and in the Holy Spirit? Do we live in consistency with our profession?

It is fundamentally important for us not to focus exclusively on Peter's being wrong and Paul's being right. We need to understand *why* Paul was right and *why* Peter was wrong. Paul's argument is not personal and vindictive, as if he were somehow jealous of Peter's ministries. Nor is his argument simply intellectual. Rather, Peter was wrong because *his theology was wrong*. Peter's practice flowed from his theology, and his theology, as a result of his reversal, was rotten. Consequently, his behavior was also wrong. Peter's new theology was no different than Judaism: salvation is of the Jews, and Gentiles must convert to Christ and to both the law and the Jewish nation in order to be acceptable to God. Paul was right because he saw in Peter's behavior the blossoming of a poisonous plant. Paul knew that justification was by faith, for both Jew and Gentile, through God's grace, and in Christ, and it resulted in the gift of the Holy Spirit. Paul knew that Peter had failed to understand the first and second elements of the gospel and that this misunderstanding distorted the whole gospel.

But perhaps we are being too hard on Peter. It may be that he was simply failing in the implications he was drawing from his theology but that his theology itself was fine. Peter, perhaps, believed that Christ was sufficient and that the Holy Spirit was more than adequate to guide one's life before God. But, it might be argued, he was *acting* in a way that denied his theology. Potential applications from this view could also be found, and this is a view, I think, that deserves some consideration.

Before we can apply Paul's message in 2:11–14 we must understand what made Peter wrong. Peter was not wrong because he reversed his behavior nor even because he demanded circumcision; we could feasibly imagine situations in the world of Judaism when Christians might go along with the command

---

20. The "even," the passive voice of the verb ("was led astray"), and the instrumental dative combine to tone down Barnabas's responsibility. Barnabas, for whatever reasons, went along with the faction but seems not to have desired it. Perhaps he held out the longest for the hope of peace. As is easily noticed, Paul does not attack Barnabas.

of God to circumcise so as not to offend the Jews (cf. Acts 16:3). Peter was wrong because he failed to perceive the implication of the gospel when applied to Gentiles. What Paul was after were misperceptions of the gospel, not people who reversed their decisions and practices.

What does this text say about *confrontation?* Some biblical scholars have found this passage embarrassing and even sub-Christian, usually because they see in Paul's behavior a combative triumphalism. Why, they ask, did Paul not seek out Peter in private? He had apparently gone private earlier (2:1–2), so why not here? Did Paul contradict himself with his desire to confront people in gentleness (6:1)? To be sure, it would be eminently helpful to have both Peter's and Barnabas's account of the incident to round off the rough edges of Paul's account. And it is surely our responsibility not to be too hard on either Peter or Barnabas in light of our own known habits toward error. We must be careful not to think that everything about confrontation can be found here; after all, Paul is not talking about confrontation abstractly!

Nonetheless, what Peter did was wrong. He compromised the gospel in trying to rearrange its essentials. It is one thing to become a Jew to the Jews; it is quite another thing to make Gentiles become Jews. And this is where Paul's point must be given full weight. We need to tolerate social differences and to be flexible with respect to minor details; but, we can never tolerate the demand of social conformity as one of the essentials of the gospel. Paul was right and Peter was wrong.

Put differently for us, we need not be overly concerned with when a person was baptized (at infancy or at a later profession of faith), which denomination one attends, which political party one prefers, what color someone may be, or which social status one has attained—these are trivial. But faith in Christ, obedience to him, and adherence to the essentials of the gospel are neither trivial nor to be taken lightly. We pronounce trivial differences tolerable; we pronounce gospel deviations wrong.

But did Paul need to rebuke Peter publicly? First, it is important for us to admit how little we actually know about this situation; second, it is just as important for us to sympathize with Paul in his portrait. Before we jump to the conclusion about Paul's supposed harshness, it might be good for us to attempt to read this story more gently and compassionately. It is possible (in my view likely) that Paul did go to Peter privately first; I do not think this is asking too much or assuming too much. Good leaders (and Paul was surely one) do not immediately jump on people. If Paul did, then it is probable that he got nowhere, or at least not as far as he wanted. Thus he went public. Yet even this public rebuke and explanation may have not won the day. Paul's relationship with Jerusalem seemed to have remained tense and strained throughout his life.

But perhaps I am wrong; perhaps Paul did get after Peter immediately in a public confrontation. Was he wrong in doing so? To begin with, we need to say that Paul's example is not impeccable and that he just may be wrong here *in his approach*. I would want to maintain that, as a principle, *what Paul taught* was right; *how he taught what he taught* may have been less than desirable. Peter was wrong in compromising the gospel; Paul was accurate in what he saw and what he had to say about Peter. But, Paul could be wrong in *going public* about Peter.

However, I would also want to maintain that there is a certain wisdom in the principle of confronting private sins privately and public sins publicly.[21] What Peter did was wrong and, left alone, would have had massive public consequences. In such situations it is probably wisest to go public—but to do so with a certain humility and gentleness (cf. Gal 6:1). I am convinced that we can hold together a direct (and uncomfortable for us) confrontation by Paul with a loving stance toward Peter, his followers, and the churches in Galatia. Try reading Galatians 2:11–14 in a gentler tone; it can be done. And when done, the entire emotion of the passage changes. I ask if it is not possible to read this with tears in Paul's eyes and a thankful, but repentant, response on the part of Peter. We do know that Peter did not ultimately part company with Paul. This tense situation may have been an important growing experience for both apostles.

PERHAPS I SHOULD say up front that this text is not about contemporary "food laws" in our society. We have all grown accustomed to the news media telling us that one more food we have been eating is not good for us and may clog our arteries (only to be countered five years later by another study that suggests the opposite), and we have also gotten used to checking the lists on boxes of food to find what percentage is fat and cholesterol (now broken into the good kind and the bad kind). But these scruples of ours were not Peter's or the Jews'. What concerned them was biblical law, living before God in a "clean" state, and keeping their national status clear with respect to these laws. We misfire when we think these legal concerns of Peter's were concerned with diet; they were about piety.

---

21. J. R. W. Stott, *Only One Way*, 53: "He did not listen to those who may well have counselled him to be cautious and to avoid washing dirty theological linen in public. He made no attempt to hush the dispute up or arrange (as we might) for a private discussion from which the public or the press were excluded. The consultation in Jerusalem had been private (verse 2), but the showdown in Antioch must be public."

Furthermore, while Peter's behavior (and misbehavior as corrected by Paul) might teach us what Mark taught us, that all food is clean (Mark 7:19), that is also not the point. I would want to maintain that this is a legitimate inference from the text but that such is not the concern of the text. The text is concerned about *social and cultural imperialism,* about *Jewish designs to protect their privileged status before God.* Accordingly, Paul's criticisms of Peter were not concerned with getting Peter to eat shrimp and other "watery swarming things," but with getting Peter to realize how grand God's plan was: God's design was for all people to come to him through Christ and in the Spirit. Paul's concerns then were to destroy social and cultural imperialism. This he does by showing how all people may be found acceptable to God simply by surrendering in faith to Jesus Christ.

The freedom of consistency. Peter learned a lesson at Antioch; if he did not, he should have. That lesson was that the demand to live according to the gospel brought with it a remarkable freedom and adventure as it penetrated the Gentile world. The life that Peter had lived was a sheltered life, enclosed within the law of Moses and protected by myriads of self-respecting Jews who lived according to the law. But Peter was converted to Jesus Christ, and he now had to live a new life in the Spirit of God. The adaptations and changes that Peter's new ministry involved were difficult for him. He needed to learn that there had to be considerable flex in this new life. What was hard to accept was that this new life was consistent: consistent with God's Spirit (though perhaps not with the law). Consistency in Christian living is not conformity and uniformity. Consistency is measured by listening to God's Word, to Christ, and to the Spirit of God.

There is a certain safety in being regulated by law and ordinances, along with a certain respectability and social blocking. When a questionable practice arises, there is security in consulting the rule book and looking up the answer, thus remaining within the group. But life in the Spirit is not so secure. Peter had trouble with this when he got to Antioch and did not have the courage to stick to his initial leadings. What was formerly regulated was now left to him to decide as God's Spirit led him.

I have often thanked God for the Spirit of God, for apart from him we would be without guidance on so many issues that confront us in our world today. The New Testament is our foundation, but it is only a foundation; the superstructure has to be constructed over and over again as we confront our society. When we face crucial political or social decisions, we go to the Bible, but sometimes we are not given direct answers; after reading it and surrendering our spirit to God's will, we need boldly to step forth as Christians and live the way we think God wants us to. When we arrive in our Antiochs, in our new situations, we need to learn to live consistently within the freedom that God's Spirit provides. For some, this is scary; for all it ought to be the adventure of living in faith.

Peer pressure. We adults are in the habit today of speaking of "peer pressure" as something that the youth of our society faces. They face the pressure of friends and acquaintances who drink, use drugs, engage in immoral sexual practices, and live lives that are essentially unholy and displeasing to God. We constantly urge them to "Just Say No" to their friends and to sin. But we forget that peer pressure is as much a part of the adult life as it is of the teenage years.

Where is peer pressure felt (at the adult level) in your church and in your life? To be sure, some peer pressure is good. If we use another term we can see this. The term *accountability* has become fashionable in evangelical circles of late. Accountability is the positive side of "peer pressure." The negative side is our focus. What we are concerned about here is that, as with Peter's succumbing to the pressures of the Jewish leaders who misunderstood the gospel, there are instances when Christians today refuse to live according to the gospel because of the potential displeasure of others. As Hudson Taylor experienced criticism for adopting the Chinese way of life, so many Christians today experience criticism for their experiments in Christian freedom. The principle is simple, and potentially dangerous: as long as we are led by the Spirit, our behavior is God's will. While it may be unspiritual (i.e., not being led by God's Spirit) for most of us to skip a Sunday morning service to play golf, it may be the precise leading of God's Spirit for a Christian professional golfer to do so as he or she serves the Lord with the gifts granted by the Lord. There are no rules and regulations here; there is only God's Word, God's Spirit, and God's Church—each offering guidance.

It doesn't seem to matter what decisions we make; someone will criticize our choices. If we are handcuffed by a fear of people's criticisms, we will never accomplish anything. Such fear is nothing more than peer pressure. Peter made a bad decision when he felt that pressure; we will too. But God calls us to a fearless obedience of his will as we live in the Spirit. What we need is courage, courage to live according to our faith and its implications rather than according to our emotions, fleeting passions, and fear of others.

The hardest implication of grace to accept is perhaps that there are no other grounds of acceptance with God other than Christ in God's Spirit. We are not accepted on the basis of our physical appearance, our financial status, our family history, our social standing, our athletic talents, our rhetorical skills, or our religious deeds and piety. We are accepted by God's grace through Christ. And here is where it is hardest: *we have a hard time treating others in a way that is consistent with the way God treats us.* God deals with us in a way that is consistent with who we are in Christ; we, on the other hand, add rules and tests for accepting others. I maintain that life in God's grace is hardest when it comes to living with and accepting others.[22] And one facet of this difficulty is learning to live in God's freedom in such a way that other's approval or disapproval is not the motivating force in our decisions. May God, in his grace, grant us the freedom to live in the Spirit.

---

22. The best book I have ever seen on Christian relationships is D. Bonhoeffer, *Life Together*, trans. J. W. Doberstein (New York: Harper & Row, 1954), esp. 40–77.

Galatians 2:15–21

WE WHO ARE Jews by birth and not 'Gentile sinners' [16]know that a man is not justified by observing the law, but by faith in Jesus Christ. So we, too, have put our faith in Christ Jesus that we may be justified by faith in Christ and not by observing the law, because by observing the law no one will be justified.

[17]"If, while we seek to be justified in Christ, it becomes evident that we ourselves are sinners, does that mean that Christ promotes sin? Absolutely not! [18]If I rebuild what I destroyed, I prove that I am a lawbreaker. [19]For through the law I died to the law so that I might live for God. [20]I have been crucified with Christ and I no longer live, but Christ lives in me. The life I live in the body, I live by faith in the Son of God, who loved me and gave himself for me. [21]I do not set aside the grace of God, for if righteousness could be gained through the law, Christ died for nothing!"

Original Meaning

SERIOUS BIBLE STUDENTS have a hard time deciding where Paul's address to Peter ends and begins to reflect theologically on what took place between the two of them. Some (reflected in the NIV) think that Paul's conversation with Peter does not end until verse 21 (but, could Peter have possibly followed this kind of argument in speech form?), while others say that verse 14 is the end. I prefer this second view and agree with those who consider verses 15–21 as a "theological reflection" by Paul on what took place at Antioch and as a theological summary of what he told Peter on that occasion. We can be sure that Peter did not have to listen to such a dense argument; but we can also be sure that what Paul says here was presented to Peter in a longer, more digestible, form.[1] Put differently, verses 15–21 is a later elaboration by Paul on what took place between Peter and him at Antioch. Knowing Paul as we do, we are forced to imagine

---

1. In a scholarly commentary, H. D. Betz has argued that 2:15–21 is the *propositio* (main thesis or proposition) of Galatians (see his *Galatians*). While it is reasonable to argue this, I prefer to see these verses as Paul's theological reflection on the incident with Peter rather than a new stage in the letter to the Galatians. Galatians 3:1 starts afresh with direct address to the Galatians while, in hindsight, 2:15–21 appears to be direct address to Peter.

him reflecting long and hard on just what was taking place at Antioch under the leadership of Peter. He no doubt spent hours that night praying and reflecting on what he said and how he would have to approach the all-too-common (but growing) problems at Antioch.

The exegesis of verses 15–21 is fraught with difficulties, both in logic and in meaning. The paragraph can be divided into two major sections: (1) The Fact of a Common Conversion Experience (vv. 15–16) and (2) The Implications of a Common Conversion Experience (vv. 17–21). In the first section Paul states (supposedly to Peter) that both of them, though Jewish, had come to the common conviction that Jesus Christ was the agent of salvation in God's plan and, secondly, that they had come to him in faith for that salvation. Implicit in this coming to Christ was the denial of acceptance with God through the works of the law (vv. 15–16).

The implications of this common conversion experience are then spelled out in sharp, theologically loaded comments. (1) The life of the Christian is not a "lawless" life in the sense of wicked antinomianism (v. 17). Finding our salvation in Christ and not in the law does not mean that Jesus Christ leads people away from the law into sin. While the regulations of the Jews are fine (cf. Rom. 7:12), the guidelines for the Christian are to be found following Christ and living in the Spirit. (2) In converting to Christ, the Christian, especially the Jewish Christian (here "I" in v. 18 refers to Peter), forfeits the opportunity of ever returning to the law as the ground of one's acceptance with God or the basis of one's morality and the guide for life. This statement is then restated in v. 19: finding acceptance with God in Christ means dying to the law (as the instrument of that acceptance). (3) In converting to Christ, the Jewish Christian finds spiritual life through death, understood here as being crucified with Christ, to the law, so that the resurrected Christ might grant his new life to the believer (vv. 19–21). And if we (Paul and Peter) have come to Christ for salvation, we have at the same time perceived that God's grace is not to be found in the law. Coming to Christ, then, is not a denial of God's grace. In what follows, I shall expound each of these implications.

As can be seen, the whole issue is the *place of the law in the life of the Galatian Christian*. Put differently and more realistically, it is the *place of Jewish distinctives and social regulations that governed Jewish behavior and separated them from the Gentiles and the Galatian converts*. We should not at this point separate these two dimensions of the law for first-century Jews; they did not perceive their social distinctives (circumcision, table purity, etc.) as something other than straightforward life under the law of Moses (moral principles). The struggle for Peter (and somewhat earlier for Paul) was how to live as a Christian Jew and how that life was to be governed. Were they to submit to the Jewish law?

And, if so, did that mean they were to remain Jews and expect converts to Christ eventually to embrace the whole law (to become proselytes to Judaism)? Regardless of how hard this perception is for us today, this was the central issue for first-century Jewish converts. Were they, in turning to Christ, abandoning their Jewish heritage, fulfilling it, or simply adding to it? Peter's struggle was similar to that of other Jews: Are we Jews? Jewish Christians? or Christians? Are we reformers of Judaism or are we starting the church?

Here is the nub of the issue for Paul as he looked at Peter's behavior in Antioch: Peter, in finding acceptance with God in Christ, apparently failed to realize the comprehensiveness and sufficiency of the new covenant in Christ and life in the Spirit. To Paul, Christ's work was complete and the law was thereby relegated to its proper time in history (see especially the notes at 3:19–25). Paul contends that Christian morality and life before God are not to be found in "observing the law"; rather, they are found in death and resurrection with Christ and in the "fruit of the Spirit." True life before God, he argues, is through Christ and in the Spirit.

Another issue of general concern to the entire paragraph is the meaning of "I" (vv. 18–21) and "we" (vv. 15, 17). Commentators are divided over whether Paul means (1) to refer to himself alone in an *autobiographical sense*, (2) to refer to all Christians in a *universal sense*, (3) or to refer to Paul and Peter as *Jews in a representative sense*. While I am keenly aware that applications almost always proceed along the line of the autobiographical sense (#1), I am now convinced that this is not what Paul means. Perhaps this is disappointing to readers who, like me, put Galatians 2:20 to memory long ago as a vivid reminder of our stance before God: we must die to self and live unto God through Christ.[2] In what follows, I will not deny this (and so our memorization time has not been wasted!). But I will suggest that there is a more nuanced meaning intended by Paul.

Since options #2 and #3 are mutually exclusive, it is best for me here simply to state that Paul's conversation with Peter begins its reflection with these words: "We who are Jews by birth and not 'Gentile sinners'. . . . " These words cannot be taken in a universal sense because not all readers are Jews. In what follows, therefore, I will assume that Paul has in mind *particularly the common conversion experience of Jewish Christians*. He is reflecting on what both he and Peter went through in converting to Christ and, of course, this rings true for every Jew who has converted to Christ (a deconfession of the law). The

---

2. Of course I believe this is still true for Christian practice; I just do not think this is Paul's particular meaning in this passage.

fact of common conversion experience leads Paul to reflect more deeply on some of its implications, in particular, on the role that the law and Jewish social regulations are to play in the life of the Jewish Christian as he or she relates to Gentile Christians and to the Gentile world at large.

The fact of a common conversion experience (vv. 15–16). In these two verses we find the *original condition* (v. 15), the *recognition of salvation in Christ* (v. 16a), and the *act of faith in Christ* (v. 16b). These are the components Paul mentions as he discusses the common conversion of himself and Peter. They were Jewish by birth but had discerned (by God's grace) that justification was in God's Messiah, Jesus of Nazareth; as a result of this discernment, they had turned to Christ in faith and turned away from the works of the law.

The original condition (2:15). As I mentioned above, this clause is important for a full appreciation of Paul's intention in this paragraph. Paul is dealing here with the perception of Jewish Christians, namely, the assumed perception of Peter and himself. To be a Jew "by birth" was a wonderful privilege because Israel had been given God's covenant and promises (Rom. 3:1–2; 9:4–5; Eph. 2:12). This privilege was valued on the part of many Jews and led, so it seems, to Gentiles being dubbed "sinners," because they neither had the law nor obeyed it (cf. Rom. 2:12–16; 9:30–31; 1 Cor. 9:21; Eph. 2:11–12; 4:17).[3] We cannot fail to see here a social consciousness in the Jewish perception of sin: Jews were righteous (because, as Jews, they were observant of the law) and Gentiles were sinners (because they neither had the law nor obeyed it). Furthermore, for the more conservative wing of Judaism, like the Pharisees, *sinners* also was a term for anyone who did not adopt their legal viewpoints on such matters as tithes, sabbaths, corpse impurities, and food laws. And it is particularly these Jewish distinctives that separated Jews from Gentiles: Gentiles were sinful in that they were uncircumcised and ate unclean food with unclean people. But Paul and Peter had the privilege of not being "Gentile sinners."[4]

The recognition of salvation in Christ (2:16a). As privileged Jews, Peter and Paul came to the conviction to "know that a man is not justified by observing the law, but by faith in Jesus Christ." This recognition is far from natural for Jews (cf. Rom. 9:30–33; 10:1–4; 11:7–10; 2 Cor 3:12–18). Paul is not saying that all Jews by nature know that justification is in Christ. Indeed, what Paul is talking about here is a rare experience, one in common only between Jews who

---

3. On the Jewish background to the association of Gentiles with the term *sinners*, cf. 1 Sam. 15:18; Pss. Sol. 2:1–2; 17:25; Jub. 23:23–24; 24:28; 4 Ezra 3:28–36. These references were found in J. M. G. Barclay, *Obeying the Truth*, 77–78, n. 7.

4. It goes without comment that Paul knew that Jews were also sinners (cf. Rom. 3:9–20) but that is not his angle here.

believe in Christ. But this rare experience was shared by Paul and Peter. In what follows we need to analyze three crucial terms for understanding this passage (and Galatians as a whole): *justification, works,* and *faith.*

Since the Reformation, no doctrine has had more importance in the church than *justification by faith.* It was Martin Luther's perception that he could be accepted by God exclusively on the merit of Christ and that if he simply trusted God's promise in Christ he would find that acceptance. Of course Luther did, and his discovery has changed the church. Justification by faith, consequently, has become a central doctrine in the church. But what does *justified* mean?[5] Broadly speaking, *justification* is a metaphor of our acceptance with God that is drawn from the world of law and jurisprudence. The dilemma people find themselves in before God is that they are guilty because they have transgressed God's law and commandments. Their desire and only hope is that God, perceived in this metaphor as Judge, will somehow forgive them, make things right, and eliminate their guilt. But since God as Judge is purely objective and altogether morally righteous, and because he cannot simply overlook sin, humans find themselves in an awful predicament. But God surprisingly forgives; his agent in this forgiveness is Jesus Christ, who legally assumed our guilt and bore the curse of the law in his crucifixion (3:13). The result of Christ's work is that humans who trust in Christ and surrender themselves to him are declared fit before God.[6] As a result of God's justifying sinners, we have a new status (no longer held accountable for sinfulness), and, through his act of accepting us, God grants us the Spirit so that we have a transformed character; that is, the person who is justified (Gk. *dikaioo*) also inevitably lives a consistent life of righteousness (Gk. *dikaiosyne*).

Paul says that he and Peter had come to the conclusion, in their conversion, that "a man is not justified by observing the law." This "observing the law" is literally translated "on the basis of the works of the law." What are the *works of the law?* Are they merit-seeking works done in order to gain favor with God? From our previous discussions it should be obvious that I do not think

---

5. For a full discussion, see A. Hoekema, *Saved by Grace* (Grand Rapids: Eerdmans, 1989), 152–91; see also G. E. Ladd, *A Theology of the New Testament* (Grand Rapids: Eerdmans, 1974), 437–50; D. J. Moo, "'Righteousness' Language in Paul," in *Romans 1–8* (WEC; Chicago: Moody, 1991), 75–86. A more popular treatment may be found in L. L. Morris, *The Atonement: Its Meaning and Significance* (Downers Grove, Ill.: InterVarsity Press, 1983), 177-202.

6. In the courtroom people may be declared "guilty" or "acquitted." Theologically considered, we can never be "acquitted" because the Judge's decision is not that we are "not guilty." Rather, the Judge pronounces us "guilty but nonetheless forgiven" because Christ has assumed our penalty. The verdict then is "guilty" but the penalty is eliminated because Christ bore it on our behalf.

Paul has in mind a person's merit-intentions (works done *in order to gain* favor with God) in this expression. Rather, as we read Galatians, we find that Paul must have in mind two ideas: (1) behavior, or work, that conforms to the law of Moses as an expression of a confession that ultimate acceptance with God is to be found through a commitment to submit to the law of Moses, and (2) behavior that separates Jews from Gentiles, namely, the works of circumcision, table food restrictions, and social regulations governing the behavior of Jews as they relate to Gentiles (cf. 2:11–14).[7] These two elements belong together: Paul knew that implicit in conversion to Christ was a confession that a proper standing before God could not be had through a commitment to the law. Christ was the fulfillment of the law and went beyond it in his revelation (Rom. 10:4; Gal. 3:19–25). To do the law after Christ was to deny his sufficient work; it was to step back in salvation-history to a period before Christ. For Paul, this was abominable and denied the very purpose of Christ's coming. Thus, Paul reasons with Peter that they were agreed that a person is not justified by observing the law; commitment to Christ negates a commitment to the law as the means of being accepted by God. Paul would say, "You cannot serve Christ and the law at the same time."

On the other hand, Paul is not against "good works." For him, "works" has three primary ideas.[8] (1) There is the *principle of works* that appears in Rom. 3:27, and here we are close to the idea of merit or doing (see also Gal. 3:12) as the way one finds acceptance with God. This sense of works Paul opposed; the principle of works is never a means of acceptance with God. (2) There is the notion of *Mosaic works, or works of the law,* as found predominantly in Galatians, that describes the behavior of certain persons who were expressing their conviction that acceptance with God could only be had if one lived according to the law of Moses (e.g., 2:3, 11–14). *What* these people were doing was perverted by *why* they were doing it: to express their faith in Moses rather than in Christ alone. There was nothing wrong with living according to the law when it was done properly; after all, Paul circumcised Timothy (Acts 16:3) and later himself took steps to be purified so as to offer sacrifices in the temple (21:26). But when one obeyed the law to

---

7. For a scholarly defense of the view that "works of the law" describe Jewish distinctives, see esp. J. D. G. Dunn, *Jesus, Paul, and the Law: Studies in Mark and Galatians* (Louisville: Westminster/John Knox Press, 1990), esp. 183–241; see also 242–64. This view has been picked up in part by J. G. M. Barclay in *Obeying the Truth* and by F. Watson in *Paul, Judaism and the Gentiles.*

8. For more discussion, see H.-C. Hahn and F. Thiele, "Work," in *NIDNTT* 3:1147–59; D. J. Moo, "'Law,' 'Works of the Law,' and Legalism in Paul," *Westminster Theological Journal* 45 (1983): 73–100, esp. the chart on p. 93; however, I demur from Moo in several important respects.

express one's confidence in it as a necessary step for acceptance by God, Paul took serious umbrage. (3) There is the idea of *good works* as found in Eph. 2:10. What Paul means here is that people are called by God's grace in order to serve him in good works, a lifestyle that is attractive, moral, and godly. We might say, for Galatians, that the "fruit of the Spirit" (Gal. 5:22–23) is a description of "good works." This kind of works is the primary thrust of how Paul thinks Christians should live.

Therefore, when we say Paul taught that justification was not by works, we need to clarify which kind of works he had in mind. In Galatians, he is concerned primarily with the second sense and perhaps at times (but perhaps not at all) with the first sense. But Paul is not, or never was, against "good works" as an adequate description of a Christian's moral life and relations with others. Indeed, Paul says we will be judged by our works (Rom. 2:5–6; 1 Cor 3:10–15; 2 Cor 5:10; 11:15).

Now to our third expression. Justification comes to a person *by faith*, not by observing the law. Perhaps no term is more misunderstood in modern evangelicalism than "faith." What is this faith that saves us? What word best describes this term? Assent? trust? surrender? commitment? Once again, we address here an issue that deserves a much lengthier treatment. In Paul's letters, faith is the necessary response required for the person who wants to live at peace with God (cf. Rom. 1:17; 3:22, 25; 5:1; 10:4), and it is held firmly in contrast to the principle of "works"—works done to secure salvation (Rom. 3:27; 4:5). This faith clearly involves an assent (a mental agreement) to certain facts: the resurrection of Christ (Rom. 4:24; 10:9) and the salvation that comes through Christ (2 Thess. 2:12; 1 Tim. 1:16). While faith for Paul has a beginning (Rom. 10:9–10; 13:11; Eph. 1:13), it is also the continual disposition of a Christian toward all that God has done in Christ (Rom. 1:17).[9] We may thus define faith as *the initial and continual response of trust in, and obedience to, Christ by a person for the purpose of acceptance with God.* William Barclay said it well: "Faith is complete trust and complete surrender to Jesus Christ. It is the total acceptance of all that He said, of all that He offered, and of all that He is."[10] Thus, when Paul uses the term "faith" (as in "justified by faith"), he is describing both the initial act of trust and the continuing disposition of trust

---

9. Because faith is continuing (and not just some one-time act of trust), Paul can call it the "obedience of faith" (Rom. 1:5).

10. W. Barclay, *The Mind of St. Paul* (San Francisco: Harper & Row, 1958), 143. See also the definition of his namesake, J. M. G. Barclay, *Obeying the Truth*, 236: "In other words, faith in Galatians is not just 'believing the gospel'; it also includes a commitment to 'obey the truth,' and cannot be distinguished from the constant attempt to 'walk in the Spirit.' " See further at pp. 235–37.

and obedience. This is why faith in Christ[11] and "works of the law" are opposites: one cannot opt for Christ's system *and* Moses' system at the same time because they are mutually exclusive options for salvation. Either one believes in Christ or one chooses to commit oneself to the law. One cannot live under both systems without destroying one or the other's integrity.

The act of faith in Christ (2:16b). Paul and Peter were Jews and came to know that people could not find justification by holding to Jewish regulations or by observing the law (the law's time was now over; see 3:19–25). They had come to the conviction that faith in Christ would justify. So they believed in Jesus Christ. Peter's conversion story is bumpy and long; Paul's is sudden and short. Peter's Christian faith began in Jerusalem (John 1:35–42), was further established in Galilee (Luke 5:1–11), came to a major point in the first confession of Jesus' Messiahship (Mark 8:27–30), floundered in the passion week (14:66–72), was revived after the resurrection (John 21:15–19; cf. Luke 22:32), and came to maturity at Pentecost (Acts 2). Nonetheless, Peter continued to stumble throughout his life (Acts 10:1–11:18; Gal. 2:11–14). However, the maturity of Peter's faith is seen marvelously in his two letters. Paul, on the other hand, was suddenly and dramatically converted (Acts 9:1–30). In spite of this diversity in actual conversion experiences, Paul sees their conversions as essentially identical: they had refused the law system and had embraced the Christ system.

The implications of a common conversion experience (vv. 17–21). There are three implications of this common conversion that will be addressed here.

(1) *The life of the Christian is not a "lawless" life in the sense of wicked antinomianism* (v. 17). Surely this was the biggest fear of any self-respecting and God-fearing Jew: the Christians, with their emphasis on the Holy Spirit as the guide for the moral life, were devaluing the law and, inevitably, would abandon the morality prescribed by the law. They (so they feared) would eventually be no different than either pagans or half-committed Jews (i.e., they would be "sinners"; cf. 2:15). Because Jews, particularly Pharisaic Jews, would have reasoned this way, Paul had to first spell out that the moral implications of converting to Christ. In essence, Paul argues that coming to Christ did not

---

11. There is a growing number of scholars who believe now that "faith of Jesus Christ" in Galatians 2:16 (and elsewhere in Paul's letters) means "the faith that Jesus Christ exercised" and not "faith in Jesus Christ." For Galatians 2:16, this view provides the objective means of salvation (Christ achieved something for us) and the subjective reception ("So we, too, have put our faith in Christ Jesus"). I tend toward the traditional view here since I take the second expression of faith in 2:16 ("our faith in Christ Jesus") as a repetition of the former expression (NIV: "faith in Jesus Christ"). For discussion, see F. F. Bruce, *Galatians*, 138–39; R. N. Longenecker, *Galatians*, 87–88.

mean that "Christ promotes sin." It was unimaginable (I suppose) for the Jew to conceive of a moral life that did not take its starting point from the law of Moses.

All of this emerges from Paul's comment that he and Peter were "justified in Christ." The act of turning to Jesus Christ in faith was, according to Paul, an act of denying that one must live under the law of Moses to find acceptance with God. And this was especially the case for Jewish Christians, typified here so clearly by Paul and Peter. The act of turning to Christ was a social act on their part: they were turning away from Judaism and turning toward something significantly different, however much it was seen as the fulfillment of Judaism. For the Jew who grew up seeing the law as the center of God's revelation, it was no small matter to turn away from the law as the means of being accepted by God. And for the Jew who sat idly by and watched other Jews turn to Christ, there was the (realistic) fear that leaving the law meant abandoning God's moral will. It meant turning to a life of sin because sin was living lawlessly, living a life that was not governed by the law or by one's interpretation of that law.[12]

This turning to Christ was an acknowledgment of a person's sinfulness—in this case, an acknowledgment by Peter and Paul that they, though raised under the covenant of Abraham, were sinners as well and in need of God's forgiveness. Their turning to Christ was a turning for righteousness (imputed), an act whereby they confessed that their morality was corrupt and insufficient. They went to Christ in order that they might be declared right before God. And so Paul's question—Does Christ promote sin? Paul's answer: "Absolutely not!" Christ does not minister sin; rather, he eliminates sin through his sacrificial work. But it is true that the gospel Paul preached was a gospel that dealt face-to-face with sin and its consequences. It seems likely to me that Paul's focus on forgiveness (and sin) had given the Judaizers pause because their system assumed forgiveness (in the temple rituals) and then focused more on morality and social relations. Paul's focus on sin and forgiveness, I am suggesting, led to their charge that Christ was one who promoted sin by inviting sinners to come to him.

The implication of Paul's emphasis here is that life in Christ is not life in sin. Rather, life in Christ, as he will elaborate in chapters 5–6, is life in the Spirit. Instead of promoting sin, Christ promotes purity, holiness, love, and attractive personalities. What was formerly found only in the law for the Jews (namely, God's will for his people) has now been fulfilled in God's great gift of the Holy Spirit.

---

12. See J. M. G. Barclay, *Obeying the Truth,* 78–79.

(2) *In converting to Christ, the Christian, especially the Jewish Christian, forfeits the opportunity of ever returning to the law as the primary orientation governing all of life* (v. 18). As suggested above, I think it is best to take the "I" here as a term representing both Peter and Paul, but especially Peter. It was Peter, after all, who had reneged on his commitment to Christ. Thus, Peter was rebuilding Judaism when he withdrew from open table fellowship, even though he had previously destroyed it when he turned away from Judaism to Christ. Peter became the "lawbreaker" when he returned to Judaism, for in going back he was adopting the law with its condemning force (3:13, 19–25).

(3) *In converting to Christ, the Jewish Christian finds spiritual life through death, understood here as being crucified with Christ to the law so that the resurrected Christ might grant his new life to the believer* (vv. 19–21). Paul says three things in this section. (a) The "Jewish Ego," the privilege Jews thought they had—but had only until Christ—died to the law. This took place when Paul (and Peter) converted to Christ. This they did so "I might live for God." What Paul is describing here is not some mystical (daily) experience. He is describing the common conversion experience of Jews: when they turn to Christ, they die to the law as the means of salvation. And the law helps in that it runs its course until Christ (3:19).

(b) The life Paul now lives for God is the result of dying with Christ (v. 20). But the life Paul lives ("I") is the life the Jewish Christian finds in Christ. It is a life of the indwelling Christ (cf. 2 Cor. 3:17) and the indwelling Spirit (Gal. 3:1–5; 5:22–23). When the Jewish Christian died to the law by dying with Christ (who absorbed the full wrath of God that came about because of the law's work), that Jewish Christian was raised a new person: a post-law Jewish Christian. That person was now indwelt by Christ and the Holy Spirit, who would now guide and control.

(c) In opting for the Christ system, these Jewish believers were not setting aside God's grace. Here we must infer that the accusation against the Jewish Christians was that they were setting aside God's grace. Surely for them this grace was understood as the law of Moses. Paul counters: "No, it is not we who are setting aside God's grace when we leave the law. Rather, you (who do not come with us) are missing the great grace of God in Christ." In fact, Paul argues that everything in their conversion was for naught if a proper standing before God could be achieved by obeying the law. If that could have been done, there would have been no need at all for Christ. But these Judaizers had indeed confessed that Christ was God's agent for salvation.

To sum up: Galatians 2:15–21 is complex. I have tried to show that it is primarily concerned with the common Jewish experience of conversion.

That conversion involved a denial of the sufficiency of the law and an affirmation of the total sufficiency of Christ. This reflection was generated for Paul by Peter's inability to understand just how sufficient Christ was. Peter's social behavior had denied his conversion experience, and Paul sternly reminded him of this very inconsistency. In Christ, Paul is saying, there is neither Jew nor Gentile, and any attempt to force Gentiles to adopt Jewish distinctives is a glaring contradiction to the heart of the gospel.

THE FIRST ISSUE deserving discussion is the matter of how we apply a text to (a now largely) Gentile Christian movement when the original text was for Jewish Christians. Can we simply skip over this passage in our haste to find something practical for our Gentile world? Absolutely not! First, we must appreciate the Jewish experience, and then we can generalize because, even though we come at the same experience from different angles and worlds, the content of the conversion is the same.

Let us try to appreciate the experience of Peter and Paul. Both grew up in Judaism—Peter in Galilee and Paul in either Tarsus or Jerusalem. Both had been trained in spirituality according to the law of Moses and both lived among Jews under such guidelines. In fact, both had been taught to revere the law of Moses with almost unbounded respect and adoration. The law of Moses was everything when it came to religious revelation. Furthermore, both Peter and Paul were apparently faithful to their religious heritage, though we would probably give the prize here to Paul's devotion. I am of the view that the heritage of both was probably heavily influenced by the Pharisaic-type of piety, though I will not defend this view here.[13]

Growing up in similar contexts, both of them found it extremely difficult to abandon the law when they converted to Christ. It was the turning to Christ that created a rift with their past and that caused Peter problems. But Jews had to learn, if they wanted to be consistently Christian, what it meant

---

13. Paul's Pharisaic background is well known (see Acts 22:3; 23:6; Phil. 3:4–6). Regarding Peter, two examples may suffice: (1) the disciples', including Peter's, serious questioning of Jesus about his offending Pharisaic traditions (Matt. 15:12), and (2) Peter's comment that he had never eaten anything unclean (Acts 10:14). This latter comment probably refers to Peter's *intention*, and not actual practice, because the laws on this were so carefully defined that it would be hard to live one's entire life without offending these traditions at some point. However, such uncleanness could be eliminated with washing and by waiting until evening. Proper standing, however, could always be retained if one did not knowingly or intentionally eat any unclean food. See above, pp. 101–2.

to be a part of the God's new people: the church of Jesus Christ. We are unfair to both of these men, especially to Peter, if we do not appreciate the difficulty of applying the gospel and letting it have full control of all of life, especially in those areas where one's social identity was at stake.

Peter was completely comfortable with the hassles and struggles he had when he was evangelizing and pastoring Jewish Christians, but it was the stress of working out the gospel among Gentiles that forced him to back away from the implications of the gospel. What Peter (and Paul) had to learn was this: the gospel is for all, it is enjoyed by faith, Christ is the Savior, and the Spirit guides. Fundamental to all of this was the simple social change: the life of the church is not to be guided by Jewish restrictions but by God's Spirit and the teachings of Jesus. This was the experience of conversion that was common to all first-century Jewish Christians. It involved death to the law as the center of life, hope, and salvation.

These racial and historical differences between first-century Jewish Christians and us do not, however, prohibit us from finding general similarities. That the gospel is for all can be appreciated most easily by non-Jews, since they have never felt the restricted fellowship of the Jews. The means of justification (faith) was probably not as difficult for them to accept as we have made it out to be. We have come to think that Jews thought only in terms of works for salvation. This is wrong. Jews thought that they were God's people because they were Jews, and, as a result, God had given them a multitude of privileges. In my opinion, salvation by "faith" was not difficult for Jews to accept. What gave them grief was salvation by faith *apart from the law*, for they thought obedience to the law was true faith (see Heb. 11). What they had to learn was that the object of their faith had changed from God's revelation in Moses to God's revelation in Christ. Christ has replaced Moses as the focus of salvation, just as the Spirit has replaced the laws of Moses as the focus of God's will.

But even with this difference, the response of humans is the same for Jewish Christians as for Gentile Christians: faith in Christ. We can easily see and apply that salvation is by faith, though we will probably not balk (as first-century Jewish Christians did) at eliminating the law of Moses as the object of our faith. (We Gentiles simply have other things in the way.) And two other features are so similar that it makes application easy: Christ is the Savior and the Spirit is the guide. There is absolutely no difference for Gentiles and Jews here, though each will come at Christ and the Spirit from different worlds.

So while I am the first to admit that this text spoke and still speaks directly to Jews about what takes place in their conversion, the abiding contents of the gospel make applications to Gentiles just as easy. What we need to do is to recognize the Jewish features of this text, sort out the ideas theologically, and then apply what abides to our world. What we have done is to find the features of the gospel that Paul is driving at, examine them in their context, and then rethink how these same features might have relevance to Gentiles.

I do think, however, that "death to the law" is not of paramount significance to a Gentile conversion, especially if we are accurate in our portrayal of the law in Galatians as involving a socially confining body of regulations. In that sense, this feature of the text applies only to Jews or to others from similar religious contexts, who grow up or convert out of a movement that sees the law as a self-defining and boundary-marking instrument. But perhaps this can be applied to those who have grown up in (or who at least were nurtured by) any fundamentalist movement emphasizing certain rules that give that group a well-defined boundary and identity. Perhaps also the principle of "death to the law" refers to anyone who has grown up in a socially defined world, where one's racial status (be it Greek, Polish, or Irish) is intimately connected to one's hope before God. In this latter case, the socially defined world is what needs to be broken down by eliminating the connection with race, and, in the former case, the legally defined world needs to be broken down by eliminating the legal boundaries being created. Both examples are addressed by Galatians.

Justification is justification in all ages. Our world is no different from Paul's when it comes to the *agent and means of justification*: justification is based in Christ's sacrificial absorption of our guilt, and we are justified only if we believe in Christ. To apply this we must first get people to sense their guilt, and this is difficult today. The 1960s generation broke down the importance of a great deal of social laws in the Western world, laws that had enabled easier presentations of the gospel, for most people were operating under some form of a Judeo-Christian ethic considered to be true and divine. Existentialism, outright apathy and despair, as well as the growth of pluralism have each made their way into our cultural perceptions of the world. Each of these has made ultimate standards for morality much more difficult to present. Thus, in this last decade of the twentieth century we are facing by and large a mass of people who have no sense of moral ultimates. It is hard for such people to sense their guilt before God because they don't sense much being right or wrong.

Robert Bellah has addressed our modern predicament and situation with penetrating insight. "In the absence," he says after addressing moral foundations in our society, "of any objectifiable criteria of right and wrong, good or evil, *the self and its feelings* become our only moral guide."[14] He is fundamentally right here. He goes on and I quote him here at length:

> If the individual self must be its own source of moral guidance, then each individual must always know what he wants and desires or intuit what he feels. He must act so as to produce the greatest satisfaction of his wants or to express the fullest range of his impulses. . . . Utility replaces duty; self-expression unseats authority. "Being good" becomes "feeling good." "I've always loved that thing that Mark Twain said about something moral is something you feel good after," Ted Oster [a California lawyer mentioned in the context] remarks, "and something immoral is something you feel bad after. Which implies that you got [*sic*] to try everything at least once. I guess I'm pretty result-oriented, and whatever produces a good result must be right, and whatever produces a bad result must be wrong." *Acts, then, are not right or wrong in themselves, but only because of the results they produce, the good feelings they engender or express.*[15]

What is the solution? There are several avenues to explore in our world. First, we need to pray for God's grace to break through in another revival. Such a revival will set free the Spirit of God to create in people a divine arrangement of what is right and what is wrong. Second, after our prayers (and during them) we need to preach and teach the truth of God's Word and God's ethical standards. Third, we need to dialogue with others about morality, and do so both at the intellectual level and in popular discourse. An issue facing our generation is, How do we make intelligent and abiding moral decisions? Is the answer to be found in majority opinion? in personal opinion? in social conventions? in the Declaration of Independence? Or is the final answer to be found only when God breaks through in revealing himself and his will, as in the Bible? It is my contention that until our society awakens morally, it will be difficult to apply the doctrine of justification. But, as any evangelist will tell you, there are many today who are searching for answers to moral questions and to a consciousness of personal sin. To these people Paul's message is a flash of glorious light.

It is probably the case for the majority of Westerners that the "legal metaphor" of justification is not as evocative and directly relevant as other metaphors (e.g., a relational one, like "reconciliation"). Accordingly, it is fundamentally important for our perception of the meaning of justification to

---

14. R. Bellah, et al., *Habits of the Heart: Individualism and Commitment in American Life* (San Francisco: Harper and Row, 1986), 76 (italics added).

15. Ibid., 77–78 (emphasis added).

examine its meaning in the ancient world. To do this, we must become historians, or at least listen to historians of Roman and Jewish justice and those who are keenly aware of the first-century meanings. As discussed above, justification denotes the process of being moved from a state of guilt to a state of acceptance with God through the sacrificial acceptance by Christ of our guilt. This situation needs to be described before applications can be made. And it needs to be adjusted and presented in such a way that it makes sense to our society. It strikes me that "acceptance by God" is a useful expression for our world, though there are certainly others, and we need to be creative about finding meaningful images for our world.

To apply the notion of works and faith, we need once again to understand what they meant in Paul's world. The biggest problem for us today is the same for each: each of these terms has been seriously colored by our definitions of "works" and "faith" that derive (naturally enough) from our social and church contexts. For instance, for far too many people "works" is a bad word, or at least a word describing a negative religious quality. "Works," it is sometimes said, is something people who do not believe in Christ do; "works" is a characteristic of those people who think they can earn their salvation by accumulating merit before God. The sadness of this assertion needs to be understood: too many have equated all works with the "works" Paul set in contrast to "faith." To be sure, Paul is against any kind of disposition toward God that suggests that we can find acceptance with him apart from Christ and faith. But in our concern to be "full of grace," we have misunderstood Paul's own teachings. Neither Paul nor anyone in the Bible was against "good works." So, for us to understand how to apply what Paul says about works, we need first to understand that there were some good kinds of works and some bad kinds. Our language and perceptions will need to change as we investigate this matter.

The same goes for "faith." Once again we have many well-intended, God-fearing preachers and teachers of the Bible who contend that "faith" is little more than credence. For these the matter to be defended is "salvation by grace." It is argued that if salvation is by grace (and not by human works) and if faith is trust, then our obedience (understood to be something after our trust is expressed) has nothing whatsoever to do with our justification and final salvation. Is this how Paul understood "faith"? I argued above that it is not at all the way Paul understood faith. A simple examination of the term *believe* or *faith* in Paul's letters will convince the reader that Paul saw faith as more than credence. He saw faith and obedience tied into one another, and he saw faith as both an initial and a continuing response of the human to God's promises. Thus, before we can apply the passage to our world, we need to be serious Bible students, checking the uses of the terms *faith* and *believe* throughout Paul's letters and the New Testament, bracketing off our presuppositions (and perhaps hopes!), and arriving at solid exegetical conclusions. This process of checking our views against the Bible and revising when we are wrong or inaccurate is the only means of understanding and progress in Bible study.

FIRST, IT IS good for us once again *to reflect on our own conversions* and to observe how we, like Peter and Paul, were moved from a state of guilt to a status of acceptance with God, completely through the merit of Christ's death. To do this it is good for us to contemplate our pre-conversion disposition toward God, his Word and will, and his people (the church). It is healthy for us here to think about our sinful habits and patterns and to deplore them as disgusting in God's eyes. It is even good for us to pause and contemplate once again the inevitable end of such a life (God's wrath). After pondering such thoughts, we need to think clearly about what Christ has done for us in his sacrifice. We need to contemplate him on the Cross, absorbing our guilt and sin and taking on himself the curse of God so that we might find forgiveness. After deliberating over such things, we can then turn to the joy we find in forgiveness and offer our deepest thanks to God for his grace in our life.

But we dare not stop here. We need to examine if we are letting the gospel of God's grace have its full implications in our life. Are we shunting off the gospel racially? Are we preventing other racial groups from enjoying God's grace? Are we discriminating against other cultures or other social groups? Are we building walls between the sexes? Or are we allowing the full message of the gospel to have its complete force?

Second, we need to apply *justification by faith through Christ* to our world by evangelizing and letting the message of justification for all (through Christ, not the law, by faith) penetrate our deepest chambers and our innermost social constructions. To do this we need to be willing, with Paul, to see all people as sinners. Ours is a conscientious and sensitive world. Consequently, we are afraid to let the world know that there is sin and that all people are sinners. Thus, the sweet work of Christ that forgives, reconciles, justifies, and redeems can have no impact because we refuse to take the first step: admit that we are all sinners.

In addition, we need to show people that God has been in the courtroom as Judge and has handed down the verdict regarding our status: we are guilty. But, he says, if we will simply look to Christ, we will be forgiven, set free, and be acceptable to him. So we need to present Christ to our world as the one who saves us from our guilty verdict.

Third, we need to spend more time in our churches, especially in adult and youth Bible studies, exploring the biblical meaning of *faith*. It is my contention that this doctrine has been seriously misunderstood in the last thirty or forty years, and, as a result, some have made shipwreck of their faith and others have ruined the vitality of churches. Let me explain. It is common today to hear that the only requirement for salvation is to "believe that Jesus Christ saves." This is true—if properly defined. However, the term *believe* has been frequently misdefined in this preaching, and the statement consequently becomes untrue. In fact, we get back to Galatians 1:8–9: the gospel is transformed through this misdefinition and the result is a heresy. So what is the misdefinition? Simply put, it is the reduction of the meaning of faith to "mere credence." That is, faith is defined as "believing that Jesus is Savior" and no more. Jesus is indeed Savior; but in order for him to become the Savior for a given person, that person must surrender himself or herself in trust and obedience for true faith to be expressed.

How can we correct this situation? I believe it can come about only through a total revolution of our thinking about what God expects of us for acceptance and for Christian living. We delude ourselves if we think because we have made some decision we are done with it and forever secure in God's eyes. We delude ourselves if we think we can live immoral lives, shack up with partners who are not our spouses, defraud others of their money, take no action to alleviate social ills in our world, and live in constant tension with our children and family members—we delude ourselves, I say, if we think we can live like this and pretend that we are at peace with God and enjoy his Son's justifying work. Those who have been justified, live justly; those who have been made holy in Christ, live holy lives; those who have experienced God's love, love others; those who have experienced God's forgiveness, forgive others; those who have been called from the world, no longer live in the world and call others to be "out with them"; those who have died to the flesh, live in the Spirit.

This principle is usually referred to in theological textbooks as the interplay of the indicative (what we are) and the imperative (what we should be). Whatever we call it, the Bible (and especially Paul!) teaches that God's people are those who have been transformed by his grace and are those who now live unto God. We are simply deluding ourselves, and the judgment of God will surely prove this, if we think this is not the way God operates.

This revolution of our thinking needs to impact our evangelistic strategies and our discipling ministries. Both deserve explanation. As for evangelism, while I feel that I may be taking on the world, I do believe that our typical evangelistic tracts are potentially dangerous here. The typical tract teaches that anyone can be saved who simply believes that Jesus Christ has come for that person's salvation. But that same tract rarely defines just what faith means and just what it implies. What is all too often assumed is that faith means little more than mental agreement. But this is not what faith means and it is not how the apostle Paul defines it. Check the concordance once again. It means total surrender in trust and obedience. Obedience is not something just subsequent to faith; obedience is the expression of faith, and faith without obedience is dead. Do we believe James 2:14–26 or not? Our evangelistic tracts, then, need to be nuanced with definitions of faith. We need to present the gospel in such a way that the commitment required is clear. Jesus Christ has come for your salvation, and you need to surrender your hope and your very self to him.

The same revolution will make an impact on our discipling ministries. (I use the term *discipling* here to describe post-conversion instruction and development, though I am not happy with the way we often use this term.) Discipling should not be the coaxing ministry of getting infantile Christians active, nor should it be the attempt by mature Christians to get "credence believers" to become "obedience believers." This approach simply sets the stamp of approval on false definitions of faith. Rather, discipling ministries should *assume that Christians are consistently obedient* and then move on to specific applications of God's will for an individual's life. Christians who do not obey will then be seen as "weird anomalies" and not as "typical underachievers"! Put differently, our discipling ministries should be given less to persuasions to holiness and more to guidance in holiness—and I say this because if we present the gospel properly from the beginning, we will not have people in our discipling classes who are not yet fully committed.

Finally, we need to explore the significance of Paul's criticism of the "works of the law." I am assuming here that there are three kinds of "works" for Paul (the principle of works, Mosaic works, and good works) and that Paul's protest here is with the second one. And let us assume here that Mosaic works were specific actions done by those under the covenant of Abraham (including some proselytes) who were, in performing these actions, demonstrating both their faith in God's system in Moses and their social solidarity with others who lived in the same way. Finally, let us assume that Paul criticizes the Judaizers for attempting to nationalize Gentile Christians into Judaism by instructing them in the way of Moses. How can we apply something like this?

First, we need to recall that Paul is more against the purpose of these actions than against the actions themselves. That is, he was thoroughly against the Judaizer who tried to get Gentiles to be circumcised if that Judaizer was contending that such had to be done in order to be accepted with God. If that is the case, we can proceed to the next point: we can apply Paul's protest *to any performance that is demanded in order to find or maintain acceptance with God*. Any such performance nullifies the sufficiency of Christ and blunts the freedom of the Holy Spirit. I will apply this to *denominationalism*.

I believe that it is virtually impossible for us today not to be a member of some denomination. There is no such thing as "generic, orthodox Christianity" that can advertise itself as absent of all party lines. Such a church lives in a dream world because reality (as we live it) is too particular, too finite, and too demanding for us not to have some drawing of lines. But there is a difference between being a member of a denomination and being a denominational*ist*. The latter defines one's church as God's best church, demands others to come to his or her church to find God's best, and criticizes other churches for their non-agreements. This is denominationalism and it is wrong. Paul would be against (and so must we) those who attempted to make people join a specific group in order to be acceptable to God.

Before I go on, I want to add that I do not, in defining myself in this way, want to say that all churches are the same. I believe that some churches are more biblical, more orthodox, more lively, more healthy, and more useful than others. But I do not think that this can be anchored into any one denomination, even if I am a member of the Evangelical Free Church of America.

How then should we live? We need to respect the doctrinal stances that divide us, especially when those doctrinal stances have been prayed over, worked at, and defined biblically, and when those doctrinal stances are taken seriously by diverse bodies. More importantly, we need to remember that we are all part of God's church and that we are together trying to reach the world with God's love and to strengthen God's people. We are united by a common life. If we will simply reflect for a moment on our sinfulness and our limitations, we should be able to admit that maybe it is we who are wrong or slightly inaccurate over the things that divides us. But we also need to oppose elements of our church and other churches that are inconsistent with the Bible. These kinds of dialogues are healthy for local communities as we seek to hold one another in line with the truth of the gospel. We also learn quickly what is important and what is not.

I end this section with a confession. When I was younger, I used to drive by different denominations and utter either imprecatory prayers about that denomination or think that it was too bad that so many people were being led astray by that church's thinking. Time has a way of making us mellow. The most shaping experiences of my life have been encounters with other churches and denominations, always leaving me with the following chain of thoughts: I wish I were in that denomination; but that denomination surely has its problems, too; no, I like where I am; I wish we could all agree. What has happened to me is probably typical. Encountering Christians of other denominations broadens us all and challenges us to think about the church in new ways.

The encounter with Christians from other denominations and persuasions makes me appreciate the wideness of God's revelation in the Bible and the fallibility of our attempts to construct the fullness of that revelation in our differing theologies. It also strengthens my confidence because I see just how big God's church actually is. Most importantly, it drives me to my knees in thankfulness to God for the greatness of his saving activity throughout the world. My church, after all, is one small piece of God's grand work of bringing people to himself. How can I but be thankful to God and tolerant of how he is working elsewhere? How could we ever demand that someone join our denomination in order to be acceptable to God?

Galatians 3:1–5

YOU FOOLISH GALATIANS! Who has bewitched you? Before your very eyes Jesus Christ was clearly portrayed as crucified. ²I would like to learn just one thing from you: Did you receive the Spirit by observing the law, or by believing what you heard? ³Are you so foolish? After beginning with the Spirit, are you now trying to attain your goal by human effort? ⁴Have you suffered so much for nothing—if it really was for nothing? ⁵Does God give you his Spirit and work miracles among you because you observe the law, or because you believe what you heard?

> ## Original Meaning

THE VAST MAJORITY of scholars see a major section beginning at 3:1 and ending at 4:31. For most, this section is considered the theological argument of Paul. I have entitled it in my outline "Paul's Theological Vindication of His Message." Furthermore, most scholars see 3:1–5 as expressing the essential argument for the entire section. Thus, I have entitled these verses "The Thesis Stated." Interestingly, however, Paul "states" his thesis here through a series of rhetorical questions, and the thesis itself is found in the implicit answers to each question. For example, Paul asks in verse 2, "I would like to learn just one thing from you: Did you receive the Spirit by observing the law, or by believing what you heard?" Now the answer to that question, according to Paul, must be "by believing what you heard." And the implication, then, is that the Spirit comes to a person when that person believes, or surrenders, to the message about Jesus Christ.

This first unit takes another tack that is not frequently found in Pauline theological arguments, namely, the entire unit proceeds by way of *argument from experience*. Paul here appeals not to logic or Scriptural foundation, but to the Galatians' *experience of conversion and Christian living*. In essence, Paul asks, "How have things religious happened to you? Did these things happen through your association with the law of Moses? Or did they occur through faith in Christ?" Paul's appeal, then, is an appeal to their experience, and from that experience to some lessons about theology. By "experience" I mean the concrete events and realities that happened to the Galatians, along with their perceptions of those events and realities. I refer, then, to the things they observed, touched, felt, and thought.

Our unit here may be divided into two parts:

1. Paul's personal question (v. 1)
2. Paul's questions about experience (vv. 2–5)

This second part has four questions: (1) the question about initiation (v. 2); (2) the question about completion (v. 3); (3) the question about persecution (v. 4); and (4) the question about miracles (v. 5). We need to look at each of these in turn.

Paul's personal question (v. 1). The "header" for this section, "You foolish Galatians!" is not intended to make friends, but neither was it perceived as a personal insult and therefore unworthy of an apostolic leader. As I said in my comments on 1:1–9, the latitude for acceptable speech in debate was much greater then than it is today. Such "name calling" and heated rhetoric is found elsewhere in the New Testament, whether on the lips of John the Baptist (Matt. 3:7–10), Jesus (Matt. 23; Luke 24:25), James (James 4:1–12; 4:13–5:6), or Paul elsewhere (2 Cor. 10–13). While we may not imitate Paul in this regard, we can learn about different but acceptable forms of rhetoric.

The term *foolish*, however, captures Paul's point: they were illogical[1] in committing themselves to the Pauline message of God's grace in Christ and then succumbing to the Judaizers' Moses-gospel. Most doubt that Paul is seriously interested here in the "who," for he already knows the answer to this question: the Judaizers. Rather, his question is rhetorical in preparation for the following exclamation: "How could you have been fooled[2] after learning about the crucifixion of Jesus Christ!"[3]

Crucifixion is the center of Paul's understanding about Jesus Christ. What may be distasteful to moderns is the center of his attention.[4] For Paul, the

---

1. The Greek term is *anoetai*. Its origin is instructive: "without knowledge" or "without reason" and hence, "illogical" and "lacking in discernment." See R. N. Longenecker, *Galatians*, 99.

2. The Greek word here is *ebaskanen*, "bewitched" or "fooled." While the word literally describes being fascinated by a magical spell, scholars debate whether the term here is being used more metaphorically ("fooled") or literally ("bewitched"). See the discussion in R. N. Longenecker, *Galatians*, 100.

3. Though the NIV has two sentences here (a question, a statement), the original Greek construction is one sentence (a question, with a longer subordinate clause about the clear portrayal of Christ's crucifixion). By separating the question from the subordinate clause and forming two sentences, the NIV leads the reader to look for more of a specific answer to the question.

4. A wonderful book has been written on the cross of Christ by J. R. W. Stott, *The Cross of Christ* (Downers Grove, Ill.: InterVarsity Press, 1986). A careful sketch of the ancient evidence about crucifixion can be found in M. Hengel, *Crucifixion* (Philadelphia: Fortress, 1977).

cross delivers from the present evil age (1:4) and murders the law, thus terminating its lordship (2:19–20; 4:5), so that we can die to the law, sin, and the world (5:24; 6:14); the cross of Christ justifies (2:21), absorbs our guilt (3:10–14), and ends nationalistic Judaism (2:19–20). We can see from this impressive list of the accomplishments of the cross in Galatians that Paul has wrapped his entire argument both *for* Christ and *against* the Judaizers around the cross of Christ. It is no wonder that early theologians of the New Testament, like Tertullian, developed the sign of the cross. In fact, Tertullian wrote:

> At every forward step and movement,
> at every going in and out,
> when we put on our clothes and shoes,
> when we bathe,
> when we sit at table,
> when we light the lamps,
> on couch, on seat,
> in all the ordinary actions of life,
> we trace upon the forehead the sign [of the Cross].[5]

John Stott states it well: "There is then, it is safe to say, no Christianity without the cross. If the cross is not central to our religion, ours is not the religion of Jesus."[6]

Whatever Paul is referring to in verse 1—whether it was the publicity of the event or the impressiveness of the event[7]—it must have been a compelling experience. Paul knew that his initial preaching of the gospel at Galatia was a memorable and powerful experience. He recalls the same event later and says that "you welcomed me as if I were an angel of God, as if I were Jesus Christ himself," and then he goes on to ask, "What has happened to all your joy?" (4:14–15). I suggest that the intensity of this experience, their conversion experience, leads Paul to appeal to it first. "What he had preached to them was so openly and clearly proclaimed that Paul is at a loss to know how

---

5. I obtained this quote from J. R. W. Stott, *The Cross of Christ*, 21. It is from Tertullian, *De Corona*, chapter 3. The entire passage is concerned with the importance of tradition in the development of Christian customs and practices. The treatise can be found in *Latin Christianity: Its Founder, Tertullian* (Ante-Nicene Fathers, volume 3, trans. and ed. A. C. Coxe; Grand Rapids: Eerdmans, 1980 reprint), 94–95.

6. Stott, *The Cross of Christ* , 68.

7. This debate revolves around the term *proegraphe* and whether it means "proclaimed publicly" or "portrayed publicly." H. D. Betz has made a persuasive case for the term stemming from a rhetorical background and hence argues for "portrayed." Thus, it has less to do with the "public nature" of the preaching and more to do with the "impressive nature" of the preaching (see his *Galatians*, 131–32, esp. note 39).

his converts could ever have failed to see its significance or to appreciate its implications for the question at hand."[8]

Paul's questions about experience (vv. 2–5). Paul now goes to a series of questions that seem to progress from earlier to later experiences in their own Christian development.

The question about initiation (v. 2). He begins with their first experience, their initiation into Christianity, their conversion. His little introductory statement is a bit naughty: "I would like to learn just one thing from you." We know that this "one thing" was a piece of bait which, if taken, would be yanked on by Paul and cost them their entire time in the waters of "Judaizing Christianity." If he gets them to answer this question honestly and therefore properly, he knows they will have to abandon the Judaizers and rejoin his group.

His question? "Did you receive the Spirit by observing the law, or by believing what you heard?" Here Paul appeals to their initial, perhaps charismatic, experience of receiving the Spirit. And he wants to know: How did they get the Spirit? By obeying Moses or by obeying the gospel of faith? Before answering these questions, we need to pause over the expression "receive the Spirit."

For Paul, receiving the Spirit is the identifying characteristic of the Christian. To be a Christian is to be indwelt by the Spirit, and to be indwelt by the Spirit is to be a Christian (cf. Rom. 8:9–11). The Spirit of God is the definition of the Christian.[9] Paul says that the Christian's very beginning is with the Spirit (v. 3), and he contends that God works among Christians through the Spirit (v. 5). Faith brings the blessing of Abraham, and this blessing is the "promise of the Spirit" (v. 14). Later, he says that those who are truly sons of God are those who have been granted the Spirit, who calls out "Abba, Father" (4:6). What Paul is talking about here may be an experience, and it may very well be a charismatic one, but it is not some experience subsequent to faith in Christ. For Paul, faith in Christ means being granted God's Spirit. This granting of the Spirit ends the age of the law. Abraham's promise is the promise of the Spirit (3:14), and when the law had run its course, God sent his Spirit (4:4–6). So it makes sense that those who live in the Spirit are not under the law (5:18).

We need to address here the comment made above that this receipt of the Spirit was perhaps "charismatic." By "charismatic" I simply mean that the Galatians may have spoken in tongues, displayed miracles, or been given

---

8. R. N. Longenecker, *Galatians*, 101.

9. On the Spirit in Paul's theology, see D. Guthrie, *New Testament Theology* (Downers Grove, Ill.: InterVarsity Press, 1981), 549–66; G. E. Ladd, *A Theology of the New Testament* (Grand Rapids: Eerdmans, 1974), 479–94, 511–30, 541–43.

prophetic utterances as demonstrations of the presence of the Holy Spirit. Historians of the early churches are well aware of the amount of charismatic activity that took place, for which we find evidence in Acts (cf. Acts 2–3; 8; 10; 18) and in the debates arising at Corinth (cf. 1 Cor. 12–14). Charismatic phenomena were neither unique nor surprising in the early churches.[10] Thus, it would not be surprising if charismatic experiences characterized, or were at least present at, Galatia. Furthermore, at verse 5 Paul confirms that miracles were taking place in Galatia: "Does God give you his Spirit and work miracles among you. . . ?" There is no question here about the presence of miracles; the debate, as will be seen below, was over the source of these miracles—from Moses through works, or from God's Spirit through faith? And observe how closely "giving the Spirit" is to "working miracles." Finally, it is just possible that the crying out of "Abba, Father" was an experience of either ecstasy or an inspired utterance (4:6).[11] Thus, I retain the possibility that Paul's appeal was not only to their conversion experience of receiving the Spirit but that this experience was also charismatic and therefore particularly memorable.

The real issue here, however, is not the experiential one; this was assumed. The issue was *how the experience took place and what triggered it*. Was it "by observing the law" or "by believing what you heard"? In discussing these two options, we observe that we are discussing an important issue for each of the four questions we are examining and so some detail is required.

First, "observing the law" is a fluent rendering of "out of [or, on the basis of] works of law." As I have often observed (and will continue to do as we go on), this expression describes behavior that conforms to the law of Moses, done in order to express the confession that acceptance with God, while it may come through Christ, is deeply dependent on obeying the specific laws of Moses. It is that behavior that is inherently cultural imperialism and that denies the sufficiency of Christ.

Now, Paul argues, if the Galatians will but look at their own personal histories, they will quickly discover that (1) they received the Holy Spirit *while* Paul was ministering to them the first time; (2) they received the Spirit *when they believed* in Jesus Christ and surrendered themselves to him; (3) they learned about Mosaic stipulations *later* from the Judaizers; and (4) while their escapade into Mosaic religion may have not eliminated their experience of the Holy Spirit and the presence of miracles (v. 5), they got no further

---

10. See esp. J. D. G. Dunn, *Jesus and the Spirit: A Study of the Religious and Charismatic Experience of Jesus and the First Christians as Reflected in the New Testament* (Philadelphia: Westminster, 1975).

11. See ibid., 239–42.

ahead when they accepted the message of the Judaizers. Thus, Paul reasons, it is best to abandon the Judaizers' gospel and to continue to walk in the truth of the gospel.

Second, "by believing what you heard" is a translation of what would literally be, "out of the hearing of faith." This, Paul infers, is how they got the Holy Spirit. Scholars disagree whether this expression means (1) "hearing about the need for the faith"; (2) "believing what you heard [the gospel]"; or (3) "hearing, that is, faith."[12] While I am inclined to accept the second or third option—the difference is minimal anyway—I am convinced that the issue Paul has in mind is the absolute contrast between a religious life based on commitment to Moses (works of the law) and one based on surrender to Christ in faith (believing what you heard).

This "one thing" Paul wanted to learn has now been raised to the conscious level by the Galatians. If they received the Spirit by faith, then they are wrong in attaching themselves now to the laws of the Judaizers; if they received the Spirit by observing the law, then Paul is wrong and the Judaizers are right. But, Paul knows, they received the Spirit earlier than the Judaizers' arrival, and therefore they have to admit right here that they received it by faith. The debate is effectively over now. Paul is the winner. Paul could end his letter right here. He didn't, so we have to go on as well.

The question about completion (v. 3). Since Paul, like any good debater, assumes that his readers are on his wavelength and agree with him, he begins with an assumption: "After beginning with the Spirit." This assumption is based on the correctness of his previous argument. Assuming that they began in the Spirit, Paul now wants to know if they are going to find perfection, or completion,[13] "by human effort." Here I must disagree resolutely with the NIV, which translates the Greek term *sarki* ("by flesh") with "by human effort." The unfortunate dimension of this translation is that it makes the reader think the issue is one of "effort" (i.e., merit-seeking) versus "non-effort" (i.e., faith). This misunderstands the import of both "flesh" and "faith" and so fails to take into consideration the function of the law for the Judaizers.

---

12. For more discussion, see R. N. Longenecker, *Galatians*, 102–3.

13. This term has generated a debate among scholars. Is it passive ("Are you being perfected" by something outside yourselves) or middle ("Are you trying to perfect yourselves" by circumcision and other Mosaic codes)? Even if the verb is probably middle, most now would argue that it is not reflexive ("perfect yourselves") but rather intransitive middle ("attaining perfection"). And, as F. F. Bruce has translated, it is also conative: "are you *trying* to attain perfection." This "perfection" is to be understood in light of historical and social context: the Judaizers undoubtedly argued that, however good Paul's gospel was, it was something short of the fullness intended by God. This fullness could be found if one not only trusted in Christ but also submitted to the law of Moses and proselytized into Judaism. Perfection, then, is nationalization.

Rather, what Paul has in mind is "flesh" in the sense of a life that is not based solely on Christ's work and the power of the Holy Spirit.[14] To live in the "flesh" is to ignore the Spirit, and, in this context, Paul may be thinking partly in terms of circumcision—the paramount religious act in the flesh, probably seen as the perfection or completion of the proselyte's faith and obedience. What dominates Paul's mind here is the notion of flesh that he uses elsewhere. Similar to Paul's message in 4:23 and 29, the Spirit and the flesh are two different domains under which a person chooses to live or, put in time categories, two different periods of time. It is the issue of two ages (before Christ and after Christ), two worlds that war against one another (5:16–18). This means that Paul sees life in the "flesh" as life under the law; in a strange twist of fate for Judaism, Paul sees law and flesh as two coordinates and Christ and Spirit as their opposites. The opposite of "flesh" in 3:3 is not "faith," as if Paul were talking about effort or reception; rather, its opposite is Spirit. In choosing to move over to the view of the Judaizers, Paul argues, the Galatians were choosing to live in the "flesh" and were revoking their claim to live in the Spirit, which is the new age inaugurated by Christ's death.

The question about persecution (v. 4). Paul's third question pertains to the early experiences the Galatian converts had in persecution. What Paul envisages is simple: after their conversion to Christ (according to the Pauline gospel), the Galatian converts experienced persecution at the hands of others (probably at the hands of Jews, perhaps also the Judaizers; see 4:29). Now Paul asks, "Have you suffered so much for nothing?" In other words, had you simply converted to Judaism immediately, you would never have experienced the persecution you encountered for converting to Christ. If you suffer as a Christian, it is for something; but if you suffer as a Christian and then toss it all away by converting to Judaism, your suffering as a Christian would be for nothing. So, he asks, was this all in vain? Paul is both shaming the Galatians and appealing to his standard argument (see 4:29; 5:11) that those who are persecuted are in the right and those who persecute are in the wrong.

The question about miracles (v. 5). His final question is simple: "Does God give you his Spirit and work miracles among you because you observe the law [i.e., 'on the basis of works of law'; see above], or because you believe what you heard?" The means has not changed: it is either through surrender to Christ or through commitment to Moses. The manifestation, however, has changed. Now it is not receiving the Spirit but the presence of miracles. The Galatians were well aware of God's powerful workings in their midst; they were no doubt proud of their "power evangelism." But, Paul queries, what triggered God's power? By now the Galatians must be either hiding in shame or

---

14. See J. M. G. Barclay, *Obeying the Truth*, 203–9; F. F. Bruce, *Galatians*, 149.

continuing the Judaizers' polemical responses by appealing to Scripture, which Paul goes on to rebut.

Paul has sustained here a vigorous polemical argument on his behalf, and it is highly appealing to the Galatians since it is drawn from their experience. Their experience, from front to back, confirms the message of Paul and counters the message of the Judaizers. God's Spirit comes to us and stays with us through faith; God's Spirit has nothing to do with "observing the law."

Bridging Contexts

INASMUCH AS THIS section is thoroughly an appeal to experience, it is best to begin with experience. We begin by observing that *certain experiences are powerful* in our lives. Not all experiences are powerful and life-changing, but some are. I am concerned here only with those major experiences in life that change us. Such experiences would certainly include crucial moments in our uprising; discovering our special talents, such as pitching a baseball or solving intricate mathematical problems; special experiences in our physical development; our marriage; our choice of career and the initial experiences in that career; changing careers; discovering that we have a fatal disease, like cancer or the HIV virus; special moments of success or failure in our life ambitions; and the few moments when we actually face that we are growing old. In addition to these, one of the more powerful experiences in life, for many, is a *religious conversion*.

Religious conversions both change our pasts and shape our futures. In them is communicated the goodness of God's love in spite of our sin, the perception of God's design for our world and how we fit in that design, and the significance of a religious community. In many churches, Christians are fond of recounting their religious conversion, and some churches make time available weekly for the recital of these experiences in life.

Because religious conversion is such a powerful experience, it can be appealed to with force and persuasion. Paul does precisely that with the Galatians. He knew that their conversion was a powerful experience; after all, he was there and was the herald of the gospel that transformed them (4:12–16). In effect, he knew the simplicity of their experience and so could appeal to it: it was triggered, through God's grace, as a result of the proclamation of being accepted by God through faith in Christ alone. They did believe and so experienced the rush of God's Spirit and the love of his forgiveness. We cannot doubt that the Galatians continued to rehearse their own conversions over and over as they reflected on the new life they found in Christ.

What we need to recognize is that experiences are powerful in life and cannot be denied as unreal. We cannot pretend that they did not happen and we cannot wish them away. I can remember a crucial week of camp when I was a teenager that forever transformed my life. Prior to that week I wanted to be a professional athlete; after that week I wanted to serve Christ, whether as an athlete or not. Prior to that week I only occasionally read my Bible, rarely prayed, and halfheartedly attended church; I did not see anything of value in Christian community and did not see God's will for my life as the most essential thing to know. After that week all these things changed: I devoted my life to praying, studying the Bible, and teaching it to others; I found Christian fellowship to be not only valuable but absolutely foundational for growth and accountability; and I saw that all that mattered in life was to do what God had called me to do.

I remember this experience as if it were yesterday: I can still see the colors of trees under which I prayed; I can still see the basketball court on which I was playing a missionary whom God used to speak to me; I can still smell the "mess hall" and hear the voices of the room. I can smell the cabin in which I stayed and I can still feel the emotions of listening to a man of God expound Scriptures, one of which was Ephesians 5:18. And over and over in my life, I have appealed myself to this experience—when I was down, when I was unsure as to what God wanted from me, when I needed encouragement after failures. I knew that God began right there a work that he would finish (Phil. 1:6). I rebounded off of this experience over and over, knowing that God would not take me so far and then be done with me. The experience was powerful and helped shape my life. Its power has enabled me to draw faith lessons from it with confidence.

But we have also learned that *experiences can be deceiving*. Paul is not here justifying *all experiences*, nor is he appealing to *every Galatian experience*. He is talking here about an experience he witnessed and knew well, and he appealed only to certain dimensions of it. So, although it is true that experiences are powerful, there is no mechanism in our system to make sure that power is attributed only to good experiences. It is simply untrue to agree with the pop singer who claims that because it feels so good, it must be right. Paul appeals, then, to a major experience (their conversion) that was witnessed by many, and he argues the predominance of faith because the "works of the law" had not yet appeared as an option for the Galatians. So while we may want, at times, to bank on our experiences and while we may, at times, want to appeal to others' experiences, we find justification for doing so only if that experience is known, confirms the point that is being made, and is in accordance with the Bible.

Paul was willing to appeal to experience in his theological argumentation. Theology without experience is sterility, while experience without theology is emotionalism. True theology is something that also needs to be experienced, and experience needs to be theologically sound; and here I am not talking only about "ecstasy" and "tongues" but about what the Puritans called our "religious affections." To know about the love of God is not enough; we need to feel it, to sense it, and to be moved by it because God wants our entire beings to be wrapped up in his love. J. I. Packer, in his truly great book on God, writes much about theology and the intricacies of what we know about God. But he says early on in his book that "we must not lose sight of the fact that knowing God is an emotional relationship, as well as an intellectual and volitional one, and could not indeed be a deep relation between persons were it no so."[15] And Pascal said: "The [bare] knowledge of God is very far from the love of Him" (*Pensées* 4.280). I would call this "love of Him" the genuine experience of God, apart from which we do not know God; and I would say that experience is crucial for the entirety of our Christian faith. And because experience is crucial, we can appeal to it. But we must do so carefully, because what some have experienced is simply not in accordance with Scripture.

Paul begins this section with an appeal to experience; this does not mean that we need to begin our polemical work and evangelistic apologetics with appeals to experience. Paul is not consciously setting out a hierarchy of logical arguments. And in these appeals, he does something that is as effective now as it was then: he grounds his appeals in rhetorical questions. Rhetorical questions are questions that are really not questions because their answers are obvious, so obvious they are not answered. The question is meant to engage the reader (or listener) in a way that forces the reader to arrive at the desired answer. It is the answer that matters, not the question. This is why throughout the commentary above I assumed answers to each of these questions. Paul assumed his readers would catch on to what he was getting at.

This form of communication is effective and could be used more than perhaps we do. The silence of not answering creates a situation when the answer is actually provided but not aloud. Such silence allows the listener (or reader) to reflect on the answer and internalize it. Perhaps some of the following rhetorical questions can be used in our applications of Galatians. Has God provided the Holy Spirit or the law as your moral guide? Is God's Spirit sufficient for guiding your life? Did God send his Son for one nation or for all? Is his Son's sacrifice intended for all people or only for white suburbanites? Does God use handicapped or only healthy people? As we look around in our church today, do we see a collection of economically similar or dissim-

---

15. J. I. Packer, *Knowing God* (Downers Grove, Ill.: InterVarsity Press, 1973), 35. The entirety of pp. 13–37 are germane to our present discussion.

ilar people? Are there people of different economic classes in our community? Does God enable only men or also women? Are we reaching only our kind or all kinds of people? Are we obeying the truth of the gospel or are we obeying a gospel that we have fashioned?

 EXPERIENCE IS AN integral part of all of our lives. We strip our Christian faith of one of its most important dimensions if we rob it of experience and pretend that Christianity is unemotional, unobservable, and untouchable. Paul knew the "witness of the Spirit" (Rom. 8:16), and so did John (1 John 3:19–20; 5:10–11). Countless Christians have experienced God's grace and cannot be persuaded that it was not God who encountered them. Paul in our passage appeals to the experience of conversion that the Galatians had when he preached the gospel to them. We should not deny this dimension of Christianity. But neither should we seek to conform all people to one kind of experience, nor should we demand that every person have some kind of powerful experience as evidence for conversion.[16]

I believe it is important for local churches to provide opportunities for Christians to stand before their brothers and sisters and recount their experiences with God, especially their conversion experiences. While there needs to be control over what can be said (I am not describing what psychologists call "group therapy"), our fears about what will be said are probably greatly exaggerated. Personal story-telling is not a kindergarten exercise but is the very structure of our life, for if we have no story we have no life. What I am proposing is that Christians be encouraged to rehearse aspects of their story and to tell of their experiences. Knowing the experience of others may help us to understand them, to pray for them, and to instruct them.

I am frequently called upon to be a coach for one of my son's local teams; sometimes it is basketball and other times it is baseball. What I have found with these young men (twelve- and thirteen-year olds at the present) is that they like stories—stories about major leaguers, about our local high school team, and about my time in Little League "decades ago" (when bats were wooden and when kids played sandlot games). Why do they like stories? Because stories capture real life in real events. The same is true of Christians, whether they are children, teenagers, or adults: we can all identify with stories. Why

---

16. See H. T. Kerr and J. M. Mulder, *Conversions: The Christian Experience* (Grand Rapids: Eerdmans, 1983), xiii–xv, for some perceptive comments on the variety of conversion experiences.

is the biography section of bookstores so popular? Because they tell stories about real people. Why did God tell so much of Israel's history in stories, why is the nature of a gospel little more than a biography, and why did Jesus tell so many stories (i.e., parables)? Because stories are important and animate the imagination. Why does a congregation suddenly become more attuned to the preacher when he (or she) provides an illustration? Because illustrations are stories that help us understand.[17] Churches that structure the story as part of its purpose will benefit greatly; churches that do not will rob its people of reality and cut off its youth from examples that can shape their lives. Galatians 3:1 is a witness to the power Paul could muster in his preaching, and that power revolved around his ability to portray Christ publicly and effectively through the spoken story about Christ.

We can appeal to experience in our theological arguments. Blaise Pascal, in his famous *Pensées*, said: "People are generally better persuaded by the reasons which they have themselves discovered than by those which have come into the mind of others" (1.10). A disease that particularly affects my own discipline, academic theology, is an unwillingness (probably to avoid the appearance of popularity) to integrate experience into one's academic work. But academic theologians ought to learn from Paul here: Paul was so astute theologically that countless scholars have spent their lives unraveling his letters and arguments so they can order their own thoughts biblically. Yet, for all his academic precision, Paul was also experiential in his approach.

How then should we appeal to experiences in ministering to others? Here I am simply assuming that Paul's example is one worth emulating without being bound to following it rigidly. We would want, first of all, to appeal to experiences about which we are aware. While Paul clearly does not tell us how he knew about their experience as the preface for his appeals, it is also clear that he knew what he was talking about (cf. 1:6–9, 11; 4:13–15) and, because he knew about it, he appealed to it. Second, we should probably follow Paul in not making lots of appeals to experience. Paul's appeals to experience as a crucial foundation for his arguments are infrequent. Third, we should probably infer the obvious and the compelling from experiences rather than clever and difficult-to-discern features. While I (individually) may learn from a specific experience something I think God wants me to know or learn, that does not warrant my dictating that same lesson for everyone who has a similar experience.[18] Fourth, what we infer from experience must

---

17. On the value of illustrations, see J. R. W. Stott, *Between Two Worlds* (Grand Rapids: Eerdmans, 1982), 236–43.

18. Take the example of Augustine, *Confessions* 8.28–30, where Augustine rehearses his conversion, how a voice came to him telling him to read from the Scriptures, and in opening Scriptures he read a passage (Rom. 13:13–14) that converted him.

be in accordance with Scripture if we are serious about our Christian theology and the authority of the Bible.

So I believe we can learn from this passage that arguments from experience can be a part of our theological argumentation. Let us take the example of a young man who was raised in a Christian home, committed himself to Christ during his high school years, left home for college, enjoyed two good years of Christian fellowship at his campus, and who also, after two years of fighting the battles against sin and the flesh, announces that he has had enough of Christianity, wants to move into his girlfriend's apartment and to participate in weekend beer parties, and overall desires to be morally unchecked. While I would not want for any reason to forget to pray through this and to remind him pastorally (i.e., firmly) of what God's Word says about purity and the final ends of life in the flesh, I believe in this sort of situation it is wise also to appeal to his experiences: the disappointment of his loving parents, his college brothers and sisters, and his local church who have prayed for him for years; the joy he had experienced in conversion, fellowship, and Christian growth; the emotional maturity that develops in waiting for the timing of God's partner; the sickening feeling that comes the morning after beer bashes; and the misery that will come to him (if he is a Christian) if he decides for an immoral lifestyle.

If we were able to take careful statistics of pastoral counseling and Christian ministry, we would, I suspect, be surprised at how frequently our appeals are to experience rather than simply to logic. In fact, as a college student I once attended a local lecture on philosophical logic by a world famous logician. He began his question-and-answer session with a statement to this effect: "You will discover, in real life, that people change their views, not as a result of logical reasoning, but as a result of arguments from authorities (if Billy Graham says so, then I believe it) or as a result of appeals to experience." In the eighteen years since that lecture, I can think of very few statements I heard in college that have been more frequently fulfilled than that one.

But we cannot think our appeals to experience are all that we need. Contextual reading of Paul's argument from experience shows that Paul did not stop here; he went on to arguments from Scripture and logic. And so should we. Our arguments from experience have no truth-backing if they are nothing more than that. They must be anchored in and carried out by appeals to Scripture and theological reasoning. Otherwise, we reduce our ministries to emotional appeals.

But I must also add that appealing to *powerful* experiences is the most forceful of appeals to experience. I include in such experiences our conversion experience (especially for those for whom it was somewhat dramatic), miraculous answers to prayer, and even outright miraculous events in our lives. Very few of our experiences are as powerful as these, and it is to such experiences that Paul appeals. We would be wise to appeal to these kinds of experience if and when we do appeal to experience.

The experience of conversion was the foundation for Paul's entire appeal here. Had the Galatians not been converted to the truth of the gospel, Paul would never have written this letter. But conversion is not in vogue right now. Perhaps because of the excesses of the 1950s and 1960s with popular evangelism appealing to superficial conversions, or a backlash to the "I've Got It" and "Born Again" movements, or the embarrassing revelations of TV evangelists, or the desire of evangelicals to be intellectually and socially acceptable, we evangelicals are not emphasizing conversion as the only true foundation of a relationship to God. Our reactions are overreactions. These overreactions are also weakening our churches when we could be strengthening them.

In our previous section we examined the need to preach and teach justification by faith since that was the essential message of that passage. Here we see that the experience of conversion is the foundation for the whole passage. Thus, while justification by faith is a doctrinal formulation of the experience of conversion, we should not avoid repetition. We need to preach the necessity of conversion, we need to teach it in our Sunday schools and in our Bible studies, and we need to evidence it in our lives.

As we have hinted before, the experience of conversion is not some formula that every Christian repeats. Some people are suddenly and dramatically converted; others are converted over years; some can never remember when they were not Christians. For each, however, conversion is a necessity because no person can relate to God until that person surrenders the entirety of his or her person to God. That surrender is conversion. I know of no better collection of conversion stories than the one collected by Hugh T. Kerr and John M. Mulder.[19] It would make a great adult Bible study topic to study this book and compare each conversion to teachings on conversion in the Bible.

Through such an attention given to conversions in the church and in the Bible, perhaps our churches will be encouraged with what is going on at the local level, and perhaps we will gain better clarifications of the nature of conversion required by God.

---

19. Kerr and Mulder, *Conversions* (see note 16). This book collects the stories of fifty different conversions, including the Apostle Paul, St. Augustine, Blaise Pascal, John Bunyan, John Wesley, Elizabeth Bayley Seton, Sojourner Truth, Charles Spurgeon, Thérèse of Lisieux, Billy Sunday, C. S. Lewis, Dorothy Day, Ethel Waters, and Charles Colson.

Galatians 3:6–14

A BRAHAM: "HE BELIEVED God, and it was credited to him as righteousness." ⁷Understand, then, that those who believe are children of Abraham. ⁸The Scripture foresaw that God would justify the Gentiles by faith, and announced the gospel in advance to Abraham: "All nations will be blessed through you." ⁹So those who have faith are blessed along with Abraham, the man of faith.

¹⁰All who rely on observing the law are under a curse, for it is written: "Cursed is everyone who does not continue to do everything written in the Book of the Law." ¹¹Clearly no one is justified before God by the law, because, "The righteous will live by faith." ¹²The law is not based on faith; on the contrary, "The man who does these things will live by them." ¹³Christ redeemed us from the curse of the law by becoming a curse for us, for it is written: "Cursed is everyone who is hung on a tree." ¹⁴He redeemed us in order that the blessing given to Abraham might come to the Gentiles through Christ Jesus, so that by faith we might receive the promise of the Spirit.

PAUL'S ARGUMENT FROM experience (vv. 1–5), his thesis that everything in the Christian life comes by way of faith and not through the works of the law, now gives way to his subtle arguments from Scripture. In fact, the present passage is the first in a series of arguments for the truthfulness of Paul's gospel (3:6–4:31). These arguments form the evidence from which Paul infers his case.

Because Paul's argument here is complex, I will summarize it briefly before getting into the exposition of individual points. In essence, Paul contends that a person's justification is by faith and not by works of the law and that this principle is not really new to the people of God. The evidence for these two ideas can be found in the Old Testament. (1) Acceptance by God solely on the basis of faith is as old as Abraham (vv. 6–7). For this point, Paul quotes Genesis 15:6. (2) Gentiles being accepted by God on the same basis as Jews is also as old as Abraham (vv. 8–9); again, Paul quotes Genesis (12:3; 18:18; 22:18). This is Paul's positive point. Paul then moves to a negative point. (3) The law does not justify because its function is to curse (vv. 10–11). Paul proves this by referring his readers to Deuteronomy 27:26 and Habakkuk 2:4. (4) In fact, the law operates under a different system—not a system governed by faith but governed by doing (v. 12). (5) Paul addresses here, in parenthetical fashion, how it is that people who are condemned (those who live under the law like Jews) can escape the cursing function of the law (v. 13). The escape hatch is found in Jesus Christ, who was cursed by God to absorb the curse of others. Paul proves this by quoting Deuteronomy 21:23. Paul then sums up his point in verse 14: the redemption Christ provides permits Gentiles to enjoy the Abrahamic blessing (his point in vv. 6–9), which is nothing other than the promised Spirit (which is the point of the argument from experience). Before I expound each of these points, I will chart out Paul's connections:

Faith → Abraham → Gentiles: Faith connects Abraham to the Gentiles.

Justification → Blessing of Abraham → Redemption → Holy Spirit: The justification Abraham experienced is similar to the redemption Christ brought, and both are considered the incorporation of Gentiles into the blessing of Abraham and the gift of the Holy Spirit.

Law → Works of the Law → Curse: The law brings a curse so everyone who commits himself or herself to the system of the law decides to inherit the curse of God, rather than the blessing of Abraham and the promise of the Holy Spirit.

Paul's argument is complex, but the following points are clear: (1) Paul is intent mainly on proving, not that merit-seeking is wrong, but that Gentiles are acceptable to God on the basis of faith in Christ rather than by observing the Jewish law. This is the point of Galatians because of the problems the Judaizers had stirred up. (2) The choice to live under the law is a choice to inherit the curse of the law because the desired items, called variously justification, the blessing of Abraham, redemption, and the promise of the Holy Spirit, come as a result of faith, whether in God (for Abraham) or in Christ (for Christians). Because this passage is so theologically rich and logically complex, I will have to explain the text in greater detail than I have normally been doing.

Acceptance by God solely on the basis of faith is as old as Abraham (vv. 6–7). The "Consider Abraham" of the NIV is a translation of a difficult expression. The Greek text reads literally, "Just as Abraham believed God. . . ." It is difficult to know what to make of the "just as" (Gk. *kathos*). There are four main options: (1) To connect it with the last clause of verse 5 and translate: ". . . or the hearing of faith, just as Abraham believed." While normally *kathos* introduces a subordinate clause, such a view is not preferable here because verse 5 is clearly a question that ends with "what you heard," and it is also clear

that Abraham did not receive the Holy Spirit. (2) To consider it as an inference and translate it, "Therefore, Abraham believed God. . . . " The obstacle
to this view is that *kathos* never means this. (3) To infer that it is shorthand
for "just as it is written in Scripture" and that it therefore introduces a new
sentence by way of proving the overall point of verses 1–5 (justification is
by faith, not works of the law).[1] (4) To consider *kathos* as an introductory
expression for an example: "Take Abraham for an example." This view is
adopted by the NIV, NEB, and JB.[2]

Abraham, at any rate, is an example of faith from the Old Testament, but
what is crucial here is that Abraham was justified by faith; that is, he was fully
accepted by God not by observing the law but by faith. For Paul to choose
Abraham is more than illustrative: Abraham was seen by Jews as the father
of their nation and the quintessential Jew.[3] One Jewish work of the era says:
"For Abraham was perfect in all of his actions with the Lord and was pleasing through righteousness all of the days of his life" (Jub. 23:10). Jewish writings saw two features of his life: (1) he was considered righteous because he
remained faithful through the test of God, and (2) Abraham's faith of Genesis 15:6 was intimately tied to his submission to circumcision in 17:4–14.
Thus, believing and keeping the covenant stipulation of circumcision were
to be done together; believing without being circumcised was contrary to
Abraham.

The significance of this background here in Galatians is that Paul proves
Abraham's prototypical role *without reference to circumcision*. Paul's emphasis (and
surely the Judaizers perceived his refusal to follow up Gen. 15:6 with an
appeal to ch. 17) is that Abraham was pronounced as "acceptable to God"
before his circumcision, making the implication clear: circumcision was not necessary. "As a result, Abraham becomes the prototype of the Gentile-Christ-
ian believer, as opposed to the Jewish (and Jewish Christian) observer of the
Torah."[4] Abraham was accepted by God *solely because he surrendered his entire life
to God's promise*.

Paul immediately applies his observation about Genesis 15:6: "those who
believe are children of Abraham." For Paul (as for John the Baptist; cf. Matt.
3:7–10), Abraham's descendants are those who simply believe; not those who

---

1. This view is held in differing ways by F. F. Bruce, *Galatians*, 147, 152, who translates
"(By faith, of course,) just as (in the words of scripture,)" and by H. D. Betz, *Galatians*, 137,
140, who translates "As [it is written]." One advantage of this view is that some early
Greek manuscripts add "it is written."

2. See R. N. Longenecker, *Galatians*, 107, 112.

3. See the helpful excursus of R. N. Longenecker on how Abraham was seen by Jews
(ibid., 110–12).

4. H. D. Betz, *Galatians*, 139.

believe and allow themselves to be circumcised. While Paul goes on in verses 8–9 to say that Gentiles are incorporated into Abraham's blessing and so become "children of Abraham," Paul also states that the "seed of Abraham" is only Christ (v. 19). That is, his particularistic reading of "seed" leads to the universalism of incorporating Gentiles (vv. 8–9) because *faith* in Christ is what connects one to God's promise.[5] But as of yet, Paul is not appealing to the inclusion of Gentiles.

I am sure that the Judaizers were offended by Paul's reduction of Abraham's response to Genesis 15:6. James, a contemporary of Paul, pointed to a combination of Abraham's initial faith (15:6) and his faithfulness to God's call when he sacrificed Isaac (22:1–19), though James was fighting another battle (those who thought credence was enough), and so he saw Abraham's faith finding its natural active completion in obedience. Paul would never deny obedience as the natural active completion of faith; but when his opponents argued that circumcision (the "work of the law" for a converting Gentile) was necessary, Abraham as an example of justification prior to circumcision came immediately to his mind. So while the Judaizers may have been offended by Paul, and perhaps James would have been bothered by such an inference unless it were clearly explained, Paul knew that he had the Judaizers by the throat. The fact is, Abraham's circumcision (Gen. 17) came *after* his pronouncement of acceptance (15:6). Thus his descendants are those who believe, those who opt for the faith system (along with Christ and the Holy Spirit); they opt out of the works system.

That Gentiles are accepted by God on the same basis as Jews is as old as Abraham (vv. 8–9). Having argued that Abraham was accepted by God because of his faith and that the true descendants of Abraham are believers, Paul now argues that *Gentiles* can be these true believers. Once again, he argues this by appealing to Scripture (Gen. 12:3; 18:18; 22:18). His logic is this: (1) Abraham was justified by faith (Gal. 3:6–7); (2) Gentiles are justified in Abraham because all nations, that is Gentiles, will be blessed in connection with Abraham (v. 8; from Gen. 18:18);[6] (3) therefore, since Gentiles are justified in Abraham's promise, they must be justified as Abraham was: that is, by faith, not works of the law.

The law does not justify because its function is to curse (3:10–11). Paul's point in verses 6–9 has been simple: Scripture teaches that Abraham was

---

5. A nice survey of how "offspring" or "seed" works itself out from the original Abrahamic promise can be found in T. E. McComiskey, *The Covenants of Promise: A Theology of the Old Testament Covenants* (Grand Rapids: Baker, 1985), 17–38.

6. The source Paul is quoting has been a matter of some debate. Either Paul is combining Genesis 12:3 and 18:18 or he is appealing exclusively to Genesis 18:18.

accepted by God because of faith; faith then is the foundation on which humans, including Gentiles, construct their relationship to God. This is his positive argument. Paul now moves to a negative argument: the law of Moses, when it governs a person's life, brings a curse rather than acceptance with God.

Verse 10 can be read as the basis for verses 6–9: acceptance with God is based on faith *because* there is no other way—the law only brings a curse, so the law cannot bring acceptance with God.[7] It can also be an inference: *since* Abraham was declared acceptable with God on the basis of faith, then it follows that those who opt for the "law system" are living under a curse since they have not followed Abraham. Whichever explanation is preferred, the net effect of these verses is to provide a negative argument: not only was Abraham declared fit for God by faith, but those who opt for the law will never be fit since the law brings a curse.

We need to explain once again the expression "who rely on observing the law." This translates *hosoi ex ergon nomou eisin* ("they who are on the basis of law"). Put more idiomatically, it means "those who commit themselves to the law" or "those who base their salvation on the law" (cf. 2:16; 3:2, 5). The NIV's use of the word "relying" here can lead to the idea of merit-seeking. But the critical point here is that Paul is not concerned with works-righteousness and merit-seeking. He is describing, in a catchy phrase, the alternative to "those who are of faith" (v. 9 reads *hoi ek pisteos*: "those who commit themselves to Christ on the basis of faith"). As in verses 2, 5, Paul is setting alternative approaches to God: either through faith or through obeying the law. But in so setting out these as opposites, Paul is not presenting various motives. J. D. G. Dunn clarifies our expression in the following words:

> The phrase refers not to an individual's striving for moral improvement, but to a religious mode of existence, a mode of existence marked out in its distinctiveness as determined by the law, the religious practices which demonstrate the individual's "belongingness" to the people of the law.[8]

In other words, this expression does not describe a specific (wrong-headed) branch of Christians but is an apt description of *all Jews*, especially those who are caught in the web of thinking that their Jewishness is sufficient

---

7. The translators of the NIV have decided the opening conjunction ("for," *gar*) functions simply to begin a new paragraph by signaling the start of a new argument. H. D. Betz translates: "By contrast, those who are men of works. . . ." (*Galatians*, 137).

8. J. D. G. Dunn, *Jesus, Paul and the Law: Studies in Mark and Galatians* (Louisville: Westminster/John Knox Press, 1990), 220.

before God. It casts a dark shadow, of course, over all ethnocentrisms and nationalisms. If "those who are of faith" are all those who, since Abraham, have trusted in God's promise, then "those who are of works of the law" are those who have chosen to base their salvation in their Jewishness, in their Jewish distinctives, and in their adherence to specific laws of Moses.

More importantly, those who are of the law are "under a curse." Why? Paul quotes Deuteronomy 27:26: because "cursed is everyone who does not continue to do everything written in the Book of the Law." It is here that the classical (Lutheran) view of the law in Paul finds its crucial piece of evidence. They argue that Paul is speaking here of the *necessity* of obeying every commandment for one's entire life and that he is assuming that *it is impossible to obey the law*; thus he can argue here (by assumption) that people who choose the law also choose a curse because they will never do what they need to do. This view is sometimes described as the unfulfillability of the law. But there are two substantial problems with this view, so substantial that the view should not be held. First, there was no Jew (eccentrics like the author of 4 Ezra aside) in history who thought that a Jew had to be sinless with respect to the law in order to be acceptable to God. This is obvious from the tabernacle and temple systems; inherent to both is the tacit admission that sinlessness was impossible and therefore confession, atonement, and forgiveness were necessary. Indeed, this is why the pious Jew repented from sin and visited Jerusalem for Passover and why the pious Jew celebrated the Day of Atonement.[9] Paul's comments on his past assume his compliance with Jewish law with respect to sin, forgiveness, and atonement (Phil. 3:4–6).

Second, Paul himself thought the law could be fulfilled by the Christian who lived in the Spirit and lived a life of love (Gal. 5:14; cf. Rom. 13:8–10). So did James (James 2:8) and Jesus (Matt. 7:12; 22:34–40). What we need to observe here is that there is a difference between fulfilling the law and obeying the law on the one hand, and being sinless on the other. Judaism did not assume that one had to be sinless. What they assumed is that the one who undertook its obligation had to obey it thoroughly, an infraction had to be confessed, and atonement had to be made. Those who did do this, like Paul (Phil. 3:4–6), were considered "legally righteous," though not sinless.

So, if Jews did not think sinlessness was necessary and if Jews, and Christians, thought the law could be fulfilled, then how is it that the "law brings a curse"? The answer to this, I think, is fairly straightforward and has to do

---

9. See E. P. Sanders, *Judaism: Practice and Belief 63 BCE – 66 CE* (Philadelphia: Trinity Press International, 1992), 103–18, 119–45, 251–57, 270–78. See also his *Paul and Palestinian Judaism: A Comparison of Patterns of Religion* (Philadelphia: Fortress, 1977), 107–47; see also 33–59.

with the *purpose of the law*. Though I must postpone our discussion of this topic until we expound 3:19–25, I can state my view here. The reason the law curses is because that is what the law does and all it can do. The law was never given *to make someone righteous* nor was it given *to give salvation or life*.[10]

What then does the quotation from Deuteronomy 27:26 mean? Probably many think that the emphasis here is on the word *everything* and that, because "those of the works of law" do not do everything, they are finally condemned. I dispute this view as outlined in the previous paragraphs. In addition to those arguments, there is no reason to place our emphasis on the word "everything." The only reason interpreters do this is because they assume that the law must be perfectly done to be acceptable with God. But this view was not assumed by Paul (or the Judaizers or Pharisees), and so it should not be assumed here. What we should see here is the connection of "law" and "curse." Then we should move on to Paul's comments in verse 11 where he shows, in fact, that salvation is by faith, not by observing the law, *because the law cannot bring salvation since it was not designed to do so* (cf. vv. 19–25).

Once again, verse 10 means that those who opt for the law are cursed because they are choosing to omit the salvation that can come only through faith in Christ (now that he has come). In choosing for the law they are left to find what they can for salvation in the law; but it will not bring them salvation. It can only condemn (v. 22).

The law operates under a different system: it is not a system governed by faith but a system governed by doing[11] **(v. 12).** Paul has established that the law does not bring acceptance with God; that, even as taught in the Bible (Hab. 2:4), it comes by way of faith. Paul now backs off to take one more swat at the law. The law, he argues, is not of faith (and faith saves); the law demands "performance." He quotes Leviticus 18:5: "The man who does these things [i.e., the law] will live by them." Here Paul contrasts the terms *faith* and *does* and, in so doing, he shows that the law *is not a system of faith*. Rather, it is a system of "doing." Once again, however, Paul does not bring in merit-seeking but *only that the law is not a faith system*. This is critical for our perception of Paul's logic.

The curse of the law fell on Christ so others might escape (vv. 13–14). Having established that acceptance with God is by faith in Christ and that those who opt for the law against Christ (as the Judaizers are in effect doing) are cursed by God, Paul now must explain how it is that Christ provides an

---

10. A fascinating subject emerges from Paul's observations here: how were pre-Christian Israelites accepted by God? Paul, I believe, does not intend to answer this question. He would say, I guess, that they trusted in God's covenantal arrangement.

11. I do not think we need here to identify "doing" with "merit-seeking works."

escape for those who have lived under the law. I take these two verses to be a parenthesis, a pastoral aside.

It is probable here that Paul is speaking especially about Jewish Christians in the phrase "Christ redeemed *us.* . . . "[12] Evidence for this view is found in 2:15; 3:23—25; and 4:4—6, and in the emphasis of Galatians on Jews. Also, it must be added that Jews saw the law as their prerogative and argued that Gentiles were neither under the law nor did they know the law (Rom. 2:12—24). Finally, Paul states that the law lasted only until Christ (Gal. 3:19); how, we might ask, could Gentiles be under the law?

Once again, we need to learn to read the letter the way Paul intended it to be heard. I would contend that it was particularly the Jewish Christian who raised, at this point in the argument, the issue of what to do with the curse they incurred in living (especially previously) under the law. Even if Paul was not specifically referring to the Jewish Christian, the deliverance from the curse of the law would be of paramount importance for the Jewish Christian. If one opts for the view that "us" refers to all people, both Jewish and Gentile Christians, one might appeal to Romans 2:14—15 and argue that, since the law was written in the hearts of the Gentiles, and since Gentiles do not live sinlessly (or seek God's method of atonement), they also are redeemed for the law's curse.[13] Furthermore, this view is strengthened by the "reversal" of the Galatians: by moving over to Judaism, they were now inheriting the law and its curse.

The term *redeemed* is drawn from the commercial world and describes "purchasing things," "buying back a captive," "liberating a slave through a ransom payment," or "securing the interests of a family by offering a fee."[14] The essential idea is that (1) people are by nature slaves to sin and under the curse of the law, (2) Christ paid the price of freedom by dying on the cross, and (3) those who trust in Christ's ransom price are set free from sin and the curse of the law.

How did Christ do this? Christ ransomed Jewish Christians from the curse of the law "by becoming a curse." What Christ did was to die the death of a transgressor (this is the point of quoting Deut. 21:23). In so doing, he becomes the transgressor because Christ was publicly crucified (cf. 2 Cor. 5:21). But because he was innocent and sinless, he can die on behalf of

---

12. This view is held by, among others, J. B. Lightfoot, *Galatians*, 139; H. D. Betz, *Galatians*, 148.

13. This view is held by F. F. Bruce, *Galatians*, 166—67.

14. See the semi-popular discussion of L. L. Morris, *The Atonement: Its Meaning and Significance* (Downers Grove, Ill.: InterVarsity Press, 1983), 106—31; see also J. R. W. Stott, *The Cross of Christ* (Downers Grove, Ill.: InterVarsity Press, 1986), 175—82.

those who have sinned and so absorb their curse. And because he was divine, he could perfectly satisfy the justice of God (see Rom. 3:21–26).

The redemption Christ accomplished not only freed Jewish Christians (Jews who believe) from the curse of the law; that redemption also made it possible for Gentiles to be incorporated into Abraham's blessing (v. 14) without nationalizing.[15] Moreover, since Christ has absorbed the curse of the law, the law's murderous power has been exhausted. This means that the era of the law has come to an end, and that in turn means that Gentiles can be accepted by God without becoming Jews, without living according to Jewish distinctives. Put differently, the cross nullified Jewish privilege; this we have already seen in 2:15–21.

Furthermore, now that the curse of the law is over, the new people of God (both Jewish and Gentile) can "receive the promise of the Spirit" (v. 14; cf. Acts 2:33). Paul began his entire argument with this gift of the Spirit (vv. 1–5), and he later sees the Spirit as the power of God's new people (5:1–26).

To sum up: (1) Paul proves here that Gentiles are acceptable to God because of faith; they do not have to live according to the law to find acceptance with God. In fact, Paul argues that the law era is now over because Christ has defeated its power by absorbing its curse. Abraham is the great example of how one is accepted with God: inasmuch as he was accepted by faith, so both Jewish Christians and Gentile Christians are accepted on the same basis. These people are "those who are of faith." Those who think they still have to obey Moses both misunderstand the purpose of the law (see vv. 19–25) and will inherit a curse; they are "those of the works of the law." (2) Paul also argues, negatively, that those who live under the law (i.e., the Judaizers and those who convert to their "gospel") are going to inherit a curse. Salvation is found only in Christ and through faith; those who add Moses to Christ nullify Christ and those who are "of the works of the law" are not living by faith. You and I would probably give anything to know what the Judaizers had to say about Paul's polemical arguments here. But we can only guess.

Bridging Contexts

THERE ARE TWO main topics discussed in this text, and it takes two different maneuvers to bring them into our world. First, we need to address the issue of Gentiles being admitted to the people of God by faith. The most important thing for Paul about Gentiles is that they were non-Jews. His perception, which came to him by

---

15. See J. B. Lightfoot, *Galatians*, 140.

revelation (cf. 1:16) and was his particular "mystery" (Eph. 3:1–13; Col. 1:24–2:3), was that God was now broadening out his people to include Gentiles. What we have, then, is a fundamental principle: universalism overrides the nationalism of Judaism. As we work through the passage, we find behind it this principle of universalism. We hurry to clarify that it was not that Gentiles were unacceptable to God prior to Christ, nor that Judaism had no place for Gentiles. This would be both inaccurate to the Old Testament presentation and potentially slanderous to Judaism.[16] What we are saying is that there is a broadening of that scope and a centralizing of the universality of the truth of the gospel.

This fundamental issue here is both theological and sociological. It is theological in that Paul claims that the inclusion of Gentiles is by faith and that their inclusion is permitted without having to nationalize (i.e., their becoming Jews). Prior to Paul, conversion to Judaism implied nationalizing as well.[17] Paul sees in his gospel a denationalizing of the people of God because all are accepted by way of faith. This theological principle has been revealed by God and pertains to the truth of the gospel. But sociologically, this notion was difficult for Jews to fathom because of how they perceived their past. To be a Jew was (and still is) a privilege. To no surprise, it was hard for Jewish Christians in Paul's day to accept a completely "nationless" construction of the people of God. But this is exactly what he was urging on his converts. Paul wanted the Jewish Christians to relinquish their commitment to the law as what defined them. I believe Paul would have tolerated circumcision for their baby boys, but I also think he would have sharply criticized such behavior if he thought such behavior was being done to express the necessity of obeying Moses in order to be accepted by God.

We can apply to our world the related ideas that the gospel is for all and that social barriers must be broken down by the gospel. We find that the principle Paul is using is that God loves "all kinds of people" and works with "all kinds"; therefore, the church cannot construct barriers to prevent the inclusion of "some kinds." We must apply Paul's message to our world by seeing if our churches and our gospel minister to all kinds who believe. We must constantly explore the implications of this kind of universalism for the church today.[18]

---

16. For Jewish attitudes toward Gentiles, see my book *A Light among the Gentiles: Jewish Missionary Activity in the Second Temple Period* (Minneapolis: Fortress, 1991), 11–29.

17. Again, see ibid., 30–48.

18. I am aware of the neoorthodox concept of universalism, which teaches that all humans will eventually be accepted by God. Paul does not teach this nor does anyone in the Bible. What we are concerned with here is the kind of universalism that teaches that anyone, regardless of race, who believes in Christ is on equal ground before God. On the

Our second topic for consideration concerns how we are to apply the message of the "curse of the law" on those "who are of the works of the law." If it is the case that "the curse of the law" is something largely incurred by Jews (and for Paul, the Jewish Christians as well), then how do we apply this to our world? I see three possibilities: (1) for the contemporary orthodox Jew who thinks the law needs to be obeyed and his nation respected for acceptance with God; (2) for the Gentile who has God's law written in the heart; and (3) for those who cross over the lines of the truth of the gospel by adding various sorts of demands on top of the gospel in order to be acceptable to God.

First, for *orthodox Jews*. I do not wish here to get involved in the ongoing discussion of the relationship of the variety of American Judaisms to Christianity with its myriad of denominations. My view is that, at the most basic level, Christianity's relationship to Judaism is unlike its relationship to all other world religions. These two religions are not opposites, though Christianity is the fullness and completion of Judaism. I base my view on Jesus' teaching on the law (Matt. 5:17–20) and on the early church's appropriation of the theology of the Old Testament as its own. Furthermore, I believe that Judaism is incomplete and that when practiced correctly, it is in search of what Christ brings.

Paul teaches that Christ is the "end [or climax] of the law" (Rom. 10:4) and that the law ended in some sense with the death of Christ and his absorption of the curse (Gal. 3:10–14, 19–25). This means that obeying the law is disobedient to Christ if that obedience is done in opposition to or completion of Christ; this, of course, is the message of Galatians. This means that the orthodox Jew fits into the mold of the Judaizers' concerns in Galatians. While Jews today are more and more sympathetic to Jesus, they remain stubbornly opposed to the configuration of theology as taught by Paul.[19] Christians need to take a stand here and lovingly and persuasively show that the glory of God's covenant is revealed through Christ and that God's promises find their ultimate "yes" in Jesus (2 Cor 1:20). I would contend that the message of Galatians on the "curse of the law" is directly applicable to contemporary orthodox

---

problem of the former kind of universalism, see W. V. Crockett and J. G. Sigountos, *Through No Fault of Their Own? The Fate of Those Who Have Never Heard* (Grand Rapids: Baker, 1991). See also the stimulating work of C. H. Pinnock, *A Wideness in God's Mercy: The Finality of Jesus Christ in a World of Religions* (Grand Rapids: Zondervan, 1992). The problems of universalism and pluralism are vexing and need to be addressed by evangelicals with seriousness and urgency.

19. On this see D. A. Hagner, *The Jewish Reclamation of Jesus* (Grand Rapids: Zondervan, 1984); and "Paul in Modern Jewish Thought," in D. A. Hagner, M. J. Harris, *Pauline Studies: Essays Presented to Professor F. F. Bruce on His Seventieth Birthday* (Grand Rapids: Eerdmans, 1980), 143–65.

Jews who believe that God accepts people on the basis of obedience to the law and its social distinctives (i.e., on the basis of being a Jew).

Second, *for the Gentile who has God's law written in the heart.* Inasmuch as God's will and law are written on the hearts of all people throughout the world— a teaching of Paul in Romans 2:14–15—we can apply the "curse of the law" to the Gentile. The unconverted Gentile feels the curse in the same way as the Judaizer and the Galatian Christian who converted to the Judaizer's ways. A conviction coming through one's conscience stings anyone who goes against what he or she knows to be God's will. There is an indirect witness to this phenomenon through missionary stories about people who know right from wrong and who have established moral codes that conform to the Judeo-Christian ethic. The point remains the same: the Gentile who has never heard about God's law can experience the curse of God's law because that person has been given an internal (call it "innate," if you will) witness to God's moral will.

Third, *for those who add demands on top of the gospel in order to be accepted by God.* This is the primary audience of Galatians, those who added to the gospel of Christ and, in so adding, compromised the sufficiency of Christ and the power of the Spirit. This type of person, whether wittingly or not, adds conditions to the covenant God has established and thus forms an adequate analogy to the Judaizers. There are *no* conditions for acceptance with God apart from surrender to Christ and life in the Spirit. Additions bring God's curse. I listed four such additions in the introduction to this book: (1) laws and regulations, (2) experiences, (3) education, and (4) cultural imperialism. Each of these could be explored for applications in our world. Our purpose here, however, is not to apply but to point out the method we need to have in order to make our applications consistent with the text.

Once again, "those of the works of the law" were primarily Judaizers and Jews. It also came to be applied to those Gentiles who converted to Judaism through the proselytizing efforts of the Judaizers. How do we apply this expression to our world? The immediate answer here is that we need to understand why Paul used this expression for these people: they were "of the works of the law" because they chose to embrace a system of religion that did not base itself exclusively on Jesus Christ. In so choosing, these people added the Mosaic law on top of Christ as the means of acceptance with God. For our application today we need to find people who (1) compromise Christ's sufficiency with their addition or redefinition of the gospel, or (2) who propose that the law is the surest means of obeying God while they dispense with the Spirit as the sure guide of God's people into the life he wants for them.

These kinds of teachers can emphasize nationalism, racism, denominationalism, or simply a legalism of Christian disciplines. Our surest way of discovering this form of heresy today is to examine how pure our systems of
thought are (in comparison to the gospel of Christ) and how cleanly we allow
them to operate in our churches. It is frequently the case that, although the
gospel is pure, its operations in a local setting are anything but clean. A
church can cloud the clear message of the gospel with all kinds of distortions
and wrong-headed notions. A church's health is defined by whether it wor-
ships God in his holiness, responds to him warmly in his love, and lives
according to his will in loving holiness. We should inspect our own systems
to see if acceptance with God is based solely on Christ and if we urge the
power of the Spirit for Christian living. If any of these principles are missing, they may be because some form of "works of the law" is at work as a virus
corrodes a computer system.

WE CAN CERTAINLY apply to our world the twin
ideas of God's revelation that the gospel is for all
and that it breaks down social barriers. Indeed,
God loves "all kinds" of people and works with
"all kinds"; therefore, the church cannot construct barriers that prevent the
inclusion of "some kinds." We must apply Paul's message about the inclusion
of Gentiles on the basis of faith to our world by examining whether our
churches are ministering to all kinds who believe. In other words, is your
church universalistic?

We can approach this problem of universalism by way of *principle*: universalism means acceptance of all, and thus we need to examine where and
where not we are accepting all. This is deductive logic: if it is true that God
loves all, we must see if we are loving all. I would like to approach this another
way since we have already proceeded by way of principle.

We can also approach this issue *historically and socially*: we can probe how
Gentiles were treated by Jews in Paul's world and then see which groups are
in a similar relationship to us. One problem here is that Jews did not treat
Gentiles in the same way in all places. For instance, some Jews formed
enclaves, like the Essenes at Qumran (they were flourishing at the time of
Paul), and had little contact with Gentiles. The entrance of a Gentile into the
congregation at Qumran would have been treated with considerable alarm,
and the Gentile would have been immediately expelled as unclean. Other
Jews living in Palestine, in a place like Nazareth, rarely came into contact with
Gentiles; when they did, they responded to them appropriately but no
doubt developed little or no relationship to them. Yet other Jews living in

Palestine, because of their business associations, had regular contacts with Gentiles. There were further variations in the Diaspora. Some Jewish communities assimilated themselves quite naturally and completely into the life of their Gentile community. The synagogue at Sardis, a few centuries after Paul, was in effect the city center. By exploring the social and historical situation we can gain insights into how the gospel might fit more appropriately in our world.

More particularly, we can say that Paul operated in Diaspora communities with Gentiles in a way that was different from the manner he had in Jerusalem, since the social meaning of interaction with Gentiles was completely different. Paul's inclusion of Gentiles in most Diaspora churches was tolerable because it is likely that proselytes had already made their social impact on Jewish synagogue communities. But his startling demand that they need not convert completely to Judaism would have been uncomfortable for the Jews still in the synagogue and for many Jewish Christians. The theological problem was simple: Would Jewish Christians let the universalism of the gospel have its full realization? And would this realization be impeded by strong-minded people of a more traditional view? This social setting is one avenue for bringing the text into our world.

I think it appropriate here to find analogies for application: what kinds of people make us uncomfortable when they are included in our churches? (Let us assume that these new people are Christians; I am not talking here about the uncomfortable feelings many Christians have when known crooks or known sinners are enmeshed into a church without signs of conversion.) To repeat, what kinds of people are uncomfortable for us?

For many churches, people who join "their" church after a long relationship with another church from a different denomination are unsettling. Sometimes this discomfort arises from a Christian practice (like the gifts of the Spirit, raising hands while singing), at other times because of doctrinal variations (like eternal security, views of the future, variant translations of the Bible), and at still other times because of suspected doctrinal deviations (like the truthfulness of Scripture or the deity of Christ). I maintain that while different denominations seem to flow naturally from human sinfulness and the inability of Christian leaders to be infallible in their judgments, it is fundamentally important for churches to maintain a unity of the Spirit when people of diverse viewpoints are worshiping and living together. We do not really need the Spirit if we are identical. But we do need his Spirit to enable various people to live in unity. God wants people of variety to worship and live together because he takes delight in seeing the Spirit of God create one new people as a witness to the world of his grace.

Let us apply this universalism here to the racial problems in the United States as an example. Some people (mistakenly) think there is no problem of race in the U.S. churches. Nothing could be further from the truth. In addition, I would argue that God does not mean for there to be "black churches," "white churches," and "Hispanic churches." The development today of the "black gospel" and the "Hispanic gospel" is, in my view, a distortion caused by what is taken to be *the* gospel: the "white gospel." When whites learn that the gospel they believe has been shaped massively by their white culture, we shall make progress.[20]

We can apply our passage to the racial issue because both of the main issues arise in the interaction of blacks and whites. There is a nationalism (we have a "white gospel") and a "works of the law" type of thing going on (we socialize into white suburbia). What Paul teaches is that the gospel of Jesus Christ is for all, all together, not all apart or each in its racial quarter. The issue separating Paul's gospel from the Judaizer's gospel was as much Jewish versus Gentile as it was Moses versus Jesus. And the issue separating black and white today is as much racial as it is religious. In fact, I would say that it is ninety percent racial; the religious elements separating blacks and whites are hardly known (besides whites being stiff in their worship style). Paul did not raise his gospel in our church and ask us to part, like the Red Sea, into two separate congregations. God gave to each of us the Spirit of God so that we could be one and worship together. The gospel of Christ allows black children to walk from Sunday school class to the worship service holding hands with little white children.

I have seen "mixed congregations" work. I also know that it takes effort to understand one another and to be flexible over issues that seem natural to one group and wrong to another. I know that the work is sometimes hurt by personal fights between leaders who have different racial, socio-economic, and ideological backgrounds. But I believe in God's Spirit and I believe God wants us to work together.

I shall make some recommendations for better working together. First, I recommend that my white readers attend a black church for awhile. I recommended this to one of my students one time, and he is now pastoring in a black church in the inner city. I also recommend that my black readers attend a white suburban church for awhile. I ask that each observe and not judge. I suggest that each ask questions of each other. Perhaps it would be good for a black church in an inner city (Aren't most in the inner cities? Have

---

20. Again, see the works of P. Berger, including *The Sacred Canopy* (New York: Doubleday, 1967).

you every asked why?) to form a relationship with a white suburban church and let pastors lead worship services and preach in one another's churches.

Second, I suggest that each person develop a raised consciousness about the issues of race. I ask that my white readers not write off Jesse Jackson every time he sees a racial issue at work. He is rarely completely wrong about the influence of race. I also ask that my black readers not write off Republican candidates as people who are only fostering white supremacy. How specifically can we develop a racially-sensitive consciousness? I know of only one way: whites get to know blacks and blacks get to know whites. Ask them to your homes and learn about each other.

I finish this section with a story. For several years my parents lived in Atlanta, and we visited them a couple of times. On one of the occasions we took a pilgrimage with our children, who were then twelve and nine, to the Martin Luther King, Jr., Center, off Auburn Street in downtown Atlanta. We visited the center, the museum, and the Ebenezer Baptist Church. We picked up literature and read a book about "M.L." But mostly we absorbed the life that he lived—a life that fought hard but peacefully for racial justice, a life that pursued God's justice both through biblical study and social work, a life that ended tragically because of the accurate gun of a racist.[21]

Our time in that center will not be forgotten. We were also surprised at the number of Atlantans we became aware of who have never been there and wondered why we would want to go there. We were disappointed that in Atlanta, the major city in the South where Martin Luther King, Jr., spent so much of his energy, segregation is still the rule *in the churches*. We were hurt because we knew that they knew that God's message was for all kinds. We knew that their cute little white children were learning to sing a song that was not having the desired effects because of their institutionalized practices: "Red and yellow, black and white, all are precious in his sight; Jesus loves the little children of the world." Their practices seemed to teach that Jesus loved only whites. Let the message of Paul about the inclusion of Gentiles into the people of God have its intended power in our world today!

---

21. Read Coretta Scott King, *My Life With Martin Luther King, Jr.* (New York: Holt, Rinehart, and Winston, 1969); J. M. Washington, ed., *A Testament of Hope: The Essential Writings of Martin Luther King, Jr.* (San Francisco: Harper & Row, 1986); Jesse L. Jackson, *Straight From the Heart*, ed. by R. D. Hatch and F. E. Watkins (Philadelphia: Fortress, 1987).

Galatians 3:15–18

B ROTHERS, LET ME take an example from everyday life.
Just as no one can set aside or add to a human covenant
that has been duly established, so it is in this case.
16The promises were spoken to Abraham and to his seed. The
Scripture does not say "and to seeds," meaning many people,
but "and to your seed," meaning one person, who is Christ.
17What I mean is this: The law, introduced 430 years later,
does not set aside the covenant previously established by God
and thus do away with the promise. 18For if the inheritance
depends on the law, then it no longer depends on a promise;
but God in his grace gave it to Abraham through a promise.

HAVING ESTABLISHED THAT Scripture confirms the
experience of the Galatians, namely, that God
grants his Spirit to people because they surrender
to Christ and not because they conform their
lives to the Mosaic law, Paul now moves to another kind of argument, an analogy or "example from everyday life" (cf. also Rom. 3:5; 6:19; 1 Cor. 9:8).[1]
Through it he makes his point once again: the law of Moses is not God's most
important revelation; that revelation is God's promise to Abraham. This
means that the response demanded of Abraham is also more significant than
the response demanded through Moses. That is, faith (Abraham's
response)—not works of the law—is the foundation of our relationship to
God (cf. Rom. 4:13–15). (It is no wonder that Paul must soon cover his tracks
and speak about the purpose of the law in Gal. 3:19–25.)

Paul compares his teaching to the legal arrangement of covenants of
inheritance. He argues that the legal system prohibits the subtraction or addition to a covenant that has been established properly. Knowing that the
arrangement God worked out with Abraham was in effect a covenant, Paul
can argue that nothing could have been added to or taken away from that
covenant (though that is not his concern here). Thus, if God established a
covenant with Abraham, the law, which was "added" 430 years later, cannot
revise the terms of the original covenant. And (here is his point), *if God's
covenant was established by faith and not by works of the law, then the covenantal relationship*

---

1. The Greek expression is "I speak according to a human manner" or "I speak the way
humans do things" (*kata anthropon lego*). On this, see H. D. Betz, *Galatians*, 154–55.

God has with the Galatians through Christ is also by faith and not by works of the law—
if Abraham is the key person in the heritage.

Paul makes several points in his discussion of covenants. (1) He states his analogy from covenants governing inheritance[2] (v. 15). (2) He clears some ground by clarifying the ultimate party of the covenantal arrangement with God (v. 16). (3) He next applies the analogy itself to the relationship of Abraham's covenant to Moses' law (v. 17). (4) By way of parenthesis, he restates his argument by analogy, this time drawing more on the language of inheritance: since inheritance laws show that one receives an inheritance as a result of a promise, it follows that the inheritance of Abraham's blessing must be by way of promise and not by way of the works of the law (v. 18).

In proceeding through this argument, Paul once again lays before his readers his two alternatives: either they must choose Abraham, with his blessings climaxed in the gift of the Holy Spirit, or they must choose Moses, with his "works of the law" and the consequent "curse of the law." *I am convinced that what Paul is doing with the Galatians is teaching them how to read the Bible properly (and, for them, differently).* They had learned to read the Bible through the eyes of Moses as interpreted by the priests and Pharisees; Paul wants them to learn to read the Bible through the eyes of Abraham. This approach focuses on God's covenant and faith as the response to God's offer in the covenant. In addition, this Abrahamic approach focuses on a universal plan of God (Gen. 12:2–3) rather than a nationalistic emphasis on Israel that comes through a Mosaic approach.

The analogy from covenants (v. 15). Essentially Paul's argument is that the way a human covenant operates is certainly the same way as a divine covenant does (an *a fortiori* argument). Although scholars today are unsure about which particular legal institution Paul is using (Roman, Greek, Jewish),[3] they are agreed that Paul's point is secure: when a covenant or testament or last will has been established—probably after the death of the testator[4]— someone cannot come along and add to it or take away from it.

A clarification (v. 16). "The promises were spoken to Abraham and to his seed." Here we must understand "promises" as virtually equivalent to the "covenant" in the analogy; Paul confirms this view of "promises" in verse 17,

---

2. It makes most sense if we see the covenant here as describing inheritance covenants. In 3:18 Paul shows that this is the kind of covenant he has in mind. See the discussions in H. D. Betz, *Galatians*, 155–56; R. N. Longenecker, *Galatians*, 128–30.

3. A survey of the possibilities and the evidence can be found in R. N. Longenecker, *Galatians*, 128–30.

4. The Greek word is *kekuromenen* ("duly established") and, as F. F. Bruce points out, testaments are not "duly established" or "ratified" until the testator has died (cf. Heb 9:15–22); see *Galatians*, 170–71. The perfect tense of the participle may confirm Bruce's view.

where he uses "covenant." Paul's analogy, then, is between the covenant of inheritance in the legal world and the covenant of promise made with Abraham.

In applying this analogy to the relationship of the Abrahamic covenant to the Mosaic law, Paul realizes that he must first prove that the Abrahamic covenant applies to the Christian era. He does this by means of a special form of interpretation (then quite common), in which he sees in "seed" (which could be either singular or plural) a "corporate solidarity" in Christ. That is, Christ is the "seed" about whom God made promises, and all those who are "in Christ" are also the "seed" (v. 29).[5] This provides an important clarification, for readers of the Bible might be led to think that the "seed of Abraham" refers to all Israelites and, furthermore, they might wonder how it is that Paul can claim that Gentiles are under the covenant of Abraham. By stating that Christ is the "seed," Paul interprets Genesis 13:15 and 24:7 in a Christian manner and reveals that the Abrahamic covenant is the one that climaxes in Christ and those who believe in him.

The application of the analogy (v. 17). Now that Paul has shown that the covenant of Abraham applies to Christians, he applies the analogy of the law of covenants of inheritance. And his point is quite simple: The law of Moses was given 430 years (Exod. 12:40—42) after the covenant was made with Abraham; therefore, since the covenant (made with Abraham, not Moses) is irrevocable, the law cannot change the arrangements God made with Abraham. This means that the promise stands firm and the mode of relating to God is faith rather than works of the law.

What is the "covenant of Abraham"? It has been customary, in theology, to prefer the term *testament* for a unilateral (one-sided) arrangement, initiated and carried out by one person, and to use the term *covenant* for a bilateral arrangement. There were two Greek terms for *covenant: diatheke* and *syntheke*, the latter clearly implying equality of partners. It is also clear that Greek translators of the Hebrew term *berith* did not want to make the covenant of Abraham to sound like a mutual arrangement of equal parties, so they chose the term *diatheke.* In the history of discussion, some theologians have stressed the unilateral nature of God's covenant with Abraham and have sometimes even preferred the expression the "testament of Abraham." And, of course, this has become the standard way Christians describe the Bible: Old Testament and New Testament.

On the other hand, since there is clearly an obligation on the part of the persons (Abraham and his corporate "seed") to commit themselves to the obligations of the covenant (i.e., circumcision, obedience to the law, surrender),

---

5. See R. Y. K. Fung, *Galatians,* 155—56.

other theologians prefer the translation "covenant." I shall use the term *covenant* because I agree that, while God's arrangement with Abraham was sovereignly initiated and established, Abraham did have an obligation to live within the parameters established by God.[6] Their relationship, however, was by no means equal, and the covenant should never be understood as a mutually agreed upon agreement.

The original promise given to Abraham[7] (cf. Gen. 12:2–3; 17:1–8) had within it eight separate promises: (1) offspring, (2) blessing for Abraham, (3) a great name, (4) blessing or cursing, depending on how one treated Abraham, (5) occupancy of the Promised Land, (6) blessing of Gentiles, (7) God being God to his people, and (8) kings descending from Abraham. This promise, I believe, was administered, in the history of God's dealing with humans, in three separate covenantal arrangements: (1) the covenant of circumcision from Abraham to Moses, (2) the covenant of Moses from Moses to Christ, and (3) the new covenant from Christ to the end of time. From this brief sketch on "how to read the Bible," we can see the crucial role Abraham played in being the one with whom God set up his promise and began his covenantal arrangements.

Promise to Abraham	Circumcision	Mosaic	New
	Abraham–Moses	Moses–Christ	Promissory Administrative Christ–Kingdom

I believe also that this centrality of Abraham is exactly what Paul sees as askew in the Judaizers; they had elevated Moses over Abraham and so, in effect, missed out on the crucial promissory nature of God's covenants with his people. Paul, as anyone can see who reads Galatians 3, wants to anchor the essence of God's mode of relating to people in Abraham and not in Moses. That is why he says that "the law . . . does not set aside the *covenant* previously established by God and thus do away with the *promise* " (v. 17).

The restatement of the argument by analogy (v. 18). The promise of an inheritance rests on the promise; put differently, it rests on the covenantal arrangement established by the person. God gave a promise of great things to Abraham. He did this, says Paul, "through a promise." If, with the Judaizers,

---

6. For discussions, see T. E. McComiskey, *The Covenants of Promise: A Theology of the Old Testament Covenants* (Grand Rapids: Baker, 1985), esp. 59–93; L. L. Morris, *The Atonement* (Downers Grove, Ill.: InterVarsity Press, 1983), 14–42.

7. For this paragraph I am deeply indebted to my colleague and friend, T. E. McComiskey, in his book, *The Covenants of Promise.*

the Galatians think they will inherit the blessing of Abraham by works of the law, then God was wrong in how he set it all up. God did not demand of Abraham to obey the law. In fact, as Paul has shown, the law was not even around; it came 430 years later. This must mean that the way to inherit the blessing of Abraham (which the Judaizers and Galatians both want dearly to inherit) is the way Abraham got it: by faith in God's promises.

Paul seems to be going further: those who commit themselves to the law as the system of salvation nullify the promises of the Abrahamic covenant; those who commit themselves to the Abrahamic covenant as the system of salvation cannot ask the law of Moses also to save them. Why then, after all, did God give the law if everything was provided in the Abrahamic covenant? Good question, one that Paul answers next (vv. 19–25).

Bridging Contexts

OVER AND OVER we have seen that Paul's concern is the same: one is accepted by God through faith in Christ and not by doing the works of the law. Once again, this is Paul's point here: the covenant of Abraham, one participated in by faith, was God's original design for people. The law of Moses, participated in by works of the law, was a secondary revelation and is not the primary way God wants us to relate to him. All of this is "old stuff" by now, and we tend to tire of applying the same message from every passage.

What is new in this passage (and the next one) is something highly important for each person: namely, Paul sets out here for us how to read the Bible and put it together, even though he does not explicitly tell us this. At times when we are interpreting a passage in the Bible, we need to see what is behind what the author is saying and distill it to find the presuppositions of the author. Usually such presuppositions are not expressed, so we have to work hard at times to find them.

I have stated some of the presuppositions Paul is using in our passage in the commentary above. What we need to observe here is that, before we can apply this passage to our world, we need to have these presuppositions before us, for these presuppositions are what propel him forward in his argument and what give his arguments their foundation. So we must ask, How did Paul read his Bible as revealed in our passage?

First, Paul presupposed that the promise, or covenant, given to Abraham was the foundation of God's revelation to his people. Why does he bring up the analogy of the legal situation pertaining to a covenant (testament) and its irrevocability? Because he knows that it fits what he knows about how God wants to work with people. In other words, he knows that the law of Moses came after the covenant with Abraham; therefore he can make the law of Moses secondary to the covenant with Abraham—so much so that he has to spend six more verses of complex argument to reveal why God gave the law. Now all of this is *based upon the priority of the Abrahamic covenant*.

Second, Paul argues that the Abrahamic covenant is one of faith and not works of the law, even though Abraham was commanded by God to be circumcised (Gen. 17:9–27). But it is also clear that Paul does not bring in circumcision here because he knows (1) that the Judaizers will jump all over his case and (2) that Abraham was pronounced righteous *before* he was circumcised (thus he assumed that circumcision was not part of the original promise; cf. v. 6; also Rom. 4:9–12).

Third, Paul also assumes that, while the law has importance for shedding light on the Christian's ethical behavior, it is not as important for Christians as the Judaizers were claiming. Paul addresses this point in verses 19–25, and we postpone discussion of this point until then.

How then are we to read the Bible in an apostolic, Christian manner? We must begin with Abraham and let the Abrahamic covenant set the agenda for everything that follows. This means we must live before God in faith and do the "works of the law" as something that demonstrates our faith in God's promise, not as something that provides acceptance with God. Furthermore, Christians, who live in the era when the new covenant administers the Abrahamic promises, do not have to live by the law, since they have something better than the law to guide them: they have the Spirit. Does this rule out the law and teach us to throw away the books of Moses? Definitely not! What Paul teaches, and I will show this in our discussion of Galatians 5, is that those who live in the Spirit do exactly what God wants and so fulfill the law. They do everything the law ever wanted us to do and more.

In summary, Paul sets out a scheme for reading the Bible, a scheme drawn along historical lines. He evaluates the concept of legal covenants of inheritance and applies such to how God's covenant with Abraham relates to the law of Moses. This application, then, is a revelation on how to read the Bible. A chart of these relationships is set out here. I am assuming here some of the points that are not made by Paul until verses 19–25 and giving emphasis to the characteristics Paul mentions regarding the period from Abraham to Christ.

God → gives promise to Abraham by faith → which is fulfilled in Christ.
People who respond properly
    respond in faith.
Moses' law obtains after Abraham
    and only until Christ.
Jews are under sin and a curse
    during this time.

The promise of Abraham gives life, and, when Christ comes, it also gives the Spirit. The law of Moses brings a curse and does not bring life.

The scheme of Paul, then, is historical (from Abraham to Christ, with an intervention by Moses), and we do not operate with a Christian reading of Scripture if we do not see God's promises in Abraham as critical and fulfilled in Christ. Christ's work is not something totally new; it is the climactic fulfillment of the promises given to Abraham. When Abraham sacrificed the heifer, the she-goat, the ram, a turtledove, and a pigeon, and when God passed between this sacrifice (Gen. 15:9–21), what Abraham did not know (but we do) is that God was setting out for his Abrahamic people his first revelation of sacrifice that would pass through the Levitical rituals, the tabernacle, and the temple, and would come to its perfect completion in the sacrifice of Christ (v. 14; Heb. 8–10). We who trust in Christ's perfect sacrifice were, in effect, standing with Abraham when he accepted God's establishment of the covenant in Genesis 15.

HOW SHOULD WE read the Bible? Let me suggest a few ways in which the normal Christian reads the Bible, and let me also suggest that few people read the Bible with the depth of Paul because they have not been taught the important category of "covenantal interpretation."

First, most of us read the Bible in a highly *individual manner*. We read the Bible for personal blessing, personal guidance, and personal instruction, and we should. But sometimes our individual desires express a rank egocentric approach to life and Bible reading. This shows up when we seek constantly to gain an emotional experience, to gain approval with God for reading his Word as a discipline, to gain honor from others for our brilliance, to find a promise for the day, or to gain insights (tricky ones at that) for sermons and talks. While I know that God uses our highly individual desires to teach us something, I also know that frequently our individual approaches lead us to find meanings that are not there and teachings that are simply not accurate. One of the goals of this series is to help us to learn to interpret the Bible more accurately, both in its original meaning and its contemporary significance.

Second, we often read the Bible *apart from contexts*. Perhaps this is a result of the convention of a Bible separated into verses rather than paragraphs. Many Christians today like to read the Bible as if it were all like Proverbs—that is, as if it contained nothing but random sayings that have almost no connection to one another. But thankfully, more and more publishers are printing

Bibles in a paragraph format rather than a verse format. I believe this will encourage reading the Bible more contextually.

An example from Galatians 3:13 may suffice. If I am correct (and many agree with me here) that "us" here refers to Jewish Christians, then at one level it is incorrect to say that Christ freed "us Gentiles" from the curse of the law. My point is not mitigated even if I admit that it can apply to "us Gentiles" indirectly through the law written in our hearts. My point is this: reading the Bible simply by verses can lead anyone with a desire for application to think that "us" means "both Jews and Gentiles." Reading the Bible in this way leads us into misreading.

Third, we often read the Bible *without a big picture*. This, of course, is part of the problem of reading the Bible apart from contexts because the "big picture" is part of the context of a proper reading. There are three major "contexts": (1) the book in which the passage occurs; (2) the essential program of how to put the Bible together; and (3) the fundamental ideas of the Bible put together systematically. Since I am concerned here with the second, I will speak briefly to the first and third before getting to the second.

One major context for reading a passage is to understand it in light of the book's basic ideas. Just as it is important for readers today to know if a given statement about the truthfulness of universalism comes from a neoorthodox thinker (who thinks that all will eventually be saved) or from an orthodox thinker (who thinks that the term means that "all kinds" but not "everyone" will be blessed by God), so it is important for us today to know if we are quoting James or Paul or Matthew when we use the term *righteousness* (sometimes translated "justification").[8] Not reading contextually too easily results in misreadings.

For Galatians we simply need to read each passage in light of the whole book and then recognize that fuller ideas may be given to us as we read more of Paul's other letters and other books in the New Testament. For now we concentrate on Paul's letter to the Galatians. At the beginning we read: "Paul, an apostle—sent not from men nor by man . . . " (1:1). If this verse began Ephesians or 1 Thessalonians or almost any other of the Pauline letters, we would not get the import from it that we get from Galatians. But that is

---

8. We cannot engage in this interesting discussion. James states that Abraham and others are "justified by works and not faith alone" (James 2:24), whereas Paul teaches that we are "justified by faith alone" apart from works (Gal. 3:6–9). And Matthew shows that we must have "surpassing righteousness" (the same term, though a noun, as "justify" in James and Paul) to enter the presence of God (Matt. 5:20). I believe these three uses of the same terms can be synthesized, but we misunderstand James if we impose Paul's definitions on him, and the same applies in the other directions.

because we know that Paul is fighting Judaizers in Galatia who deny Paul's divine calling and who assert that Paul is nothing more than a Jerusalem missionary who has abbreviated the message of Jerusalem in order to gain more converts. So when Paul says "not from men" in verse 1, we gain a sharper focus as to what he is saying *because we know the context of the book, the context of what such expressions mean in their larger context of meaning*.

Another part of the "big picture" is our overall view of theology. We believe that the message of the Bible is unified and that, somehow, it can all be put together in a synthetic way. Anyone who believes this will want to synthesize seemingly discordant passages. I take but one example from Galatians (again from 3:6–9) and compare it to James 2:14–26. Paul teaches that justification is by faith alone, while James teaches that justification is by works and not by faith alone. At a formal level, this is a contradiction; but at a deeper theological level it is harmonious. Put together, which is part of the big picture, what we find is that while justification is by faith, saving faith is a faith that works. Paul needs to focus on one because he is doing battle with Judaizers who think a person must obey Moses to be justified; James needs to focus on the other because he is doing battle with some who said that simple creedal faith justifies. While each emphasizes one extreme, at a deeper level they can be put together by defining saving faith in a broader way. We must learn to read the Bible in such a way that our conclusions from one book do not contradict our conclusions from another book.

The third area of the "big picture" (the middle one in the list above) is our overall program of putting the Bible together. My reading of literature allows me to (over)simplify the possible approaches into two. The first teaches that God has always operated in one way with his people, and that way is outlined in the covenantal arrangement with Abraham. The second teaches that God has operated in different ways in different periods of history. The first is usually called "covenant theology"; the second, "dispensationalism."[9] I am

---

9. Three major books are T. E. McComiskey, *The Covenants of Promise*; C. C. Ryrie, *Dispensationalism Today* (Chicago: Moody, 1965); D. P. Fuller, *The Unity of the Bible* (Grand Rapids: Zondervan, 1992). Fuller is one of the few today who emphasize that law and grace are not opposites, and he shows that such an opposition is at the heart of both dispensationalism and covenant theology. He steers another course, one that is much closer to covenant theology than to dispensationalism. A convenient summary of classical covenant theology is M. H. Smith, "The Church and Covenant Theology," *Journal of the Evangelical Theological Society* 21 (1978): 47–65. More advanced readers will want to examine J. S. Feinberg, *Continuity and Discontinuity: Perspectives on the Relationship Between the Old and New Testaments. Essays in Honor of S. Lewis Johnson, Jr.* (Westchester, Ill.: Crossway Books, 1988), esp. 37–86, 131–78, 181–218, 221–59.

We must not think, however, that only "Scofield Bible readers" are dispensationalists (though they are a primary example of people who so read the Bible). Rather, anyone who

aware that this is an oversimplification of the issue. After all, some covenant theologians point out some of the "discontinuities" between the Old and New Covenants while emphasizing the "continuities." (Continuities and discontinuities usually apply to such ideas as the relationship of Israel to the church: Is Old Testament Israel now the church, or are they two completely different groups?) Correspondingly, some dispensationalists, while they clearly show the "discontinuities," also point out the "continuities." I must add that both systems emphasize the covenant, with the covenant theologians emphasizing the one covenant and the dispensationalists emphasizing the variety of ways (covenants) God has worked in history.

Furthermore, dispensationalism today is not what it was two and three decades ago; great changes are taking place.[10] I fit myself more into the covenant group, though I, with Daniel Fuller, do not want to stress the opposition of law and grace. I will expound more of a covenant approach in the paragraphs that follow because I believe that verse 15–18 are rooted in Paul's own form of covenant theology. What I want to emphasize in my discussion is the absolute importance of the Abrahamic covenant in reading the Bible from cover to cover.

Readers of the Bible need to understand the importance of God's promise to Abraham (Gen. 12:2–3; see also 13:14–17; 15:1–6; 17:1–8): that God would make him into a great nation (the theme of Israel), that God established his relationship with his people through a sacrifice (15:7–21), that God would bless Abraham and make his name great, that God would treat people the way people treated Abraham, and that God would bless the whole world through Abraham (the theme of universalism). We see also that what was expected of Abraham was faith (15:6) and obedience (17:9–21). What we find is that God's original promise to Abraham is the foundation of all his relationships with people from that time on and into eternity. In Abraham's promises we find the plan of God, his grand scheme of things for the world. God has entered into a relationship with his people, sworn by an irrevocable oath, and this is the only way people enter into fellowship with God. We also discover that Moses' law does not replace the Abrahamic promise, but it clarifies what God wants of his people who do believe in him. I believe that

---

makes radical distinctions between various periods in salvation history, at least one for the Old and New Covenants, can be classified under this general heading. Thus, the contemporary liberal theologian who positively dislikes the Old Testament may be described, however unwittingly, as in some sense a dispensationalist, for he or she may focus exclusively on Jesus Christ and the new relationship with God that he taught.

10. A recent book that seeks to record the modern changes in dispensationalism is C. A. Blaising and D. L. Bock, *Dispensationalism, Israel and the Church: The Search for Definition* (Grand Rapids: Zondervan, 1992).

in reading the Bible through Abrahamic covenant categories, we suddenly grasp the totality of the Bible—what God is doing and what he wants to do with his people.

What readers of the Bible can do here, if they wish to gain a grand perspective of what God is doing, is to trace his promises given to Abraham through the entire Bible in their daily Bible readings.[11] I suggest then that each person have a separate sheet of paper for each of the eight themes listed above and, while reading, make observations from separate chapters in the Bible on how these promises are working themselves out in the Bible. Is the option of reading the entire Bible through the eyes of the category of the covenant of Abraham only one among many? While surely people can read the Bible using other categories, this category is the one Paul used, and it therefore becomes an apostolic reading of the Bible. Remember, the heart of Paul's mystery was in effect a new reading of the Bible; his mystery related to the relationship of Gentiles and Israel to the promises of God given to Abraham. I can think of no better way to approach the Bible than through the covenant of Abraham.

The next step is to relate the fullness of the new covenant to the Abrahamic promise and covenant. What response is expected to God's promise to Abraham, and what is the response expected for the new covenant? What is the means of establishing the promises to Abraham and the new covenant? Who is the covenant of Abraham designed for, and for whom does God establish the new covenant? (Thus, what is the relationship of Israel to the church?) Other particular questions come to mind: What is the relationship of God's promise to Abraham that he would bless or curse people depending on how they relate to Abraham, on the one hand, and, on the other, how Jesus says something similar about how people respond to him (Matt. 10:32–33) and to his disciples (10:40–42)? Is there a relationship between the land promised to Israel (Gen. 13:14–17) and the world (Rom. 4:13; 8:20–21; Rev. 19:11–16)? One final question: What is the relationship of the law of Moses (which came 430 years after Abraham but is surely God's revealed will for his people) to the teachings of Jesus and Paul about God's indwelling Spirit? We shall touch on this question in our interpretation of the next passage.

---

11. For help, I recommend that readers find some of these references in T. E. McComiskey's tracing of these themes in *The Covenants of Promise*, 15–58.

Galatians 3:19–25

W

HAT, THEN, WAS the purpose of the law? It was
added because of transgressions until the Seed to
whom the promise referred had come. The law was
put into effect through angels by a mediator. ²⁰A mediator,
however, does not represent just one party; but God is one.

²¹Is the law, therefore, opposed to the promises of God?
Absolutely not! For if a law had been given that could impart
life, then righteousness would certainly have come by the law.
²²But the Scripture declares that the whole world is a prisoner
of sin, so that what was promised, being given through faith in
Jesus Christ, might be given to those who believe.

²³Before this faith came, we were held prisoners by the law,
locked up until faith should be revealed. ²⁴So the law was put
in charge to lead us to Christ that we might be justified by
faith. ²⁵Now that faith has come, we are no longer under the
supervision of the law.

I BELIEVE THIS section is the most important passage in the book of Galatians for understanding
the nature of Paul's theological argument against
the Judaizers. This passage tells us more what
lies behind Paul's arguments than any other passage. In fact, it is one of the
most important passages in all of Paul's letters when it comes to understanding the relationship of Christianity to the law of Moses, no small issue
for first-century Jewish Christians.

But being important does not necessarily mean it is easy to understand.
The debates that scholars have generated on this passage alone amount to
shelves and shelves of evidence, arguments, and debates. Due to the complexity of Paul's argument I can do no more than state my views here. Rarely
will I be able to argue even partially for the positions I take, and even more
rarely will I interact with opposing viewpoints at more than a superficial level.
Those who wish to follow up the debates and ponder the issues more completely will have to read in the works mentioned in the footnotes. I will begin
with an outline and then expound each section of that outline.

I. The Question About the Historical Purpose of the Law (vv. 19–20)
   A. The question (v. 19a)
   B. The answer (vv. 19b–20)
      1. The purpose of the law (v. 19b)
      2. The temporal limitations of the law (v. 19c)
      3. The circumstances of the giving of the law (vv. 19d-20)
II. The Question About the Historical Function of the Law (vv. 21–25)
   A. The question (v. 21a)
   B. The answer (v. 21b)
   C. The reason for the answer (vv. 21c–25)
      1. The inability of the law (v. 21c)
      2. The function of the law in history (v. 22a)
      3. The function of the promises in history (v. 22b)
      4. The explanation of the function of the law (vv. 23–25)
         a. Time elements of the law (v. 23)
         b. Effect of the law (v. 24a)
         c. Result of the law's effect (v. 24b)
         d. Suspension of the law (v. 25)

The Question About the Historical Purpose of the Law (vv. 19–20)

PAUL'S FIRST QUESTION arises naturally for every law-revering Jew: If it is the case that Abraham's covenant is paramount for God's relationship with his people, what then was the purpose of the law? Why did God even give the law if Abraham's covenant was adequate? Paul knew that many (perhaps most) Jews had lived as if the law were the foundation of one's relationship to God and the Abrahamic covenant were only the beginning of that relationship. He also knew that most thoughtful Jews would have argued for some sort of "progressive revelation": what God began in Abraham he perfected through the revelation to Moses. So it is no surprise that Paul would be interrogated thoroughly about how he saw the law in God's plan of redemption. Furthermore, the argument from analogy (vv. 15–18) was only an illustration of what Paul had already argued: that the Galatians themselves experienced everything good by faith rather than works (vv. 1–5), that Abraham himself was justified by faith (vv. 6–9), and that those under the law were under a curse (vv. 10–14). It is no wonder Paul had to pause and clarify the basis for everything: the law was never intended by God to do what the Judaizers were asking it to do, nor was it ever intended to be the socially restricting instrument it had become.

It would also have been natural for thoughtful Jews to wonder if Paul believed at all in the authority of the law of Moses; if they concluded that he did not, it would also have been natural for them to think of Paul as a deviant. This means that Paul's answer in this section is fundamentally important for the success of his mission and even more important for his own apostolic authority. If he cannot come up with an adequate response, Paul is done, the Judaizers will win, and the Galatians will convert to Judaism.

The *question* Paul raises ("What, then, was the purpose of the law?") is easy to understand. His *answer*, however, takes some unraveling. There are three cords wound together. He begins by talking about the *purpose* of the law (v. 19b), moves on to the *temporal limitations* of the law (v. 19c), and then concludes with some inferences from the *circumstances* surrounding the actual giving of the law to Moses (v. 19d–20). Before proceeding to expound these, I think it might be helpful if we sketched over the way Christians have seen the role of the law and how it relates to Christians today.

Essentially, there are three answers to the purpose of the law in the history of the church. (1) The first sees the law *abrogated* by Christ and the new era inaugurated by the Spirit. For these people, the law no longer has any binding relationship to Christians; it belongs completely to a bygone era. While this view has sometimes been associated most significantly with an early heretic, Marcion, one need not deny any central Christian doctrines to espouse this view. (2) The second view contends that the law was God's *first but incomplete revelation of his will* and that his will has now been completely revealed through Christ and through the teachings of the New Testament as inspired by the Holy Spirit. For these people, the law is God's will, but it is not completely his will for his church. Furthermore, Christians, while they are not subject to the law or "under the law," find in the law preliminary principles for living but find also that, in living in faith and in the Spirit, they do all that the law asked for and more. (3) The third view is that the law of Moses *remains prescriptive* for the church as well. The law, for these people, was the revealed will of God for his people and remains that will; however, these people also contend that God's will cannot be performed properly unless one has the Spirit of God. Then the Christian does what God wants, and that is revealed in the law.

How important is our view on the law? Very important! Theologians have distinguished three "uses" of the Law: (1) in society as God's moral check and guideline for civil law; (2) in history and personal life as God's means of revealing sin in order to drive people to trust in his grace; (3) in the church as a guideline for Christian ethics. Our concern here is primarily with the so-called "third use of the law" (*tertius usus legis*).[1] Do we check our lives against the Ten Commandments or not? Do we seek out Exodus, Leviticus, and Deuteronomy when we seek to live honorably before God, or do we seek out what Jesus wants of us and what God's Spirit is saying to us (as confirmed through the New Testament)? Do we have any arguments for social issues in our day (e.g., capital punishment, marriage and divorce laws) that can be derived from the New Testament, or do we have to go to the Old Testament for such answers? This brings us right back to Paul's question: Why did God give the law? Did he give it for us (as Christians) or only for Jews of a bygone era? Our answer to the question about the importance of this discussion is clear; we must find how the law relates to us today.

First, Paul answers the question by stating the *purpose of the law* (v. 19b): "it was added because of transgressions." Scholars here are divided: Should we translate "It was added *because of* transgressions," or "It was added *for the purpose of revealing* transgressions"? Put differently, which came first: sin or the law? Did God add the law because the people were sinning, or did the people suddenly learn that they were sinning because God gave the law? Later Paul states that the law does not give life (vv. 21–22) but is a teacher (v. 24); elsewhere he says that "through the law we become conscious of sin" (Rom. 3:20; cf. 7:7) and that when there is no law there is no sin (4:15; cf. 5:13). Romans 5:20 states that "the law was added so that the trespass might increase" (cf. 7:13). Thus, I conclude with many who see the *purpose of the law* as being that it was given in order to reveal certain kinds of behavior as sinful.[2] The law, then, was a judging instrument for the people of God; through its written code they learned that certain behavior was contrary to God's will. We might diagram it thus:

Abraham — Israel's bad behavior — Law of Moses — SIN.

---

1. Since Luther and Calvin, there has been great debate on this "third use of the law." See J. Calvin, *Institutes of the Christian Religion*, ed. J. T. McNeill; trans. F. L. Battles (Philadelphia: Westminster, 1975), 2:348–66. A Lutheran view is seen in J. T. Mueller, *Christian Dogmatics* (St. Louis: Concordia, 1955), 470–85; a Reformed view is seen in L. Berkhof, *Systematic Theology* (4th ed.; Grand Rapids: Eerdmans, 1941), 612–15; and a more charismatic (renewal) view can be seen in J. R. Williams, *Renewal Theology: Salvation, the Holy Spirit, and Christian Living* (Grand Rapids: Zondervan, 1990), 100–17, esp. 115–16. This entire issue is explored in depth in the articles and responses by Greg Bahnsen, Walter Kaiser, Jr., Douglas Moo, Wayne Strickland, and Willem VanGemeren in *The Law, the Gospel, and the Modern Christian: Five Views* (Grand Rapids: Zondervan, 1993).

2. So F. F. Bruce, *Galatians*, 175; R. N. Longenecker, *Galatians*, 138; R. Y. K. Fung, *Galatians*, 159–60. Thus, I would amend the NIV to read: "it was added to reveal transgressions."

The second part of Paul's answer on the historical purpose of the law pertains to *the temporal limitations of the law* (v. 19c): "until the Seed to whom the promise referred had come." Here is Paul's most radical statement: the law was to govern God's people for only a certain number of years. In other words, God gave the law (1) to reveal bad behavior as transgression of his moral law but (2) only until Messiah had come. Thus, our diagram:

Abraham — Israel's bad behavior — Law of Moses — SIN — Christ.

Finally, Paul speaks about the *circumstances of the giving of the law* (vv. 19d–20) and infers that the law is inferior to the promise because of these circumstances. The underlying assumption here is that an arrangement between a person and God that has mediators is inferior to an arrangement that has no mediators, because the latter arrangement is directly from God. Paul is also assuming that the arrangement with Abraham, the covenant established through Genesis 12 and 15, is one that had no mediation; for that reason alone it is superior.

The first comments in verse 19d-e assume that God gave the law through angels[3] and that the mediator himself was Moses.[4] Thus:

GOD

X X X X X X X X X X X X (Angels)

Moses

Israel at Sinai

is inferior to:

GOD

Abraham

The law, then, has a dual mediation: angels stood between the people and God, and so does Moses. This means that the law is inferior to the promise of Abraham and that the Judaizers must be wrong in arguing for the prior-

---

3. See also Acts 7:38, 53; Heb. 2:2. That angels were involved in the giving of the law at Sinai is not clear in the Old Testament (cf. Deut. 33:2 and the Septuagint version of Pss. 102:20; 103:4). But this view was apparently common in Judaism (cf. Josephus, *Antiquities* 15:136). For discussion, see F. F. Bruce, *Galatians*, 175–76; R. N. Longenecker, *Galatians*, 139–40.

4. On Moses as mediator, see Exodus 20:19; Deuteronomy 5:5; Hebrews 8:6; 9:15, 19. See again R. N. Longenecker, *Galatians*, 140–41.

ity of Mosaic law. But note that this is a point tacked on by Paul. His first point is that the law was given (1) to reveal sin (not to bring life to God's people), and (2) to reveal sin only until Christ came (and the Spirit, who convicts; cf. John 16:7–11).

The Question About the Historical Function of the Law (vv. 21–25)

PAUL MUST NOW address the issue from a slightly different angle: having established that the law was given to reveal sin and for only a limited time, he must now ask another question: Is the law actually working against the purposes of God in the Abrahamic promise (v. 21a)?

The answer (v. 21b). Again, the question makes the issue explicit, but the explanation involves considerable complexity. Paul's answer is simple: "Absolutely not!" But the Judaizers are not satisfied and Paul knows that. He has just spent the better part of twenty verses putting the law in its place and, in their view, he has depreciated it. Furthermore, merely saying that the law is not contrary to the promises does not mean that Paul is cleared of their charges. So Paul must explain.

The reason for the answer (vv. 21c–25). Paul first states four basic things here: he speaks to the inability of the law first (v. 21c), then to the function of the law in history (v. 22a), next to the function of the promises in history (v. 22b), and finally to an explanation for the function of the law (vv. 23–25). I will look briefly at each.

First, Paul talks about *the essential inability of the law to bring saving life* (v. 21c). Here once again the Judaizer will be upset: Jewish history and tradition had elevated the law to that which God uses to redeem his people. Mishnah Aboth 2:8 says, in an interesting list of wisdom, "lots of Torah, lots of life," and then says, "If he has gotten teachings of Torah, he has gotten himself life eternal."[5] The law and knowledge of it is what separated Israel from the rest of the sinful world and what marked them out as God's holy people. But Paul counters their elevation of the law. He performs this countering move by assuming that the Judaizers were Christians, and so he assumes that justification is by faith (and not by works of the law). Assuming this, he says, "If a law had been given that could impart life, then righteousness would certainly have come by the law." But righteousness did not come via the law, because the promise was given to those who, like Abraham, believed. In effect, Paul's

---

5. This text is clearly from a period much later than the New Testament and Paul. I use it here simply to illustrate what was probably believed by many faithful law-observant Jews in New Testament times.

argument is that the law is not intended to bring life;[6] therefore, the Judaizers cannot be demanding the Galatians to follow the law of Moses *in order to be accepted by God.*

Paul now moves on to discuss *the function of both the law and the promises in history.* In these statements he simply repeats (in different words) what he has already stated or assumed in verses 19–20. The function of the *law* (v. 22a) was to declare "that the whole world is a prisoner of sin." That is, the purpose of the law[7] was to reveal sin (cf. v. 19). The law did this in order to clarify the function of the promises in history (v. 22b): "so that what was promised . . . might be given to those who believe." Paul here relates the condemning function of the law with the life-giving function of the promise.

To further our diagram above, we offer the following (updated) chart:

God	God	
	Angels	
	Moses	
Abraham		CHRIST
Life ----Israel's bad behavior --------Law of Moses-------SIN----		Life
Faith	confining all (Jews?)	Faith

|---- Era of the law --------|

Works of the law

The next three verses (vv. 23–25) outline Paul's *explanation of the function of the law.* He largely restates what has been said before about both the purpose of the law and its time limitations, but this time he uses other terms. He deals with the time elements (v. 23), the effect of the law (v. 24a), and its result (v. 24b). The conclusion of the entire section concerns the suspension of the law (v. 25).

First, Paul speaks of *the time elements of the law* (v. 23). At verse 19 Paul had said that the law was to "reveal sin" until the Seed had come; now he says the same thing but uses different expressions for both elements. Instead of "Seed," Paul uses "faith"; instead of "revealing sin," Paul uses "held prisoners." But there is no essential difference in what he is saying. The law reveals Israel's sinfulness and, in effect, holds Israel as prisoner. The "Seed" is Christ, and when Christ comes it is the era of faith. While some readers might think that "faith" here is the personal response of an individual, that is not what Paul means. He is now talking about the *era* of faith as eclipsing the era of "works

---

6. Life here means spiritual life (cf. Rom. 8:11; 1 Cor. 15:22, 36; 2 Cor. 3:6).

7. Paul uses the term "Scripture" for "law" here. This is the obvious implication of the parallels between v. 23 and vv. 24–25.

of the law," just as the era of the law is superseded by the era of Christ and the Spirit. To do the "works of the law" is to live in the wrong era.

Second, he addresses *the effect of the law* (v. 24a). The law held those under it (probably Jews) as prisoners and locked them up. What this means[8] is that "the law was put in charge to lead us." This latter expression is a free translation of what literally translates, "the law has become our pedagogue [Gk. *paidagogos*]." A "pedagogue," while sometimes used to describe a positive image, here describes the law's confining and imprisoning work—as is seen in verse 25, where we are no longer under the pedagogue (that verse parallels the law's imprisoning work of vv. 22–23), and in 4:2–3, where the time under a pedagogue is compared to a time of children being enslaved. Thus, the effect of the law was that it was an imprisoning pedagogue *eis Christon* ("unto Christ").

This last expression has two possible meanings, the differences of which are great. The first takes it in an educative function: "the law was our pedagogue to lead us to Christ." This view is a common, traditional view, which sees the law as pointing out our sins so we will cry out for God's grace in Christ.[9] But besides the fact that Paul is not talking here about "individual experience" but rather about "salvation history," he does not teach in Galatians that this is the purpose of the law. True enough, Paul does teach that the law "reveals sin" and "imprisons," but he does not say that it does these things to "lead us to Christ" but to condemn us. The second view is therefore to be preferred: "the law was our pedagogue *until* Christ." This view is not only the majority view today but is also contextually more compatible.[10] The line of thinking about the law in verses 19–25 is temporal: the law had a limited function (revealing, imprisoning) for a limited time (until the Seed, until Christ). Notice the time dimensions: "until the Seed" (v. 19), "before this faith came" (v. 23), "until faith" (v. 23), "now that faith has come" (v. 25). Our text only makes sense if "to Christ" means that the law had a confining ministry until the era of Christ came.

Third, Paul turns to *the result of the law's effect* (v. 24b). The word order of the Greek sentence is important in order to gain Paul's point: "that on the basis of faith we might be justified." All of Paul's argument assumes that the Judaizers agree that justification begins with faith in Christ; they also mistakenly assume that the "works of the law" perfect that faith. But now that Paul has

---

8. Galatians 3:24 begins with *hoste;* "what all this means" is our paraphrase of this word.

9. See above, footnote 1. It has been especially emphasized by Lutherans, but Reformed theologians give it considerable emphasis as well.

10. So F. F. Bruce, *Galatians*, 183; R. N. Longenecker, *Galatians*, 148–49.

shown that the law pertains to a limited time, he can say that justification is solely by faith because "works of the law" now pertain to a bygone era.

Finally, Paul draws it all together by speaking of *the suspension of the law* (v. 25). His words in this verse are strong. He claims that the era of Christ eclipses the era of Moses because the era of Christ is the climax of the promise of Abraham. The law had a limited purpose, and this purpose was only for a limited time—until the Seed had come. The expression "under the supervision of the law" once again translates the term *paidagogos* ("pedagogue"). As in verse 24, this term here does not define a positive role for the law. Rather, it refers once again to the "condemning" and "imprisoning" function of the law (cf. vv. 22–23). So, in effect, Paul says that once faith came, the law could no longer condemn us. Why? We can only reason that it is because Christ (who starts the age of faith) absorbed the curse of the law (cf. vv. 10–14).

To use Paul's words, I now use "an example from everyday life" (v. 15). I often compare the role of the law in history to the role typewriters have played in the development of word processing. The technology and idea of a typewriter was eventually developed into an electronic, faster, and far more complex computer that does word processing. But when typing on a computer, one realizes that one is still using the old manual typewriter's technology. Further, one realizes that the computer far transcends what the typewriter was. Everything that a typewriter wanted to be when it was a little boy (and more!) is now found in the computer. This compares to the law. Everything the law wanted to be when it was young (as revealed to Moses) is found now in Christ and in life in the Spirit. Thus, when a Christian lives in the Spirit and under Christ, that Christian is not living contrary to the law but is living in transcendence of the law. And it is for this very reason that life lived primarily under the law is wrong.

When the computer age arrived, we put away our manual typewriters because they belonged to the former era. Paul's critique of the Judaizers is that they are typing on manual typewriters after computers are on the desk! He calls them to put the manual typewriters away. But in putting them away, we do not destroy them. We fulfill them by typing on computers. Every maneuver on a computer is the final hope of the manual typewriter. "Now that faith/Christ has come, we are no longer under the supervision of the law"— but not because the law is contrary to the promises; rather, it is because the law is fulfilled in Christ and the Spirit in a manner similar to the way a typewriter is fulfilled in the technology of a computer. And I am profoundly thankful for both!

Put together, Paul argues that the Judaizers are wrong (and those Galatian Christians who follow them) because they do not understand why God gave the law. They do not know that it was designed to turn Israel's bad behaviors into transgressions of God's law. Nor do they know that it was given for only a short period; we might talk here about the "parenthesis of the law." Consequently, they do not know that everything for salvation and acceptance with God is established in Abraham. Consequently, they do not know that imposing the law after Christ has come is a gross stepping back in God's plan of redemption to a previous era. It is B.C. lifestyle in an A.D. period. Essentially, Paul's argument against the Judaizers is historical and biblical: they do not understand what God's plan of salvation was all about as he progressively revealed himself, beginning with Abraham and continuing with Moses until Christ (see also Rom. 6:11–14; 7:7–13; 11:25–32; 2 Cor. 3:7–18; Phil. 3:2–11).

Bridging Contexts

THE BEST PLACE to begin is with Paul's conclusion: "We are no longer under the supervision of the law" (v. 25). As I stated above, "supervision" here refers to the imprisoning ministry of the law. I think this statement is similar to Paul's statement, written a few years later, to the Romans: "Therefore, since we have been justified through faith, we have peace with God" (Rom. 5:1). It is also similar to Romans 8:1–2: "Therefore, there is now no condemnation for those who are in Christ Jesus, because through Christ Jesus the law of the Spirit of life set me free from the law of sin and death." Those who trust in Christ are immune from the curse and condemnation of the law. Its "pedagogical" (imprisoning) role has come to an end with the arrival of Christ.

The obvious implication of the suspension of the law for Galatians is that the Judaizers are doubly wrong: not only have they misunderstood the purpose of the law (it was to reveal sin, not give life), but they have also not understood that it now pertains to a bygone era. Thus, the concern of Paul is once again established: we gain our identity before God on the basis of our faith in, and faithfulness to, Jesus Christ, not on the basis of our conformity to Mosaic law. This can be moved into our world quite simply, as we have done so frequently in this commentary. Yet another argument against legalizing movements and concerns in the church today is that the era of the law is over. Since we have worked the theme of legalism in the world and churches today so often in the previous pages, it would be good for us to move our applications here in a slightly different direction. What I will do in our "Bridging Contexts" and "Contemporary Significance" sections is to explore the significance of the suspension of the law for moral life today.

The tendency here is extremes. It is frequently stated that Christians are not under the law, but there are Christians who think they must reconstruct the world on the basis of Old Testament law.[11] But in what sense are Christians not under the law? Are Christians exempted from the law being a preliminary sketch of God's moral will? Or are they exempted from it being their sure guide to a noble life before God? We should note that Paul never excuses Christians from disobeying the law because they are not "under the law." Instead, Paul expects Christians to live the law by living "under the Spirit" (v. 18). Jesus taught something similar for his followers (Matt. 5:20; 7:12; 22:34–40). So being freed from the law does not mean being freed from every purpose, use, or implication of the law of God. Furthermore, it is clear from the numerous quotations from the Old Testament found throughout Paul's letters (as in Gal. 3:6–14) that Paul does not think the law is suspended in every sense. The law remains authoritative for him, and he quotes it as the foundation of his arguments.

So as we move to our world with Paul's statement that now that faith has come we are no longer under the law, we know that the law has not been destroyed and annulled. Rather, it is no longer the *primary arrangement for acceptance with God*, and it is no longer *a means of separating Israel (the people of God) from other nations in some exclusive sense.* The law is not the "contractual obligation" under which the Christian lives. It was not designed to give us life before God (v. 21). But it remains valuable—highly valuable—for our clarification of ethics, as long as it is understood in light of what Paul teaches about its fulfillment (Rom. 10:4), the "law of Christ" (Gal. 6:2), and the impact that the Holy Spirit has on our relationship to the law (cf. chaps. 5–6).[12]

Furthermore, any reasonable reader would agree that Paul's statement that the law "was added because of transgressions," meaning "it was added to reveal transgressions" (see above), remains a continuing function of the law. If the law is holy and good (Rom. 7:12), then it follows that it still reveals God's

---

11. This is the position of the theonomists; for example, see Greg L. Bahnsen, "The Theonomic Reformed Approach to Law and Gospel," in *The Law, the Gospel, and the Modern Christian: Five Views* (Grand Rapids: Zondervan, 1993), 93–143. Two carefully worked out positions on the place of the law in Christian living can be seen in Knox Chamblin, "The Law of Moses and the Law of Christ," and Douglas J. Moo, "The Law of Moses or the Law of Christ," in *Continuity and Discontinuity*, ed. J. S. Feinberg (Westchester, Ill.: Crossway, 1988), 181–202, 203–18. See also Moo's "The Law of Christ as the Fulfillment of the Law of Moses: A Modified Lutheran Approach," in *The Law, the Gospel, and the Modern Christian*, 319–76. Moo's latter work and my view sketched in this chapter differ only in minor details; the general view that the law is no longer the direct authority for Christians is the same.

12. An attempt to work this out can be seen in W. C. Kaiser, Jr., *Toward Old Testament Ethics* (Grand Rapids: Zondervan, 1983).

will, albeit not the fullness of that will. And if it reveals his will, then it will reveal sin. And if, in addition, the law has been given by God to increase sinfulness to God's people (cf. Rom. 5:20), it most likely will continue to do so. I think, then, that while the law has been suspended as a "contractual obligation" or as the "covenant between people and God," it has not been suspended as a preliminary statement of God's will, nor has it been suspended as a moral check on all human behavior. To revert to my typewriter-computer analogy, when we use a computer we are conscious that what is before us is a typewriter nonetheless (even if it is much more). It is a development of that typewriter, but it is the typewriter that has been developed. So I believe the law retains its functions of (1) giving us a sketch of God's moral will for us and (2) convicting people of their sin. But how these two uses of the law work themselves out for people who are filled with God's Spirit is even more important; I will touch on this issue below and later at 5:16–26. General conclusions in Paul's letters must be understood in such a way that they do not conflict with the message of Paul and the Bible.

Once again we are confronted by a text whose primary purpose was to speak to a Jewish problem, the problem of being under the law. This was not a problem for Gentiles since they neither knew the law nor lived under it the way Jews did. It was Jews who raised the questions about the purpose of the law in history and how the law relates to the Abrahamic promises. Jewish privilege seemed to be undermined (cf. Rom. 3:9–20; 9:1–5). But we have two points to make in defense of the view that the law of God, and specifically its purpose of condemning people as sinful, is just as applicable to Gentiles as it is to Jews.

First, I made a point earlier that Gentiles have the law written in their hearts (see Rom. 2:14–16). Thus, at some level, they are also responsible to God's moral will. Now it may not be clear precisely what they know about God's law, but it is clear enough from Paul that they know enough to get in trouble. "Hence, even though the Gentiles do not have the law publicly given to Israel, they have it in all essentials privately."[13] Our point remains valid here. If the law was designed to reveal sin, then it follows that, to the degree that Gentiles know God's law in their hearts and consciences, their sins also have been revealed. Second, Paul says in verse 22 that "the whole world is a prisoner of sin." This expression "whole world" is a translation of *ta panta* ("the everyone/everything," "the whole world"), and the majority of commentators think this describes not just Jews but "everyone in the world without distinction." So while it is reasonable to think that really only Jews are under the

---

13. J. R. Williams, *Renewal Theology: God, the World, and Redemption* (Grand Rapids: Zondervan, 1988), 239–40, quotation taken from 239.

law, it still follows (for reasons Paul does not say here) that "everyone" has received the law's sentence of condemnation for not following it.

These two reasons allow us to say that it is fairly natural for us to think that all humans have sinned, whether they have transgressed God's written law (which they have heard in the Bible somehow) or God's law written in the human heart. If we add, on top of this, the inflaming conviction of God's Spirit (John 16:7–11), then it is also clear that we have every right to think that most humans know they are sinful (whether they suppress this or not). This is a great platform on which to build evangelism.

ONE OF THE most significant implications of these verses is the conclusion that God's law (meaning the law of Moses—primarily Exodus, Leviticus, and Deuteronomy) has been in some sense suspended for the Christian. The Mosaic law is a preliminary glimpse of God's will for his people. How then do we work out moral problems today in light of this view of the law? Perhaps we could try to work out a moral problem in the light of what we know about verses 19–25.

First, Christians must begin with two assumptions: (1) that faith is the response God wants of us if we are to be accepted by him and that this faith works itself out in obedience;[14] and (2) that life in the Spirit (under the Spirit) is our primary mode of operation as we seek to live obediently before God. This has an important corollary: *Christians who are seeking God's will do not turn first of all to the law of Moses for direction.* Instead, they listen to God's Spirit and to the teachings of Jesus ("the law of Christ"; see 6:2); both of these teach them that they are to "love God" and "love others." In following the Spirit and Christ, the Christian will always do what the law tried to tell them to do. Thus, they will actually do God's will.

What if there are no directions in the New Testament, and what if the Spirit does not seem to speaking with clarity? This question about the Spirit deserves some discussion. I want to begin by saying that few Christians today believe that the Spirit of God is the central focus for Christian ethics.

---

1. Since Luther and Calvin, there has been great debate on this "third use of the law." See J. Calvin, *Institutes of the Christian Religion*, ed. J. T. McNeill; trans. F. L. Battles (Philadelphia: Westminster, 1975), 2:348–66. A Lutheran view is seen in J. T. Mueller, *Christian Dogmatics* (St. Louis: Concordia, 1955), 470–85; a Reformed view is seen in L. Berkhof, *Systematic Theology* (4th ed.; Grand Rapids: Eerdmans, 1941), 612–15; and a more charismatic (renewal) view can be seen in J. R. Williams, *Renewal Theology: Salvation, the Holy Spirit, and Christian Living* (Grand Rapids: Zondervan, 1990), 100–17, esp. 115–16. This entire issue is explored in depth in the articles and responses by Greg Bahnsen, Walter Kaiser, Jr., Dou-

I believe, in fact, that Christians treat the New Testament more like a second Mosaic law than as a witness to God's Spirit leading his new people. Paul saw the Judaizers as "law-centered," and he wanted a church of people who were "Spirit-centered." But we cannot be detained by this perspective, since we are assuming that Christians do believe in the Spirit's guidance, can follow it, and will do what God's Spirit says.

I continue the question asked above. What if the New Testament teaching and the Spirit's prompting seem to conflict with the law of Moses and the witness of the books of Moses? How then do we operate? I could go on and on about principles of moral conduct, but it is probably best for us to proceed by working through the biblical evidence for a specific example, for in that way the newness of Paul's ethic is seen more clearly. So we shall look at one test case—how Christians today should participate in *international warfare*.[15]

The main question is: Should Christians go to war? It is not my purpose here to resolve what has become, at times, a bone of contention among Christians (though if I could resolve the issue once and for all, I would). My purpose here is more limited. I want to examine *how we make such a moral decision as Christians in light of Paul's view that the law has been suspended*. In other words, we are concerned here with method and not with answers, though some answers will be suggested. Because of the need to illustrate the complexity of moving from the Old Testament into our world, I will need to spend more time on this issue than would otherwise be done.

I begin with a partial sketch of how this moral issue is treated today in evangelical churches. Fortunately, there is no impending war that could cloud our thinking on the issue. Unfortunately, however, too many conservative Christians have infrequently taken this issue as a serious one. Certainly life is precious, and the taking of another person's life is a serious act with lifelong consequences for the one who takes that other person's life. Murder itself is prohibited by God (Exod. 20:13) and no Christian would want to be involved in murdering another person. While I am not necessarily arguing that bloodshed in war is murder, I do believe we can agree that murder is wrong and so the taking of another person's life must be treated as a moral issue.

---

15. Two books that procedurally have no specific agenda other than exposing Christians to all sides are: (1) R. G. Clouse, ed., *War: Four Christian Views* (Downers Grove, Ill.: InterVarsity Press, 1981), which has contributions by H. A. Hoyt, M. S. Augsburger, A. F. Holmes, and H. O. J. Brown; each responds to the others views; (2) J. A. Bernbaum, ed., *Perspectives on Peacemaking: Biblical Options in the Nuclear Age* (Ventura, Calif.: Regal Books, 1984), which was published under the direction of the Christian College Coalition. This latter book contains the papers given during a conference on the subject at Pasadena in the spring of 1983. Both books are models of Christian discussion of difficult, emotional, but crucial issues that face us.

Once again, unfortunately, in the last fifteen years in the United States particularly, patriotism has become connected to the center of Christianity for many people. Though I believe that it is good to be patriotic, to submit to our governing authorities, and to pray for them (so Rom. 13:1–7; Titus 3:1; 1 Peter 2:13–17), I also believe that patriotism at times has to bow to submission to God's will (Acts 4:1–22). So we need to think about how Christians are to respond to international conflict, not just "fall in line" with the government. There may be times when we will agree (and go to war) and times when we will not (and become conscientious objectors). Regardless, we must think through the issue before God and ask what he would have us do.

One final point: economical advantage in the Western world is not the sole foundation for making a decision about international conflict. Ours is a materialistic world, and I hope everyone agrees with me here. Indeed, I am not sure that we are all as aware as we ought to be of how economically driven and motivated our political and international decisions actually are. There have been those who have argued (forcefully at times) that some, even most, of U.S. involvement in international conflict has been exclusively motivated by self-interest in economical matters. I am one who thinks that such concerns often motivate our government; I am also of the view that economical concerns are not necessarily bad. What we need here is Christian thinking on the matter. When our government decides that international conflict is appropriate and necessary over a certain issue, then it is fundamentally important for Christians to determine whether or not they will be involved for such a motivation. Perhaps at times Christians will decide to go to war (just war theory) and at other times not. What we must do is make that decision before God on solid biblical grounds, not just for personal economical advantages.

I see four basic approaches that Christians have taken. What I mean here is not four positions, but four ways of making decisions about Christian involvement. The first approach seeks for the texts *about patriotism, usually limited to zeal, and the pursuit of justice* in the whole Bible (e.g., Num. 25; Joshua–Judges; 1 Kings 18–19; Rom. 13:1–7; 1 Peter 2:13–17), and contends that, since the Bible enjoins the people of God to be patriotic and to pursue justice, then Christians should be and do the same; this means participating in war. It is obvious that some major leaps are involved in this move from Bible times to the twentieth century. To name but three considerations: (1) Patriotism to a nation that is theocratic (as Israel was) is much different than to a nation that is secular and democratic. (2) The texts that speak of "submission" to government are spoken in contexts of peace and by people who, at times, were willing to disobey government (e.g., Peter at Acts 4:1–22); thus they should not be taken as blanket endorsements of governing authorities. (3) Why patriotism means willingness to go to war and do combat is not clear. Is there perhaps some other way of being patriotic? How, after all, is a Christian patriotic? Some Christians, as most readers would know, refuse to swear an oath of allegiance to any "flag" since their only allegiance is to Christ. In spite of some important points raised by this approach to the whole issue, patriotism is too narrow of an angle on the biblical evidence, and there are too many ill-defined maneuvers here.

A second approach has been to examine Old Testament *texts on war* as the critical biblical evidence. As might be expected, three conclusions have followed. (1) For some, the Old Testament evidence on war (e.g., Deut. 7; 20; Joshua–Judges; 1–2 Samuel)[16] leads them to think that God initiates wars, guides them, and stands behind the victors; thus, war must not be seen as immoral. Since the God of the Old Testament is involved in wars and since the Christian God is the same God, then it follows that Christians can also be involved in wars. Usually this means there is a demand to be discerning of which side God is on and which side is right, and then participating on that side (just war theory). (2) Others contend that Christians must encourage a more enterprising approach: they may have to be on the side of an aggressive government that is making the world more just and equitable (crusade/preventive war theory). (3) Still others have contended that Old Testament wars, while they certainly existed, are unlike any kinds of wars fought today because the wars of Israel were actually spiritual wars fought by the Lord himself.[17]

This approach to the issue of war deserves some response, though I can give such only briefly here. First, I commend this approach for tackling what I believe to be some of the most important evidence that has to be considered: the Old Testament texts describing not only warfare but God's initiation and support of such. But, second, I must admit that this is where a Christian approach to the matter is fundamentally important. While it may be true that God participated in war in the Old Testament period, what is the responsibility of Christians in the New Testament period (our era)? It is interesting (and perhaps illuminating) that no one in the New Testament is a known warrior for Israel, and no one is known for military violence as a Christian. In fact, church historians are generally agreed that early Christians

---

16. A sketch of Old Testament wars can be found in K. N. Schoville, "War; Warfare," in *NISBE*, ed. G. W. Bromiley (Grand Rapids: Eerdmans, 1988), 4:1013–18, and, in the same encyclopedia, P. C. Craigie, "War, Idea of," 4:1018–21.

17. This view has been expounded by M. C. Lind, *Yahweh Is a Warrior* (Scottdale, Pa.: Herald Press, 1980).

only at the end of the second century A.D. became involved in the militia of Rome, and then with censure from some.[18] To step back in our argument, we still need to address the issue of how we relate Old Testament concepts of war to New Testament concepts of "following Jesus" (who did not fight in a war) and "life in the Spirit."

A third approach has been to examine *biblical texts on peace and peace-making*, make them operative and dominant, and then argue that Christians must live in a peaceful way. Of course, texts that have been given priority are Matthew 5:9, 38–42 and the records of martyrdom (e.g., Acts 12:2). Once again, there have been only a few basic options: (1) pursuing peace means denouncing every involvement by the Christian in war (pacifist view); (2) pursuing peace means nonviolent forms of involvement (modified pacifism, or nonviolent resistance, or nonresistance view), or (3) pursuing peace means military build-up (peace-through-strength view). But once again, approaching the matter this way is stunted. Who is to decide that the approach is exclusively through the idea of peace? Does seeking peace (Matt. 5:9) imply no participation in military? Was that in Jesus' mind at all? And, how can people who believe in the Bible decide simply to omit the Old Testament evidence for war? Once again, we are confronted with a significant problem in the way we approach the whole question.

A final approach I will call the *individualism approach*; this one is so much a part of Western culture that Christians have unknowingly accepted it without thinking about its long-term impacts. This view simply says that participating in war is up to the individual who must make a decision before God and is accountable before God for his or her decision. This approach is both very modern, where blanket toleration and pluralism are rampant and where moral absolutes are usually denied, and quite unbiblical, because it seeks to let the person become the sole authority and refuses to let the Bible speak where it can. How do we get out of all of this?

I make several suggestions in the paragraphs that follow that are (1) based on the view Paul has of the priority of the Abrahamic covenant over the Mosaic law and the new covenant as the climax of the Abrahamic covenant, (2) rooted in evidence of all sorts, and (3) ultimately reliant on the view of Paul that Christians live "under the law of Christ" and "in the life of the Spirit."

First, it is fundamentally important that the Christian base his or her lifestyle entirely on faith in Christ, obedience to Christ, and life in the Spirit. This means that Christians do not go first of all to the Old Testament texts

---

18. See the survey of the evidence in L. J. Swift, *The Early Fathers on War and Military Service* (Message of the Fathers of the Church 19; Wilmington, Delaware: Michael Glazier, 1983).

to find God's will. They are not bound to Mosaic law, even if they are bound to God's will. Jesus promised a Counselor who would guide (John 14–16), Pentecost fulfilled that promise (Acts 2), and Paul showed just how the Spirit was to operate (Gal. 5). Jesus also taught his disciples to "fulfill" the law by loving God and loving others as the sure tests of that obedience (Matt. 22:34–40; cf. 7:12). This is where the Christian begins: with obeying Jesus in loving God and others, and with submitting to the Spirit.

May those, then, who submit to the Spirit and follow Jesus involve themselves in international conflict? This is a good question, one that Christians must spend time discussing. How does the cross of Christ fit into God's overall design for the Christian's essential lifestyle? Is it not the case, perhaps, that "self-denial" (exemplified in the cross of Christ) is the fundamental norm of Christian living? We need to consider this more than we have.[19]

Second, I would also suggest that the newness of the age of Christ and his gift of the Spirit renovates the Old Testament theocratic kingdom and functionally eliminates the Old Testament passages on war as paradigms for Christian activity.[20] I believe this is an implication of Paul's teaching on the law (which prescribed how Israel was to engage in warfare and how the Lord would be behind Israel) and of how it has been suspended by, and fulfilled in, Christ. The message of Galatians is that God works with all kinds now, that God is no longer operating in a nationalistic sense, and that God's people are comprised of all those who believe, whether Jew or Gentile. I believe that this universalism means that God *is no longer exclusively behind one nation*.

This means that Old Testament principles of how God stands behind Israel (his times against Israel were designed to provoke Israel to repentance, not to vindicate other nations) are suspended as well, since God is no longer behind one nation. In other words, the message of universalism in Galatians effectively suspends the biblical concepts operating behind the concept of war (Israel is God's nation and God therefore fights for Israel). What we are getting at here is one possible implication (I do not pretend to think I am absolutely correct here) of the "suspension of the law" according to Galatians 3:25 and how it might apply to the Christian who is struggling over how to participate in international conflict.

Third, the Christian's first priority in life is to follow Christ, evangelize the world with the good news of God's love in Christ (as Paul did), and live

---

19. A challenging book in this regard, applied to the issue of war, is R. J. Sider, *Christ and Violence* (Scottdale, Pa.: Herald Press, 1979).

20. For a different view, see P. C. Craigie, *The Problem of War in the Old Testament* (Grand Rapids: Eerdmans, 1978), who sees the Old Testament wars as a revelation of God's will and activity but not his moral being.

a life of submission to the Spirit. What I find in the pages of the New Testament is no trace of military activity as evidence of the Spirit and no trace of military activity as evidence of following Christ. Does this mean that all participation in international conflict is unchristian? It is my view, which I humbly submit to you, that Christians can be involved in international conflict only as an extension of God's calling in their life to follow Christ, to live in the Spirit, and to evangelize the world, and, furthermore, only in ways that are consistent with the cross of Christ and the revealed will of God.[21]

Does this exclude violence and warfare itself? I believe so. How can Christians put to death others for whom Christ has died (who are not believers), and how can any Christian put to death a fellow believer? In the latter case it would be to render to Caesar what is clearly God's; in the former, it would be to render to Caesar what may become God's. We have no way out. Behind this position is the universalism taught in the book of Galatians which, I submit to you, erodes the social barriers that are erected in times of international conflict.

We have moved a considerable distance from Paul's message of justification by faith, which he proved by appealing to the priority of the Abrahamic covenant. While the most important implication of our passage is that justification is by faith and not by observing the law, we also saw that Paul was operating with an entirely new reading of the Bible that "put the law in its place." Our movement from that world into our world concerned itself in this passage with this notion of Paul's about the law. We have argued that Paul was quite radical in this regard and that we as Christians need to explore its implications. I have attempted one such exploration into the field of the Christian participation in international conflict. May God guide us, through his Spirit, as we seek to live today as followers of Jesus!

---

21. A classic test-case, of course, is Dietrich Bonhoeffer who, though largely pacifistic in beliefs, involved himself to the point of death in the resistance to Hitler.

Galatians 3:26–4:7

YOU ARE ALL sons of God through faith in Christ Jesus, ²⁷for all of you who were baptized into Christ have clothed yourselves with Christ. ²⁸There is neither Jew nor Greek, slave nor free, male nor female, for you are all one in Christ Jesus. ²⁹If you belong to Christ, then you are Abraham's seed, and heirs according to the promise.

^{4:1}What I am saying is that as long as the heir is a child, he is no different from a slave, although he owns the whole estate. ²He is subject to guardians and trustees until the time set by his father. ³So also, when we were children, we were in slavery under the basic principles of the world. ⁴But when the time had fully come, God sent his Son, born of a woman, born under law, ⁵to redeem those under law, that we might receive the full rights of sons. ⁶Because you are sons, God sent the Spirit of his Son into our hearts, the Spirit who calls out, "Abba, Father." ⁷So you are no longer a slave, but a son; and since you are a son, God has made you also an heir.

IN THE BROADER context of the book of Galatians, our section is the third argument Paul offers to the Galatians for his view that (1) both acceptance with God and the continuance of a relationship with him are (2) based on faith (3) for people of all kinds, and (4) not on doing works of the law to perfect that relationship. He had stated his whole theory in 3:1–5. His first argument was rooted in the Old Testament (vv. 6–14), and his second argument was an "example from everyday life" (vv. 15–25). This third argument is from "sonship," which contains another "example from everyday life" (4:1–2) and ends with a pastoral appeal to agree with him (4:8–20). This appeal will be the focus of our next chapter.

Essentially, the argument from sonship may be put like this: (1) Faith in Jesus Christ makes a person a "son of God," and this obtains for everyone (3:28); (2) being a "son of God" means that a person is also a member of Abraham's seed, because one becomes associated with Christ, who is the Seed of Abraham (v. 29). Since believers are members of Abraham's seed, (3) they are also "heirs according to the promise" (3:29). This connection, faith → son of God → Abraham's seed → heir of the promise, is then explained and illustrated further by appealing to the human institution of a son becoming an adult male and, as an adult male, inheriting the father's promise. Such an analogy compares to the history of Israel: when Israel was under the law, Israel could be compared to a "slave-like" son, who was still immature and unable to enjoy the benefits of adulthood. But when Israel became an adult male (i.e., when God fulfilled his designs through Christ), Israel was set free from its slavery to the law, so that Israel might become a son with full privileges (and Gentiles would be included too). Throughout this entire argument Paul emphasizes universalism (cf. 3:26–28): the Judaizers had restricted God's acceptance to those who were Jews or who would join Judaism by following the works of the law; Paul says that God accepts all on the basis of faith in Christ.

I believe Paul's argument is rooted in the early Christian baptismal experience (cf. v. 26) of learning, by faith, to call God "Father" (cf. 4:6–7 with 3:26–27). Such an experience makes one conscious of being a son of God. On this basis, Paul argues that sonship implies something: being an heir of Abraham and of his promises. This is Paul's polemical point: if you are a son of God by faith (and you know this by the experience of calling God "Father"), you are also an heir of the covenantal promises to Abraham; you have become an heir by faith, not by observing the law. Once again rooting his point in their experience, Paul proves that their lives as sons of God and heirs of Abraham are by way of faith, not works of the law. Paul goes on to stress that this faith is the means of acceptance for all (v. 28). Therefore, once again, the Judaizing Christians have got it wrong. Nationalistic restrictions are done away with for those who know that acceptance by God is through faith.

Paul's argument in this passage is fairly straightforward. After a statement of his point that all can be sons and heirs by faith (vv. 26–29), he gives an analogy (4:1–2) and applies that analogy to the Galatians (vv. 3–7). Because Paul's most important points are scored in 3:26–29, the commentary section will focus on those verses.

Thesis Stated (3:26–29)

PAUL'S MAIN THESIS is that the Galatians are sons of God and heirs by faith in Christ (v. 26). He then restates his point by saying that all who were baptized have put on Christ (v. 27). That Paul was most concerned with the word *all* in both verses 26 and 27 becomes obvious by his explanation in verse 28: in Christ there are no racial, social, or sexual distinctions, because all are one. The implication of the "allness" of verses 26–28 is brought out in verse 29: those who belong to Christ are both the seed of Abraham and heirs.

Statement of sonship (v. 26). Paul's beginning with "You" is sudden and somewhat unexpected, since he has been focusing on Jewish Christians and their experience of moving from "under the law" to "life in the Spirit." However, that Paul ultimately has in mind not just a new Judaism (i.e., a Jewish church) is clear from how he moves freely from one group to the larger group (the universal church), and sometimes without giving notice. In fact, in 4:1–7 the focus is blurred, so much that at times we are unable to know which group is in focus (cf. 4:6).

The use of "sons of God" is important for the Galatians' experience, for they learned to say "Abba" to God through conversion (4:6). Earlier, Paul had expressed that those who believe are "children of Abraham" (3:7), but now he points out that they are "sons of God." In Galatians, Paul uses such terminology only at 4:6–7, and it may well be that the analogy to a son in verses 1–2 has prompted Paul's use of the term here. Being a "son of God" is a special promise by God for the last days and describes that special relationship of intimacy that the people of God can have with God (cf. 2 Cor. 6:18). As Paul describes those who are "sons," we should not pick up "manly" or "male" traits. Rather, in Paul's letters "son" is especially related to both Jews and Gentiles (Rom. 9:26) who have been set free from the law (Gal. 4:1–7), who now live by faith in Christ (3:7, 26) and in the Spirit of God's glorious freedom (cf. Rom. 8:14), and who await God's final redemption (Rom. 8:19). The last thing on Paul's mind when he used the term *son* was "manliness."

We are closer to Paul's intention if we find his emphasis on the word *all*, since this is the first word of the sentence in Greek (see 3:8, 22, 26, 28; 6:10). This is the word the Judaizing missionaries would have heard as particularly jarring. Their cause was to get these "half-converts" to become "full converts" by persuading them to adopt the code of Moses as the completion of God's instruction. Now Paul tells them that "all" become sons of God through faith. The "allness" of God's plan, the universalism, was predicted long ago (v. 8) and, while that plan awaited its fulfillment in Christ, the law confined "all" (v. 22). When Christ came and people believed in him, "all" became "one," thus ending the national restrictions that governed Jewish behavior (v. 28). As a result of being part of God's people, Christians are to do good to "all" (6:10).

Restatement of sonship (v. 27). As Paul restates his thesis of sonship, he makes several parallel comments, as this chart shows.

Sons of God	through faith	in Christ Jesus
United with Christ	in baptism	
Put on Christ		

What is important for our analysis of verse 27 is to realize that Paul sees faith as being expressed originally in "baptism" and becoming "sons" as the baptismal experience of being "united with Christ" and "putting on Christ." Paul is probably thinking that, since Christ is the Son of God, being united with him and putting him on is what sonship is all about.

Some will no doubt have problems with the observation that faith and baptism are parallel expressions for Paul. Among many free churches in the world, baptism has taken on a secondary importance and is too often confined to "nothing more than an entrance rite" into the church. While it is clear that Paul makes a fundamental difference between external rites and internal reality (cf. Rom. 2:25—29; Phil. 3:3; Col. 2:11; cf. Gal. 5:6), and can even suggest that baptizing was not his purpose (1 Cor. 1:13—17), baptism was in the early church *the initial and necessary response of faith*. To be sure, their world was more ritual-oriented than ours and consequently got more out of rituals than we probably do.[1] Nonetheless, we dare not make baptism "nothing more than a ritual of entrance," for it was for the earliest Christians their first moment of faith, and we know of no such thing as an "unbaptized believer."[2] Baptism was not necessary for salvation, but faith without baptism was not faith for the early church. The Galatians knew this, and so Paul appealed to their experience.

The early baptismal ceremony was, in effect, a dying with Christ and a rising with Christ (so Rom. 6:1—14). This was its symbolic virtue: it dramatized salvation. Furthermore, the ceremony was frequently associated with two moral ideas: the putting away of sin and the putting on of a new life (cf. Rom. 13:12, 14; Eph. 4:24; 6:11—17; Col. 3:5—17).[3] To be "clothed with Christ" perhaps refers to the early Christian practice of stripping and then reclothing oneself in a white, liturgical robe after the baptismal ceremony, thus symbolizing disrobing oneself of sin and then putting on the virtues of Christ.[4]

---

1. On rituals and symbols, see the foundational study of the cultural anthropologist Mary Douglas, *Purity and Danger: An Analysis of the Concepts of Pollution and Taboo* (London: Routledge & Kegan Paul, 1966), and the more recent study of B. J. Malina, *Christian Origins and Cultural Anthropology* (Atlanta: John Knox, 1986), 139—65.

2. The most complete analysis of baptism I have seen is G. R. Beasley-Murray, *Baptism in the New Testament* (Grand Rapids: Eerdmans, 1962). A positive portrayal of the "grace of baptism" can be seen in G. W. Bromiley, "Baptism," in *The Evangelical Dictionary of Theology*, ed. W. A. Elwell (Grand Rapids: Baker, 1984), 113—14. He follows up this article with articles on believer's and infant baptism (pp. 114—17). The commentary of F. F. Bruce (*Galatians*, 185—87) has a good discussion of the issues as they bear on Galatians.

3. See H. D. Betz, *Galatians*, 188—89.

4. So Justin Martyr, *Dialogue with Trypho*, 116, ed. A. C. Coxe (Ante-Nicene Fathers; Grand Rapids: Eerdmans, 1979) 1:257.

One more connection needs to be observed. As noted above, "sons of God" in verse 26 parallels the expressions "united with Christ" and "have been clothed with Christ" in verse 27. I would also suggest that the baptism of the Galatians (v. 27) was the moment in which they learned to call God "Abba" (cf. 4:6–7) and so, in effect, learned that they were all "sons of God" (3:26). Paul is now ready to make his point: the Judaizers are wrong because they do not realize that at their baptism the Galatian converts learned that they were sons of God.

The explanation (v. 28). Before drawing his conclusion, Paul pauses to explain what he means by "all" in verses 26–27. Here he sets out his cultural, social, and sexual mandates. These are set out "in Christ Jesus," and we must first look at this expression.

What does it mean to be "in Christ Jesus"? In Galatians this idea is expressed in various ways: "in Christ" (1:22; 2:17), "in Christ Jesus" (2:4; 3:14, 26; 5:6), and "in the Lord" (5:10). Sometimes the "in Christ" expression means nothing more than "by Christ" (2:17; 3:14; 5:10), and once it conveys the special relationship a group of local churches has to Christ (1:22). The other instances signify the "location of believers": they are "in Christ" (2:4; 3:26, 28; 5:6). This usage is sometimes called the "mystical 'in'" in Paul. If what we mean by mystical is not just, or even primarily, ecstatic, this term is appropriate, for Christians have been swallowed up into Christ so that they live in him and out of a relationship to him. To be "in Christ" is to be in spiritual fellowship with him through God's Spirit. This is one way of defining what a Christian is: one who is "in Christ." While the ideas are not identical, to be "justified" is a different way of speaking of the same reality that takes place in being "in Christ." Both expressions indicate the new relationship to God that Jesus Christ brings through the Spirit.

Those who are "in Christ Jesus" are those who believe in him; those who believe in him come from all walks of life, from every nation, and from both sexes. The problem the Judaizers had with Paul was that he did not properly (in their view) construct the church because he was breaking down the line between Jews and Gentiles. No doubt, they argued that this line was made by God when he called Abraham (Gen. 12). Paul now shows that faith in Christ obliterates such distinctions, and so he sees in the seed of the gospel a tree that has within it three mandates: a cultural one, a social one, and a sexual one.[5] Thus, Paul goes beyond the concerns at Galatia by expressing what may have been an early Christian slogan that he endorses here and else-

---

5. I borrow these expressions from R. N. Longenecker, *New Testament Social Ethics for Today* (Grand Rapids: Eerdmans, 1984) and point to his book for a fuller development of each of the themes.

where (cf. Rom. 10:12; 1 Cor. 7:17–28; 12:12–13; Eph. 2:11–22; Col. 3:5–11).[6] The revolution of Paul begins through Christ's work and participation in him through faith.

Scholars have often observed that a Jewish blessing that was prayed daily by some Jews is reversed here: "Blessed be God that he did not make me a Gentile; blessed be God that he did not make me ignorant [or a slave]; blessed be God that he did not make me a woman" (Tosefta Berakoth 7:18). This is possibly a first-century prayer; the distinctions behind it were certainly made at times by Jews and by others.[7] In any case, Paul is surely responding to such a demeaning classification of humans.

The cultural mandate:[8] "neither Jew nor Greek." We have addressed this mandate over and over. Paul set his face against anything that demanded a cultural and national conversion to become a Christian; no one had to become a Jew to become a Christian. This feeling of national distinctiveness on the part of the Jews was broken by the blood of Christ (cf. Eph. 2:13), which effectively annulled the curse of the law and its regime (Gal. 3:10–14; Eph. 2:14–15). The new era brought with it (and in its mighty wake) a cultural revolution. Cultural divisions are to have no part in the church of Jesus Christ. All humans must be treated in light of God's love in Christ, not in light of their cultural past.

It goes without saying that the road to the elimination of such divisions for the first Christians was rocky and full of pitfalls. Paul describes one example in Galatians 2:11–14, and the Judaizers were seeking to fight against this essential point of the gospel. Peter had troubles elsewhere (Acts 10:1–11:18), but eventually the church of Jerusalem was willing to say that "God has granted even [note this term!] the Gentiles repentance unto life" (Acts 11:18).

The social mandate:[9] "neither slave nor free." Slavery was widespread in the ancient world among Gentiles and Jews. It was generally different from, though it included, the mistreatment of racially different slaves as evidenced in the United States in the seventeenth to nineteenth centuries. For the ancient Roman world there have been estimates that slaves comprised as much as thirty-three percent of the population. Slaves were gained in numerous ways: purchase, indebtedness, capture in war, and birth. Regardless, the

---

6. R. N. Longenecker (*Galatians*, 157) states that the "second and third couplets have no relevance for Paul's immediate argument."

7. For "others," see F. F. Bruce, *Galatians*, 187–88. He refers to one text of Thales that speaks of his gratitude for not being born a beast, woman, or barbarian.

8. See R. N. Longenecker, *New Testament Social Ethics for Today*, 29–47; H. D. Betz, (*Galatians*, 190–92) provides a wealth of background evidence and ideas.

9. See R. N. Longenecker, *New Testament Social Ethics for Today*, 48–69; H. D. Betz, *Galatians*, 192–95.

number who were treated fairly and kindly appears to be an exception rather than the rule. The Old Testament developed rules of kindness to slaves (cf. Lev. 25:39–55).

Our social mandate in Galatians can be taken in two ways: as a social statement for the abolition of slavery as an institution or as a declaration of the irrelevancy of the institution in Christ. In light of 1 Corinthians 7:21–24 and Philemon, it seems best to see Paul giving a declaration of the second option: the irrelevancy of one's social status for acceptance with God and life in the church. As with culture or race, so with social status: there are distinctions but they are irrelevant. Nonetheless, the social mandate explodes with social possibilities. "In Christ," Paul says, the slave becomes our "brother" (Philem. 16). Both freedmen and slaves have the Spirit and are in the body of Christ (1 Cor. 7:21–24). In fact, it is indeed likely that in the early church slaves were leaders, and their owners submitted to them in the context of the church.[10] As R. N. Longenecker observes: "The phrase is also pregnant with societal implications. And undoubtedly some early Christians realized, at least to some extent, the importance for society of what they were confessing."[11]

While Paul did not set up here a social agenda, he created an atmosphere that would eventually lead to the abolition of slavery throughout the whole world. In the history of the church, various movements (among the later movements we name the Quakers) sought to implement the abolition of slavery completely. With the rising tide of the civil rights movement in the 1950s and 1960s in the United States, the entire issue took on new significance for the church. While progress has been slow, much slower than it should be in the church, there has been progress. We can only pray for further courage to live our lives in a way that is consistent with the "irrelevance" of slavery in Christ. Social classes ought to have no bearing on the church's work.

The sexual mandate:[12] "neither male nor female."[13] For some reason, the sexual mandate has been even more explosive than the cultural and social ones.

---

10. F. F. Bruce (*Galatians*, 189) points to Onesimus who, though a slave, may have become the bishop of Ephesus.

11. R. N. Longenecker, *New Testament Social Ethics for Today*, 51.

12. Ibid., 70–93; H. D. Betz, *Galatians*, 195–200. See also K. R. Snodgrass, "Galatians 3:28—Conundrum or Solution?," in *Women, Authority and the Bible*, ed. A. Mickelsen (Downers Grove, Ill.: InterVarsity Press, 1986), 161–81, with responses by S. C. Stanley (pp. 181–88) and W. W. Gasque (pp. 188–92). The entire book is a good one to read on the debates about women in the church. From the more traditional side, see the excellent essay of S. L. Johnson, "Role Distinctions in the Church: Galatians 3:28," in *Recovering Biblical Manhood and Womanhood: A Response to Evangelical Feminism*, ed. J. Piper and W. Grudem (Wheaton: Crossway, 1991), 154–64.

13. Paul's pattern is slightly interrupted here. Whereas in the first two pairs he says "neither . . . nor", here he says "not male *and* female" (the NIV retains the "nor"). Some have seen in this change a completely different idea, namely, the elimination of sex distinctions

Again, we need to observe that Paul spoke these words in a given historical and social context, a context that clearly believed in the *inferiority of women*. Whether we quote texts from the Greco-Roman world (Galatian context) or from the Jewish world (the context of Paul especially and of some Galatians), there was a widespread conviction that women were inferior. The Jewish historian Josephus wrote, for example: "The woman, says the law, is in all things inferior to the man" (*Against Apion*, 2.201). Paul's agenda in verse 28 assumes this context. Why else would he point to "neither male nor female" as his third pair of things that have been abolished in Christ?

This principle of inferiority worked itself out in many ways. I mention but a few. Women were talked about in rude and condescending ways; they were not to be taught the law; they were to tend to their children; they were not considered reliable witnesses in court; they may have even sat in seats separate from men in synagogues. One could paint even a grimmer picture if one desired. I have not because I am also aware that women were at times given positions of leadership (for example, Phoebe in Rom. 16:1–2) and, in actual practice, I suspect that women were given more respect than the surviving literature suggests (see the story of Priscilla in Acts 18).[14] But positive ideas are not behind Paul's desire to see "sinful" walls broken down.

So it was inferiority of women working itself out in religious communities that Paul opposes with this statement "neither male nor female." In the same way that there was to be no cultural/racial distinctions and no social status prejudices, there was to be no sexual prejudice. For those who are in Christ, antagonisms, criticisms, snide remarks, subtle insinuations, and overt prejudices must end, for in him male and female are one. I believe that, as is the case with slavery, so with women, Paul provides an agenda that would take years for the church and society to implement properly and honorably before God.

The implication (v. 29). Paul concludes with an implication of being a son of God. Since the Galatian believers are "in Christ" and since Christ is the Seed of Abraham (v. 19), then it follows that the Galatian believers are also Abraham's seed. And if they are Abraham's seed, then they also inherit Abra-

---

completely. However, it is much more probable that "and" comes from the Gen. 1:27 (Greek) text Paul was quoting and so amounts to the same idea as in the other pairs. See F. F. Bruce, *Galatians*, 189–190. But what Paul has in mind is not the relationship of a husband to a wife but of men to women in general.

14. For more evidence and judicious assessment of such evidence, see R. A. Tucker and W. Liefeld, *Daughters of the Church: Women and Ministry from New Testament Times to the Present* (Grand Rapids: Zondervan, 1987), esp. 19–87, for Paul's time period. See also B. Witherington III, *Women and the Genesis of Christianity*, ed. A. Witherington (New York: Cambridge, 1990), which summarizes his two previous scholarly books on the subject of women.

ham's promise—a relationship with God that entails his blessing and goodness. So Paul concludes that the Judaizers are wrong because of the intrinsic connections he spells out: Abraham – faith – Christ – seed of Abraham by faith: both Jews and Gentiles. What the Judaizers wanted was the promise of Abraham, but they thought they had to follow the law of Moses in order to get it; Paul, however, knew that one received the Abrahamic promise by faith. That the Galatian believers knew that God was their father was sufficient proof for Paul.

The Analogy and Its Application (4:1–7)

PAUL'S THESIS, WHICH we have treated in a more thorough fashion than usual, is now illustrated with an analogy and then applied. Until Paul says "What I am saying is . . . ," we may not have been able to understand his logic. But now we see that in 3:26–29, Paul has set up his basic point that sonship demonstrates that the Judaizers are wrong. These next two verses (4:1–2) show us how he makes the point. A child who is destined to inherit an estate is no different than a slave as long as he is a child (until twenty to twenty-five years old), for he cannot inherit that estate until he becomes an adult. During this period he is subject to the "guardians and trustees," but only until the father's set time of inheritance.

In verses 3–7 Paul applies this analogy to make a point about Israel's history that is almost identical to the point made in 3:15–25: namely, the "childhood period" is the period of the law and the "inheritance period" is the time inaugurated by Jesus Christ. Full rights (i.e., freedom from the law) do not come until after Christ's work is done. The time of the law is a time of slavery; the time of Christ is a time of freedom. What Paul does not say, but what he implies, is that the time of slavery was a time of "works of the law" and the time of Christ is the time of "faith."

First application: we were enslaved (v. 3). "When we were children" is Paul's description of Jewish life under the law (and perhaps Gentile life under the "law written in their hearts"). But Paul says they were enslaved "by the basic principles of the world." What does this expression mean?

The only other place Paul uses this term[15] in Galatians is 4:9, where he is describing a return to either pagan life with its tribal/national religions (cf. v. 8) or to the Mosaic laws regarding "special days and months and seasons and years." We can gain more insight into the meaning of this expression by comparing "basic principles" to the negative dimensions of the previous era

---

15. The Greek expression is *hypo ta stoicheia tou kosmou* ("under the basic elements of the world"). Its use in Colossians 2:8, 20 has obviously different senses.

as described in 3:15–25. Here it must refer to the law that came after the promise (vv. 15–18), to its sin-revealing purpose (v. 19), to its temporal limitations (v. 19), to its inferior status because of its need for mediation (vv. 19–20), to its inability to bring life (v. 21), and to its imprisoning function (vv. 22–25). Thus, it is best to see "basic principles" as a reference to the law in its negative and suspended features.

Once again, the Judaizers would have been offended at Paul's rather disparaging view of the law. How can Paul, we imagine they might have asked, say the law was nothing but the "ABCs" of God's revelation? I believe Paul has worked this out quite carefully: it is because he sees Jesus Christ as the climactic fulfillment of the Mosaic revelation. To revert to my typewriter illustration, the former era is nothing but a time when Jews hammered out their ABCs on a typewriter; the new era is a fulfillment of that machine and an entirely new agenda is in order: not just ABCs, but sentences, paragraphs, chapters, and books are now in order! That old typewriter (the law) is a "basic principle" compared to the fullness of the computer age (Jesus Christ and God's Spirit)!

Second application: we were made sons (vv. 4–5). As with the time set by the father for the maturation and inheritance for his son, so also with God. When the "time had fully come," God sent his Son so that the inheritance could be had. The expression "fully come" is the completion of the "basic principles" of verse 3. God sent his Son, and this Son lived under the law (though not under sin) so that he could absorb the curse of the law, exhaust the fumes of God's wrath, and redeem those under the law. Once the Son had done this, the barrier was knocked down between God and people (and between peoples), and they could become "sons of God" (v. 5). Their sonship is tantamount to governing the "whole estate" (v. 1), as Paul will show.

Third application: we are heirs (vv. 6–7). Being a "son of God" means having God's Spirit, which is the promise of Abraham (3:14); this is what the Judaizers want too. The Spirit of God enables the son of God to cry out "Abba." "Abba" is the Aramaic term for "father" and became the special language of Jesus for addressing God (Matt. 6:9–13; Mark 14:36).[16] Jesus' prayer language was followed by the early church; thus, the early Christians saw addressing God as "Abba" as their distinctive mark. It marked them off, as circumcision marked off male Jews, in a way that made them realize they were the "sons of God."

If, therefore, the Galatian Christians are calling God "Abba," they are "sons of God"; the ability to call God "Abba" is evidence of being a son of God. This

---

16. The classic study of this was done by J. Jeremias, *The Prayers of Jesus* (London: SCM, 1967), 11–65. See also J. D. G. Dunn, "Prayer," in *DJG*, 618–19.

means they are no longer "slaves," living in the old era (typing on a manual typewriter). And since they are sons, they have the inheritance.

We can now fill in Paul's logic: since believers have the inheritance by faith, they do not need to live out the "works of the law"; therefore the Judaizers are wrong in urging what amounts to a nationalistic view of God's work, and it need not be followed.

ONCE AGAIN, WE have arrived on the same shore: acceptance with God is based on faith in Christ and not on observing the law. Everyone who believes, whether Jew or Gentile, slave or free, male or female, is accepted by God. On the contrary, the Judaizers have duped the Galatian converts into thinking that they needed to convert "all the way to Judaism," that is, to a particular nation, in order to be fully acceptable to God. But Paul stands firm with the grace of God, through Christ, in the Spirit, by faith—for all. This has been his message from the beginning. But Paul has gotten to the shore this time on a different boat: the boat of sonship. He has explored the theme of sonship, and the experience of sonship that the Galatians knew all about, to argue his case.

How do we apply this theme of *sonship* to our context? Ours is a day that has been deeply influenced by what is often described as "women's liberation." I am completely for the "liberation of women" and for the liberation of everyone and everything—as long as "liberation" means "slavery to Christ" (Gal. 1:10; cf. Rom. 12:11; 14:18) and to one another in love (Gal. 5:13). We as Christians need to sympathize with the plight of women in the history of the civilized world and to understand the impact that some awful institutions have made on how they have become what they are. Indeed, feminists have accused the teaching of the Bible, and Paul is not exempted here, of both fostering and establishing the oppression of women. While feminist interpreters of Scripture praise the "insight" of Paul here in 3:28, they also point out that neither Paul himself (see 1 Cor. 14:34–35; Eph. 5:22–33; 1 Tim. 2:8–15) nor other New Testament writers grasped the implication of this call to liberation here. They argue that as the church took a long time to grasp the equality of races (and so ended slavery), so it is taking too long to do the same for women: liberate them from the bondage of male dominance and from a patriarchal world.

Why bring this up? Because these same critics of the biblical message contend that calling God's children "sons" is also patriarchal, condescending, and expressive of a male-dominated worldview. They say that they do not want to be called "sons" since they are not males; they want to be called "daughters." God, they argue, is not a "male"; thus, they urge sensitive people to abandon "chauvinistic language" that was used by God accommodatingly in the Bible and translate such expressions with "sexless" terms, like "children." This is exactly what the NIV had done at 3:7. What should we do?

I wish to make two points, the first about *translation* and the second about *sensitivity*. In our final section I shall try to "update" the message of Paul about sonship for our world. First, the matter of *translation*. What is an acceptable translation of the word *huios* ("son"), which refers to a male child? This word does not refer to a girl, and it is different than the term "child" (which largely describes the developmental stage of a person). Furthermore, there was something in the reference to a son that would not have been conveyed in the term "child" or "daughter," namely, the privileges inherent to becoming a man and inheriting a father's estate (in a patriarchal world). Thus, in preferring the term "child" (as the NIV does at 3:7) something is lost. Is it best to lose something so as not to be offensive? I think not, at least not in this case. There comes a point when translation is no longer translation; it becomes "updating" or "paraphrasing" or "contextualizing."

I am all for each of these maneuvers in our interpretation and in our application; I am not, however, for the translation of any text that would harm the original message. No matter how important it is for us to make the gospel relevant, there comes a point when we must not tamper with the message so as to make it relevant. I believe this applies to the matter of sonship in Galatians. While I am deeply disturbed by patriarchy and chauvinism, I do not believe that the way to eradicate them from society is to retranslate ancient texts so as to give the impression that they never existed. Instead, I would prefer to see "footnotes" or special devices (e.g., using all caps to make one sensitive to the issue: SONS OF GOD is "non-sexist" in implication) in popular translations, especially pew Bibles, that call attention to issues that press against the church today.

Second, the matter of *sensitivity*. Having said that I prefer not to retranslate the whole Bible so as to avoid all traces of patriarchy, I am also of the view that it is fundamentally important for Christians to be sensitive and to be as "nonsexist" in their language as possible (with the above proviso). Not only should we be sensitive; we need also to change structures so that oppression of women is eliminated, just as we have been actively against cultural and racial biases.

So to move into our world with the message of Paul about sonship means, first of all, to cut through the rhetoric of patriarchy and male dominance while at the same time respecting what translation actually is. Then we need to find out just what "sonship" and "inheritance" meant for the Jewish world (and the

Galatian context), so that we may have a firm grasp of what Paul meant. To repeat what was said in the "Original Meaning" notes, the term *son* does not necessarily mean something about "manliness" in the sense of "macho." Here many interpreters (and some feminists) go astray: they begin with what "son" means today, or what it means in their reconstructed patriarchal world, and then proceed to show just how chauvinistic the text can be.

Without getting into the obvious patriarchy of the ancient world, I still contend that the way to do a study of a word and its associates is not by looking at what "son" means in our world or even what "son" can mean in a patriarchal world. What we need to do is to see how Paul uses the term *son* and then *trace the connections and connotations he provides for his readers.* These are the ideas we will want to focus on. I am convinced that for Paul "son" does not have the senses that many feminists think it has. To be sure, it comes from a patriarchal world in which men were superior to women and sons superior to daughters. But, and here is my point, the *assumptions aside,* Paul does not exploit these features of the meaning but other less patriarchal and more positive ideas.

Sonship denoted for Paul the special intimacy that God's people can have with him, the freedom those people experience from the bondage and curse of the law, as well as the filling of the Spirit that God enables. In addition, the theme of sonship also speaks to the hopeful stance of the believer as he (or she!) awaits the fullness of salvation that comes when brother time gives birth to sister eternity. These are the ideas that need to be explored as we think about our sonship in Christ. As we apply the message of sonship, we need to be both historically accurate and pastorally sensitive, expressing a very real patriarchal idea in a way that does not offend our sensitivities and that focuses on those features that are significant to the author.

A second feature of our text that strikes the reader is the emphasis on "all," the theme of universalism, in the "thesis" section of his argument (3:26–29). Nowhere else in Galatians does Paul spell out the vastness of the love of God for all. He says you are "all" sons of God (v. 26), for "all" of you were united with Christ (v. 27), and "there is neither Jew nor Greek, slave nor free, male nor female, for you are *all* one in Christ Jesus" (v. 28, italics added). Regardless of who you are, if you believe, you get to inherit the Abrahamic promises (v. 29).

How do we move this message of universalism into our world? We have already applied the universalism of Paul to our day in the areas of racism (the social mandate of v. 28) and denominationalism (the social and cultural mandate of v. 28). One area we have not explored is how the universalism of Paul applies to the sexual mandate of verse 28: "neither male nor female." We will therefore explore this here.

I have seen several ways people have sought to "apply" New Testament texts about women in our world.[17] The first we call the *"condemn and dismiss" approach*. What takes place here is the conclusion that the New Testament evidence is almost exclusively chauvinistic (most, however, exclude v. 28 by claiming more than it actually teaches) and therefore to be condemned as a product of its time. It must thus be dismissed after we have learned the lessons it has taught us about oppression. Most readers will see in this view one that can hardly maintain a firm grasp of evangelical theology, and so most evangelicals have dismissed the view itself.

A second approach I shall call the *mutual equality but functional subordination view*. This is the traditional view, espoused throughout the history of the church. For those who hold this view, the New Testament teaches both equality before God in status (v. 28) and functional subordination in office (e.g., 1 Tim. 2:11–15). Thus, these proponents see two strands in the New Testament they think can be woven together by positing that, while God accepts women in the same way he accepts men (by faith in Christ), that acceptance does not revolutionize social differentiation and differing roles for the sexes. It follows that the roles for women in the church are almost always seriously lessened by this view.

A third view may be called *evangelical and feminine liberation*. While this view wants to submit to Scripture (as is not seen in the first approach to these texts), it also recognizes the cultural conditioning of the text of the New Testament and seeks to eliminate it as we move the truth of God into our modern world. Furthermore, under this approach is a recognition that our society is considerably different than Paul's.

How should we proceed? Let me suggest a model that we can use that may be compatible, at the outset, with both the second and third approaches. To begin with, we must do our homework on the ancient world (what were the lives of women like around the Mediterranean Sea?) and on the New Testament texts themselves. We must understand *what the text meant in that world* before we can have any hope of moving it into our world. Much work has gone on in this area in the last few decades.[18] The foundation for this series of commentaries is that the ancient world is not identical to ours and that to

---

17. A readable and comprehensive guide to modern studies can be found in R. A. Tucker and W. Liefeld, *Daughters of the Church*, 401–34.

18. The most recent work in this regard is R. C. Kroeger and C. C. Kroeger, *I Suffer Not a Woman: Rethinking 1 Timothy 2:11–15 in Light of Ancient Evidence* (Grand Rapids: Baker, 1992). It is a particular failure of the work cited above of J. Piper and W. Grudem, *Recovering Biblical Manhood and Womanhood*, that they do not devote sections to women in the ancient world, nor do they have extensive treatments of the problems on moving the ancient data into our world.

apply the ancient text to our world requires patient historical work so we can discern what the text meant.

Another part of this step is a very careful examination of what Paul says about women. More frequently than not, readers of the Bible and professional interpreters (who should at least know better) decide that one text is superior to another; thus, they make one set of texts fit into their descriptions of another set of texts. On this particular issue, some take Galatians 3:28 as the most important truth of Paul about women, make texts like 1 Corinthians 14:34–35 and 1 Timothy 2:11–15 fit into that text, and end up making Paul the first feminist. Others operate in the opposite direction and end up squeezing all the juice out of Galatians 3:28 to the point that it says absolutely nothing new (God loves all people). The only legitimate way to do serious biblical theology is to believe all the texts and fit them into some reasonable whole. As for verse 28, if we are going to examine Paul's view of women properly, we must say that for Paul "equality in Christ" is not necessarily "elimination of distinctions of roles" for his time.

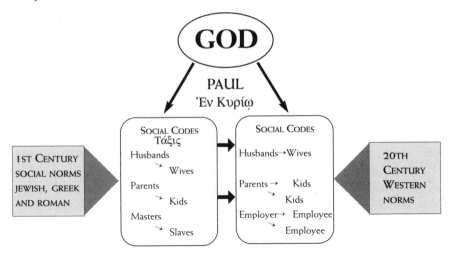

Second, as a result of this historical work, we must *compare that social world to our social world* and, in particular, compare the role women had in the ancient world to the role they have in our world—and the modern world differs considerably. To do this we need to read books on our culture and on women in our culture.[19] With a good picture of both worlds, we need to compare them, see how Paul's teaching "fits" into our world (or how it does not

---

19. A standard anthology of writings, though now slightly dated, is N. Glazer and H. Y. Waehrer, eds., *Woman in a Man-Made World: A Socioeconomic Handbook* (Chicago: Rand McNally, 1977).

"fit"), and then start to work with the business of applying. We quickly discover that women's roles were different in that world from what they are
today. We learn that the New Testament, and Paul, were influenced by such
things as the prevailing social norms (many say this is what Paul is talking
about in 1 Cor 11:2–16) of the Jewish, Greek, and Roman worlds, which
came to them as self-evident truths and conventions. Today we think it is
wrong (in most of the Western world) for men to wear dresses, but men in
Africa wear outfits that are entirely feminine when looked at from our viewpoint. We think these things are rights and wrongs, even though they are
social conventions, rules we play by. This order of Paul's society was seen as
under God's providential arrangement, and we see the same in our world.
What we need to do is to compare social norms, see how Paul's statements
fit into those social norms, and then make applications.

The third step is to recognize that *development takes place over the centuries* in
social structures. The social structures of the first century were not any more
God-ordained than the ones in our age. It may be that at times ours are better, but may it be that at times theirs were better? Along with the development that has occurred over centuries comes change, and along with change
comes the necessity of interpreting and applying for a different world.

One example will suffice to make our point about change. I know of only
one or two small denominations that believe in foot washing and, unless the
rest of Christendom is wrong and they are right, I do not see God refusing
to bless his people because they are not washing one another's feet. Jesus, of
course, commanded this practice (John 13:12–17), and evidently it was
practiced in the early church (1 Tim 5:10; Augustine, *Letters* 119.18). In spite
of Jesus' direct words and the early church's testimony to obedience to his
words, Christians of all ages and places have no problems dismissing it as a
custom of an ancient world that can be accomplished in other ways today.
In particular, I was taught that hospitable reception of a person is an equivalent. So we were taught to stand when others enter our home, greet them,
and do whatever was necessary to make them comfortable (take their coat
and hat, get them some tea, etc.). I think this is correct. But the process of
interpretation is one in which we explicitly eliminate a command of Jesus and
substitute in its place a cultural equivalent.

"Cultural equivalent" is the key here. Other examples might come from
our permission for women to wear jewelry (just go to church on Sunday!),
even though Peter prohibited it (1 Pet. 3:3–6), and our complete disregard
of Paul's comments on the theological grounding of short hair for men and
long hair for women (1 Cor. 11:2–16). I suggest that applying texts on
women involves a similar process: serious biblical and sociological study of

women in the ancient world, the Pauline letters, and our world; careful comparison of the roles of women in both worlds; identification of change and development; and finding cultural equivalents.

Speaking of development and change leads to yet another idea: the idea of progressively working out what Paul says. I know of few people who think slavery is right. But Paul evidently did not think it was completely wrong; thus he encouraged slaves to remain as slaves and commanded masters to treat their slaves kindly. He certainly did not think the gospel brought a social revolution by way of abolishing slavery. And yet, for moderns, slavery is wrong. Most Christian interpreters think the Bible taught a kinder view of slaves than the ancient world (which is surely generally true) and that Paul's statement in verse 28 provided the statement that would eventually lead to the abolition of slavery. For these interpreters there is a progressive unfolding of the actual working out of God's will, with only part of that progression caught in the Bible. Perhaps it is the case that what Paul said in verse 28 about women will unfold in history in the same way as the slavery statement has. Perhaps as humans have been freed from the awful grasp of ownership by other humans, so also women will be freed from their bondage to social inferiority.

I believe these are the steps we need to use before we can talk about women in the church, before we have truly and responsibly applied Paul's statement in Galatians 3:28 to our world. What we will see is that the cultural conditioning of the ancient world led Paul to apply his view of the equality of women with men in certain ways that did not harm the preaching of the gospel (hence his restrictions at 1 Cor. 11:2–16 and 1 Tim. 2:11–15). But when those cultural conditions changed, his applications would have changed; and so I am of the view that the statement of verse 28 is fundamental to Paul's entire approach and that it should be to ours as well.

In this section we have looked at two issues: sonship and the equality of women according to Galatians 3:28. In our next section, I will look at sonship and seek applications for Paul's teaching in our world. The above discussion on women will suffice for our purposes—because of space constraints and because the discussion above on women points us in the directions we need for applications. After all, the passage we are considering is about sonship.

WE BEGIN WITH *a new view of sonship.* To make this message relevant to our world we need, as I said above, to be sensitive to sexist language. So my proposal is that, while we retain the term "son," we make it non-sexual. To be a "son" of God does not mean to be "manly" or "masculine." It means:

Being intimate with God. In our world, being a "son of God" is not similar to being "intimate with God." But according to Paul, a "son of God" is one who learns to call God *Abba* because God has given his Spirit to his sons. Calling God *Abba* is the most intimate language of the family in the Jewish world. This was the first term a Jewish child learned (along with *imma*, "mommy"), and it can be translated "daddy." While "daddy" is accurate, there is more to it than the language of a child. The father, the *abba*, in Judaism was also a commanding authority figure for the Jewish family, and children were taught never to disagree with and always to honor him. Thus, the term *abba* is not just the prattling of a child, not just the language of little children with their loving fathers playing games and talking sweet things; rather, it is the term that Jews used for their relationship to their fathers that involved both relational intimacy and honorable respect.

A "son of God" is one who relates to God both with love and with respect. We develop intimacy with God through prayer—prayer that explores God's relationship to us and our relationship to God, prayer that is trusting and vulnerable to God's promise and sure word, and prayer that is designed to live before God obediently and lovingly. We develop intimacy with God through a lifestyle that remains in consistent conversation with God as each day progresses. Instead of diddling our time away with thoughts of fleeting things as we drive the car or wash the dishes or go for walks, we can spend our time in those activities talking to God and listening to him speak to us as his children. We can pray and learn to know God.

We also develop intimacy with God by reading his Word, believing it, obeying it, and sharing it with others. But mostly, we learn to be intimate with God by trusting in him and learning through that trust that he is loving and good. God desires that we desire him. In that desire he is delighted, and we become delighted in his delight. Loving God's delight is what intimacy is all about, and that is what it means to be a son of God.

Being free from the curse of the law. To be a son of God means that we (both Jews and Gentiles) have been set free from the curse of the law, that we have moved from the B.C. era to the A.D. era (shall I mention typewriters and computers again?!), and that we have left the age of tutors and guardians to being led by God's Spirit. I believe analogies help here.

As parents we tag along with our children when they are young because we know they are too irresponsible to make good decisions. Parents, of course, differ on when they start letting children make their own decisions, but I am not talking about tagging along with our children when they go to college, get married, and start their careers. When our kids are young, we help them up the steps on a slide so they do not fall off; we accompany them to the bus stop so they do not venture onto the street; we accompany them to sporting games so they are not taken advantage of; we look after their homework so they get it done on time; we drive with them (as we recently did with our daughter Laura) so they will learn to drive responsibly and not peer out the window for their friends; and on and on. Children must get tired of being looked after, and it must feel good when they get to school (away from their parents), when they get to summer camps, when they go to college, and when they finally leave home and set up their own establishment. That feeling of relief from "being looked after" and "constantly corrected" is similar to what Paul meant by being a "son of God." A "son of God" is one who has been set free from tutelage and turned loose with God's Spirit to guide them.

No longer suffering the guilt of being a sinner before God, no longer fearing the awful wrath of God, and no longer being sentenced by God as cursed—that is what it means to be a "son of God." Anyone who senses his forgiveness before God, anyone who knows he (or she!) has been welcomed into God's big family, anyone who knows that the law cannot condemn them because Christ has absorbed the law's curse, is a "son of God." We are sons of God solely because Christ, the Son of God, has made us part of his family by dying on our behalf.

Being led by God's Spirit. Because we have become sons of God, God sent his Spirit into our hearts. I doubt very much whether we can know the order in which these things happen: rather, conversion is a complex event in which God works and we respond, and because God works and we respond, certain good things happen to us. These good things can be defined in a host of ways. Paul, for one, raided the ancient vocabulary to describe what took place—he used terms like salvation, justification, reconciliation, and propitiation (strange terms for us). But essentially what took place was that God "took us back" and "accepted us" (terms that make more sense to us).

The great gift God gave to us because we are his sons is the gift of the Spirit. Paul says that anyone who is a Son is "led by the Spirit" (Rom. 8:14). While Paul does not connect "sonship" with being "led by the Spirit" in Galatians, he certainly thinks they are connected because he sees Christians as sons (Gal. 3:26–4:7), and he sees Christians as those who are "under the Spirit" (5:16–26). A son of God, then, is one who is "led by God's Spirit."

Legalists are led by the law; hedonists are led by their desires; materialists are led by their possessions. But sons of God, Christians, are led by the Spirit. What prompts their actions, what stirs their emotions, what guides their behavior, and what determines their careers is God's Spirit. Furthermore, sons of God do not fear and worry about where the Spirit will lead them.

They know that God's Spirit will lead them perfectly into God's will and God's blessing so they march behind confidently and joyously.

Are you a "son of God"? Are you intimate with God, are you free from the law's awful curse, and are you led by God's Spirit? You can become one by faith. "You are all sons of God through faith in Christ Jesus" (v. 26).

Galatians 4:8–20

FORMERLY, WHEN YOU did not know God, you were slaves to those who by nature are not gods. [9]But now that you know God—or rather are known by God—how is that you are turning back to those weak and miserable principles? Do you wish to be enslaved by them all over again? [10]You are observing special days and months and seasons and years! [11]I fear for you, that somehow I have wasted my efforts on you.

[12]I plead with you, brothers, become like me, for I became like you. You have done me no wrong. [13]As you know, it was because of an illness that I first preached the gospel to you. [14]Even though my illness was a trial to you, you did not treat me with contempt or scorn. Instead, you welcomed me as if I were an angel of God, as if I were Christ Jesus himself. [15]What has happened to all your joy? I can testify that, if you could have done so, you would have torn out your eyes and given them to me. [16]Have I now become your enemy by telling you the truth?

[17]Those people are zealous to win you over, but for no good. What they want is to alienate you [from us], so that you may be zealous for them. [18]It is fine to be zealous, provided the purpose is good, and to be so always and not just when I am with you. [19]My dear children, for whom I am again in the pains of childbirth until Christ is formed in you, [20]how I wish I could be with you now and change my tone, because I am perplexed about you!

PAUL IS A good pastor; thus, he cannot wait until the end of his "sermon" to make some applications. While he still has one more argument (4:21–31) to go through until he has presented his complete case, he nonetheless jumps into the significance of his arguments thus far. He has argued from the Old Testament (3:6–14), the nature of covenants (3:15–25), and from sonship (3:26–4:7). Our section, the application, belongs to the argument from sonship but goes well beyond it to become an application of his entire argument.

This section can be neatly divided into two (uneven) sections: (1) The Problem (vv. 8–11) and (2) The Plea (vv. 12–20). The Plea is rather random and emotional. In it Paul appeals to his own example and to his own role in their reversion to Judaism (vv. 12–16); then he explains what is actually going on at Galatia (vv. 17–18) before appealing once more in a more emotional tone (vv. 19–20).

The Problem (vv. 8–11)

ELSEWHERE PAUL DESCRIBES the past of his Gentile converts in less than positive terms (cf. Rom. 1:18–23; 1 Cor. 12:2; Eph. 2:11–13; 1 Thess. 4:5). Here he does the same: "Formerly,[1] when you did not know God, you were slaves to those who by nature are not gods." Put differently, there were two religious dimensions of their religious past: (1) they did not know the God of Israel, the true God of the world,[2] and (2) the gods they did know were "by nature . . . not gods" (cf. 1 Cor. 8:4–6). These expressions confirm that the Galatian converts were formerly Gentiles.

Paul goes on to state that now that they are converted, they have *a good beginning.* He corrects his own language in his description of their conversion: "But now that you know God—or rather are known by God. . . ." This correction is designed, not to teach that they did not know God, but to put the emphasis where Paul usually puts it: on God's sovereign grace as the initiating force in conversion. He insists that people do not seek God (cf. Rom. 3:11: "no one who searches for God"); rather, God seeks people. Humans are so caught in their sin and so in love with their sin that they do not seek holiness and love in and of themselves (cf. 1 Cor. 8:3; 13:12; 1 John 4:19: "We love because he first loved us" [cf. v. 10]).

That good beginning *has now become a bad situation;* that is the Galatians' problem. In spite of having received the knowledge of God, they have reverted back to their former ways. Paul wants to know, "How is it that you are turning back?" What he says here may be the most radical statement he makes anywhere about the law. The Galatians had had a typical pagan past (ignorant about the true God and worshiping non-gods). They had converted wonderfully as a result of Paul's preaching (3:1), but now they were "turning

---

1. The Greek word is *tote* ("then" or "formerly"); this word is often used in contrast to "now" (or "presently" in British English), as in 4:9 (see Rom. 6:20, 22; 7:5–6; 1 Cor. 13:12 [different terms but similar]; Col. 1:21–22). All of this may go back to the prophet Hosea in 1:6, 9; 2:1, 21–23.

2. This is a common complaint of Jews who lived in the Diaspora and who saw their environment as "ignorant of the true God" (see Jer. 10:25; Acts 17:20, 23; Eph. 4:18; 1 Peter 1:14).

back to those weak and miserable principles" (cf. 1:6; 3:3).[3] Here Paul describes their "new-but-bad situation" with the term *principles*, the same term he used in 4:3 for the Jewish past under the law. Furthermore, in verse 10 he mentions what is by almost every reckoning Jewish observances[4] of holy days and seasons (cf. Rom. 14:5–12; Col. 2:16–17). What is revolutionary here is that Paul considers "moving into Judaism" as nothing other than a reversion to "paganism," to "non-gods" (cf. Gal. 1:6). He asks, "Do you wish to be enslaved by them all over again?" Their move from idolatry to Christianity and now to Judaism is for Paul no different than a venture back into "idolatry" or "paganism."

R. N. Longenecker says it well:

> Beyond question, Paul's lumping of Judaism and paganism together in this manner is radical in the extreme. No Judaizer would ever have accepted such a characterization of Torah observance; nor would those in Galatia who acceded to their message. . . . For Paul, however, whatever leads one away from sole reliance on Christ, whether based on good intentions or depraved desires, is sub-Christian and therefore to be condemned.[5]

F. F. Bruce adds that this viewpoint is given "not as an exaggeration in the heat of argument but as the deliberate expression of a carefully thought out position."[6] Incidentally, Paul's willingness to lump together both unconverted Jew and Gentile under the "elemental principles" encourages our application of the text of Galatians, which so often addresses the Jewish Christian problem, to all groups today. Every human being, Paul would say, is captive to the "element principles" in some way and is only set free by Jesus Christ.

This bad situation leads to *Paul's fear*: "that somehow I have wasted my efforts on you." Paul had worked hard on the Galatians' behalf and for the universalism of the gospel. He risked rejection and censure in a private meeting (2:1–10), and he publicly rebuked Peter (2:11–14). He risked his life in missionary work (cf. 4:12–16) and experienced a great deal of criticism from the Judaizers. Any pastor knows the heartache and fear that come when a parishioner wavers, stumbles, and even falls away. That is all Paul is

---

3. These "principles" were "weak" in that they were powerless to rescue from sin and give spiritual life (see Rom. 8:3; Gal. 3:21), and "miserable" (or "poor") in that they were unable to provide the richness of God's blessing (cf. Gal. 4:1, where the boy is nothing more than a poor slave until manhood, at which time he inherits the blessing).

4. The term, a present middle verb, Paul uses here describes "minute observance"; so J. B. Lightfoot, *Galatians*, 172.

5. R. N. Longenecker, *Galatians*, 181.

6. F. F. Bruce, *Galatians*, 203.

saying here, and he will say similar things to other churches and try to rectify the problems (1 Cor. 4:16–17; 1 Thess. 3:5). His fear and frustration now give way to a plea.

The Plea (vv. 12–20)

AS ALREADY MENTIONED, Paul's appeal here is random and emotional. He calls the Galatians to follow his own example (v. 12a) and states his own personal role in their reversion (v. 12b). He goes on to remind them of the way they responded to him initially (vv. 13–16). Then he explains the situation at Galatia so they will know what is really happening (vv. 17–18). Finally, he makes an emotional appeal or wish that finishes off his argument (vv. 19–20).

Paul's example (v. 12a). Later, Paul will remind both the Corinthians and the Thessalonians of his own example (1 Cor. 2:1–5; 11:1; 1 Thess. 1:2–10) as a foundation on which he can construct his appeals. Those appeals began with the technique he uses here with the Galatians: "Become like me, for I became like you." Most likely Paul means something like this: "Become like me by freeing yourself from the law of Moses, just as I abandoned the law of Moses as God's dominant revelation for his people" (cf. Gal. 2:15–21). The second clause, "for I became like you," would then mean: I became like you Gentiles when I abandoned the law, accepted that I too was a sinner, and then turned to Jesus Christ (again, 2:15–21; see also 1 Cor. 9:19–23).[7]

Another interpretation sees here a theory of communication: "Become like me, for I became like you" is the appeal of a pastor who has fully sympathized and identified himself with his congregation. Again, evidence for this is 1 Corinthians 9:19–23. However, in this view the emphasis is given to *motivation* rather than theological grounding.[8] Even if I would agree that a secret to communication is identification and sympathy, I find this view of the verse to be more modern and less in tune with the essential problem Paul is facing: the Judaizers persuading the Galatians to live under the law.

Paul's role in their defection (v. 12b). "You have done me no wrong." What does Paul mean here? Is it nothing but a trusting comment, as between friends: "Friends agree not to hurt one another and you have not hurt me"?[9] I think not. Rather, Paul is stating that, in moving over to the Judaizers and abandoning the truth of the gospel as Paul preached it, they were not hurt-

---

7. See J. B. Lightfoot, *Galatians*, 173–74; H. D. Betz, *Galatians*, 221–23 (who also appeals to the relationship of friendship to understand the appeal of Paul); R. N. Longenecker, *Galatians*, 189.

8. See the comments of J. R. W. Stott, *Galatians*, 112–13.

9. So H. D. Betz, *Galatians*, 223.

ing Paul.[10] While the Judaizers might appeal to personal arguments, like "Don't leave or you will injure us," Paul knows that leaving his gospel is not leaving him; on the contrary, it is leaving God (1:6; 4:12a). This requires a good (to use our term) "self-image" and a solid confidence that not many have but the apostle did: he knew that he was a servant of God, not the center of God's work, and he knew that rejecting him was more importantly rejecting God (cf. Matt. 10:40–42).

Paul's reminder of their initial response (vv. 13–16). In spite of the fact that their departure is not taken personally by Paul, he reminds them of how they had previously responded to him, in the hope that they will repeat it, abandon the Judaizers, and once again align themselves with the universalism of the gospel.

When Paul originally preached the gospel to them, he did so "because of an illness" (v. 13), which was a "trial" to them (v. 14). What was this illness? There have been many guesses but no consensus. Some of the guesses are that he had malaria, epilepsy, or an eye disease. The evidence is incomplete, and we do not know even that it was the same as the "splinter" of 2 Corinthians 12:7. What we do know is that it was "because" of this illness that Paul ended up in Galatia. It is possible that he needed help that could only be found there (i.e., some kind of doctor) or that the conditions there were favorable for his recuperation. The illness was obvious and certainly the kind that could be offensive to an audience (hence, a "trial to you").

More importantly, the illness did not bother the Galatians (vv. 14–16); they looked beyond it and saw in Paul's preaching the truth of God because his message was attended by the power of the Holy Spirit (cf. 1 Cor. 2:4–5; 4:20; 1 Thess. 2:6). In fact, they received him as if he were an angel (Gal. 1:8);[11] even more, they received him as if he were Jesus Christ himself. This idea of being received as if one were Jesus Christ may well be connected to the theme of apostleship (see notes on 1:1). Apostles were personal representatives, and receiving such a person was tantamount to receiving the sender (cf. Matt. 10:40–42).

Paul says they were so receptive that they would have given their eyes to him, had they been able to (v. 15). It is this verse that has led so many to think Paul's "illness" was an eye disease; this is possible but hardly certain. H. D. Betz, in fact, shows that the theme of friendship in antiquity often associates such things as giving one's eyes as a demonstration of the depth of one's commitment to a friend.[12]

---

10. So R. N. Longenecker, *Galatians*, 190.
11. Paul was treated as if he were a god in Acts 14:11–20, when he preached at Lystra.

Reminding the Galatians of their former commitment (and friendship) to him makes the present situation unbearable for Paul: "What has happened?" (v. 15), and "Have I now become your enemy by telling you the truth?" (v. 16). This whole situation, Paul thinks, needs clarification for them, so Paul proceeds to that.

Paul's explanation of the situation (vv. 17–18). Paul contends that the Judaizing Christians (i.e., "those people") "are zealous to win you over." They want to "alienate you [from us],[13] so that you may be zealous for them." This term *zeal* is highly important for understanding the Galatian context. When used negatively, this term describes an emotion of "jealousy" and "intensity" that seeks to remedy a situation, frequently with violence. We are aware that there was a "party of Zealots" during the Great War (A.D. 66–73), whose sole ambition, through use of violence, was to defeat Rome and establish Jerusalem as the place that worshiped one God.[14]

Were the Judaizers violent Zealots? I am of the view that, though the term "zealous for you" can mean nothing more than "working hard to proselytize you,"[15] the term here describes the intensity of their action as well as the general national character of that action. In other words, while these Judaizers were not themselves using warlike violence to make full converts, they were part of a larger movement that was intensely nationalistic which, under better conditions, might erupt into violence. Physical force may have been used in Galatia (cf. notes on 2:14 and 6:12). This, I believe, is the natural inference from "compel you to be circumcised" in 6:12, where we will see that the real "zealots" are still back in Jerusalem and those "zealots" are putting pressure on the Judaizers to compel synagogue associates to conform to the whole law. What is clearer is that their orientation is highly nationalistic, and so Paul uses the term "zealous for you." We must remember that the central feature of their zeal was Israel and the law—and especially the law of circumcision. Circumcision was the act that separated the Jew from the Gentile. In essence, therefore, their "zeal" was nationalism.[16]

This helps define the meaning of "alienate" here: "to alienate you [from us]" means "to enter you, through circumcision, into Israel," "to allow your passage from one group into another." The Judaizers' goal, of course, was that

---

12. See H. D. Betz, *Galatians*, 226–28. He recounts a story of Lucian that involved the friendship of Dandamis and Amizoces and how Dandamis had his eyes removed in order to release Amizoces from capture. This bothered the released one so much that he also removed his eyes.

13. These words are implied.

14. On this see W. J. Heard, "Revolutionary Movements," in *DJG*, 688–98.

15. This appears to be the consensus (e.g., see F. F. Bruce, *Galatians*, 211–12).

16. See J. D. G. Dunn, *Jesus, Paul, and the Law*, 133–36.

the Galatians might be "zealous" for them: devoted so much to the law that they would carry on their agenda of separating God's people from the Gentile world by constructing the barriers that Jesus Christ had broken down. Their action, however, was "for no good" (v. 17): that is, it would not lead to acceptance with God as Paul has outlined from the beginning of the letter.

Paul now pauses to interject a note about "zeal": it is good to be zealous if one is zealous for God, as some of the saints of Israel had been (cf. Gen. 34; Num. 25:10–13; 1 Macc. 2:19–27, 50, 58; 2 Macc. 2:58). It is "for no good," however, if one's zeal is nationalistic and contrary to the promises of Abraham. And their zeal ought to be expressed for God "always" and not just when Paul was with them. We can only guess that their conversion must have led to an outpouring of commitment to everything Paul had taught them. Paul now senses that this "zeal for the gospel" has flagged and needs to be rekindled.

Paul's wish (vv. 19–20). Paul now expresses a wish to be with them so he can rectify things. We see here the heart of a pastor (much like the pastoral section 2 Cor. 2:14–7:4). His goal was clear: "until Christ is formed in you" (v. 19; cf. 2:20; 2 Cor. 3:18). He wanted the Galatian converts to grow in the Spirit until the image of Christ was formed—actually "transformed"—in them (cf. Rom. 12:1–2; 13:14; Eph. 4:23–24; Col. 1:24–2:5; 3:10). This would be a life of the Spirit, not the law; it would be centered in Christ, not Moses; it would be the universalism of the Abrahamic promise, not the nationalism of the Judaizing view of the Mosaic law.

Paul's description of the Galatians' situation leads him to think of his pastoral role to be one like giving birth to children. While he implies new birth here, he also implies that the opponents had caused what, in effect, might be considered an abortion. Paul must now "again" (v. 19) go through the process of leading them to the faith they once embraced.[17] He wants them to grow into Christ.

But for them to grow, Paul senses that he would have to be there and "change my tone"—from this stern warning and harsh language to the gentleness of a love that would persuade them over to his side and "alienate them" from the Judaizers. Paul's letter, he implies, is a weak communication in comparison to his mighty presence.

---

17. It is far wiser not to speculate here whether Paul thought an apostate could once again be born again. I doubt very much Paul thought that, and I am also sure that such an idea was not in his mind here. He is thinking more at a church-corporate level than at an individual-personal level.

Bridging Contexts

PAUL'S EMOTIONAL APPEAL is no different than many emotional appeals that pastors, teachers, parents, and friends make today. Because it is so like what happens today, it is not hard to make applications of the general nature of this passage. What we see operating here is a pastor, and we can learn lessons from Paul as pastor. In fact, the text points us in that direction when Paul says, "Become like me, for I became like you." Putting this Pauline statement together with others about "imitating him" (cf. 1 Cor. 4:16; 11:1; Phil. 3:17; 4:9; 1 Thess. 1:6; 2 Thess. 3:7, 9) makes pastoring a natural application. So we can learn lessons about pastoring, or caring for others, from the example of Paul.

Although at one level this particular command to the Galatians to become like him is simply a statement of Paul for them to follow him, and maybe only in a particular manner, when we examine it in the context of his own teachings of a similar nature, we find a pattern. Paul thought he was a good example of how to follow Christ and, though he surely thought following Christ was the ultimate aim, he encouraged young Christians to learn to live as Christians by following him. Thus, particular statements can become general patterns when we trace them through other passages in Paul's letters.

When we approach a passage, however, what do we do to find the transferable lessons? Several techniques are recommended. (1) Some direct statements have straightforward applications. "Become like me" is not hard to understand: Just as Paul lived apart from the law, so must we. (2) Sometimes the situation behind the statement or idea may be similar to ours. In our passage, we may find a situation of Paul's (failing converts) to be similar to ours (failing converts), and so we learn to respond to the situation in a way similar to Paul's. The same applies to Paul's illness; how can we apply this? I see his illness as an "impediment to communication" that God simply walked over in his desire to get to the hearts of the Galatians. We can apply this by finding similar "obstacles to communication." (3) We may need at times to examine one passage in light of others of the same kind to get a fuller picture of the idea so application might be made. We have suggested this for the notion of imitating Paul. (4) We may learn that some things Paul did are not for us. Whether it is his authority or his social and historical context, sometimes his world is so different that we cannot make an imitation of him possible. (5) Sometimes the motivations of Paul can be discerned; assuming that an apostle is worthy of imitating, we can infer from his motivations that our motivations should be similar.

As mentioned above, this is an emotional appeal. But we need to observe that this is not the only kind of appeal Paul could make. He could be also very reasoned, even complex and esoteric, in his argumentation (cf. 3:6–4:7; 4:21–31). Peter knew there were hard things in Paul to comprehend (2 Peter 3:15–16). So while Paul is emotional in this passage, emotional appeal was not his only tactic. He knew when to be intellectual and when to be emotional, just as he knew when to be a Jew and when to be Gentile (1 Cor. 9:19–23).

PAUL'S EMOTIONAL RESPONSE here is, without doubt, a critique of the "dry as dust" approach some advocate for teaching and preaching. Inasmuch as the gospel of Christ stirs our emotions, we should try to stir the emotions of those who hear it. Inasmuch as the message of sin pricks our consciences, so we should seek to convict others of sin. Inasmuch as the love of God is soothing and ennobling, so we should flood our people with a sense of their dignity because God loves them. The emotions attached to, and inherent in, a text ought to be there, and we ought to bring them out. Otherwise, we do not read the Bible aright. We dare not pretend that the Bible is a book for academics, designed only for intellectual stimulation and debate. The Bible is a book of reality, and part of reality is emotion.

The main issue in this "Contemporary Significance" section is on **imitating Paul**. I would first of all recommend that readers of Paul set out the passages in which he talked about following him and see just what he wanted them to follow. These passages include Galatians 4:8–20; 1 Corinthians 4:16; 11:1; Philippians 3:17; 4:9; 1 Thessalonians 1:6; 2 Thessalonians 3:7, 9. Read these and make a list of the things Paul asked others to imitate in his practices.

A question needs to be asked while doing this exercise: Is there difference between an apostle and a pastor in spiritually nurturing others? Surely there is. Do these differences negate or tone down any of the observations about imitating Paul? There is one so important that I want to record it here: that an apostle has a kind of authority that neither pastors nor parents nor "disciplers" dare to think they have. I believe that we will need to be careful in "imitating Paul," and one sure way of guaranteeing that we are being careful is to recognize right up front that we are not as authoritative as he was.

Second, I would like to apply this principle of "following Paul," or "learning from his example," to Galatians 4:8–20. What can we learn about pastoring, or caring for the spiritual welfare of others, from Paul's own example? Here are four considerations.

(1) *His goal and ours*: to form Christ in others (v. 19). Paul's goal was not to have people say he was a great evangelist; not to have the approval of others; not to have the sanction of Jerusalem. His goal in working with people was to have Christ formed in them. In verse 12b we find that Paul was not "personally hurt" when the Galatians succumbed to the Judaizers, and in verse 16 he shows that he was willing to be an "enemy" if he had to be in telling them the truth. These two statements can only come from someone who sets out in ministry only to please God and not be bothered by human rejection. What does Paul want in others? As I outlined above, this would be a "Spirit-led life" and a "Christ-centered existence." What is our goal?

We are, no doubt, as seduced as Paul was to gain the approval of others. We may begin with no desire but to serve God, but we find, after a few good experiences, that the approval of others is gratifying. The approval of others, I believe, can be cancerous. Before long we look forward to it and find, after even longer, that we are partially motivated by it. How do we see this? When we are disappointed when people do not approve of us.

Let me give an example of a Sunday school teacher. This teacher labors hard for her adult students and works hard so that the students will learn and grow. Unconsciously for awhile, she labors solely to serve God and exercise her gifts. After some of the sessions she observes that some of her students are growing and giving her the satisfaction of knowing that she has been instrumental in their growth. She continues. After a few months (or years) she observes that the affirmations are not as frequent nor as intense. Later she begins to take note of a general lack of affirmation. At this point she begins to sense a "lack of appreciation" and so begins to be a little rougher with her class. The story will go on and her feelings will escalate into bitterness and even possibly quitting, unless she realizes that she has gotten trapped into thinking that the goal of her teaching was to please others. She can recover quickly, I believe, once she realizes that her goal is to urge that people "live in the Spirit" and "make Christ the center of their lives." People's responses almost never measure whether we are serving God properly. To change the focus of this application, let me suggest that pastors for a while not stand at the back of "their church" after preaching, in order to see if they are getting dependent on congratulations.

At the same time, let me pause to remind us that our ministries are designed to help others. And I am not wrong, I think, in saying that it is both normal and acceptable to find a certain enjoyment in finding out that we have been helpful to others. The issue is simple: what is our motivation? Do we serve to be approved by others or do we seek God's approval?

(2) *His ground and ours*: an identical personal experience (v. 12). Paul could call the Galatians to become like him because he had become like them. That is, he had learned to live apart from the law; he wanted them to do this as well. Here is a fundamental principle in ministry. We will never be as effective with people as we should be until we have experienced what we are advocating. It is also the case that what we have experienced is frequently what we like to talk about. Nonetheless, we will often find ourselves "in trouble" if what we are talking about is not something we have actually lived through. As it makes little sense for someone who has never mothered or fathered to stand on a pedestal and talk about childrearing, so it makes little sense for someone to talk about "living apart from the law" who has been living a life of legalism. This ground of experience for teaching and influencing is found in all disciplines of life. It forms the basis for a cherished idea throughout our churches: namely, we want experienced people ministering to us.

Can you imagine the looks on the faces of a nominating committee at a local church when they interview a young person for an opening who has never attended church regularly, never taught a Sunday school class, never led anyone to Christ, never been married and so never raised children, never been on a church committee, never led a song or prayed publicly, and also never preached a sermon in a church? When that young person says that attending seminary is qualification enough, a church board is more than justified in urging that person to "go out and get some experience."

(3) *His intensity and ours*: the pain of childbirth (v. 19). I don't know what it is like to give birth, but I have been there for the birth of both our children. (The birth of our son, Lukas, was painful enough for me that a nurse had to attend to me to keep me from fainting!) What I know is that it is laborious (no pun intended!) and painful. A child sees the world only as the result of a great deal of effort.

Paul's pastoral experience led him to see "nurturing others in spiritual things" as similar to giving birth. He knew it was laborious and painful; he knew it took a lot of worrying and trusting in God; he knew it took a lot of attention to details and concern for people. In short, pastoring is much like mothering. While some church traditions call pastors "fathers," and rightly so, it is surprising that more do not call them "mothers"! Giving birth and mothering are both *very intense work*. Reading Galatians from cover to cover in one sitting may wear a person out when we recognize how intense Paul was in this letter. His letter is only a sketch of what he could be like (so he tells us in v. 20)! Here he talks not only about his theology, but also about his feelings for them, about his hopes for them, about his disappointments over them, and about his frustrations. For another example of Paul's pastoral intensity, read Colossians 1:24–2:5.

Those who work with the spiritual lives of others know what Paul is talking about. It means laborious prayer for them—praying here to avert one sin and praying there to stave off another problem. It means intellectual discussions that seek to answer questions that young Christians seem always to have.

(4) *His situation and perhaps ours*: a repulsive illness (vv. 13–14). Whatever Paul's illness was, it was apparently repulsive. Paul writes "even though my illness was a trial to you"; this can only mean that they saw in his illness something difficult to live with. This created tension between Paul and the Galatians and made communication difficult. Nonetheless, God's Spirit overcame the problem, and the Galatians were converted and taught the truth of the gospel.

We can apply this by finding an analogy: whatever impedes communication due to a shortfall on the part of the leader can be overcome through the Spirit. In my life I have seen God use all kinds of people: from preachers with speech impediments to athletes with physical handicaps to disciplers with problems in communicating. While we would not want to sanction "communication handicaps" as the surest way for God to use a person, we should also remind ourselves that God can use, and has used, some mighty weak vessels in communicating the gospel.

The problem then stares us in the face: we like tall, thin, handsome (male) pastors who have articulate speech and deep voices; we like them clean-shaven and well-dressed. In addition, we like it if they are compassionate and gentle and stimulating from the pulpit. Our exaltation of this "type" works itself down into our consciences, and individuals feel the call if they "fit the description," while others feel decidedly unwelcome if they do not. Our perceptions of whom God uses can thus become a disgusting typification of cultural values rather than perceptions rooted in biblical values and traditions.

I once heard a pastor preach and wondered, on watching him the first few minutes, how he could ever have "made it" as a pastor. Here was a tall, gangly man whose body had some mysterious and spasmodic jerking, while he seemed to stammer and stutter not infrequently as he sought to deliver the sermon. After "getting used" to this odd type of preaching I become thunderstruck at the eloquence of his message and the profundity of his experience of God's grace. Later I learned that he was, in fact, a mighty pastor with a powerful ministry in a large parish. What had been a "trial" to me became an invisible barrier to the grace of God.

Galatians 4:21–31

TELL ME, YOU who want to be under the law, are you not aware of what the law says? ²²For it is written that Abraham had two sons, one by the slave woman and the other by the free woman. ²³His son by the slave woman was born in the ordinary way; but his son by the free woman was born as the result of a promise.

²⁴These things may be taken figuratively, for the women represent two covenants. One covenant is from Mount Sinai and bears children who are to be slaves: This is Hagar. ²⁵Now Hagar stands for Mount Sinai in Arabia and corresponds to the present city of Jerusalem, because she is in slavery with her children. ²⁶But the Jerusalem that is above is free, and she is our mother. ²⁷For it is written:

"Be glad, O barren woman,
    who bears no children;
break forth and cry aloud,
    you who have no labor pains;
because more are the children of the desolate woman
    than of her who has a husband."

²⁸Now you, brothers, like Isaac, are children of promise. ²⁹At that time the son born in the ordinary way persecuted the son born by the power of the Spirit. It is the same now. ³⁰But what does the Scripture say? "Get rid of the slave woman and her son, for the slave woman's son will never share in the inheritance with the free woman's son." ³¹Therefore, brothers, we are not children of the slave woman, but of the free woman.

THIS MOST INTERESTING "use" of the Old Testament forms Paul's final and, from his view, climactic argument for his case against the Judaizers. The latter thought God's work with Gentiles was incomplete if it did not have both a component of trust in Jesus Christ and of commitment to the Mosaic law. Paul contends that acceptance with God involves *only* the component of Jesus Christ. The time of Moses is passé.

But, he argues in this last argument, if one reads Scripture "allegorically," one will see that the stories of Abraham-Sarah-Isaac along with the stories of Abraham-Hagar-Ishmael teach the point he has been making. God's way is through promise, not through the "flesh." This final argument from the law (i.e., the Pentateuch) complements his previous three arguments: from Scripture texts (3:6–14), from covenants (vv. 15–25), and from sonship (3:26–4:20). As well, Paul anchors his argument in the patriarch Paul thinks is paramount: Abraham, not Moses.

Some scholars have observed that ending a discussion with a "fancy allegory" was highly recommended by some skilled debaters in the ancient world. By returning to the method of beginning with a question (as he started the section at 3:1–5), Paul allows the readers of his letter to "figure it out themselves." His "allegorical story" urges them to read the story themselves, figure out its meaning, and then apply the lesson to themselves. This is rhetorically sound.[1] Furthermore, ending an address with an illustration has commended itself as a most profitable way of closure from time immortal.

The passage divides itself neatly. (1) The Question (v. 21): Do you really know what the law says? (2) The Biblical Material (vv. 22–23). What the law says is now stated: Abraham's relationship with two women form the basis of how the whole law is constructed. That construction involves either "promise" or "flesh" (NIV: "ordinary way"). (3) The Interpretation (vv. 24–27): Abraham's two women, Hagar and Sarah, correspond to two covenantal arrangements with God. One is a promise covenant (Sarah-heavenly Jerusalem-freedom), while the other is a "flesh" covenant (Hagar-law-slaves-earthly Jerusalem). (4) The Application (vv. 28–31): those who are being persecuted now correspond to those who were being persecuted then. Since those "then" were the sons of promise, those who are being persecuted now likewise are "sons of promise."

While this paragraph is not hard to interpret, it is hard to figure out how Paul got so clever to find this allegory.[2] It is easiest perhaps to make two lists of correspondences, lining up the person or thing under one covenant with

---

1. See the comments and quotations of ancient debaters in H. D. Betz, *Galatians*, 239–40. While some of these debaters thought it best to rank arguments from strongest to weakest (this would make our text the weakest of arguments), others thought an "indirect argument" and one that forced the reader to figure it out could be very effective.

2. Philo of Alexandria had already found similar contrasts in an allegorical way. He saw Abraham and Sarah as virtue, Isaac as higher wisdom, Hagar as lower learning of the schools, and Ishmael as sophistry. See his books *Abraham*, 68; *On Flight and Finding*, 128, 209–10; *On the Change of Names*, 255. Philo's entire works are more often than not allegorical interpretations of Old Testament passages. A full description of Jewish exposition of the Hagar-Sarah story can be seen R. N. Longenecker, *Galatians*, 200–206.

its "antitype" in the other.[3] Some correspondences are not explicitly stated, and so I have had to suggest them. What is not stated but what is clearly implied is that Paul is on Sarah's side and the Judaizers are on Hagar's.

LAW	CHRIST
Abraham	
Hagar Covenant	Sarah Covenant
Ishmael ("flesh")	Isaac ("promise")
Persecutor	Persecuted
Children-Slaves	Children-Free ones
Mount Sinai	(Mount Zion? Golgotha? Heaven?)
Earthly Jerusalem	Heavenly Jerusalem
in slavery	in freedom
Judaizers	**Paul**
Old Covenant	**New Covenant**

Before we expound this text, it might be good for us to examine whether this is an allegorical interpretation or a piece of typological interpretation. Definitions are critical here and, I suppose, the final difference is not that great for determining meaning. But it is worth our while to see if Paul is seeking hidden meaning (allegory) or simple correspondences that occur according to God's plan of redemption (typology).[4]

H. D. Betz has, I think, offered the best definitions I have seen for these two terms.[5] *Allegory*: "allegory takes concrete matters mentioned in Scripture

---

3. The order of these associations is arranged in an inverted manner (called a "chiasm"). I reproduce the chart of R. N. Longenecker, *Galatians*, 213. The As, Bs, Cs, and Ds each correspond to one another. See his discussions of each. Thus:

```
A      Hagar
    B       Mount Sinai
        C        slavery
             D        the present city of Jerusalem
             D´       the heavenly Jerusalem
        C´       freedom
    B´      (Mount Zion)
A´     our mother
```

4. It does not solve our problem to appeal to the Greek term *allegoroumena* (NIV: "taken figuratively") and say that it is therefore "allegory." The Greek term here could refer to a wealth of methods.

5. See H. D. Betz, *Galatians*, 239. A similar definition is found in R. N. Longenecker's most helpful book, *Biblical Exegesis in the Apostolic Period* (Grand Rapids: Eerdmans, 1975), 127. Longenecker's book has a brief survey of Jewish methods of exegesis. See also F. F. Bruce, *Galatians*, 217.

and tradition (mythology) to be surface appearance or vestiges of underlying deeper truths which the method claims to bring to light." *Typology*: "Persons, events, and institutions of Scripture and tradition are taken as prototypes of present persons, events, and institutions, which are explained as their fulfillment, repetition, or completion within a framework of salvation history." Betz concludes that Paul's method in verses 21–31 is a mixture of these methods of Bible study. While Paul clearly *emphasizes correspondences* (typology), he may hint that such is the *deeper meaning* of the Old Testament narratives (allegory). I agree with Betz that it is probably too restrictive to Paul's method to limit it either to allegory or typology, though the emphasis ought to be given to the typological. What we do know is that Paul's approach to the Old Testament was revolutionized through his Damascus Road encounter with Christ. From that moment on, he learned to reread the Jewish Bible in light of its fulfillment in Christ. His reading of the Bible is "Christocentric" through and through.

It is just possible, though we must guess at it, that Paul's use of the allegory here was determined by a similar appeal on the part of the Judaizers to Abraham's son Ishmael, who was one of the fountains of the Gentiles. They may have argued that Abraham's descendants were his "fleshly" descendants, namely Jews, and that the Galatians then needed to become Jews. Paul counters that Abraham's true "fleshly" descendants are actually in the line of Hagar and Ishmael, not Abraham. The real "seed" of Abraham is Christ and his people.[6]

The question (v. 21). If Paul is indeed responding to the Judaizers' own use of the Sarah-Hagar story, what he is doing here is setting out the "real meaning" of the story by showing that Hagar is connected in the Old Testament with "flesh" and that "flesh" is opposed to Spirit. Those who wish to be "under the law" (live according to the Mosaic law in such a way that Christ is eclipsed) need to learn to read the law in light of what God has done in Christ.

The biblical material (vv. 22–23). Paul alludes here to texts in Genesis 16, 21, and 25. There we learn that Sarah's frustration over not having children led her to encourage Abraham to have children through her servant, Hagar, a custom that was apparently acceptable at that time (cf. 30:3–13). She had a son named Ishmael, but Hagar herself became disrespectful of

---

6. On this, see the engaging discussion of C. K. Barrett, "The Allegory of Abraham, Sarah, and Hagar in the Argument of Galatians," in *Essays on Paul*, ed. C. K. Barrett (Philadelphia: Westminster, 1982), 154–70. He has been followed in general by F. F. Bruce (*Galatians*, 218) and R. N. Longenecker (*Galatians*, 197–219).

Sarah; thus, Sarah punished her. Hagar fled Sarah's anger, though she eventually returned. Ishmael, as promised by God (16:12), was disliked by the descendants of Sarah, departed from living with them, lived in the wilderness of Beersheba and Pharan (21:14–21), and eventually became the titular head of the Arabs.

Paul fastens his attention on (1) the two women, describing one as the "slave woman" and the other as the "free woman" (which fits his polemical agenda), and (2) the births of the two boys—one in the "ordinary way" and one "as the result of a promise."[7] Sarah's encouragement of Abraham is considered in the Old Testament as "unbelief" and by Paul as "fleshly." This latter sense is not fleshly in the sense of "lust" but in the sense of "not living according to the promise of God" to form a nation from him (Gen. 12:2–3).

The interpretation (vv. 24–27). As we diagrammed above, these two women correspond to two covenants. Hagar is in the covenant established on Mount Sinai (the place of giving the law) and her children are all slaves (the state of those who live under the law; cf. 3:26–4:7). Jerusalem corresponds to this Mount Sinai, for since its inhabitants live under the law, its people are slaves. Such an association would have been shocking to the Judaizers and to all Jews. To think that Paul would say that those who "obey the law" are for that very reason in the line of Ishmael! Surely this was more than they were used to hearing:

Hagar → Ishmael → Mount Sinai's law → Jerusalem → Slave inhabitants!

This was a major revolution on how to read one's past.

But Paul goes on. Sarah's seed has a covenant established in the "heavenly Jerusalem." The children of the "barren woman" is from Genesis 11:30, where Sarah is described as "barren." But this Sarah is connected to Isaiah 54:1 by the word "barren" (cf. also Isa. 51:2). In 54:1 we have promises of God that he would restore Zion. Thus, Isaiah is predicting the future Jerusalem. In fact, by associating their being the true Jerusalem in the sense of fulfilling 54:1, Paul is saying that those who believe in Christ are living in the new era, the era of fulfillment. They are "more" numerous, meaning that God has blessed them more.

The application (vv. 28–31). "Now you, brothers, like Isaac, are children of promise." Here Paul makes his application to the Galatian situation. He does so in a most interesting way, again arguing from experience: The way the two boys treated each other also corresponds to the present day. Just as

---

7. The NIV "ordinary way" is from *kata sarka*. This expression means for Paul "life outside the Holy Spirit." See notes on 3:3.

Isaac was persecuted by Ishmael,[8] so "believers in Christ" are persecuted by the "Moses plus Christ Judaizers."[9] Put differently, you can figure out whose side you are on by figuring out who is being persecuted and who is persecuting. The persecutors are wrong (1:13, 23) and the persecuted are right. What is the solution? As Sarah expelled Hagar and her son (Gen. 21:10), so the Galatian believers ought to expel the Judaizers. This ought not to be taken as a broadside against all Jews and against all of Judaism. It is a particular comment directed at a specific group of people: the Judaizers, who were trying to impose the law of Moses on Gentile converts.

The conclusion Paul draws skips from verses 28–29 to verse 31 (v. 30 being a kind of "pastoral exhortation"): since we are the persecuted, we are "children of the free woman" and not sons of the "slave woman." This means that the Judaizers are wrong in their insistence that the law must be adopted in order to become a "son of Sarah."

Bridging Contexts

IT IS PROBABLY easiest to begin with Paul's method of interpretation because that method is what gets him to his conclusions. We have noted his conclusions over and over (acceptance by faith, not by conforming to the law of Moses). What changes here is Paul's method. The apostle interprets Scripture in a way that is most unlike what we are taught to do. Can we do what Paul does here?

Our usual pattern of interpreting Scripture is to begin with discovering the *meaning of a text in its context* and then to proceed to its *application in our context*. In essence, our procedure is to "fuse contexts," to put together the ancient world and our world by importing the message of the ancient text into our world. John Stott describes the task of interpreting the Bible, applying it to our world, and preaching it as one of "bridge building."[10] We are taught to hold the Bible in one hand and the newspaper in the other, to grasp

---

8. There is no explicit reference of Ishmael actually persecuting Isaac in the Old Testament. There are two explanations: (1) the statement in Genesis 21:9 that Ishmael was "playing with" Isaac was understood to mean "teasing" and then throughout Jewish history came to mean "persecution," or (2) the history of conflict between Arabs and Jews was enough to attribute such to the head of the Arabs, Ishmael (e.g., Judg. 8:24; Ps. 83:6). See R. N. Longenecker, *Galatians*, 217; F. F. Bruce, *Galatians*, 223–24.

9. The use of the persecution theme may refer to no more than social harassment. However, I suspect that it confirms our view that both Peter (Gal. 2:14) and the Judaizers may have used force (2:3; 4:18; 6:12).

10. See J. R. W. Stott, *Between Two Worlds: The Art of Preaching in the Twentieth Century* (Grand Rapids: Eerdmans, 1982), 135–79.

the timelessness of the gospel together with the timeliness of its relevant applications, or to read the languages of the Bible and speak the languages of our culture.

The foundation for this approach—and this is the procedure of this series of commentaries—is first to *examine the text in its context.* We begin with exegesis of words, of phrases and clauses, of sentences, of paragraphs, and of biblical books in their respective contexts. We cannot bring forward to our world a message until we have found the message in the ancient texts.

But this is exactly what Paul is not doing. The original context is neglected for, so far as we know, the original Sarah and Hagar did not stand for covenants. How do we respond? With one of three possibilities: we are wrong and Paul is right; Paul is wrong and we are right; or it is not a matter of "right or wrong" but simply a procedure that we no longer use and one that Paul used only rarely, fully aware that what he was doing was not "exegesis," and only for a specific reason.

Are *we* wrong in pursuing the "original meaning" of a text? I think not. The foundation for the quest for original meaning (call it the "historical aspect of exegesis") is our respect for God's Word given in space and time, our respect for what God said *then.*[11] This historical aspect ties us into "what was actually said and what actually happened" and gives us a standard for measurement. Without this historical aspect, there are no controls over what the gospel is and what should be said in the name of God. If the text means whatever anyone wants it to mean, then it has no meaning for everyone; it has only meaning for individuals. So I am fully persuaded that we are not wrong. But neither am I persuaded that Paul was wrong.

The third option is best. Paul was doing something here that was acceptable for his age, he was aware of what he was doing, and he knew he was doing it for a specific context. Furthermore, what he was doing is not recommended for us if we are seeking original meaning. If, as many scholars today think, Paul was simply turning a Judaizing argument on its head, then it becomes completely clear that Paul was not doing something on his own initiative. To use the words of 2 Corinthians 11, Paul was "playing the part of the fool"; he was "playing their game," and he did it better. They had started the problem by saying a true child of God had to be Jewish, and they appealed to Abraham. They also said the line of Gentiles goes back to Ishmael, not Isaac. So Paul, by investigating the matter more seriously, showed that Ishmael was the "son of slavery." Consequently, those who adhered to

---

11. For a technical discussion of scholarship on the issue of "meaning," see G. R. Osborne, *The Hermeneutical Spiral: A Comprehensive Introduction to Biblical Interpretation* (Downers Grove, Ill.: InterVarsity Press, 1991), 366–415.

the slavery of the law were following in the tradition of Ishmael. True children of God are in the line of Sarah. If, as I say, Paul was responding to this sort of situation, then we have no problem at all.

Furthermore, it seems likely to me that the rarity of this kind of procedure in Paul (cf. elsewhere at 1 Cor. 9:9–10; perhaps at 1 Cor. 10:1–11) shows that he knew it was a departure from the normal rules of interpreting the Bible. Frequently, Paul interprets the Bible in a way consistent with our "historical aspect," if we leave out of the question our concerns with tracing background first (which we need to do because we live two thousand years or more later). Paul sought to understand a text in the original languages (either Hebrew or Greek) and according to the normal rules of grammar and syntax. But here he dabbles for the moment in a procedure that his opponents had used and one that was "in vogue" at his time.

I am of the view, then, that what Paul does here is not wrong; but neither are we wrong in contending that the "historical aspect" of interpretation is fundamental to proper study of the Bible. Paul did something that we cannot really imitate and in a context that is not ours. On the other hand, it is not wrong for us to relate the gospel by using the figures of the Old Testament, as long as we do not contend that such is the original meaning. I have frequently heard sermons and Bible studies based on Old Testament texts that, after restating the original meaning and context, said almost nothing about original meaning but that still spoke to me about what God wanted of me. To be sure, sometimes these well-meaning folks thought they were doing exegesis, and they were wrong. Nonetheless, these sermons simply used an Old Testament figure and the narrative about him or her in order to restate the gospel of Jesus Christ.

Such "restatements" are far less frequent today than they were twenty years ago because church attendees today do not know their Bibles as well as people did twenty years ago. Allusions to Old Testament figures are not given as much because neither the preachers nor the listeners have immersed themselves deeply enough in the pages of the Old Testament. How many in our churches today would pick up immediately on the implications of names or stories like those of Ichabod, Ehud, Hezekiah, or Hosea? What if I were to say that Paul responded to the Galatian defection the way Eli and his daughter-in-law responded to the messenger and pronounced the districts of Galatia to be inhabited now by Ichabods (read here 1 Sam 4:1–22)?

I see no reason why we cannot make allusions like these, allusions that restate the message of the gospel in terms of Old Testament figures and events. There is no reason, so far as I am concerned, why Christians cannot express the gospel by using the characters and events of the Old Testament. This is, in effect, a retelling of an Old Testament narrative in terms of the

Christian gospel. Thus, I see no reason why we cannot find analogies to the gospel in Old Testament stories *as long as we are aware that what we are doing is not historical exegesis but application and rereading*.

A second issue here to discuss is Paul's assumption that those who are in the right are the ones who are being persecuted (vv. 28–31). Is this always the case? The answer to this question is simple, though difficult to work out in actual living. After all, persecutors are not always wrong and the persecuted are not always right. But more often than not in Paul's day, those who were doing the persecuting were wrong and those who were getting persecuted were right. This led to his general assumption that the persecuted were on God's side. But before we can move this idea that the persecuted are right, we have to perform several steps. First, we need to sketch the context of this teaching[12] and understand its overall thrust; then we can find comparable "persecutions" in our world.

We think immediately of Daniel's three friends, who resisted the attempt of King Nebuchadnezzar to make everyone bow down before his idol. They were thrown into a fiery furnace, but God delivered them (Dan. 3). Later Daniel himself was thrown into a lion's den for praying to the God of Israel; once again, God delivered him (Dan. 6). Others suffered, not only for their life of obedience, but also for their fearless prophecies and warnings (cf. 1 Kings 18; 22:13–28; Jer. 26:20–24). One major book of the second century B.C. was dedicated to the heroic efforts of the martyrs (1 Maccabees). We find a veritable table of martyrs and their sufferings in Hebrews 11:32–38: these things they suffered because of their faithfulness to God.

Jesus himself was the prototypical martyr of God. His enemies tried to silence his preaching (Luke 4:29) and find fault with his practice or teachings (Mark 11:27–33; 12:13–17, 18–27, 28–34). His crucifixion was seen by outsiders as the moment when he was finally put away; it was seen by God as the act whereby he brought those outsiders near. Jesus said that those who are persecuted are blessed by God (Matt. 5:10–12) and that those who were in the line of the prophets would be treated just as poorly (23:33–39). This reflected also the experience of Jesus and the early churches (Acts 4:1–22; 5:17–42; 6:9–15; 7:51–8:3; 9:1–2, 23, 29; 12:1–5). Paul too had many experiences of persecution (cf. Acts 13:8, 45, 50; 14:2, 4–7, 19; 16:19–34; 17:5–9, 13; 18:6, 12–17; 19:9, 13–16, 23–41; 21:27–28:28) and even listed them (2 Cor. 11:23–27). He is of the same view as the others: those who follow Jesus Christ will suffer persecution (2 Tim. 3:12). Peter too warned about impending persecution (1 Peter 3:8–17; 4:12–19), and James revealed that

12. A nice survey is that of T. Lewis, "Persecution," in *Dictionary of the Apostolic Church*, ed. J. Hastings (New York: Charles Scribner's Sons, 1918), 2:168–86; see also G. W. Bromiley, "Persecute," in *NISBE*, 3:771–74.

some Christians were being economically persecuted (James 5:1–6). The book of Revelation is a series of pictures that counter the evil of the world with God's vindication of his people and making all things right (Rev. 7:14–17; 19:1–22:6).

So to understand this assumption on the part of Paul, we must understand its context. The context was one of Christianity being right, of Judaism and the Roman empire in general being irritated over Christianity and its messengers, of various local groups persecuting individual Christians, and of Christians perceiving that they were being persecuted because they were Christians. Michael Green, in his masterful study of evangelism in the early churches, says it well:

> At whatever level in society it was attempted, evangelism in the early church was a very daunting undertaking. It was a task involving social odium, political danger, the charge of treachery to the gods and the state, the insinuation of horrible crimes and calculated opposition from a combination of sources more powerful, perhaps, than at any time.[13]

This was their context. How did they respond?

Their successful strategies of "coping" with persecutions were rooted in several complementary ideas: (1) that Christ was persecuted; (2) that God's messengers were persecuted all along for their proclamation of his message; (3) that God's people have frequently suffered the wrath of ungodly people because they are faithful to God's will; and (4) that God will eventually vindicate his people by making things right, both by his own action of establishing justice and by raising his people from among the dead. The early churches coped with opposition because they had God's mind on what was going on. They feared God, not people; they knew this life was not all; they took courage from Jesus' example and from the many who were opposed in the life of the church.

Contemporary Significance

I WANT TO look here at the theme of *persecution.* How do we cope with opposition to the truth of the gospel, whether as general unbelief or as overt hostility to the one relating the truth of the gospel? In our passage, as we have seen, Paul appealed to persecution as part of the history of God's faithful people, and therefore it could be used as a test of one's faithfulness. Can we use this today?

---

13. Michael Green, *Evangelism in the Early Church* (Grand Rapids: Eerdmans, 1970), 47. This quotation is his summary of a chapter on the "Obstacles to Evangelism."

First, we need to define what "persecution" is. *Persecution is opposing a Christian for either obeying God or for declaring God's will and truth.* We are not talking about the financial struggles of the wealthy in a materialistic society nor about a flat tire on the way to work that cuts into a person's plans for the day; neither are we talking about adolescents struggling with parents or parents being disappointed when their children do not attain the status the parents desired. While all these intrusions in life have their part to play in the development of Christian character, these are not persecutions. One quick look at the events referred to in the paragraphs above on the biblical teaching on persecution will quickly prevent the reader from thinking about persecution as such mundane things as struggles with adolescents. We treat with disrespect our Christian brothers and sisters who are experiencing genuine persecution when we class our "flat tires" with their being run from town, being fired, and being killed—for the sake of the gospel.

Here is *our problem*: there are many Christians today who live in a country that is not overtly hostile toward Christianity or toward the proclamation of the gospel. One can attend Christian grade schools without social hassle, attend a Christian college without social reprisal, marry a Christian, and then carry out a calling in the context of a Christian institution. These kinds of people may never suffer persecution in their life. For these people, the message of Paul that assumes the persecuted are in the right is *almost totally irrelevant*, and we need to admit it. For such people, learning about persecution may be encouraging, and it may provide for them categories for coping if they ever encounter persecution. For them one of Paul's last statements is simply not a part of their experience and therefore probably not accurate: those who follow Jesus Christ will suffer persecution (2 Tim. 3:12). In my view, it is indeed theoretically possible to follow Christ and not suffer persecution.

Paul is not wrong, however. For we find that the context of the Bible and the social situation in which he spoke these words show them to be a general truth that may not be true in every imaginable situation. But I also find that while it is "theoretically possible" to follow Christ and not be persecuted, it is indeed rare. So while it is possible for Paul's teachings and assumptions to be practically speaking irrelevant, it is more than likely that these teachings are not irrelevant and that those who follow Christ will find the message of the Bible on persecution practical.

If we pursue Christ in the *realities of our world*, we will quickly discover that there are types of persecution awaiting followers of Christ. These persecutions will confirm Paul's assumption that the persecuted are right. Where will we find these? I would like to suggest that, at the general level, the *Zeitgeist* (or "spirit of the age") is against the truth of the gospel. Just thinking about our society makes one think of "pluralism" and "the gospel of toleration." Both of these concepts are directly contrary to the truth of the gospel. Both are against any concept of "absolute truth." If *pluralism* means there are "plural options" in the pursuit of right and wrong, in the pursuit of the good life, and in the pursuit of final acceptance with God, then the message that Jesus Christ is God's only agent for salvation will clash with pluralism, and such clash may lead to persecution. If *toleration* is the keynote of social, political, and religious policies, then it becomes clear that Christians face a stacked deck. While they may be loving, they do not agree that toleration is the keynote, nor do they think that tolerating sin and false truth claims is proper.

In other words, there is a general conflict of worldviews when it comes to a Christian and a non-Christian in our modern world. While we cannot enter here into a description of the "world" in Pauline thought, it is instructive to remember that the entire Bible witnesses to the notion that the world is opposed to the gospel as darkness is opposed to light (John 3:19–21). The world is opposed to God (1 Cor. 1:18–25) because God is truth and reveals the world's essence and orientation away from God (Rom. 3:19). This means that the Christian cannot expect to find in the "world" an ally to the gospel. Opposition can only be expected. There is a general conflict.

But a general conflict does not mean persecution except at the most basic level. But—here is where the rub comes—*the minute a Christian is willing to state his or her case for the truth of the gospel, at that very moment persecution of some kind will frequently appear.* How? It can be subtle and it can be overt. Subtle oppositions come by way of frowns, raising eyebrows, social exclusion, gossip, blacklisting, and maneuverings so a Christian will not be promoted. Overt oppositions to our willingness to speak up comes in many forms: from negative social comments to hostile comments, from economic sanctions to career firings, and from physical pressure to overt putting to death. I find, however, that the most difficult persecution to deal with is subtle. The fear of being disapproved and therefore talked about is something most Christians would simply like to avoid. The result: we fail to speak up and to be faithful. I give two examples, one from a world in which Christians subtly put pressure on other Christians and one from a world in which someone puts overt pressure on a Christian.

Recently, I was watching a Christian TV program broadcast a discussion among pastors and psychologists over a sensitive topic in our society: sexual addictions. After the host sketched the horridness of the topic, he turned it over to the panel to make their remarks. It began in a way that is so typical for psychologists that I risk a stereotype. Their very important starting point was that the person must be accepted, the person must understand that God loves him or her, the person must understand that he or she has a past that has led to this unacceptable behavior, the person must understand that the therapist cannot cure the problem until that person wants to change, etc. As the discussion progressed, I sensed that very little progress was being made and, more importantly, few uniquely Christian ideas were being spoken (except, of course, that acceptance is important).

In this situation a pastor chimed in and, rather hesitatingly, suggested that the Bible considers this kind of problem "sin"; then, getting bolder, he argued that Jesus Christ and the power of the Holy Spirit were the essential cures for this kind of unacceptable behavior. At this very point in the discussion the others began to nod their heads in agreement, and eventually all came around to a fundamental agreement.

My point here is not to suggest cures for sexual addictions, except to say that I believe the biblical solution is fundamental; but I suggest that psychologists are most useful in diagnosis, analysis, and progress for such problems, but also that the word that was uneasy for them to speak was "sin." They did not want to sound "unprofessional" and did not want to be thrown into the category of certain psychologists and pastors who think psychology has nothing to offer the Christian world. In their desire to remain respectable (not a bad desire when exercised properly), they hedged on the biblical message. I mention this because I know this is a problem for Christian psychologists—and I respect this profession greatly (my wife happens to be one!). What I see here is subtle pressure to use the right terms so carefully that, at times, there is an unwillingness to call something what the Bible calls it—"sin"; and then that same Bible promises forgiveness to the one who renounces such sin. Thus, because they want to protect the integrity of their discipline and to remain respectable in their field, and because they know that for many problems a quick cure (surrendering to Christ or the Holy Spirit) is simply not effective,[14] Christian psychologists subtly put pressure on others and themselves in such a manner that at times they end up refusing to state the truth of the gospel.

In the context of Galatians 4:21–31, I wish to make this observation: when Christian psychologists willingly stand up for the truth of the gospel as the foundation for emotional and mental health and sense an opposition to what they are doing, they will also experience the truth of Paul's words. They

---

14. I am persuaded that this is the case. For many problems lengthy sessions with a therapist, exploring one's history and working through emotions and problems are needed. But I also believe that the gospel of Jesus Christ and the power of the Spirit are what lie at the foundation of emotional and mental health. This is what it means to believe in Christianity!

will confirm the truthfulness of the gospel by seeing that it is opposed by those who do not trust in God.

Overt pressure from others is easier to detect but perhaps more difficult to accept. I was speaking with a man recently who told me of how he had married a Lutheran woman (he was formerly a Roman Catholic) and of how the change of churches was different. He then, with a little bravado, told me of how he had recently "corrected" his new pastor after the pastor had preached on salvation in Christ alone. He told me how he approached the pastor and how he had informed the pastor that he was not going to hear any more of this "one way to salvation" stuff. He then continued with a brief dissertation on how it is morally wrong for Christians, and anyone for that matter, to think they knew the truth and how it was wrong for anyone to think that God would accept only Christians. His emotions were getting stronger and more intense. He then looked at me and said, "Don't tell me only Christians are going to heaven. That's not Christian. You don't believe that, do you Scot?"

I have to admit that I didn't want to become the brunt of another tirade. Nor did I feel, at that moment, like getting into a lengthy discussion about truth, about God's revelation in Christ, and about what was "Christian." For this man it meant "being nice and tolerant and full of good works," but it certainly did not mean being orthodox. I did say, however: "I believe, my friend, in Jesus Christ, and the Bible teaches that we are accepted by God *only* through Jesus Christ." I felt uncomfortable (as anyone talking with him about this subject would have), but I also sensed a liberation, for in willingly declaring the good news in Christ there is a sense of liberation. I felt that it did not matter to me if he liked me; I knew that it was more important to follow Christ than to be accepted by him. Yet I valued his friendship (and still do). In subsequent conversations I have learned that he was (over)reacting to an unfortunate past (where only Roman Catholics could be Christians) and that he considered himself a believer and a Christian. At the time I was not convinced that he was a Christian (at least in an orthodox sense), and I experienced the pressure that every follower of Christ experiences: standing up for Christ in the midst of pressure to deny the truth of the gospel.

Once again I make the same observation: in standing up for the gospel and in boldly stating its contours, the Christian will find the truth of Paul's words: those who follow Christ will suffer persecution. That is to say, the experience of opposition is for the Christian a confirmation of the truth of the gospel. The experience does not confirm it; the gospel confirms itself through the opposition.

When we go through such experiences, we need to learn to look at them the way the earliest Christians looked at them. (1) We need to realize that we are simply walking right behind Jesus. It is encouraging for the persecuted to know that they are being treated as Jesus was treated. (2) We need to remember that God's people have always been opposed. Who do we think we are that we suppose we can live obediently and not follow in the steps of those who were opposed? (3) We can root our confidence in the hope of God's final vindication and our resurrection. Come what may in the present, we know that in the end God will put all things right. This includes our own resurrection and a glorious eternity in the presence of God. This hope ought to animate our spirits as we face opposition to the gospel.

We must return, however, to our opening observations about the *absence of persecution* in too much of the modern Christian world. It has a basis: the desire for acceptance. This desire is exactly what Paul spoke against in Galatians 1:10, and it is exactly what the Judaizers were rooted in: acceptance back home in Jerusalem. This desire is so strong in our own world that it infects our willingness to follow Christ. Indeed, our desire for acceptance works against the opportunity of confirming our faith through being opposed. In her helpful book, *Out of the Salt Shaker and Into the World* ,[15] Becky Pippert distinguishes between the Christian being "obnoxious" and "offensive" in our relationship to the world. She rightly contends that being obnoxious is wrong; being offensive is normal. She writes: "If anyone was guilty of being offensive, it was Jesus—not me. It was *his* idea that he was the only way to God, not mine." And she finished an imaginary conversation with an unbeliever with this thought: "I know, and isn't it amazing that Jesus actually said so many narrow things? Wouldn't it be intriguing to study him to discover why he made such egotistical claims?"[16]

The gospel, properly understood and persuasively presented, is offensive to sinful people. There is no getting around this. To be a follower of Christ means an inevitable conflict, and that means being offensive. We should not shirk the opportunity; it is not we who are actually being rejected (Matt. 10:40–42). Through the experience of being opposed, however, comes the confirmation that we are simply being treated the way all of our faithful brothers and sisters have been taught. Since Day One, God's people have been opposed. "It is the same now," wrote Paul (Gal. 4:29).

---

15. Becky Pippert, *Out of the Salt Shaker and Into the World* (Downers Grove, Ill.: InterVarsity Press, 1979), esp. 15–31.

16. Ibid., 27.

Galatians 5:1–12

I T IS FOR freedom that Christ has set us free. Stand firm, then, and do not let yourselves be burdened again by a yoke of slavery. ²Mark my words! I, Paul, tell you that if you let yourselves be circumcised, Christ will be of no value to you at all. ³Again I declare to every man who lets himself be circumcised that he is obligated to obey the whole law. ⁴You who are trying to be justified by law have been alienated from Christ; you have fallen away from grace. ⁵But by faith we eagerly await through the Spirit the righteousness for which we hope. ⁶For in Christ Jesus neither circumcision nor uncircumcision has any value. The only thing that counts is faith expressing itself through love.

⁷You were running a good race. Who cut in on you and kept you from obeying the truth? ⁸That kind of persuasion does not come from the one who calls you. ⁹"A little yeast works through the whole batch of dough." ¹⁰I am confident in the Lord that you will take no other view. The one who is throwing you into confusion will pay the penalty, whoever he may be. ¹¹Brothers, if I am still preaching circumcision, why am I still being persecuted? In that case the offense of the cross has been abolished. ¹²As for those agitators, I wish they would go the whole way and emasculate themselves!

PAUL'S CALL FOR freedom in verse 1 is the essence of his message to the Galatians. The purpose of Christ's work was to set Jews free from the curse of the law and to allow Gentiles to enjoy the same liberation by breaking their chains to disobedience and sin. No words can overstate the significance that the notion "freedom" has in this letter

In the overall structure of Galatians our passage begins a major section. In his first major section (1:10–2:21), Paul has attempted to prove the legitimacy of his message by demonstrating his independence, while his second section (chaps. 3–4) had the same proof in mind—using theological arguments. In this final section (5:1–6:10), Paul applies his message to the situation of the Galatians. They had been infected by a virus that contended one was not accepted by God until one had not only surrendered to Jesus Christ but also to Moses' law. Paul's inoculation contains the antidote: when one turns to Jesus Christ, one turns away from Moses and begins living under the dominion of Christ and the Spirit, whom the Father has sent into one's heart. Those who are of Christ, Paul argues, are free from the law.

It should be pointed out that chapters 5–6 are not tacked onto a polemical treatise by Paul with no apparent connections.[1] While it is true that chapters 1–4 emphasize the problem of Mosaic legalism and chapters 5–6 emphasize not using freedom as an excuse for sin, there is more connection than meets the eye. The issue from cover to cover in Galatians is twofold: Who are the true people of God (Israel or the church) and how should they govern their lives (by obeying Moses or by following the Spirit)? Paul contends for "church" and "following the Spirit." This last conclusion had created problems for his Judaizing opponents, and their charge was surely that Paul, in arguing that God's people should follow the Spirit and not follow the law, did not give the Galatians adequate guidance. They questioned Paul's essential view of Christian ethics and wondered if the Spirit was sufficient and adequate for moral guidance and for fighting off the "flesh." Paul wards off this very problem: while Christians are to live in the Spirit and not under the law, their lifestyle should be holier than those in Judaism and more loving *because of the presence of the Holy Spirit in their lives.* To return to our analogy, those who work on computers should, he argues, be more effective than those who hammer away on manual typewriters.

This last section of Galatians begins with a thesis statement (v. 1), and then Paul applies that thesis of freedom to several different issues: (1) circumcision (vv. 2–12), (2) Christian liberty (vv. 13–15), (3) flesh and the Spirit (vv. 16–26), (4) bearing burdens (6:1–5), (5) sharing (v. 6), (6) sowing (v. 7), and (7) doing good (vv. 8–12). In this chapter of our commentary, we will look at the thesis (5:1) and its application to the practice of circumcision (vv. 2–12). Our next section will look at the second and third issues.

The Thesis: Free at Last (5:1)

THIS THESIS HAS two elements: the statement of freedom (v. 1a) and the implication of freedom (v. 1b). In other words, you are free; therefore, do not get caught up in the Mosaic law.

The Greek words of this verse are more potent than the NIV's attempt to render it in English. Following the Greek word order, we translate woodenly: "For freedom Christ set you free." There are only four words in Greek: (in

---

1. This view of the book has been admirably demonstrated by J. M. G. Barclay, *Obeying the Truth: A Study of Paul's Ethics in Galatians* (Edinburgh: T & T Clark, 1988).

order) "freedom," "you," "Christ," and "set free." The first and last, the two places of a Greek sentence where emphasis can be found, are concerned with freedom—one a noun and the other a verb. The verb is in the aorist tense, which tells us not when or how they were set free, but *that* they were set free. His main focus is with the *fact of their being free at last*.

Everything we understand in this passage, and ultimately everything we "take home" from Galatians, hinges on our ability to perceive what the term *freedom* means in this letter. As H. D. Betz has said: "As a result . . . 'freedom' is the central theological concept which sums up the Christian's situation before God as well as in this world. It is the basic concept underlying Paul's argument throughout the letter."[2] So we turn to a study of freedom in Galatians and in Paul's letters.[3]

First, we should observe that "being free" is a *relationship with God*: in the presence of God we are "free" from the curse of the law (cf. 3:10–14; 5:1, 13) and a "sin status" (Rom. 6:18, 20, 22; 8:2) so that we can live as his "free children" (Gal. 4:21–31). Second, "being free" is the *result of the death of Jesus Christ*: we were captive to sin and the law, but Christ's death redeemed us from the curse of the law (2:4; 3:13; 5:1; cf. John 8:36). The language of "freedom" is tied into the language of "redemption" (cf. 1:4; 3:13; 4:5).[4] Third, "being free" is *life in the Spirit of God*: "Now the Lord is the Spirit, and where the Spirit of the Lord is, there is freedom" (2 Cor. 3:17). These three ideas are put together later by Paul in Romans 8:2: "because through Christ Jesus the law of the Spirit of life has set me free from the law of sin and death." We get nowhere in talking about freedom until we comprehend that it is through and through a *work of God in our lives through Christ Jesus and in the Holy Spirit*. Freedom is not being turned free to be whatever we want (i.e., egocentrism); nor is it some kind of "self-discovery" or "self-authentication" (that, too, is egocentrism); rather, it is being incorporated into the life of God, which he mediates to us through Christ and allows us to enjoy in the Spirit.

These first three ideas about freedom may be called the "theological dimension" of freedom.[5] We now turn to the "human dimensions." Fourth,

---

2. H. D. Betz, *Galatians*, 255.

3. See J. Blunck, "Freedom," in *NIDNTT*, 1:715–21; R. N. Longenecker, *Paul, Apostle of Liberty: The Origin and Nature of Paul's Christianity* (reprint edition; Grand Rapids: Baker, 1976), 156–208; J. R. W. Stott, *The Contemporary Christian*, 46–56.

4. An excellent study of the connection between redemption and freedom can be found in E. J. Epp, "Paul's Diverse Imageries of the Human Situation and His Unifying Theme of Freedom," in *Unity and Diversity in New Testament Theology: Essays in Honor of George E. Ladd*, ed. R. A. Guelich (Grand Rapids: Eerdmans, 1978), 100–116.

5. The normal Greco-Roman view of "freedom" referred more often to liberation from vice or pleasure in the sense of becoming a "master of one's life." It had nothing to do with

there is a *polemical dimension* to freedom. Freedom is something that Christians know about, that Christians enjoy, that Christians experience, and that the Judaizers have not known, and cannot know, until they give up their hold on the law of Moses (2:4; 4:21–31; 5:1). This is a major emphasis of Galatians. The Judaizers had come into the Galatian scene and preached the revelation of God through Moses, and they were arguing that the Galatian Christians had to submit to the law of Moses to perfect their relationship with God. Paul returns the volley with pace: the law of Moses was for a limited time (until Christ) and for a limited purpose (to reveal sin); therefore, the Galatians must not submit to the law. Instead, they must surrender to Christ and live in the Spirit. This makes them "mature sons" (3:26–4:7) who have the Spirit (4:7) and who can live in freedom of adults. The freedom of an adult implies that they no longer have to live under the tutelage of a supervisor (4:1–7). Thus, this freedom in Galatians has a decided polemical slant: it is something the Judaizers are trying to steal.

Fifth, we need to observe in Paul that "being free" is *personal and existential in the sense of being liberated to be what God wants us to be and to do what God wants us to do.* This category is slightly modern, but I think this is what Paul is getting at.[6] He teaches that freedom in Christ is being set free from the power of sin and death (Rom. 6:7, 18, 22; 8:2). This idea of "sin" is the bondage to sin that sinners find shackled around their wills and consciences. This shackle has been broken, and it can only be described as personally liberating—liberating the person to do what God wants. In 5:16–26 we find a description of what happens to a person's inner life (and outer relations) when the Spirit takes charge. I believe this is the "to be" of our category. "Being free" is being set free "to be" what God wants us to be. While the law is one thing that tethers us to our sinful nature, sinners are also shackled to sin by spiritual forces beyond their control; "being free" involves breaking this shackle as well (Eph. 6:10–18; Col. 2:15). In general, we might say that "being free" is the liberation of a person's spirit from everything that shackles it to sin and ugliness; "being free" is the liberation of a person's spirit to do what God wants, to be what God wants, and to enjoy the life God gives us on this earth.

But, paradoxically, this freedom *from* is at the same time a freedom *for* and a liberation *to*. One is not set free to do whatever one wants. Rather, one is set free to do what is right and to be what one ought to be. In the Christian

---

the view of freedom in Paul where it is a divine work of grace. See the quotations and observations in A. J. Malherbe, *Moral Exhortation, a Greco-Roman Sourcebook* (Library of Early Christianity; Philadelphia: Westminster, 1986), 158–59.

6. So also R. N. Longenecker, *Paul, Apostle of Liberty*, 171–73; H. N. Ridderbos, *Paul: An Outline of His Theology*, trans. J. R. DeWitt (Grand Rapids: Eerdmans, 1975), 258–65, 288–93; J. R. W. Stott, *The Contemporary Christian*, 52–56.

sense of freedom there are definite limitations. The great German pastor, Helmut Thielike, states this sharply when he says that "real freedom, on the other hand—the freedom 'to become what one should'—must be defined as a definite form of bondage or obligation, in a word, as what one *should* do. Real freedom is a bondage and nothing else."[7] Thus, those who have been set free have become slaves of Christ (1 Cor. 7:22; Eph. 6:6), God (Rom. 6:22), and righteousness (v. 18).

Finally, "being free" has *social implications.* Those who have been set free by God, through Christ, and in the Spirit are those who live out this life of freedom by loving others (Gal 5:6, 13–15) and by developing relationships to others that are marked by such things as kindness and goodness (vv. 22–24). This freedom, I believe, is what supports the conclusion of Paul that in Christ there is neither Jew nor Greek, slave nor free, male nor female (3:28): those who live in freedom have learned to neglect the barriers that social conventions have taught us in order that we can pursue God's will (see also 1 Cor. 9:19–23). While it is clear from Paul's letters and life that Paul did not apparently have a political agenda in his idea of freedom, it seems only reasonable that what he believed to be true in one's relationship with God and others (freedom) would begin to work itself out in how Christians saw their relationship to the wider world. Thus, I am of the view that the modern concepts of "freedom," "civil rights," and "liberty" are deeply indebted to the Pauline notion of freedom and are, in one way or another, an extension of that concept. Those who have been set free want freedom to obtain for all dimensions of life.

In short, for Paul "freedom" is the very heart of the gospel: God sets us free through Christ and in the Spirit, so that we can love God and others. E. J. Epp has described the comprehensiveness of freedom in Paul's thought admirably:

> The implications of this Christian freedom as Paul develops it are vast and far-reaching, but essentially he sees freedom as a reality effected in and through the Christ-event, which has broken the power of sin and neutralized the individual hostility against God; which at the same time has covered the guilt and stain of sin and erased the past; which has crushed all enslavement to self, to religious convention, to the present powers of evil, and to cosmic forces; and which has triumphed over every force that dominates humankind, including human mortality itself. But that is only one side of the Pauline coin—

---

7. H. Thielicke, *The Freedom of the Christian Man: A Christian Confrontation with the Secular Gods,* trans. J. W. Doberstein (Grand Rapids: Baker, 1975), 14.

the "freedom *from* what?" side; there is also the significant "freedom *for* what?" side, and this many-faceted emphasis in Paul, though it can be simply stated, is infinitely complex in its outworking: a Christian is now free to obey God in a radical fashion by serving his fellow human beings in selfless love.[8]

The *implication* of Christ setting us free is the negative side of the letter of Galatians: "Do not let yourselves be burdened again by a yoke of slavery" (v. 1b). This refers either (1) to Jewish Christians once again falling under the law of Moses as the governor of life, or (2) to Gentile Christians who have been set free in Christ from one form of slavery (to sin as pagans) and who are now turning to another form of slavery (to Judaism without Christ). The evidence of 4:8–9 seems to favor the second interpretation. What we learn from Paul's comment here is that freedom must be retained, protected from contamination, and renewed at all times.

Application of Thesis to Circumcision (vv. 2–12)

PAUL NOW APPLIES his thesis of the Christian being a truly free person to the issue of circumcision, the most blatant issue facing the Galatians. Will they follow Paul's "law-free" gospel or will they succumb to the teaching of the Judaizers, which combined the gospel of Jesus Christ with the gospel of Moses? He begins with an assertion (v. 2) and then explains it (vv. 3–6). After this he applies his message of freedom to the Galatians (vv. 7–12).

The assertion (v. 2). Because he is the apostle (1:1), Paul says "Mark my words! I, Paul. . . ." Two points in his words need to be addressed: what do "let yourselves be circumcised" and "Christ will be of no value" mean?

The expression "let yourselves be circumcised" does not simply refer to the rite of circumcision being performed on a Jewish or Gentile male. Paul will say in verse 6 that "neither circumcision nor uncircumcision has any value." To Paul neither of these matters. But here he seems to contend that circumcision does matter. Why? To begin with, Paul uses the middle voice here, expressing the notion of "submitting oneself to the rite in a personal way." But simply being circumcised is not the issue. Rather, it is their *reason for circumcision* that provokes Paul. If the Galatians go ahead with circumcision *because of the influence of the Judaizers*, they will be confessing, in the act of submitting to the rite (hence the middle voice), that they think Christ is insufficient, that the Spirit is not a good guide for living, that Moses needs to be obeyed for acceptance with God, and that one needs to become a Jew to

---

8. E. J. Epp, "Paul's Diverse Imageries of the Human Situation and His Unifying Theme of Freedom," 114.

become a child of God. This is what Paul reacts to in our letter—not circumcision *per se*, but to circumcision when done as a confession of faith in the Mosaic law and the superiority of the Jewish nation (cf. Rom. 2:25).

So Paul spells out the ramifications: "Christ will be of no value." As in 2:21 where Paul stated that if a proper standing with God came as a result of obeying the law, then Christ's coming was useless, so now: if they confess their faith in Moses through being circumcised, then Christ has no value for them. That is to say, Christ will not deliver them from the present evil age (1:4) or from the curse of the law (3:13), nor will they become children of Abraham's promise for those who believe (3:6–9, 19–25; 3:26–4:7).

The explanation (vv. 3–6). Paul now needs to back up a bit and explain what he means by "Christ will be of no value." He makes three points: if they go to the law now, (1) they will be obliged to do the whole law, (2) they will be separated from Christ and grace, and (3) they will miss what really counts: faith.

(1) *They will be obligated to do the whole law* (v. 3). "Again" refers to the assertion of v. 2, not to some previous statement Paul had made regarding the law. In opting for the law of Moses the Galatians would become "obligators" to the entire law. He is making a threat: assuming the law means one *must* keep the whole law, and *that means eliminating Christ.*[9] This expression is no different than the other terms Paul has used for those who are "under the law": they are in bondage (2:4; 4:1–7; 5:1), they are under a curse (3:10–14), they are enclosed (3:22–23), they are under sin (3:22), they are under a pedagogue (3:24), they are under the elementary principles (4:3, 9), and they become nothing more than Ishmaels (4:21–31). The foundation for his point here is historical (the law pertains to a previous era, the "manual typewriter age"), social (the Jewish nation is not the sole place of God's work), and hermeneutical (the law when properly understood does not bring acceptance with God). They become debtors to the whole law, and that means condemnation *because that is only what the law can do.*

I doubt very much that Paul means to say that if they opted for the law, they had to do it all perfectly (and if they did it would bring them acceptance). No Jew believed that Jews had to be sinless in order to be acceptable to God. Rather, the law itself provided for those who did not live it properly

---

9. This observation comes from a technical study of E. P. Sanders, *Paul, the Law, and the Jewish People* (Philadelphia: Fortress, 1983), esp. 27–29. Sanders correctly observes that the traditional view of verse 3 makes two assumptions that neither Paul nor any Jew ever states. These assumptions are those about obeying the law (the second and third are false): (1) one must keep it all; (2) one cannot do so; (3) there is no forgiveness of transgression; (4) therefore accepting the law necessarily leads to being cursed.

(the atonement system). Nor do we have other evidence in Galatians that Paul thought Jews had to obey the law flawlessly to be acceptable to God. What we find in Galatians is that opting for the law is a misunderstanding of what the law was supposed to do (3:19–25)—a choice to live in an inferior era under an inferior system and a choice to think that God's work was still nationalistic. Thus, it seems to me likely that "obligated" means "cursed," for that is all the law can do for a person (3:19–25).

(2) *They will be separated from Christ and grace* (v. 4). Paul's point about "obligation" to the law is now restated. That this is a restatement shows that the traditional view of verse 3 is inaccurate. This restatement simply contends *that those who opt*[10] *for the law's system opt out of the Christ system or the grace system*. Put differently, they are choosing another way of becoming accepted by God, and the one they are choosing (the law of Moses) will not do the job. So the issue is which system are they relying upon: how is a person accepted by God and how shall people live as God's people?

Verse 4 brings up a sensitive issue for many. Is Paul saying here that in being alienated from Christ and in falling "away from grace" these Galatians converts have lost their salvation? First, I want to say that Paul is not thinking in individual categories here. Rather, he is thinking in terms of systems: the system of the law of Moses will bring a curse and not acceptance with God; the system of Christ or grace will bring acceptance with God. Second, the expressions are identical: being alienated from Christ is identical to falling away from grace. Third, in making these two points, we inevitably raise the issue of losing one's salvation. I do admit that, though the verse is not concerned directly with this issue, it certainly does arise the moment one thinks of the person who does opt for circumcision. What are the implications of this verse for that decision?

No interpreter of the Bible worthy of the term contends for a viewpoint on this important topic by appealing simply to one verse (e.g., v. 4 here). Such a topic requires an exhaustive analysis of two topics in the Bible: God's protection of his people and human responsibility before God. The person must study not only passages on assurance (e.g., Rom. 5:1; 8:28–39; 1 Cor. 1:8–9;

---

10. We should not give emphasis to the NIV's use of the term "trying" and conclude that Paul is against "effort" here. The word "trying" is not in the original Greek; the expression is simply the verb *dikaiousthe* ("you are justified"). Since it is a present tense, many conclude that it is also "conative" (i.e., describing "attempted action") and thus translate it, "trying to be justified." While the action may be "conative," the emphasis is not on the word "trying." Rather, the present tense is used to describe action that has not yet been completed. He sees the Galatians as in a period of decision and perhaps transition and addresses them "as they walk by his soapbox."

2 Cor. 5:5) but also passages that seem to imply a possibility of falling away (1 Cor. 9:27; Gal 5:4; Col. 1:21–23; Heb. 6:4–6; 10:19–39).[11]

For those who are of the view that one cannot lose salvation (Calvinist view), verse 4 describes a person who has never been fully committed to Christ or who has never experienced genuine, saving faith.[12] For those who are of the view that one can lose salvation (Arminian view), this verse describes a Galatian convert to Christ who, if he or she opts for the law of Moses, loses his or her relationship to God in Christ and therefore forfeits salvation.[13] I believe the overall teaching of the New Testament assumes that Christians will persevere; there are numerous utterances of the assurance that they can have of their final destiny. But I am also of the view that there are enough "terrifying" passages to make one think apostasy is a real possibility and that in the case of apostasy one can "forfeit one's salvation."[14] I wish, however, to make a theological and a pastoral remark. Theologically, I believe the *only sin that can sever a Christian's relationship to God through Christ is the sin of apostasy.* Apostasy is a violent act on the part of a fading Christian who denounces his or her relationship to Christ and refuses to submit to God's will. Such an act is not haphazard or unconscious; it is intentional and known, and the one who makes such a decision vaunts in it. Pastorally speaking, I am fully persuaded that the person who wonders if he or she has committed this sin has not committed it. The one who has apostatized knows it and proudly glories in it.

(3) *They will miss what really counts: faith* (vv. 5–6). If the Galatian converts opt for the law of Moses and express that choice by personally undergoing circumcision, they will miss out on what really matters: the faith they previously exhibited (3:1–5). Paul assumes here the conclusions to his first argument: from first to last their experiences showed that everything good came as a result of faith, not as a result of observing the law. The Galatians,

---

11. Two books, fully documented with evidence, one from each side, are: I. H. Marshall, *Kept by the Power of God: A Study of Perseverance and Falling Away* (Minneapolis: Bethany Fellowship, Inc., 1969), and J. M. Gundry Volf, *Paul and Perseverance: Staying In and Falling Away* (Louisville: Westminster/John Knox Press, 1990).

12. This is the view of W. Hendriksen, *Galatians*, 37–39, 196.

13. I. H. Marshall, *Kept by the Power of God*, 110. He states: "Submission to circumcision indicated a cessation of faith in Christ," and, "It was the expression of an act of repudiation of God's grace manifested in Christ."

14. I have written a complete essay on the evidence of Hebrews; the study is technical, but I believe it can be used by anyone who wants to get to the heart of the issues. See "The Warning Passages of Hebrews: A Formal Analysis and Theological Conclusions," *Trinity Journal* 13 (1992): 21–59. Here I work through the evidence of Hebrews on four topics: the audience, the sin being described, the exhortations, and the consequences of the sin.

Paul warns, will be cursed because it is "by faith we eagerly await through the Spirit the righteousness[15] for which we hope." What "counts is faith"; circumcision is neither here nor there (cf. 6:15; 1 Cor 7:18–19). And this faith is found "expressing itself through love" (Gal 5:6)—the topic Paul addresses in verses 13–15.

It has been said that verses 5–6 are a masterful summary of Paul's whole letter. I agree. Here we find (1) faith, (2) the Spirit of God, (3) justification, (4) future hope, (5) love, and (6) the polemics against circumcision. This is Galatians.

The application (vv. 7–12). These verses are not tightly organized. Instead, Paul juts in one direction and then in another. He summarizes his theology and ethics as well as his pastoral exhortations.

Using a metaphor from the world of track and field, Paul wonders over whoever has "cut in on" the Galatians and thereby kept them from the successful run of "obeying the truth" (v. 7). Ancient runners did not run around an oval track in lanes as in our day; instead, there was a post at a set distance away and they ran to that post and back. If a runner "cut in" on another runner, especially in the final few yards before the post, that forced the second runner to trip or slow down.[16] Paul likens the Judaizer's activities to such unsportsmanlike activity: they were cutting in on the Galatian's progress toward their final goal and slowing them down. Although Paul asks "who," he knows who they are and needs no answer (cf. 3:1).

Next Paul evaluates this kind of activity (vv. 8–9), stating that it does not come from God and that just a little of it will cause large problems. Once again Paul ties in the messenger to the one who sends the messenger (cf. 1:1; Matt. 10:40–42): because the Judaizers' message is not from God (as Paul's is), such activity is not from God.

We then see Paul's confidence expressed pastorally (v. 10a): "I am confident in the Lord that you will take no other view." He would probably forgive us for asking if this is more rhetorical and pastoral than it is accurate. Paul has expressed on several occasions grave concern over the Galatians, but here

---

15. This future acquisition of righteousness (same Greek word as "justification") shows that Paul knows the Christian has only been inaugurated into salvation. While he believes we are justified (Rom. 5:1), he knows that full justification still awaits the believer (Gal. 5:5). On this see esp. G. E. Ladd, *A Theology of the New Testament* (Grand Rapids: Eerdmans, 1974), 441–43.

16. For athletic contests in the ancient world, see esp. H. A. Harris, *Greek Athletics and the Jews* (Cardiff: University of Wales Press, 1976); C. E. DeVries, "Paul's 'Cutting' Remarks about a Race: Galatians 5:1–12," in *Current Issues in Biblical and Patristic Interpretation: Studies in Honor of Merrill C. Tenney Presented by His Former Students*, ed. G. F. Hawthorne (Grand Rapids: Eerdmans, 1975), 115–20.

he seems to revert to another view of them: he thinks they will listen to him, forget the Judaizers, and continue in the way of Christ and the Spirit. I am of the view that, while Paul had confidence in his readers, when he pondered the problems from other angles, he lost that confidence. Thus, this statement is probably strategic in his entire letter: he becomes positive in order to help them make a good decision.[17]

His confidence in the Galatians means that Paul can warn the Judaizers about what will eventually come about: final judgment[18] (v. 10b). Most commentators observe that, though Paul uses a singular ("whoever he may be"), such a singular is "generic" and there are more than one person involved (see 1:7; 5:12).

Without signal, Paul suddenly responds to one of the criticisms the Judaizers have been making (v. 11): that is, "if I am still[19] preaching circumcision" only makes sense if the Judaizers were contending that Paul did demand circumcision. How this was taking place we can only surmise. My guess is that the Judaizers contended that, though Paul did not demand circumcision while he was with the Galatians, he would have done so had he been able to stay longer and spend more time teaching them the "whole counsel of God." Then he would have gotten to the necessity of obeying the law. Thus, they must have contended that Paul's message was as nationalistic as theirs; it just took Paul longer to get there. Their job, then, was simply to clean up after Paul and make sure that everything was put in order.

Paul's response includes his oft-made assumption: those who are persecuted are right (see comments on 4:21–31). And, since he is being persecuted *by the Jews*, he must be right. If he were preaching circumcision, the cross of Christ would be unnecessary (2:21; 5:2). That "offense," he says, has not been removed, and that is why I am being persecuted. Paul "cuts off" any possibility that he has ever preached circumcision; for him the gospel and circumcision are incompatible alternatives to defining the people of God.

Finally, Paul sarcastically urges the Judaizers to go the whole way (v. 12). If they are going to get involved with this purifying act of circumcision, they

---

17. An analysis of such passages in Paul's letters can be found in S. N. Olson, "Pauline Expressions of Confidence in His Addressees," *Catholic Biblical Quarterly* 47 (1985): 282–95. Other passages like this one are Romans 15:14; 2 Corinthians 7:4, 16; 9:1–2; 2 Thessalonians 3:4; Philemon 21.

18. That this is condemnation becomes clear by reading 2 Corinthians 11:15 and 1 Thessalonians 2:16 along with Galatians 1:8–9.

19. This refers either to his preconversion days of demanding circumcision of all who wanted to associate with Judaism (cf. Acts 9:1–3), to some supposed (but incorrect) period after his conversion and before his Gentile ministry when he did expect converts to be circumcised, or to the seeming ambivalence Paul could have on the issue (cf. Acts 16:1–3; 1 Cor. 9:20; Gal. 5:6).

ought to go the whole way, become eunuchs, and end the matter there! One scholar has wryly described some of Paul's comments in verses 1–12 as "Paul's cutting remarks": the Judaizers are concerned with "cutting around" (the literal meaning of the Greek word for circumcision), while his remarks about "cutting in" on runners can now be applied to his more sarcastic remarks about "cutting off" in verse 12.[20] Classing the Judaizers with eunuchs is a way of discrediting and disparaging them. Those who are eunuchs are "cut off" from the Jewish people (Deut. 23:1). Is Paul hoping for their exclusion?

ᐧᐤ

On this sour note Paul ends his first application of his main point: being in Christ is living in freedom. Living in freedom means not being caught up in the Mosaic law that demanded circumcision.

THERE IS MUCH to apply here, too much. We have combined Paul's marvelous statement on freedom (v. 1) with his first application (vv. 2–12). While his thesis statement is concerned with one idea, freedom, the application section brings up several paths along which we could travel looking for applications. We could talk about analogies to circumcision, exploring analogies that are not only ritual but have similar symbolic value: an entry rite that demonstrates one's confession and a group's view of how one is accepted by God (baptism, walking down the aisle, raising one's hand in a service, etc.). We could also examine the implications of adopting a system other than Christ or explore analogies to the Galatian apostasy. We could find methods of opponents who seek to "cut in on us" and how infecting such methods can be for a church. We could even seek for applications through following Paul's method of responding to his opponents. Thus, does verse 12 justify sarcasm? While each of these can be fruitful for a study of this passage, I will focus on freedom since it is the thrust of Paul's letter and is the foundation for the applications that follow. So to freedom we now turn.

Before we can apply the message of freedom to our lives, we must understand what Paul was getting at and how it is defined or understood in our world. I begin with the latter,[21] surveying three notions of freedom in our soci-

---

20. See C. E. DeVries, "Paul's 'Cutting' Remarks about a Race: Galatians 5:1–12."

21. A tremendous survey of freedom can be found by tracing the theme of "Liberty" through the *Great Books of the Western World*. Mortimer Adler's outline of the topic and its many references in the *Great Books* can be found in *The Great Ideas: A Syntopicon of Great Books of the Western World*, ed. M. Alder and W. Gorman (Chicago: Encyclopaedia Britannica, Inc., 1952), 1: 991–1012.

ety: individual freedom, social freedom, and personal psychological freedom. I do not pretend that these three senses are exhaustive nor that they are mutually exclusive. Those who pursue "individual" freedom may have been turned on to "psychological" freedom too. But they are typical of how our culture thinks of itself and what kinds of ideas it brings up when asked about freedom.

I mentioned previously that young adults must feel a tremendous relief when they leave home, if that home was marked by a certain overconcern on the part of the parents. One thing these children feel is "freedom." They now feel free from their parents' rules and regulations; they no longer have a curfew, no longer have to be screened on their phone calls, no longer have to ask permission about where to go and with whom. They can do what they want and when they want to. They can do anything they want to. This is how many college students (or young adults who leave home) define freedom. For these people freedom means an absolute control of one's life, *an individual freedom.* In most cases, it is no different than simple egocentrism or narcissism.

I hasten to add that this form of freedom is not just for young adults. Robert Bellah's team of scholars has examined the problem of individualism in American society at a much broader level. Especially adults in our society are caught up in the myth of the individual: the individual is the main form of reality. Individualism, it is argued, developed from both a biblical and a civic responsibility to others. But the erosion of both of these moorings has turned the Western individual loose. Bellah and others are now arguing (properly I think) that such an individualism "also weakens the very meanings that give content and substance to the ideal of individual dignity." He continues, "We thus face a profound impasse. Modern individualism seems to be producing a way of life that is neither individually nor socially viable. . . ."[22] For these people, freedom is "doing what I want," and it is "finding oneself."

Put differently, it is independence, autonomy, and personal sovereignty. Theologically, such a definition of one's personal ambition smells of profound sinfulness. This view of life defines freedom as the absence of limitations and the presence of self-sufficiency and power. Mortimer Adler asks, however, "The real question here seems to be a metaphysical one. Can any finite thing be absolutely independent?" And he goes on to say that "God has the

---

22. Robert Bellah, et al., *Habits of the Heart: Individualism and Commitment in American Life* (New York: Harper & Row, 1985), 144. See esp. 55–84, 142–63. See also his team's *Individualism and Commitment in American Life: Readings on the Themes of Habits of the Heart* (New York: Harper & Row, 1987), 51–95. I believe Bellah's *Habits of the Heart* is must reading for anyone who wants to understand contemporary Western society.

freedom of autonomy which cannot belong to finite things."[23] He has it right. What this kind of freedom often results in is nothing less than human pride and the attempt to make oneself like God by presuming that one can become absolutely independent, self-sufficient, and autonomous.

One manifestation of such an individualism is the pursuit of "financial independence," which is often nothing more than an economic expression of one's desire to be unrelated to the rest of society and the demonstration to the rest of the world (which is rarely watching anyway) that one is successful. In all this, the language of duty to one's fellow human being or the language of duty to God's will have no capacity to speak to a person who finds freedom only in doing what one wants or in finding oneself. This kind of individualism is creating and determining one's destiny; hence, the typical Western adult is involved in a moral, social, and religious breakdown.

Bellah, after surveying the aspirations of several people whom he examined in his social survey, sums it all up:

> Freedom is perhaps the most resonant, deeply held American value. In some ways, it defines the good in both personal and political life. Yet freedom turns out to mean being left alone by others, not having other people's values, ideas, or styles of life forced upon one, being free of arbitrary authority in work, family, and political life. What it is that one might do with that freedom is much more difficult for Americans to define.

He concludes, "In some sense . . . freedom to be left alone is a freedom that implies being alone."[24]

For others, "freedom" means the *breaking down of social structures* that are perceived to be oppressive or obstacles to equality and justice. These are good goals to have, and freedom surely involves the tearing down of social injustices.[25] There are many politicians whose sole goal in life is this kind of freedom, and we should applaud their efforts on our behalf. Such obstacles naturally include environmental issues that foster tension in communities, racial prejudices that determine public policies, sexual discrimination that

---

23. M. Adler, "Liberty," in *The Great Ideas: A Syntopicon of the Great Books of the Western World*, volume 1, in *Great Books of the Western World* (Chicago: Encyclopaedia Brittanica, 1952), 2:993. In the *Great Books*, a good example of this can be found in J. S. Mill, *On Liberty*, 43, 263–323, where Mill particularly examines the idea of political freedom, but he does this with a highly egocentric concept at its base (see esp. 293–302).

24. Robert Bellah, et al., *Habits of the Heart*, 23.

25. For the American scene, I recommend reading the political ideals that shape our views as expounded by M. J. Adler, *We Hold These Truths: Understanding the Ideas and Ideals of the Constitution* (New York: Macmillan, 1987), esp. 51–61 (on happiness) and 123–30 (on freedom).

influences pay scales, and international imperialism that can keep some countries from development or force weaker nations down on the economic ladder. Such injustices need to be opposed, and the work for freedom in these areas is altogether good.

But there often comes an imbalance. The struggle for social justice is, for many, the struggle of God against demonic powers, and the establishment of social justice is seen as God's salvation. This struggle can take place in social realms, racial realms, and sexual realms; and each is a struggle. The most eloquent, and frequently referred to, spokesman for this "liberation theology" is Gustavo Gutierrez. This Latin American scholar argued that there were three levels of liberation: the social aspiration of oppressed people, the human aspiration of developing a new man and a different society, and the spiritual aspiration of being set free from sin through Christ. He goes further: "This is not a matter of three parallel or chronologically successive processes, however. There are three levels of meaning of a single, complex process, which finds its deepest sense and its full realization in the saving work of Christ."[26] Few readers, I would guess, could disagree with this. But the problem is that few of the practitioners of Gutierrez put to work the importance of the "deepest sense" and in its place equate the social and human processes with the spiritual process. While social freedom is certainly an aspect of the Pauline notion of freedom, it is not the totality, and for liberation theologians and activists the concept of freedom is far too materialistic to embrace the fullness of the biblical variety of evidence.

Yet another perception of freedom is highly individualistic: the freedom of self-actualization.[27] This may involve freedom from conformity to family expectations and the status quo, from some rushing psychological or physical dependency on habits or drugs, or to the process of becoming fully alert to one's potential. I refer here to what we could call *psychological freedom*. Once again, Robert Bellah catches the spirit of this vision of freedom well when he describes "Margaret":

> For Margaret, as for others influenced by modern psychological ideals, to be free is not simply to be left alone by others; it is also somehow to be your own person in the sense that you have defined who you are, deeded for yourself what you want out of life, free as much as possible from the demands of conformity to family, friends, or community.[28]

26. Gustavo Gutierrez, *A Theology of Liberation*, trans. C. Inda and J. Eagleson (London: SCM, 1974). I quote from page 37, but the reader is referred to the larger section (pp. 1–42).

27. This view of "freedom" is particularly associated in psychology with Carl R. Rogers. A summary of such "Person-Centered Therapy" can be found in R. J. Corsini, ed., *Current Psychotherapies* (3d ed.; Itasca, Ill.: F. E. Peacock, 1984), 142–95.

28. Robert Bellah, et al., *Habits of the Heart*, 23.

I am not opposed to becoming psychologically independent of our parents, our addictions, or our pasts so that we become "individuated" or personally responsible adults. But for many, the process of becoming a free-thinking individual, the process of growing up, or the process of working through one's past (with its possible serious hindrances) is the essence of freedom and the goal of life. It is fundamentally important for every individual to be able to look in a mirror, admit who he or she is, and embrace that person. This is knowing ourselves. But self-knowledge is not biblical freedom. Knowing ourselves is only a step in learning to know who we are before God and learning what we can be through Christ and in the Spirit. Mental and psychological health is not biblical freedom any more than eliminating racial prejudice is the Millennium. The Bible sees psychological health as a product of learning who we are (sinners), surrendering our egos to Jesus (conversion), and becoming what God wants (obedient Christians). To be sure, the process of acquiring psychological health can be turbulent and temporarily devastating for some; it therefore deserves special attention. Nonetheless, I maintain that psychological freedom is not the goal but the result of God's grace.

Each of the above-mentioned models of freedom that are fashionable in our society today are part of what the Bible defines as freedom. But we are wrong if we equate these quests with Paul's call to freedom. To gain our bearings on where we are headed, we need to remind ourselves of how we can properly apply the Pauline idea of freedom: first we need to examine what the apostle meant in his context, then what it means in our day, and finally we can integrate Paul's message into our society, both informing our culture and correcting it. We have stated Paul's view and briefly sketched three concepts of freedom in our society. In our next section we shall make some applications.

WE MUST RECALL our brief outline of the idea of freedom in Paul's letters before going any further. There are two dimensions to freedom in Paul, a *theological* dimension, and a *human* dimension. The theological dimension includes a relationship with God through Christ and in the Spirit, and the human dimension includes both a personal and a social aspect. Paul's emphases were on the freedom from the curse of the law and on the freedom for all persons to be part of God's family (3:28). We must also recall what we said about the typical perceptions of freedom in our society: it can be individual, social, or psychological.

What we need to perceive is that Paul's view of freedom is not our society's view of freedom. In fact, they are almost direct opposites at times. For the apostle, freedom involves "slavery to God and his will," while for moderns freedom means doing whatever one wants; for Paul, freedom begins only in a relationship with God through Christ and in the Spirit, while for moderns freedom means being alone; for Paul, individual, social, and psychological freedom is the glorious outworking of what God can do in a person through Christ and in the Spirit, while for moderns these forms of freedom are the determining goal of life; for Paul, freedom was *inter*dependence, while for moderns it is *in*dependence. Put differently, we cannot apply freedom in Paul to our society until we see that the two are at odds with one another. This forces us to decide: "We have only to choose between bondage to the Father, which makes us free, and bondage to the powers of this world, which enslaves us."[29]

How then do we apply this? First, people must see what they need to be free *from* before they can become free. The message of Paul is that we are bound to the law and its curse, to sin, to self, and to an evil world. Galatians 1:4 is Paul's first comment about freedom in our letter: "who gave himself for our sins to rescue us from the present evil age." Here we have all four: Law is implied in sin, self in the words "our" and "us," and the world in "present evil age." No one becomes "biblically free" until one accepts that he or she is enslaved to sin, self, and the world. It does no good to tell a prisoner who lives out his life on a lush resort, playing golf during the day and dancing the night away with wine, women, and song, that he needs to be set free if the things that he enjoys most are constantly available. If, however, his greatest desires are "on the outside," then he can be set free from his deprivation to do them. So also it does no good to tell persons they need to be set free from sin if they do not realize how awful their state is. As John Stott says, "True freedom is freedom from my silly little self, in order to live responsibly in love for God and others."[30]

Let me put this differently: we cannot apply freedom to our world unless we share the gospel with our world. This means we cannot proclaim our message of freedom until we proclaim the reality of sin. The great theologian, Augustine, once said: "The will is then truly free, when it is not the slave of vices and sins."[31]

Second, we must inform our world *for* what they are set free through Christ and in the Spirit. People are set free to serve God, to follow Jesus, and

---

29. H. Thielicke, *The Freedom of the Christian Man*, 28.

30. J. R. W. Stott, *The Contemporary Christian*, 55.

31. Augustine, *The City of God*, 14.11.

to live in the Spirit. Once again, this is not what our society wants, but it is exactly what the true Christian wants. Our society wants to be left alone, to tear down social barriers, and to find oneself. Jesus wants us to be left *with him and his people,* to break down barriers in society *as a reflection of God's love in our hearts,* and to find oneself *in denying ourselves before God.* As Thielike states: "For Christians, freedom, as distinguished from enslavement under the law, arises as a result of my being empowered to be a responsible child of God and to learn to will what God wills. Freedom here becomes the unimpeded spontaneity of love."[32] And Mortimer Adler adds: "Man cannot be more free than when he succeeds, with God's help, in submitting himself through love to the rule of God."[33]

What will this freedom be like when we find it? The person who is truly free is a person who (1) trusts, loves, and obeys God through Christ and in the Spirit, (2) loves and serves others, and (3) lives before God with a clear conscience as he or she grows before God in holiness and love. So I agree with our age: there are at least three dimensions of freedom. We need to be free individually (so we can be *who* God wants), free socially (so *all* can see the glory of God), and free psychologically (so we can *relate* to God and others authentically and clearly).

We can achieve this threefold sense of freedom through Christ and in the Spirit. (1) We must be frankly honest before God about ourselves. The Bible calls this confession. Until we face up to who we really are (sinful, imperfect people who live in the constant pain of our imperfection), we cannot be free. This is not a "solidarity confession" (I, with everyone else, am a sinner) but a "solitary confession" (I, though maybe no else be with me, am a sinner). When we come to God on his terms, admitting who we truly are, we will gain access to his freedom.

(2) We must come to God honestly by relying on what he wants us to rely on: Jesus Christ. Only then will we experience the freedom God wants. Jesus Christ is the way God opens up for our line to freedom. Jesus did this through his death, which tore down barriers and cleansed us from sin and imperfection. When we trust in God's "appointed one to be trusted," we find the freedom of God.

(3) We must then "live in the Spirit." God's Spirit is God's appointed way of being renewed, of being healed, and of being made complete. The Spirit animates our lives before God so we can be and do what God wants us to be and do.

---

32. H. Thielicke, *The Freedom of the Christian Man,* 15.
33. M. J. Adler, "Liberty," 995.

When we come to God and live before him through Christ and in the Spirit, we live in freedom. Three things then happen to us. We are personally set free from our sin and our unfortunate past (though it may take some therapy and time for healing), we are set free to serve others so that social barriers are broken down, and we become what we always wanted to be though we never knew what it was. Thus, we become psychologically, socially, and individually free. For such persons, legalistic invasions, cultural imperialisms, racial prejudices, and denominational fixations do not cause alarm, for they know, in the Spirit and through Christ, they can live above them and through them.

But these three dimensions of freedom contrast with our society in their actual manifestations. Let's take the issue of "individual freedom." While our society sees this as "being left alone" or as "finding oneself," the Christian does not see it this way. The Christian knows that he or she has been set free by God through Christ and in the Spirit, not simply to become a solitary island with a stony appearance in the waters of life. Rather, it means knowing one's place before God and others. Our identity does not come from discovering ourselves but from knowing God and learning to relate to others as children of God. To be sure, Christians become individually free, but only in order that they might become part of a community. Christian freedom does not seek isolation but fellowship.

Social freedom, while appearing similar because the Christian stands side-by-side at an abortion clinic with a non-Christian social activist or with a non-Christian in a courtroom arguing out a case for justice, is not the same. The Christian wants there to be justice because God is just, not because justice is some metaphysical reality; the Christian wants to tear down sexual discrimination, not because he or she is a social "do-gooder," but because in the gospel of Jesus Christ "there is no male nor female." And so each active involvement on the part of a Christian is a Christian witness to the social impact of the gospel of Jesus Christ. Social justice is not an end in itself; it is a means of declaring the work of God for the Christian.

Christians have been set free psychologically so they can be healthy in their relationship to God, to others, and to themselves. I put the last one last because the Bible turns our society's values on their head. Self-discovery is only one of three reasons God sets us free. There is nothing more enjoyable to God than to see his people mentally healthy: healthy in all their relationships. But once again we see that freedom is freedom *for* something: for relating to God, to self, and to others. It is not personal absorption and ego-staring. It is the freedom of God's Spirit, blowing with his gentle spirit into our psyches so that we can be healed before God and others.

What Paul wants us to be able to work out in our world is an ability to cut down the minimizing of freedom. What hampers our living in the freedom of Christ? What bites into our freedom in the Spirit? Perhaps the most obvious one for all of us is *social custom*. Why is it that a local church has a set time for the Sunday morning service, usually between forty-five minutes and an hour? I suspect that it is social custom—generated over years of experience of the need to get home before the "roast burns," to get home so the afternoon can be spent in the way planned, to get home to watch an NFL football game, to get home in time so the family can travel to a local lake, etc. But how binding would such a social convention be if God's Spirit suddenly broke into a service and created a renewed sense of the holiness of God and the fellowship of the Spirit? How binding? Probably too binding. Our social convention would be pressed by some and the result would be a stifling of the good work of God.

My contention here is that whatever cuts into the freedom of God's Spirit needs to be cut out. We need to have services whose times are not determined by social convention, we need to have fellowships that are not segregated by social race, we need to have churches that are not restricted by cultural background, and we need to have ministries that are not hedged by sexual identity. We need to have all things led by the Spirit of God; and where the Spirit is, there is the freedom of the Lord.

Paul's whole message in Galatians may now be summarized: Be free, through Christ and in the Spirit! When we come to God through Christ and in the Spirit, we are free at last. Thank God, Almighty! We are free at last.[34]

---

34. These words are similar to those on the tombstone of Martin Luther King, Jr., who in his death found that he was finally free from the oppression of racial prejudice. I use the words here in memory of his great work but with a different focus. His words come ultimately from a spiritual and were publicly used in his speech before the Lincoln Memorial. See "I Have a Dream," in *A Testament of Hope: The Essential Writings of Martin Luther King, Jr.*, ed. J. M. Washington (San Francisco: Harper & Row, 1986), 217–20 (the words used are on p. 220).

Galatians 5:13–26

Y OU, MY BROTHERS, were called to be free. But do not use your freedom to indulge the sinful nature;[1] rather, serve one another in love. [14]The entire law is summed up in a single command: "Love your neighbor as yourself." [15]If you keep on biting and devouring each other, watch out or you will be destroyed by each other.

[16]So I say, live by the Spirit, and you will not gratify the desires of the sinful nature. [17]For the sinful nature desires what is contrary to the Spirit, and the Spirit what is contrary to the sinful nature. They are in conflict with each other, so that you do not do what you want. [18]But if you are led by the Spirit, you are not under law.

[19]The acts[2] of the sinful nature are obvious: sexual immorality, impurity and debauchery; [20]idolatry and witchcraft; hatred, discord, jealousy, fits of rage, selfish ambition, dissensions, factions [21]and envy; drunkenness, orgies, and the like. I warn you, as I did before, that those who live like this will not inherit the kingdom of God.

[22]But the fruit of the Spirit is love, joy, peace, patience, kindness, goodness, faithfulness, [23]gentleness and self-control. Against such things there is no law. [24]Those who belong to Christ Jesus have crucified the sinful nature with its passions and desires. [25]Since we live by the Spirit, let us keep in step with the Spirit. [26]Let us not become conceited, provoking and envying each other.

BECAUSE PAUL DEMONSTRATED that acceptance with God is based on faith in Christ, not on works of the law—and he got into all kinds of arguments as to why this was the case—he con-

---

1. The NIV consistently translates the Greek term *sarx* with the expression "sinful nature" here. The more usual translation for this word is "flesh," and we should read that here, for "flesh" and "Spirit" are flag terms for the two ages. Furthermore, "flesh" has connotations that "sinful nature" does not, such as a connection with the law and circumcision as well as being a part of the era that has been eclipsed by the coming of Christ. See J. M. G. Barclay, *Obeying the Truth*, 110–19, 203–9, 227–28.

2. The NIV prefers "acts" for the term *erga;* this term is normally translated "works."

tended that the life of faith in Jesus Christ and life in the Spirit is characterized by *freedom* (5:1), freedom especially from the law and its curse. He then
showed what this freedom meant regarding circumcision (vv. 2–12). His main
point was that submitting to circumcision meant abandoning Jesus Christ and
the grace of God. Paul now applies the doctrine of freedom to the issue of
fighting off the "flesh" (Gk. *sarx;* translated "sinful nature" in the NIV; we will
use the word "flesh" throughout this chapter). The antidote to the flesh is living in the Spirit, not obeying the law of Moses. God's people, he argues, are
marked by the Spirit of God rather than the law. This is how they are
defined and this is how they live: in the Spirit. While chapters 1–4 might be
characterized as "life through Christ," chapters 5–6 might be characterized
as "life in the Spirit."

The section before us is concerned with the significance of freedom for
battling the flesh. It may be broken into four units. (1) Paul calls us *to the life
of freedom from the flesh* (vv. 13–15): living in freedom means not indulging the
flesh but living in love (cf. v. 6). (2) He restates his call to freedom by a *call
to a life in the Spirit against the flesh* (vv. 16–18). (3) He *expounds on the life in the flesh*
(vv. 19–21). (4) He *expounds on the life in the Spirit* (vv. 22–26).

Before we examine these verses more carefully, we must sketch the setting of this section. I shall do so under two different topics: (1) the Judaizers' problem with Paul's view of life in the Spirit, and (2) the rabbinic context
of the Pauline view of how to do battle with the flesh.

(1) What was the Judaizers' problem with Paul's view of living before God
by conducting one's life "in the Spirit"? Some have argued that the letter of
Galatians actually battles off two separate problems at Galatia. One problem
was legalism, addressed by Paul in chapters 1–4, and the other was libertin-
ism, antinomianism, or outright immorality as an option for Christian
lifestyle. I argued in our last section that it is most unlikely that Paul would
argue against one group of people in the first two-thirds of the book and then
turn to another group of people in the last third. Such a structure of the book
would leave the first group with no application and the second group with
no theology. Paul does not operate like this. Furthermore, it is quite within
our grasp to imagine how these two issues can be put together.

The Judaizers, we suspect, claimed that the Galatian converts needed to
adopt the whole law to be accepted by God because in so doing, they would
express their trust in the entirety of God's revelation and provide themselves with an adequate moral guide (the law). I suspect this latter point was
appealing to the Galatian converts. H. D. Betz puts it well: "In the absence
of a code of law, how should one deal with transgression?"[3] And J. M. G. Bar-

---

3. H. D. Betz, *Galatians*, 273.

clay adds: "With no law to distinguish right from wrong, and no rituals to deal with transgressions and provide assurance, their security and self-confidence were somewhat shaky."[4] The Judaizers had a ready answer: assume the yoke of the law. In assuming these laws, the Galatians would then acquire a social identity: Jewish proselytes who were part of Judaism, a religion recognized by Roman law.

They then argued (I suggest) that Paul was teaching an abbreviated gospel (Jesus without Moses) in order to gain their initial hearing; but had he stayed longer, he would have gotten them into a catechism of the law of Moses. Therefore, they ought now to accept the law to finish off Paul's work in their midst. Furthermore, I suspect they argued that if the Galatians were to think hard about it, "life in the Spirit" was profoundly inadequate by itself. For one, it would lead to immorality faster than anything they could think of, and it would never be able to counter the forces of the flesh in their lives. But if they were to adopt the law, all would be solved: no immorality, no problem with the flesh, and full acceptance with God—not to mention acceptance with Jerusalem and the nationalists! This, I believe, is how the Judaizers made their case. And the Galatians bought it, and the emphasis Paul gives to factions in 5:13–26 makes me think that factionalism, or partisanship, is the focus of these verses (cf. 5:15, 26, and 20–21). Paul's letter is what we have of their telephone conversation—just one end of it, but Paul says enough for us to catch on to what they were saying to him.

(2) One of the issues the Judaizers countered Paul with was the issue of the flesh. Judaism's moralists had thought long and hard over how people are to ward off the forces of the flesh and, though very little of the evidence from the first-century discussion has survived, we do have some significant evidence from the later rabbis who can be brought in to illuminate Paul's own response. How did the Jews, and especially the rabbis, envision the obedient Jews fighting off the flesh?[5] All Jews, as well as Greco-Roman moralists, recognized the human propensity to sin and knew that transgressions took place. What was desirable was the capacity to fight off such inclinations to sin. The rabbis contended that every human being had two desires: the *yetser tob* and the *yetser hara* (the good impulse and the evil impulse). Such an idea is found in a non-rabbinic text that may come from before the first century A.D.: "If the soul wants to follow the *good way*,[6] all of its deeds are done

---

4. J. M. G. Barclay, *Obeying the Truth*, 71.

5. The standard treatment of this can be found in W. D. Davies, *Paul and Rabbinic Judaism: Some Rabbinic Elements in Pauline Theology* (4th ed.; Philadelphia: Fortress, 1980), 17–35; I am greatly indebted to his work here.

6. The original does not have "way" but only "good." One might infer the idea was "impulse" as well.

in righteousness and every sin is immediately repented" (*Testament of Asher* 1:6). The rabbis were convinced that this battle took place in the heart and that the *yetser hara* sought to lure people into sexual sins and idolatry (observe their emphasis in vv. 19–21). Most importantly, the rabbis contended that "the chief means of protection against the evil impulse was the study of the Torah" and repentance.[7] Furthermore, some rabbis thought that in the age to come the evil impulse to sexual immorality and idolatry would be destroyed. Is it not likely that Paul is saying that the "age to come" has come in Christ and that on the cross the evil impulse (i.e., the flesh) was put to death (v. 24)?

Several things come together here and, in my view, provide a more accurate picture of the social and religious context out of which Paul was speaking. The Galatian converts were insecure about their moral guidance and in particular about how to fight off the flesh. The Judaizers, having been taught that the law of Moses is God's moral guide, contended that it would enable the Galatian converts to fight off the flesh. Paul contends that the flesh has actually been put to death *already* and that the means of moral guidance has *already* been given: God's Spirit. For Paul, just as Jesus was the fulfillment of the law, so the Spirit is the replacement (and fulfillment) of the law as God's instrument for moral guidance. In other words, the Spirit takes the place of the law for the Christian. This is the historical context of Paul's application of the idea of freedom to the battle with the flesh.

A Call to a Life of Freedom from the Flesh (vv. 13–15)

IF MY SURMISINGS above are close to accurate, then Paul's call here to a life of freedom that does not indulge the flesh is directed at the Judaizing claim that life apart from the law always leads to indulgence. Paul contends that a life of freedom is a life of loving others (the essence of the law!) and not indulging the flesh. Thus, the call to freedom (v. 13) restates the earlier call to freedom (v. 1) but takes the implication of freedom now in a different direction. Whereas before freedom did not lead to circumcision, now it does not lead to indulging the flesh.

After the call to freedom (v. 13a), Paul orders his thoughts in a chiasm:

A. Do not use freedom *for the flesh* (v. 13b)
   B. Instead, use it for *love* (v. 13c)
   B.´ *Love* is the summary command (v. 14)
A.´ *Flesh* is seen when you fight with one another (v. 15)

---

7. W. D. Davies, *Paul and Rabbinic Judaism*, 22–23 (the quotation is from p. 22).

To facilitate explanation, I shall look first at flesh and then at love.

The criticism of Paul's blanket endorsement of "Freedom and Spirit ethics" is that it may lead to indulging the flesh, to anarchic behavior, and to life completely out of line with the law of Moses. But Paul insists that freedom should not be used "to indulge" (Gk. *aphormen*) the flesh. This Greek expression for "to indulge" is metaphorical and picturesque. It is sometimes translated "an opportunity for" (RSV), "an excuse for" (New Century Version), or "a base of operations for" (The New Translation). The term was originally a military description of the army's "base of operations" or a "starting point" for some kind of military maneuver, but it also acquired a metaphorical sense of "opportunity," "pretext," or "occasion."[8] Paul uses it elsewhere for sin taking opportunity for sin (Rom. 7:8, 11), for an opportunity for boasting (2 Cor. 5:12) or comparison (11:12), and for an opportunity for Satan to find fault in the community (1 Tim. 5:14). One papyrus records a daughter who says, "I never miss *an opportunity* to write to you [her father] about both my health and the health of my family."[9] Though believers are free, that freedom is not to become the platform for living sinfully.

Once again, to live "in the flesh" is fundamentally living outside the realm of the Spirit of God. "Flesh" is not effort necessarily (though that could be involved); rather, "flesh" is unspiritual life. Thus, "flesh" becomes closely attached to living "under the law" because, as Paul explains throughout his letter (see at 3:19–25), allowing one's life to be governed by the law is choosing not to live under the governance of the Spirit. Flesh and law belong to an era that is now past; the new era is characterized by the Spirit and Christ. Furthermore, moderns need to understand that when Paul uses "flesh," he is not thinking primarily in terms of "body" and the inferiority of the body in comparison to the spiritual aspect of human nature. This is a Platonic notion, not a biblical one. What Paul has in mind is the "total person living outside of God's will and apart from God's guiding influence through the Spirit."[10]

As stated above, verse 13b corresponds to verse 15: indulging the sinful nature fosters internal dissensions. Actually, verse 15 is a sentence in which

---

8. See the discussion of J. P. Louw and E. A. Nida, *Greek-English Lexicon of the New Testament Based on Semantic Domains* (New York: United Bible Societies, 1988), 1.247–48, where it is classed under the semantic domain of "Trouble, Hardship, Relief, Favorable Circumstances" with the subdomain of "Favorable Circumstances or State." They list such words as "peace," "calm," "truly favorable," "favorable opportunity or good occasion," and "to succeed."

9. BGU II. 632.11. The translation is mine from J. H. Moulton and G. Milligan, *The Vocabulary of the Greek Testament* (Grand Rapids: Eerdmans, 1930), 99.

10. A nice discussion of this can be found in R. N. Longenecker, *Galatians*, 239–41.

the conditional aspect is fulfilled in an imperative. Paul says literally: "If you keep on biting and devouring each other you, watch out or you will be destroyed by each other." Technically, Paul could have said: "If you keep on biting and devouring each other, you will be destroyed by each other." The addition of "watch out for" puts emphasis, emotionally, on the sin. The problem of the Galatians is typically human: egos enter into the debates between people and before long the issue is who is going to win; it becomes *who* is right, not *what* is right.

This was a major issue at Galatia: there were lots of internal fights, as a quick survey of 5:1–6:10 proves. In 5:1–12 we find the apparent need for the Galatians to make a decision over which group they would join, and the focal point of entering the Judaizing faction was circumcision. In the same verses we find ringleaders (vv. 7–10) and false accusations against Paul (v. 11). In verses 13–26 we find the emphasis on factions and strife: they were quarreling at a major level (v. 15). The wording of conflict in verses 16–18 is probably a reflection of the conflicts in the churches. In Paul's list of sins in verses 19–21, he emphasizes interpersonal ones (of the fifteen sins listed, eight concern interpersonal relationships); similarly, his emphasis on "the fruit of the Spirit" is clearly on interpersonal relations (vv. 22–23). At the end of his list he further indicates conflict in the words, "Let us not become conceited, provoking and envying each other" (v. 26). In chapter 6 we find emphases on pride (6:1–5), miserliness (v. 6), and being thoughtful of others (vv. 7–10).

When we think of the Galatian churches, we should not think of a fork in the road, with Paul going down one road and the Judaizers down the other, each beckoning the Galatian travelers to make the right decision as they come to the fork. Rather, we should think of Paul and the Judaizers on the stage platform, having made their cases for their systems, and the Galatian congregation at war with one another, forming separate enclaves here and having proud, vociferous leaders claiming minor victories there. We should think of rivalries, of separate house churches not speaking with one another, of spiritual pride on the part of those who have been circumcised (just a "cut above" the rest!), and of slogan after slogan being bandied about in the communities. The picture we draw is sad—sad because they had adopted the pattern of letting their freedom become a launching-pad for indulging the flesh.

On the contrary, Paul says, their freedom is to be a platform for serving one another in love. While I cannot get into a long excursus about "love" in Pauline theology, I do want to summarize the three main lines of his teaching. For Paul (1) love is defined by Christ's sacrificial giving of his life in love (2:20), (2) love is inspired by God's Spirit (5:22–23), and (3) love is expressed in doing good and in interpersonal relationships in society, especially in the church (5:13–14; 6:10).[11]

In our passage, Paul says two things about love: (1) the Galatians are to "serve one another" in love, and (2) the entire law of Moses is summed up in the commandment from Leviticus 19:18: "Love your neighbor as yourself." There is no question about what Paul is doing here: he is taking away the law of Moses in the letter to the Galatians as passé, but he does so by way of fulfillment. He tells the Galatians that their desire for moral guidelines is the best guideline. If you live in the Spirit, he writes to them, you will have love (5:22), and living in love is far better than the law because it is the fulfillment of the law (v. 14). Just as typing on a computer is the fulfillment of typing on a manual typewriter, so living in the Spirit and love is the fulfillment of living in the law of Moses.

Paul's entire ethic can be handled in three simple expressions: the Galatians are to live in love (vv. 6, 13), or in the Spirit (v. 22), or under the law of Christ (6:2). These are all the same; and each is the fulfillment of the law of Moses (and better). Here he allows the will of God with respect to our relationship to others to be distilled down into the word "love." But this love of Paul is not passion. It is the love of God for us that changes us so we can serve one another in love.

According to Leon Morris, "My first point, then, is that we know love in the New Testament sense only because we see it in the cross; my second point is that to see this love is to be affected by it."[12] This is the love Paul is talking about: God's love for us in Christ (2:20) enables us to be filled with God's Spirit, who then generates the fruit of love in us as we relate to others. Because it is the Spirit of God who awakens love in our hearts, it is not something we can claim as our own. Being able to love others is not the result of discipline; it is a miracle. And love works as the dynamic of human relationships, as Paul knows. Morris ends his book with a question: "Where is there a system that works better than the way of Christian love?"[13]

A Call to a Life in the Spirit Against the Flesh (vv. 16–18)

AFTER MAKING HIS point that freedom is not an excuse for indulging the flesh, Paul clarifies what he means by a life of freedom. Such a life, he says, is living in the Spirit. But this life is a war, a war between the Spirit and the flesh. But this war is not some "personal psychological struggle" or the "struggle

---

11. There is no better biblical study of love than that of L. L. Morris, *Testaments of Love: A Study of Love in the Bible* (Grand Rapids: Eerdmans, 1981).

12. Ibid., 276.

13. Ibid., 279.

within a person's soul." Rather, as E. P. Sanders has said, "The war . . . has to do with which power one—body and soul—belongs to."[14] The powers are "flesh" and "Spirit."

Once again, Paul arranges his thoughts in a chiasm:

A. Live by the *Spirit* and you escape flesh (v. 16)
    B. The *conflict* is between flesh and Spirit (v. 17a)
    B.´ The *conflict* prohibits doing God's will (v. 17b)
A.´ Be led by the *Spirit* and you escape law (v. 18)

This structure permits a ready understanding of this passage. Paul is dealing here with opposites. When a person lives in God's Spirit, he or she escapes the power of flesh (v. 17a) and the power of law (5:18).[15] Once again, Paul connects law to flesh and to the former era (3:3; 4:21–31; 6:12–13). But this life of the Spirit is a battle—a battle over God's will; those who are engaged in it recognize that flesh and Spirit are opposites. When one lives in the flesh, one does not do what God's Spirit wants.

In general we see something fundamentally important here as to how Paul depicts the Christian life. It is life in the Spirit, the life of a person who is surrendered to letting the Spirit have complete control. But we see here also that one does not gain this life by discipline or by mustering up the energy. One does not huddle with oneself in the morning, gather together his or her forces, and charge onto the field of life full of self-determined direction. Rather, the Christian life is a life of consistent surrender to the Spirit.

What Is the Fleshly Life? (vv. 19–21)

PAUL GOES ON to explain what he means by "life in the flesh" and "life in the Spirit," giving a list for each. Listing vices and virtues was common among moral teachers in the ancient world, and I give some parallels in Paul's letters that readers may want to examine: 2 Corinthians 6:1–10; 8:1–7; Ephesians 4:1–10; Philippians 4:8–9; Colossians 3:12–17; 1 Timothy 1:9; 6:4–6; 2 Timothy 3:2–4; Titus 3:3.[16] The lists were used as a characterization of someone or some idea, and they were not used as a lawbook.

---

14. E. P. Sanders, *Paul and Palestinian Judaism: A Comparison of Patterns of Religion* (Philadelphia: Fortress, 1977), 553–54.

15. To be "under the law" means (1) to live under it as the governing principle of life; that is, one orients his or her entire life around the law of Moses. (2) It also means to be under the curse of the law (3:13) and its sin-revealing, confining powers (3:19–25). That is, when a person lives under the Spirit, he or she is not going to be held accountable to the law's system and has been set free from its nastiness.

16. See also A. J. Malherbe, *Moral Exhortation, A Greco-Roman Sourcebook* (Library of Early Christianity; Philadelphia: Westminster Press, 1986), 138–41.

More importantly, the lists here of the works of the flesh and the fruit of the Spirit are not abstract listings, nor are they comprehensive. Rather, they are context specific. *In the context of church conflict, the observer will find the manifestation of the flesh in such things as factionalism and will find that the Spirit, when in control, will produce such things as love and patience.* In other words, we interpret these lists incorrectly if we take them out of their context and pretend that they are complete listings of either the flesh or the Spirit. These are the kinds of things Paul wants to focus on because he is concerned with conflict. Had he written to the Ephesians, he would have had other items in both lists.

Paul divides the "works of the flesh" into four areas that we cannot discuss in detail:[17]

(1) sexual sins: "sexual immorality, impurity and debauchery";

(2) religious sins: "idolatry and witchcraft";

(3) social sins: "hatred, discord, jealousy, fits of rage, selfish ambition, dissensions, factions and envy";

(4) drinking sins: "drunkenness, orgies, and the like."

These four areas are typical areas for problems of excess. The third area appears to be Paul's focus, for it has more detail than the others—the social sins that the flesh was working in their midst. The flesh destroys fellowship, unity, and holiness. What is most important, and what sounds like Jesus, is Paul's final word: "those who live like this will not inherit the kingdom of God" (v. 21). Whether a person made some kind of profession of faith, whether a person had a charismatic experience, or whether a person endured a great deal of suffering does not matter *if he or she lives in the flesh* (cf. Matt. 7:15–27; 2 Cor. 5:10; James 2:14–26). One's final standing before God, Paul contends, is directly related to whether or not a person lives in the flesh or in the Spirit.

What Is the Life in the Spirit? (vv. 22–26)

PAUL'S LISTING OF the "fruit of the Spirit" does not seem to have any particular order, though some have proposed an order. J. R. W. Stott sees in these nine virtues three groups of three: attitudes to God, others, and self, while J. B. Lightfoot sees dispositions of the mind, qualities governing human relations, and principles of conduct.[18] We do need to comment on the terms *fruit* and *love*, but we are not able to spend time with each word.

---

17. So J. R. W. Stott, *Only One Way*, 147–48; detailed comments on each manifestation of the flesh can be found in R. N. Longenecker, *Galatians*, 254–57, who agrees with many others in thinking this list is random and chaotic (see pp. 253–54).

18. J. R. W. Stott, *Only One Way*, 148–49; J. B. Lightfoot, *Galatians*, 212–13. R. N. Longenecker (*Galatians*, 260) views these virtues as unordered.

Paul describes "flesh" under the term *works*, while he sees the Spirit's work as "fruit." The former is plural while the latter is singular. Is there anything significant in the change of terms or the change of number? Above all, it must be observed that *works* has been a term of negative associations in Galatians and that Paul probably delighted in associating the "works" of the flesh with the "works of the law" (2:16; 3:2, 5, 10). The change of terms to "fruit" evokes a different image: from one of human responsibility to one of divine enablement. The image of fruit has a certain sense of passivity to it; it is the Spirit of God who produces such things, and they grow in the life of the Christian.

However, while this may be one reason for the change of terms, it is also clear that Paul sees evil as having fruit (6:8) and thinks that the Christian is responsible to let the Spirit be operative in his or her life. Note that Paul shoulders the responsibility of the Spirit's fruit onto the Christian: "have crucified their flesh" (v. 24), "let us keep in step" (v. 25), and "let us not become conceited" (v. 26)—not to mention verses 13, 16, and 18. It is possible that the *unity* of the fruit is emphasized in the singular while the *chaotic multitude* of sins of the flesh is represented in a plural noun. On the other hand, "fruit" can be seen as a collective plural; if so, there is nothing significant in the change to a singular.

While "love" is not the only "fruit" of the Spirit, it is the most important to Paul (cf. vv. 6, 13–14; also Rom. 5:5; 1 Cor. 13; Col. 3:14).[19] It summarizes the demand of God's law (Gal. 5:14), endures forever (1 Cor 13:13), and unites all the virtues of life (Col. 3:14). Fundamental to Paul's view, however, is that love comes from God's Spirit (cf. Rom. 5:5). Moreover, as we look over this list, we observe the reverse of the list of the works of the flesh. Whereas the flesh destroys fellowship; here the Spirit creates fellowship, unity, and holiness.

As if summarizing his whole point, Paul says that (1) those who have surrendered themselves to Jesus Christ "have crucified the flesh" and so should not be involved in the works of the flesh (v. 24); (2) those who have been given God's life by the Spirit and Christ (cf. 2:20; Rom 8:9–11) should march according to the Spirit's orders (Gal 5:25); and (3) those who live in the freedom of the Spirit should not be conceited and so fight with one another (v. 26). Once again, we end up with Paul's emphasis in this context: Galatian factionalism.

---

19. See J. R. W. Stott, *The Contemporary Christian*, 146–48; on the fruit of the Spirit see pp. 146–57.

Bridging Contexts

I KNOW OF no Christian parents or youth leaders, or for that matter any pastors, who seriously believe what Paul teaches in verses 16–26, that the sole foundation of Christian ethics is dependency on the Spirit and a life of freedom in the Spirit. In my life, which at the time of the publication of this book will be about forty years—nearly twenty-five of which has been spent actively in the evangelical movement and beyond—I have met only one person who ever expressed this view of Paul in a definitive and, to him, practical way. That person was F. F. Bruce, and our family was privileged to spend an afternoon with him while we were living in Nottingham during the time of my doctoral program. After receiving an invitation for us to visit him and his wife, we traveled by car from Nottingham to their home in Buxton. I spent the majority of my time in the car wondering just what I could ask a scholar whose work has been hailed as some of the finest in our century. I had been warned that Professor Bruce was quiet and modest and that it might take work on my part to keep the conversation going. So I prepared some questions, not of course in writing but in my mind. He met us at our car, hospitably ushered us into his home, and introduced us to his wife; I then introduced my wife and our two children, Laura and Lukas, to them.

After our pleasantries were exchanged and after a light tea, I could tell it was "question and answer time." I began with some warm-up questions about what he was working on (he had just finished his commentaries on Galatians and Philippians) and what he thought of some of the issues I was working on (Jewish missionary activity). I then asked the question I wanted him most to answer. I asked him about women in the church. My question was something like this, "Professor Bruce, do you think women should be ordained?" His response I shall remember forever. He said, "I don't care much for ordination. But what I can say with regard to the exercise of women's ministries in the church, is this: *I am for whatever brings freedom in the church. I am for whatever brings the freedom of the Spirit in the church of God.*" His answer seemed so nebulous, so full of holes, so full of problems, and so full of unanswered questions. As I have subsequently reflected it, however, I am sure I was wrong in my puzzlement. His answer is *very biblical, very Pauline, and very much like Galatians.* In fact, his answer is so much like Galatians that his answer must be right.[20]

What I am saying is this: while Professor Bruce's comment is uncommon, it corresponded to Paul's view of the essence of Christian living. It is a view

---

20. Not long before that conversation Professor Bruce had published a survey of the letters of Paul that was titled, in England, *Paul: Apostle of the Free Spirit;* this book came out in an American edition with the title *Paul: Apostle of the Heart Set Free* (Grand Rapids: Eerdmans,

that few are willing to live with. How can we condemn the Galatians for being unwilling to live according to Paul's view of ethics if we have the identical problem? How can we accuse the Galatians of being gullible and of embracing what was clearly an inferior system when we are unable and unwilling to live with the open-endedness of the Pauline view of Christian freedom? Are we perhaps as guilty of "legalism" as they were? Do we perhaps also want legal guidelines and Mosaic law? These questions are worth pondering.

We must first convince ourselves that God's Spirit is a sufficient guide for moral life before God. We must thoroughly grasp God's goodness in his granting to us the Holy Spirit as the sure guide to holiness and love. To do this we need to read Galatians once again with an open mind, and then proceed to Paul's other letters (this makes really good sense if Galatians is the first of Paul's letters), to see what Paul has in mind there when he speaks of "life in the free Spirit."

Furthermore, it is not that Paul did not have available rules and regulations to appeal to: he could have gone to Moses for some moral guidelines or even to Jesus. He could have appealed to such texts as the Sermon on the Mount (Matt. 5–7) or to specific texts in the Old Testament (e.g., Lev. 11:44–45: "Be holy, because I am holy"). He did not, however, and he knew that in not doing so he was leaving these as options. He did not see the teachings of Jesus as new laws,[21] nor would he appeal to the law of Moses as binding on the Christian. Instead, Paul described the essence of Christian living as "freedom in the Spirit."

To be sure, Paul knew that when a person was controlled by the Spirit, that person was holy. He also knew that a person who lived in the Spirit lived in a loving way. Thus, he knew that the Old Testament moral guidelines and the teachings of Jesus on holiness, righteousness, and compassion would be confirmed by anyone who lived in the Spirit. This is important to remember. Paul's statement that the law of Moses cannot condemn anyone who lives in the Spirit shows that he knew that life in the Spirit would not and could not lead to moral anarchy (cf. v. 23). However, even with this important qualification, Paul stressed that true living before God was a life in the Spirit and a life of spiritual freedom. The question for us is direct: Is our ethic an ethic of freedom in the Spirit or is it much more like that of the Judaizing invaders?

1978). He told me in that conversation that he was not happy with the American title because, for him, freedom was something that was connected to God's Spirit, not just some heart experience. That he entitled his book with "Free Spirit" confirms my impression that for Professor Bruce, freedom and the Spirit were of the essence of Christian living. Anyone who reads his personal memoirs will find the same; see his *In Retrospect: Remembrance of Things Past* (Grand Rapids: Eerdmans, 1980).

21. A good book in this regard, though not always easy to read, is A. E. Harvey, *Strenuous Commands: The Ethic of Jesus* (Philadelphia: Trinity Press International, 1990).

We begin to apply our text today when we answer "Yes" to the following question: Is God's Spirit a sufficient guide for Christian living? If you answered "yes," pass go.

Another way of looking at this matter is to pause to question whether we think that all our "good traits" are the result of God's grace or not. Do we think it is we who have made us capable to think? to walk? to write? to speak? to relate to others? to create imaginatively in our careers? to expend tremendous amounts of energy in our vocations and avocations, in our activities and in our relationships? If we do, we are not on the side of Paul. According to Paul, everything, from back to front and from beginning to end, is by faith, in the Spirit, and through Christ. It is only by extension of this basic principle that Paul's teaching on the Spirit becomes immediately clear: our moral guide is the Spirit because everything good in our life is the result of God's work on our behalf. I quote from F. F. Bruce in another context:

> The Letter to the Galatians can be thought of as so completely devoted to the theme of justification by faith that its teaching on the Holy Spirit may be overlooked. In fact, its teaching on the Holy Spirit is so interwoven with its teaching on justification by faith that the one cannot be understood without the other, any more than in real life the justifying grace of God can be experienced apart from the Spirit.[22]

To facilitate application, it would be good to have before us a brief survey of the Spirit in Galatians on both the social and the theological context of the text.[23] (1) The Spirit of God is what the Christian receives at conversion (3:2, 3, 5, 14; 5:25), and this was evidently made known through charismatic experiences (see comments on 3:1–5). Such an experience makes the convert a "son of God" who can call God *Abba* (4:6). Indeed, the reception of the Spirit is what the entire Old Testament looked forward to as it came to fruition in the universal plan of God (3:13–14). To live in the Spirit is to live in the age when God inaugurates his kingdom.[24] (2) Those who are "in the Spirit" are persecuted by those in the "flesh" (3:4; 4:29). (3) Those who

---

22. F. F. Bruce, "The Spirit in the Letter to the Galatians," in *Essays on Apostolic Themes: Studies in Honor of Howard M. Ervin Presented to Him by Colleagues and Friends on his Sixty-Fifth Birthday*, ed. P. Elbert (Peabody, Mass.: Hendrickson, 1985), 36–48 (quotation from p. 36).

23. An overall treatment of the Spirit from a practical and mildly charismatic (and Anglican!) side is M. Green, *I Believe in the Holy Spirit* (Grand Rapids: Eerdmans, 1975). For a two-page summary of all that the New Testament teaches I have never seen anything like D. F. Wells, *God the Evangelist: How the Holy Spirit Works to Bring Men and Women to Faith* (Grand Rapids: Eerdmans, 1987), 7–8.

24. See esp. G. E. Ladd, "The Holy Spirit in Galatians," in *Current Issues in Biblical and Patristic Interpretation: Studies in Honor of Merrill C. Tenney Presented by His Former Students*, ed. G. F. Hawthorne (Grand Rapids: Eerdmans, 1975), 211–16.

are "in the Spirit" exercise hope for the coming establishment of God's right-eousness and their own declaration of fitness before God (5:5). (4) Those who are "in the Spirit" are victorious over the "works of the flesh" (vv. 16–18, 19–21) and so live a life full of the manifestation of the Spirit (vv. 22–23). For this victory to occur, Christians need only submit to, or walk in step with, the Spirit (v. 25; cf. 6:8).

Thus, for Paul "life in the Spirit" begins at conversion with the gift of the Spirit, continues as it is sustained by that same Spirit, and waits for the final establishment of God's kingdom in the Spirit. It is all in the Spirit. "If Paul was rightly described, in the title of a recent book, as the 'apostle of the free Spirit,' Galatians might be described, with equal justice, as the *epistle* of the free Spirit."[25]

I pause here to admit discouragement. I do not know about you, but when I look through the list of virtues in the fruit of the Spirit, and when I exam-ine such teachings on the Holy Spirit in the light of the whole letter, I become befuddled over the church. How can we confess Jesus Christ and the fellowship of the Spirit and live in so much tension in the Christian world? Why is the Christian church so torn and divided, here over theology and there over practice? Why do we know so much of personalities and so little of Christ? Why is it that the decisive argument against the church for so many is that the church is full of hypocrites, full of dissensions, and full of denom-inationalism? To be sure, I am aware that the children of the flesh will find any argument possible to use against the truth of the Spirit (because light and darkness do not mix; cf. John 3:19–21). But nonetheless, the argument is com-pelling at times and it hurts. Why is it that Christians claim to have the Spirit but show little of his power and his love? Why is it that Christians claim to live in the Spirit but spend so much of their time "out of step" with the Spirit? It is my prayer that God will renew his work of the Spirit and that this chap-ter will be used by God to that end.

I MUST BEGIN here with a bit of irresistible humor about the Galatian social context. One of my students recently gave me a book called *The Garimus File: A Back-Door Look at the New Testament,* by Gary Stanley, an obvious wit.[26] In his attempt to communicate the mes-sage of the New Testament to the youth of modern times, the author decided

---

25. F. F. Bruce, "The Spirit in the Letter to the Galatians," 48.

26. Gary Stanley, *The Garimus File: A Back-Door Look at the New Testament,* illustrated by John Hawk (San Bernardino, Calif.: Here's Life Publishers, 1983). I express my thanks to Cheryl Hatch, the student who gave me this book, for the delight I have found in it.

to introduce Galatians by imagining the kinds of graffiti that would have been written on city walls by the various parties and factions in Galatia.[27] I quote here from some of his imagined (but highly penetrating) graffiti. One reads: "The only good Gentile is a circumcicized one." Next to this comment is a Christian's comment: "Abraham was a gentile," but this was supplemented by a Judaizer with: "Yea, but he was circumcized." Some Paulinist came along and commented on the whole debate: "So what?" (cf. Gal 5:6). At another place on the wall it reads: "LONG LIVE THE LAW," which is crossed out by some Christian who wrote: "Long live life!"—to which someone depressed added: "Life stinks!" Under this some Christian wrote: "The law stinks," and some Judaizer came along and crossed that out and wrote: "Gentiles stink!" On another part of the wall it reads: "Jews are just a cut above the rest" (obviously written by a circumcised Jew). A Christian wrote: "Grace isn't cheap but its free," but someone else crossed this out, perhaps a Judaizer, and wrote: "Nothing is free."

Someone wrote a poem about Paul:

There was a young man named Saul
Who changed his first name to Paul.
   It didn't make him an apostle
   or anything colossal,
Just a fellow with an awful lot of gall.

Next to this graffito was a string of sayings about freedom: "Free me!," "Free Beer" (crossed out with "Nothing is free" written in its place), "Freedom is a myth," and "A promise is a promise" (alluding to Paul's view of God's covenant with Abraham). Another one reads: "The best fruit is fruit of the vine," to which someone added: "Amen!" (cf. 5:22–23). A picture of a fish has a hook in its mouth and a graffito reads: "Suckers get hooked." The Judaizing wing made this comment on those who got hooked into Paul's gospel (here symbolized in the fish symbol).

Stanley has a great imagination; but it is also quite accurate as to the kinds of slogans that might have been exchanged. In context and tone, these slogans aptly capture the atmosphere at Galatia. This, I believe, is a creative method of applying Galatians: thinking of how the various Galatians might have written graffiti on the walls of the cities in which they lived. Such a method forces us to think of the message as well as of catchy phrases that condense various viewpoints. Such a method could be continued for each chapter and for other books relating conflicts.

---

27. Ibid., 28–29.

There are several options before us about what to apply. The most common approach to this passage is to focus on the individual dimensions of the fruit of the Spirit and to seek to make this list a character-building piece of instruction. This approach lists the nine virtues and spends perhaps a week on each one to see if a person will improve his or her Christian character by practicing the presence of these characteristics. Since many others have done this, I need not do it here; and, while this is fine, I am also convinced that such an approach is slightly misguided. To repeat what has been said earlier: this list of the fruit of the Spirit is not comprehensive but is contextually determined. This is an important list for a church that is full of conflict—the key issue behind the whole letter!

Besides, there are many other ways the Spirit manifests himself in the lives of individuals and in the life of the church. Does not the Holy Spirit work holiness, justice, and righteousness, to name but a few? And surely there are more manifestations of the flesh than those listed here. I need not wear this remark out. While I think it is profitable to see if the fruit of the Spirit is in our lives, I also believe it is important to see just what the Spirit is doing in our lives and to see that as his fruit as well.

We could also explore the idea of the Christian life as a battle. Most of us wear some battle scars, and so we are fully aware of the pitfalls of following the Lord. Galatians 5:16–18 speaks to this issue most clearly. We could "muster" together all the military imagery of Paul on ethical conflict (like Eph. 6:10–18) and come up with "Paul's Ethical War Strategies." We would not want to exclude Jesus' temptation here (Matt. 4:1–10).

What we will concentrate on in this section is "conflict mediation in the church" and Paul's approach to it. Of course, we are not talking about what modern sociologists, psychologists, and administrators are talking about, but the issues are similar and Paul's teachings are more than adequate to solve the majority of problems. And, of course, we have to simplify (which is not necessarily bad) because Paul is simple here. Our applications cannot get into a taxonomy of every conflict in the Bible, of how the people worked through them, and of what God's Word says about each one. We are dealing with Galatians, and with only one text at that; but we do believe that Paul's directives here are profoundly important for managing conflict in the church. Perhaps if we listened less to sociologists and more to the Bible, we would be further ahead in our conflicts.[28]

Furthermore, we need to understand the nature of this Galatian conflict: it was theological (through Christ or through the law?); it was social (Jews

---

28. The issue, regardless, is people and their egos, not theories about how to solve the problem. If you want to solve a problem, you can; if you don't want to solve it, no matter what theory you use, you can't.

or Gentiles?); it was sexual (male or female?); and it was undoubtedly tied into the power of various personalities. It resulted in factions in the Galatian churches, factions that were at one another's throats. This context is what Paul found when he wrote this letter. His solution was *to live in the Spirit.*

Situations of conflict today are found between spouses, between parents and children, between denominations, and between various groups in local churches (to name a few). Is Paul's teaching relevant to these various conflicts today? Yes, I believe so. But how?

First, conflict mediation teams will always remind us that when there is tension, the first order of business is *to clarify the issues.* This is what Paul does in the letter: he explains the problems that are confronting them, in both theological and social terms. I do not take this point from sociological theory; this is common sense that works itself out in every conflict that is solved. This is how we solve problems with our children and problems at work; this is how we solve problems with our spouses; and this is how we solve problems in the church. Paul did not know any specific theory about "conflict management," but he did know that he had to get all the options on the table before he knew which one to choose. I believe Galatians can be seen as a letter that seeks to explain the options (albeit in a highly persuasive manner) and to clarify the issues that confronted the Galatians churches.

Second, it does no good to talk about the Spirit's sufficiency as moral guide if we are not all agreed that the Spirit of God is the chief leader of our lives. We must agree here. Unless the two parties *can stop and remember the sufficiency of the Spirit,* there will be no progress. This is the hardest step for all those seeking to find peace and for those called in as arbitrators. Why? Because in that admission comes an intuition that one is going to get steamrolled into an answer that will roll over one's egocentrism or cherished viewpoint. We find this in theological arguments: if a theologian admits that he has been wrong, he knows that he will be embarrassed and have to change a lot of his ideas (which may have been getting him a lot of press!). In the history of the church, there have been few theologians who have publicly changed their minds, and I believe that it has often been so because of the stubborn egos of scholars. The church has suffered from this immensely. So rare is it that one scholar's magazine article was recently introduced in an editorial remark with "he is a scholar who is known for changing his mind."

The same problem faces marriage partners and church groups. If one church group willingly admits that the Spirit will be the guide, they are surrendering their power to make the decision. People who have vested interests (our expression for "desires of power") do not like to surrender their decisions to someone else. Furthermore, in surrendering to the Spirit people are willingly giving the matter over to the God of the Bible and to his Word. More often than not, they know what the Bible says about their personal arguments and their personal desires. And also more often than not, they know they are partly wrong.

In other words, management of conflict gets nowhere until the parties come to terms with the fundamental solution to conflict: an admission that the Spirit of God is to be the guide and director of the issue. What the Spirit wants is what the people should want, regardless of their desires.

Third, the parties need to *stop and examine what the Bible teaches about the problem*. Of course, I am aware that the Bible does not address everything under the sun, but it does address many things that divide us. It does not talk about carpet colors for churches, just as it does not talk about the Mastricht Treaty in the debate over the European economy. But the Bible does speak clearly *about dissensions and divisions in the church*. It does not matter what the issue is; divisiveness and fighting is wrong for the Christian church. So while we may disagree over the kind of organ we are going to buy (and how much it is going to cost) and over certain unimportant theological issues, we cannot get into fights about them. We must submit ourselves to this word of the Lord: "But the fruit of the Spirit is . . . peace" (v. 22); and where the Spirit of the Lord is, there is not only freedom (2 Cor. 3:17) but also peace. Likewise, we know that in situations of conflict, the Spirit is not at work the way God wants. There ought to be peace and joy, there ought to be kindness and gentleness, but often there is not. When the parties submit to these virtues of the Spirit, then genuine progress can take place. Fightings stop, and that is major progress regardless of the outcome.

Fourth, the parties must *stop and trust that the guidance that the Lord gives is sufficient*. Here I am talking about the willingness of the parties to call in an arbitrator (whether it be the Bible, a friend, a church board, or whatever), listen to the Spirit, and trust that that solution is what God wants. Moderns have a tremendous problem here. The Western world is enthralled with its individualism and its freedom (see our discussion of freedom in "Bridging Contexts" and "Contemporary Significance" at 5:1–12); thus it has a hard time (some might call it impossible) allowing others to make decisions for them.

Yes, at times the arbitration may go against our wishes. But do we sincerely think that we are always right? We must always salt and pepper our positions with the possibility that we are wrong. We must always pursue *what* is right and not *who* is right, and we must never pretend that we are always right. In submitting to the decision of arbitrators (and Paul stepped in here as the arbitrator whether they wanted him or not!), we have to exercise trust. This trust is ultimately in the guidance of the Spirit of God. Do we genuinely believe that God's Spirit is a sufficient moral guide?

I mentioned in the paragraph above that I believe God guides us through his Spirit. I also mentioned several ways that happens. It remains for me to fill this out in a little more detail. I believe that the Spirit of the Lord guides us usually in one of four ways: through circumstances, through other Christians, through the Bible, and through prayer and/or spiritual intuition. It is not unusual for those who are being trained in Christianity to want to become like the person training them; thus, if that person has been to seminary, then they should go too. We have lots of students at Trinity whose first impulse to go to seminary came from a desire to be like their leader. It is also not unusual for churches with a major emphasis on missions to raise up from their church lots of missionaries. Circumstances, in other words, often are used by God to guide us. More often than not, however, in situations of church conflict, the leading instruments of God's guidance will be how he speaks in his Spirit through other Christians, through the Bible, and through prayer. The issue, however, remains the same: Do we really believe God's Spirit is a sufficient guide?

Factionalism is wrong because it is incompatible with the Spirit who brings fellowship and peace. Perhaps I am overstepping my bounds here, but I shall venture a view on denominationalism. I am fully appreciative of the diversity of people and their viewpoints. I am thoroughly convinced that our human minds are fallible and unable to make infallible judgments about many things. So we "see darkly" at times. Our fallibility has led to denominations.

But having said this, I still find that there are too many denominations and too much factionalism in the church. There are too many factions because there is too little trust in the Spirit of God and too little living in the Spirit. God is not pleased when his people split over insignificant issues. Let me suggest that churches should never split over whether one should be baptized as an adult or as a child; we may disagree, but I cannot see that issue as so crucial that it touches on our common acceptance by God. Let me also suggest that our churches should never split over whether one should play contemporary music or classical music; again, we may disagree, but we should be big enough to handle one another, to learn from one another, and to grow in our appreciation of the different gifts God gives to his people. As long as something is consistent with the Bible, church traditions, and God's moving of his people, how can we divide over the matter? To be sure, when someone tells me that Jesus Christ is not our means of acceptance with God, I believe we should part. But I do not believe we should part company over minor issues, nor do I believe we should ever fight about issues. Debate, reason, discussion, disagreement—yes; fight, war, provoke—no.

At Galatia there was tremendous strife among the people because the Galatians had surrendered their lives to the flesh in the name of freedom. They had begun to devour one another personally in their desire for power and control. The flesh was given the upper hand. Paul entered into this terrible battle and bequeathed to them a message and letter that still has its impact to this very day. Its message is that when God's people live in the free Spirit, they do not war with one another, rather, they bring glory to God, who wants them to enjoy the fellowship he promises. This comes from the Spirit.

Galatians 6:1–10

BROTHERS, IF SOMEONE is caught in a sin, you who are spiritual should restore him gently. But watch yourself, or you also may be tempted. ²Carry each other's burdens, and in this way you will fulfill the law of Christ. ³If anyone thinks he is something when he is nothing, he deceives himself. ⁴Each man should test his own actions. Then he can take pride in himself, without comparing himself to somebody else, ⁵for each one should carry his own load.

⁶Anyone who receives instruction in the word must share all good things with his instructor.

⁷Do not be deceived: God cannot be mocked. A man reaps what he sows. ⁸The one who sows to please his sinful nature, from that nature will reap destruction; the one who sows to please the Spirit, from the Spirit will reap eternal life. ⁹Let us not become weary in doing good, for at the proper time we will reap a harvest if we do not give up. ¹⁰Therefore, as we have opportunity, let us do good to all people, especially to those who belong to the family of believers.

Original Meaning

IF IT WAS difficult at first to find direct relevance for 5:1–26 to the situation at Galatia, it is even more difficult for 6:1–10. Here we have what appears to be four random thoughts (bearing burdens, sharing with one's teacher, sowing and reaping, and doing good), so random that they not only seem unrelated to one another, but also unrelated to the situation at Galatia. Is this accurate? I think not. A close examination of the verses confirms what has been stated by John Barclay: "We can also safely conclude that these various maxims are by no means irrelevant to the Galatian churches but are intended to meet their general problems of strife and division."¹ What we find here, then, is an interplay between two themes: personal responsibility and mutual accountability—both emerging from the context of communal strife.

---

1. J. M. G. Barclay, *Obeying the Truth*, 167. See also the survey of options in R. N. Longenecker, *Galatians*, 269–71.

What I would add here is that these two themes are rooted in Paul's call to freedom (5:1, 13). It will be remembered that such freedom was freedom from the law, that this freedom was unsettling for the converts, that they wanted some kind of moral guideline, that the Judaizers contended that the absence of the law of Moses would throw the Galatians into moral confusion, that the Galatians became quite divisive over the problems, and that Paul countered this with the so-called restriction of freedom: it is not a license for sin (v. 13) but an opportunity for love (vv. 13–14). Such a life of freedom is life in the Spirit (vv. 13–26). In the present section, Paul now gives some *concrete illustrations of what it means to live as a Christian individual within a community when that community is guided by freedom in the Spirit.*

To be sure, Paul applies this notion of "freedom in the Spirit" to more than one topic here, but each of them is related to the Galatian context of strife and to the two themes stated above. The flow of the verses seems to be as follows: living in the freedom of the Spirit precludes conceit (5:26), so spiritual people should bear one another's burdens in humility (6:1–5), bear one another's burdens to the degree that they financially support their teachers (v. 6), and recognize that God will hold them accountable for how they have treated others (vv. 6–10). The specifics of how all these ideas are connected to the divisiveness at Galatia will come out in the paragraphs that follow.

Spiritual People Should Bear One Another's Burdens (vv. 1–5)

I BEGIN BY trying to put together these verses, perhaps the hardest unit when it comes to the matter of the flow of the ideas. Paul begins by stating *a problem: restoring a sinful brother* (v. 1). This is followed by *the underlying principle* to solve the problem, namely, that spiritual people (i.e., those who "live in the Spirit") need to be responsible for one another and look after one another (v. 2). The next three verses refer to the *problem of pride* (vv. 3–5). When restoring others, spiritual persons may be tempted to pride (cf. v. 1b). After insisting that they bear one another's burdens (v. 2), Paul returns to his point about being tempted and brings up the matter of a person thinking too much of himself in the process of restoration (v. 3). The solution to this is simply to examine one's actions and see if he (or she) is living "in the Spirit" (v. 4a). One does not need to assess one's standing before God by comparing oneself to others (v. 4b). This leads Paul to yet another principle underlying his point about pride: in the end, each person must stand before God for how he or she has lived (v. 5). To do this means becoming personally responsible.

The problem: Restoring a sinful brother (v. 1). When Paul wants his readers' special attention, he calls them "brothers" (3:15; 4:12; 5:11). In so doing he makes a claim on them as well: if I can call you "brothers," I can assume you will live the way God wants, and this means "living in the Spirit." One problem that sometimes arises for those who live as a community of people who are striving to live in the Spirit is that someone falls into sin or begins to manifest "the works of the flesh" (5:19–21).[2]

In this situation, the community should take it upon itself to restore such a person because this is one way a family expresses its love. But Paul's emphasis here is not *that* this restoration should be done but *how*. His emphasis is on the word "gently"; though this is a good translation for *en pneumati praütetos* (lit., "in the spirit of humility"), it masks the key word "spirit." I am persuaded that Paul is making a connection here to the "fruit of the Spirit" in 5:23 ("humility"); he enjoins the Galatians to restore (cf. 1 Cor. 1:10) the sinning brother under the influence of "the Spirit who provides humility."[3] Gentleness is crucial for restoration, and only the spiritual, those under the Spirit, should be involved. "One of the reasons why only spiritual Christians should attempt the ministry of restoration is that only the spiritual are gentle."[4]

In so doing, however, those restoring must watch out for themselves because they "also may be tempted" (v. 1b). As made clear above, I think the temptation here is to pride because of verses 3–4, which carries on Paul's point. While some have argued that the temptation would have been to the specific sin that the erring brother was trapped in, that does not seem as likely as the view I have offered.[5] Regardless, this is the problem Paul is emphasizing; he is not as much concerned here with the sinner as he is with the restorer.

We can only guess, but guess we will, that the Judaizing controversy created problems of pride among the leaders in Galatia. Evidently those who were in charge of restoring the sinful were doing so by calling attention to themselves, to their goodness, and probably to their confession of Moses. In carrying out restoration in this manner, they were comparing themselves to those who were not performing such a ministry (cf. v. 4). This suggests that

---

2. Paul uses a term for "sin" here that is normally associated with the transgression of the law (*paraptoma*).

3. I am not against the view that "spirit of humility" means no more than "gently" or "in humility" and that the Holy Spirit is not in view; but I do think the connection with 5:23 is hard to avoid and, in light of Paul's emphasis on the Holy Spirit in Galatians, I think the interpretation I give in the text is to be preferred. Note that Paul is addressing those who are "spiritual" (6:1). These are those who are "living in the Spirit" and who are not living under the law; thus, he is talking to those at Galatia who have not succumbed to the Judaizers. See F. F. Bruce, *Galatians*, 260.

4. J. R. W. Stott, *Only One Way*, 161–62.

5. So also J. M. G. Barclay, *Obeying the Truth*, 158.

the Judaizers had gained the upper hand in the churches by finding allies in the leadership.

The principle: Love one another (v. 2). Underneath Paul's point about restoring others "in the Spirit of gentleness" is the basis for such behavior: the "law of Christ," which is to live in the love of the Spirit[6] (cf. 5: 6, 14, 22; James 1:25; 2:12), means loving the sinning brother by carrying his burden to help him on the way. The expression "law of Christ" is surprising in its formulation since Paul has spent a great deal of time dismissing the law as the Christian's guide. Nonetheless, his willingness to say Christians are under the "law of Christ" and not under "the law of Moses" is entirely reasonable, once we understand that "law of Christ" is nothing other than (1) submission to the teachings of Jesus that fulfill the law (Matt. 5:17–20) and (2) life in the Spirit, which is essentially love and which itself fulfills the law of Moses (Gal. 5:6, 14, 18, 22). The Christian's law is following Jesus, that is, living in submission to the Spirit.[7]

A specific example of following the law of Christ is to carry the burden of a brother or sister. Paul is here addressing those who are restoring, and so we must envision the restorer as a person who undertakes not only to point out problems and sins, but also to carry the responsibility of helping that person become free of that entanglement. Here we find Paul's theme of mutual accountability. The Christian, when seeing a sister stumbling into sin, does not go to the other side of the road in the way the Levite and Pharisee did in the parable of the good Samaritan (Luke 10:25–37). Rather, like the Samaritan, the Christian approaches the sister "in the Spirit of gentleness," does whatever he or she can, and so works through the problem with that sister until she learns to live "in the Spirit."

The principle, then, of restoration is loving one another. Christians are responsible for one another and, because of the love of God that comes to them through the Spirit, they carry one another's burdens when those burdens are too difficult for one person to carry.

The problem of pride (vv. 3–5). As mentioned above, the problem that occupies Paul's attention while addressing restoration is pride on the part of the restorer. Pride is wrong (v. 3), and each restorer should check himself or herself out (v. 4a) and not find personal status by comparison with others, especially with sinning brothers and sisters (v. 4b). In the final analysis, each person is responsible before God for what he or she has done (v. 5).

---

6. Cf. here H. D. Betz, *Galatians*, 299–301.

7. On this question, see D. J. Moo, "The Law of Moses or the Law of Christ," in *Continuity and Discontinuity: Perspectives on the Relationship Between the Old and New Testaments. Essays in Honor of S. Lewis Johnson, Jr.*, ed. J. S. Feinberg (Westchester, Ill.: Crossway, 1988), 208–17; R. N. Longenecker, *Galatians*, 275–76.

Our only comment here is addressed to the tension between carrying each other's burden (Gk. *ta bare;* v. 2) and carrying one's own burden (Gk. *to idion phortion;* v. 5). The issue is not contradictory but two sides of one coin. Christians need to help one another in the struggles of life, but each Christian will also have to answer to God individually. Part of that individual responsibility is carrying the burdens of others. Before God one cannot look around at others and thereby find grounds for justifying oneself. That Christians will be judged by God for their works, their actions, and their motives is taught elsewhere in Paul's letters (cf. Rom. 2:6–16; 14:12; 1 Cor. 3:8; 4:1–5; 2 Cor. 5:10).

Spiritual People Should Support Teachers (v. 6)

HAVING DISCUSSED THE problem of a sinful brother and the process of restoring him without getting caught up in the web of pride, Paul closes with an underlying principle: each person must stand before God and be personally responsible. But this raises a problem that Paul knew all too well: those who are full-time teachers cannot really live completely independently; they need the financial support of others. So Paul now curbs his idea that everyone should carry his own load with the idea that an exception is granted to teachers: they need support because they cannot always carry their own load. This verse, then, is little more than a parenthetical remark—a footnote if you will, and one whose logic is not so easy to discern.

The only issue is whether or not Paul has in mind financial sharing. The vast majority of commentators think the issue is financial and I agree. Paul elsewhere speaks to the rights of those who minister the Word to be rewarded with financial support (cf. 1 Cor. 9:14; 2 Cor. 11:7–12; Phil. 4:10–19; 1 Thess. 2:6, 9; 1 Tim. 5:17–18), even though Paul himself refused such help (1 Cor. 9:12–18; 2 Cor. 11:7–12; Phil. 4:10–20; 1 Thess. 2:9; 2 Thess. 3:6–13). Paul drew on Jesus' own teachings (Matt. 10:10 par.; Luke 10:7). F. F. Bruce puts it succinctly: "The teacher relieves the ignorance of the pupil; the pupil should relieve the teacher of concern for his subsistence."[8]

This little statement is a revelation about early Christian teaching and teachers, whose primary responsibility was to pass on traditions from the apostles and to interpret those traditions for their churches.[9] Here we find that teachers worked full-time in their ministry so that they could study and

---

8. F. F. Bruce, *Galatians*, 263.

9. A survey of the data can be found in J. D. G. Dunn, *Jesus and the Spirit: A Study of the Religious and Charismatic Experience of Jesus and the First Christians as Reflected in the New Testament* (Philadelphia: Westminster, 1975), 282–84.

teach effectively; they were apparently being disrespected in the Christian community to the degree that their students were not taking care of them. Such treatment was inconsistent with "life in the Spirit" because it was unloving and unkind (5:22–23). We can guess that such disrespect was an extension of the Judaizing controversy: perhaps the teachers were part of the Pauline wing of the churches and were now being neglected by the Judaizing wing. Such a result of factionalism would not be surprising.

Spiritual People Are Accountable to God (vv. 7–10)

AFTER THE PARENTHESIS of verse 6, Paul gives the foundation of his instructions in verse 5, that people will have to stand before God. His point here is clear: since we will stand before God, we must live now before God, and that means living in the Spirit. Put differently, we must do good to all people, especially to the church, which may well have been neglected by those caught up in the divisions at Galatia.

That the antithesis of flesh and Spirit has been in Paul's mind since he began these injunctions at verse 1 becomes clear with verse 8. What we envision here is a divisiveness that was leading to shunning sinning brothers and sisters, to arrogant leadership, to comparing one's righteousness with another's, and to outright ugly treatment of teachers. Such kinds of behavior are "works of the flesh" (5:19–21).

So Paul enters with the strongest foundation that one can perceive: God is the Judge,[10] and people cannot sneer at him. Paul knows that "moral indifference would be an imperfection in God, not a perfection."[11] If a person lives to the flesh, that person will "reap destruction" (condemnation); if a person lives "in the Spirit," that person will "reap eternal life." What Paul is saying is what I have said on numerous occasions in this book: while works do not save us, no one is saved without works. Why? Very simply, because works are the sure indicators of a person's heart, orientation, and status before God. Every judgment in the Bible is a judgment according to works (cf. Matt. 7:13–27; 16:27; 22:1–14; 25:1–46; 2 Cor. 5:10; Rev. 20:11–15). A person's final standing before God will be determined by that person's relationship to Jesus Christ as revealed in his or her works. While it is absolutely true that our grounds of acceptance is the sacrifice Jesus Christ made on our behalf, our connection to that sacrifice is by way of a faith that works itself out in the many good works in a person's life.

---

10. See J. I. Packer, *Knowing God* (Downers Grove: InterVarsity Press, 1973), 125–33.
11. Ibid., 130.

So Paul speaks of "doing good," because doing good is what it means to sow "to please the Spirit." We should not become weary in doing good because, he repeats, our judgment is based on this ("we will reap a harvest if we do not give up"; v. 9). Paul then argues that the Christian is to do good "to all people," regardless of their culture, nation, or sex (3:28). But the Christian's deeds of mercy are especially (though not exclusively) to be directed toward "the family of believers."

In sum, Paul interweaves two highly fundamental ideas for Christian ethics: mutual accountability and personal responsibility. Indeed, John Barclay sees the alternation between two themes as the structural impulse behind our section.[12] He uses the terms in a reverse direction (personal accountability to God and corporate responsibility to others), and I shall change them to my terms to ease understanding. His structure (changed in terms only) is as follows:

The Heading (5:25–26)
A. Mutual accountability (6:1a)
    B. Personal responsibility (v. 1b)
A. Mutual accountability (v. 2)
    B. Personal responsibility (vv. 3–5)
A. Mutual accountability (v. 6)
    B. Personal responsibility (vv. 7–8)
A. Mutual accountability (vv.9–10)

Bridging Contexts

BEFORE THE READER of the Bible launches out into his or her world with the messages of personal responsibility and mutual accountability, he or she needs to have a firm grasp of the essentials of this text and of what it meant when Paul said it. This means a careful delineation of the text in its context and of what Paul meant by crucial expressions like "mutual accountability," "personal responsibility," and "living in the Spirit." To do this means to read his letters and the book of Acts to see just how Paul worked out his ideas. We are not fair to Paul if we take his terms (e.g., "carry one another's burdens"), distill them into our own ("mutual accountability"), and then start inferring what mutual accountability means today when our applications are not Paul's. It takes patience and industry to be a faithful applier of Scripture—the patience of much study to answer our own questions about application and the industry of intensive group study to come to terms with all that we need to have in our hand to get the job done.

12. J. M. G. Barclay, *Obeying the Truth*, 146–77, esp. 147–55.

I want to explore this approach a little more completely here. A great deal of abuse has been dispensed in the name of *mutual accountability*. Some have argued straight from mutual accountability to Christian communities (we tend to use the word "communes" here) and have pointed sharp fingers at the vast majority of Christian churches. But this is surely wrong for, as any reader can see, Paul did not establish communes in which there was complete economical partnership and the sharing of all possessions. To be sure, Christians living with one another, sharing their possessions, and so producing a team effort in their witness to the saving activity of God is a *possible application* of the concept of mutual accountability.

Furthermore, I find places like Reba Place Fellowship in Evanston, IL, Sojourners Fellowship in Washington, D.C., and the Jubilee Fellowship of Germantown in Philadelphia, Pa., to be inspiring, encouraging, and challenging.[13] Their simplicity, their focus on things eternal, and their wholesome relational atmosphere certainly challenge the normal Western capitalistic complexity with its focus on things material and its stunting of personal relationships. On the other hand, to claim that this communitarian form of life is the *only* biblical model is simply wrong, for it is not the only model to be inferred from the Bible. Agreed, such a lifestyle can be rooted in biblical principles, and the people who so choose can live effectively for the kingdom of God in this form; but such a lifestyle is not the only way to describe how early Christians lived. In fact, I am prepared to argue that such a lifestyle was indeed abnormal in the ancient world and rare among Christians.

But refutation of this lifestyle is neither my desire (since I find it wholesome and clearly an effective form of life) nor my purpose. Rather, what I want to point out is that claiming such a lifestyle to be rooted in the biblical sense of mutual accountability is not accurate because this is not the kind of communities Paul left behind when he declared his ethic of "carrying one another's burdens." To be fair, of course, I should point out that these communities do not base their existence and concepts on Galatians 6:1–10, but on texts like Matthew 6:25–34; Luke 9:57–62; Acts 2:43–47; 4:32–5:11; 2 Corinthians 8–9; Ephesians 4:28; and 1 Timothy 6:9–10. Nor do I want to suggest that their whole foundation is the sense of mutual accountability, though I am sure this is fundamental to their ideas. Rather, my goal in

---

13. For a description of biblical principles that function behind such communities, I recommend reading R. J. Sider, ed., *Living More Simply: Biblical Principles and Practical Models* (Downers Grove, Ill.: InterVarsity Press, 1980). The book is a collection of short and readable chapters on both biblical principles and the various ways many have applied these principles. There are chapters on family simplicity as well as on how to be more biblical economically in the professional life.

this section is to point out a possible misapplication (community lifestyle is mandated) of a biblical idea (mutual accountability) and to point out that the surest way of applying such a principle correctly is to see how Paul applies it. What mutual accountability can look like in our world will be explored below.

Yet another typical reading of this passage, especially one focusing on verses 4–5, 7–10, is one that explores the implications of *personal responsibility*. Paul speaks here of such things as each person testing his (or her) own actions to make sure that pride is not present, of each person carrying his (or her) own load, and of the correspondence between each person's life and actions to God's final assessment of that person. This has led some to a Western sense of personal individualism because context has been neglected. For these people Paul is saying that they are accountable to no one but God; that pastors have no rights inquiring into their past, their present, or their plans for the future; that religion is exclusively a private matter, like politics and sex;[14] and that, since they stand before God alone, they are to live alone. But once again we see an interpretation that is fundamentally sound at first but one that goes astray because it neglects two things: the wider context (where personal responsibility before God is surrounded by a mutual accountability) and the way Paul himself actually lived.

To take but one example: while Paul was fiercely independent in his sense of calling and his perception of the gospel (see chaps. 1–2), he was willing to submit his ideas and his calling to the wider churches to see if he was running in vain. Paul says, "But I did this [i.e., laid before them the essentials of his gospel] privately to those who seemed to be leaders [whom Paul was willing to brush aside if necessary; cf. 2:6], for fear that I was running or had run my race in vain" (2:2). He then, gleefully I think, says that these same leaders "gave me and Barnabas the right hand of fellowship" (v. 9). Once again, a principle (personal responsibility) needs to be understood in context and in terms of the realities of life as Paul applied that principle.

These two themes, mutual accountability and personal responsibility, fight against a major Western feature of life that I have already examined, namely, individualism.[15] Mutual accountability forces many of us to abandon our sense of being alone and forces us to reach out to others. It makes the neighbor stand up and say, "I truly am a neighbor and must be neighborly." It makes the person abandon the natural (modern) impulse of letting all others do their own thing and pushes that person to invade another's life. It

---

14. See the clever portrayal of this in O. Guiness, *The Gravedigger File* (Downers Grove, Ill.: InterVarsity Press, 1983), 71–89.

15. See above, pp. 254–55.

also forces the neighbor to allow his or her life to be open enough to others to be invaded, to be a neighbor in a genuine sense. To be a neighbor means to be both neighborly and receptive to neighborliness.

Also, Paul's message fights against the tenacity so many Westerners have with respect to their personal responsibility. While each claims this as an inalienable right, it forces each of us to face the fact that, though we are individuals, we are not solitary individuals. We are individuals in need of community, in need of others, and in need of fellowship. To be human is to relate to God and to others. Our personal responsibility before God does not relieve us from accountability to others, nor does it put us on a deserted island to live a solitary life. These are Western problems that need to be faced, and the message of Paul—a mutual accountability that does not deny personal responsibility and a personal responsibility that includes a mutual accountability—stares our world in the face.

I make one more observation regarding personal responsibility. In our culture we have become acutely aware of the origins and causes of our behavior. I am aware, for instance, that certain aspects of my personality come from what I learned from my father and my mother; I am aware as well that some of my traits (both good and bad) appear in my two children. This is a common perception today. But in this process, at times *there is an implicit excuse* for our personality traits or our behavior. "I cannot help it," one might cry, "because this was how I was raised." Or, "You would not blame me if you knew my past." We must sympathize here with the obvious reality that what we do and who we are result from what others have made us, and we should not refrain from recognizing that certain bad dimensions of people are not solely their fault. But what the Bible teaches is that *we are personally responsible for everything we are and for everything we do, regardless of the causes and problems we might have*. This, of course, leads to an entire feature of application: urging people to accept responsibility for everything they do and are. Paul teaches that we must "bear our own burdens" in this regard.

WHILE THE EMPHASIS of Paul is clearly on mutual accountability and personal responsibility—and I shall look more at these themes below—there are other comments made by Paul here that can be directly applied to our day. For instance, verse 6 exhorts the student to share his financial resources with his or her teacher. This is neither a suggestion nor a commandment, but it is nonetheless a principle that was broadly applied by Paul. John Stott pointedly discusses two dangers in the application of this principle: abuse by the minister and abuse by the congregation.[16]

Regarding abuse by the minister, even though Paul exhorted students to share with their teachers (cf. also 1 Cor. 9:14; 1 Tim. 5:17), he himself refused to accept their offers (1 Cor. 9:12–18; 2 Cor. 11:7–12; Phil. 4:10–20; 1 Thess. 2:9; 2 Thess. 3:6–13), so that he could preach the gospel without any kind of hindrance. I see two abuses possible, one financial and one relating to character. Financially, Paul was not suggesting that teachers/ministers could demand salaries and benefits. What they could expect was that their needs would be taken care of, not that they could dictate economical policies regarding their livelihood. His directive here is intended for the student/congregation to obey, not for the minister to demand. As for a character problem, Stott contends that it is too often the case that ministers who live off the financial benefit of others become lazy and neglectful of their duties. These may be found at the golf course too frequently, on vacations too often, or discharging their work load to others in the name of delegating responsibility or "lay ministry."

The other area of abuse is by the congregation. This can take on several colors. It can lead to the feeling of employment on the part of the congregation or church board and result in the congregation believing it can control the teacher's ministry. "They pay the piper, they say; so they must be allowed to call the tune."[17] It can also lead to a feeling of control over what the minister buys and how he spends his or her money. But while I firmly believe in a minister's accountability to his or her charges, I also believe that a minister should have the character to spend his or her money wisely and be trusted in these matters. One minister might need a set of golf clubs, another might think a new car is in order, while still another might spend more money on clothing; each will have his or her own hobbies and interests. (By the way, John Stott's is bird watching, a fascination that has occupied many others, including the author of this book.) A final area of abuse by the congregation could be a sense of arrival. Some church members operate as if their contribution to the minister's salary finishes off their obligations in the church's ministries. They behave (never, I suppose, would they confess this) as if this is their "ministry": they believe they have arrived.

What about *mutual accountability* and *personal responsibility*, the main themes here? I can think of no better example of how to combine these two themes than by looking briefly at the life of Dietrich Bonhoeffer and his writings. His story deserves to be told in some detail. Bonhoeffer, the son of a famous psy-

---

16. J. R. W. Stott, *Only One Way*, 167–69.
17. Ibid., 169.

chiatrist at the University of Berlin, studied theology at both Tübingen and Berlin and eventually landed a post as a lecturer in theology at Berlin. This was 1933, and Hitler was on the rise. Bonhoeffer saw in Hitler a madman bent on destruction, and so he opposed him. His opposition forced him to leave Germany and to pastor two German congregations in London. While there, he was called by the Confessing Church of Germany (the Lutheran churches opposed to Hitler's plan) to be the leader of an illegal seminary that would train pastors for ministry in the Confessing Church.

He decided to return to Germany and lead a small group of students in Zingst. Then they had to relocate in Finkenwalde. There they studied together, lived together, and worshiped together. After writing three of his most famous books in this context (*Life Together, The Cost of Discipleship,* and *The Prayer Book of the Bible: An Introduction to the Psalms*),[18] the Nazi authorities closed the seminary and banned Bonhoeffer from writing. A brief visit to the United States endeared him to many on this side of the ocean, but he knew his calling was to return to Germany and oppose the *Führer.* He returned to become part of the resistance movement, both by speaking in clandestine groups and by writing things that would later be published. But on April 5, 1943, he was arrested with other family members who were in the resistance. He spent time in the prisons at Tegel, Buchenwald, Schönberg, and finally at Flossenburg, where he was hanged. The day before his hanging he had given a sermon on the text, "with his stripes we are healed." He died as a witness to the concrete responsibility necessary for the Christian as well as to the commitment a Christian must have to others.

His book describing and defining how Christians must live together is called *Life Together.* This profound little book stirs the reader to this day as he or she is confronted with the implications of Christian fellowship. My worn, marked, and tattered copy has brought me many insights into personal relationships and challenged me over and over. The first two chapters cover "Community" and "The Day with Others." Since I would like simply to republish the entire contents, I must restrain my quotations.

Before quoting from Bonhoeffer, I pass on Eberhard Bethge's comment on attending Bonhoeffer's lectures:

---

18. I am dependent here on the introduction to *Life Together,* ed. J. W. Doberstein (San Francisco: Harper and Row, 1954), 7–13. The definitive biography of Bonhoeffer was written by his student, E. Bethge, *Dietrich Bonhoeffer* (San Francisco: Harper and Row, 1970). A marvelous selection of his works can be sampled in J. DeGruchy, *Dietrich Bonhoeffer: Witness to Jesus Christ* (San Francisco: Collins, 1988). Another moving, and shorter, biography is E. Robertson, *The Shame and the Sacrifice: The Life and Martyrdom of Dietrich Bonhoeffer* (New York: Collier Books, 1988).

The first classes at Zingst were, for the newcomers, a breath-taking experience. Suddenly the realization burst upon them that they were not there simply to learn new techniques of preaching and instruction, but were to be initiated into something that represented altogether revolutionary prerequisites for those activities.[19]

The essential course for his students revolved around his stunning lectures on discipleship, now published as *The Cost of Discipleship*.[20]

Here, then, is a sampling of Bonhoeffer's inspiring thoughts about community from *Life Together*. The foundation for Christian community and for accountability is Jesus Christ. "It is grace, nothing but grace, that we are allowed to live in community with Christian brethren."[21] "One is a brother to another only through Jesus Christ."[22] "Not what a man is in himself as a Christian, his spirituality and piety, constitutes the basis of our community. What determines our brotherhood is what the man is by reason of Christ."[23]

But Bonhoeffer knew the realities of life together, that it would involve disappointment with others, frustrations, and anger. Thus, he argues, we must dispense with illusory fantasies about some ideal state of communal life. "When the morning mists of [these] dreams vanish, then dawns the bright day of Christian fellowship."[24] Thus it becomes clear that Christian fellowship is not ordinary human love and not possible apart from the Spirit of God. He says: "Human love produces human subjection, dependence, constraint; spiritual love creates *freedom* of the brethren under the Word."[25] And he concludes: "It is not the experience of Christian brotherhood, but solid and certain faith in [this] brotherhood, that holds us together."[26]

These harsh realities of life together led Bonhoeffer to a chapter entitled "The Day With Others." He legislates for his students that "Common life under the Word begins with common worship at the beginning of the day."[27] And so, "at the beginning of the day let all distraction and empty talk be silenced and let the first thought and the first word belong to him to whom our whole life belongs."[28] This "common" (in the title of the book itself) wor-

---

19. E. Bethge, *Dietrich Bonhoeffer*, 369.

20. This is the most profound book I have ever read on Christianity: *The Cost of Discipleship*, trans. R. Fuller (New York: Macmillan, 1963).

21. *Life Together*, 20.

22. Ibid., 25.

23. Ibid., 25.

24. Ibid., 28–29.

25. Ibid., 37.

26. Ibid., 39.

27. Ibid., 42.

28. Ibid., 43.

ship included the Word of Scripture, hymns of the church, and prayer. After this, the Christian must go to work, but this must be done in constant communion with God. "Then from this achieved unity of the day the whole day acquires an order and a discipline."[29] Later he will say that life together involves the ministry of holding one's tongue, of meekness before God and others, of listening, of helpfulness, of bearing one another's burdens, of proclaiming the Word to one another, and of the ministry of the authority of service.

While Bonhoeffer's experience cannot normally be ours (who of us lives in this kind of community?), his principles retain their force. Christians form a community, a real community of sinful persons who have become attached to God through Christ and in the Spirit, and their community is their new life. They must live responsibly before God in freedom but with accountability to one another. They must confront one another because "nothing can be more cruel than the tenderness that consigns another to his sin. Nothing can be more compassionate than the severe rebuke that calls a brother back from the path of sin."[30] Bonhoeffer died as a martyr of Jesus Christ because he lived responsibly before God as an individual and because he was sustained by the fellowship of mutual accountability.[31]

I finish here with some thoughts on the importance of God being the judge as a foundation for our faith and ethics. C. S. Lewis began his famous radio lectures with this idea as implicit to all. Hidden in the consciousness of every human being is the concept that we ought to do certain things but that we do not always do them.[32] That "oughtness" is an innate sense of God's judgment, and it functions to motivate all humans to live properly. Now some will tell us that we do kind things to others because such action is good and right and because others deserve it; this is called altruism. Christian ethics, I suppose, has an element of altruism in it, but it is fundamentally wrong to think that the foundation of the Christian lifestyle is some supposed altruism. Instead, the foundation for Christian behavior is the grace of God that awakens us, the love of God that stirs us to action, and the holiness of God that stiffens our resolve to obey him. And behind each of these is the fact that

---

29. Ibid., 71.

30. Ibid., 107.

31. While editing this chapter a former student of mine, Evi Haüselmann, now busily serving the Lord in Switzerland, sent me the recent publication of the letters exchanged between Dietrich Bonhoeffer and his fiancée, Maria von Wedemeyer, while he was in prison. These letters, mostly unpublished, shed a new ray of light on the life of Bonhoeffer. Another book worthy of poring over is *Dietrich Bonhoeffer: A Life in Pictures*, ed. E. Bethge, et al. (Philadelphia: Fortress, 1986).

32. See C. S. Lewis, *Mere Christianity* (New York: Collier, 1952).

God will be our judge, that we will give account to him for everything done in the body, and that God is altogether honest and completely just.

This thought is uncomfortable for many. "How can a loving God punish?" they ask. The answer once again is context. The God of love in the Bible is also a God who is altogether holy and who will never act contrary to his holy and loving nature. Thus, the only foundation for acceptance with God is his method: his Son, Jesus Christ, expressed God's love in dying for us, but he had to die for us because God is holy (Rom. 3:21–25 discusses this). This means that God's justice is expressed in the cross as much as God's love is.

The message of Paul here is that God will judge us *justly*. This should create fear, holy fear, on our part. C. S. Lewis commented once that "our fear is precisely lest the judgement should be a good deal more righteous than we can bear."[33] It will be, but we are not to shrink from the concept of being judged. Instead, we are to trust in Christ all the more and stand with confidence before God, knowing we have done what God has called us to do— not perfectly (that is never demanded for the Christian), but honestly and with integrity that we have done what God has asked.

And Paul says that God will judge us *on the basis of our life*, whether it was "in the Spirit" or "in the flesh." This means, as I said above, that the final judgment, the judgment that will determine our entry into God's blessing, is rooted in our works. To be sure—and here I emphasize to the point of being pushy—the basis of our acceptance with God is what Christ has done on our behalf. But for God to assess whether we are attached to Christ, he will simply scan the evidence of our lives: Is it one of living "in the Spirit" or of living "in the flesh"? Those who live "in the Spirit" do so by faith and obedience; those who live "in the flesh" have sins aplenty to show for their time on earth.

The judgment of God, then, is a motivational force for the Christian. Someday we shall stand, each of us, before God. That realization makes us different and changes our lives, or it ought to. I do not know how this will happen (and those who claim they do "know too much," because they know more than what God has said), but I do know this much: we must each give an account and "the one who sows to please his sinful nature, from that nature will reap destruction; the one who sows to please the Spirit, from the Spirit will reap eternal life" (v. 8). Let us not garble this demand of God on our lives by minimizing the judgment; behind the judgment stands a holy and loving God who will always act in accordance with his love and his holiness. Judgment is inevitable for such a God.

---

33. C. S. Lewis, *Christian Reflections*, ed. W. Hooper (Grand Rapids: Eerdmans, 1967), 123.

Galatians 6:11–18

SEE WHAT LARGE letters I use as I write to you with my own hand! [12]Those who want to make a good impression outwardly[1] are trying to compel you to be circumcised. The only reason they do this is to avoid being persecuted for the cross of Christ. [13]Not even those who are circumcised obey the law, yet they want you to be circumcised that they may boast about your flesh. [14]May I never boast except in the cross of our Lord Jesus Christ, through which the world has been crucified to me, and I to the world. [15]Neither circumcision nor uncircumcision means anything; what counts is a new creation. [16]Peace and mercy to all who follow this rule, even[2] to the Israel of God.

[17]Finally, let no one cause me trouble, for I bear on my body the marks of Jesus.

[18]The grace of our Lord Jesus Christ be with your spirit, brothers. Amen.

MOST READERS OF the Bible scan the endings of letters because they think they have read the important stuff already, they think the conclusions to letters are merely conventional (Why get hung up on "Sincerely yours" when everyone says it?), or they are intent on getting on to their next book in the Bible. While no one should deny the conventional nature of a letter's ending, Paul's endings are not typical.

Regarding Galatians, Paul's conclusion is important for understanding his letter because in it (as in the introduction; 1:1–9) he emphasizes his main points. In fact, Hans Dieter Betz argues that the conclusion to Galatians is "most important for the interpretation of Galatians. It contains the interpretive clues to the understanding of Paul's major concerns in the letter as a whole and should be employed as the hermeneutical key to the intentions of the Apostle."[3] I do not know if we can go this far, but it is striking how many

---

1. The word translated "outwardly" is more literally translated "the flesh." See the footnote on the NIV text of 5:13.

2. Or, "and." See notes below.

3. H. D. Betz, *Galatians*, 313.

scholars have argued that the conclusion to Galatians is especially important for understanding the letter. We will examine why.

After analyzing all of Paul's letters, Richard Longenecker notes seven items that frequently occur in Pauline conclusions.[4] The following table, and some of the evidence from other Pauline letters, lists those items and whether or not such an item is found in Galatians.

Feature	References	Galatians
Grace Benediction	Rom. 16:20; 1 Cor. 16:23; Eph. 6:24	6:18
Greetings	Rom. 16:3–16; 2 Cor. 13:12; Col. 4:15	absent
Peace Wish	Rom. 15:33; Eph. 6:23; 2 Thess. 3:16	6:16
Signature	1 Cor. 16:21; Col. 4:18; Philem. 19	6:11
Concluding Summary	1 Cor. 16:13–18, 22; 2 Cor. 13:11	6:12–17
Request for Prayer	Rom. 15:30–32; Eph. 6:18–20	absent
Doxology	Rom. 16:25–27; Phil. 4:20; 2 Tim. 4:18	absent

As can be seen from this chart, Paul's conclusion to his letter to the Galatians does not contain the greetings, request for prayer, or doxology section that are often found in his other letters. Furthermore, his emphasis here is the "Concluding Summary." In no other Pauline letter do we find such an emphasis. Most scholars infer that a deviation from this "typical pattern" reveals Paul's hand and emphases.[5] Such a deviation may indeed be a lead for finding an emphasis, but two points must be considered. (1) If Galatians is Paul's first letter, then it is wrong to speak about "deviation," for no pattern has been yet developed for the letters. (2) It is simply not the case that these are "patterns" in the sense of set habits. While most letters contain most features, no letter contains all of them, and the order is apparently random. It is better to suggest that Paul's own "habits" developed over time and that only in his later letters can we approach the matter by way of finding deviation.

Be that as it may, any reader can see Paul's emphasis here: one final time he evaluates the issue of the Judaizers (vv. 12–17). This conclusion brings everything to a head. What confronts us here is Paul's adamant opposition to the nationalism of the Judaizers and their cultural imperialism. He is set against any presentation of the gospel that does not let surrender to Christ and life in the Spirit have their full sway. All that matter now, after Christ and the Spirit, is the "new creation."

---

4. R. N. Longenecker, *Galatians*, 287–88, where full evidence is cited.
5. See ibid., 287–88.

Paul ends this letter, then, with (1) a signature (v. 11), (2) a concluding summary that contains both a final glancing blow aimed at the Judaizers (vv. 12–13) and an expression of what he, in contrast, aims at (vv. 14–17), and (3) a grace benediction (v. 18). Each deserves some comment.

Paul's Signature (v. 11)

NOW THAT THE letter has come to its formal ending, Paul insists that he can do the writing. Thus, he takes the pen from his secretary (called an amanuensis). It was customary for ancient authors to use a secretary because they were trained to write quickly, neatly, and in limited space. Paul used secretaries elsewhere, and sometimes his conclusions reveal it (cf. Rom. 16:22; 1 Cor. 16:21–22; Col .4:16–18; 2 Thess. 3:17).

But what does it mean that Paul used "large letters"? There are three options: (1) Paul had bad eyesight that left him with trouble in writing—this is based on reading 4:13–16 as a reference to an eye disease, and I remain unconvinced that such is the best reading; (2) since Paul was absorbed in a craft, he never learned to write well—this is unlikely since many agree today that Paul was well-educated and writing well would be part of that education; (3) Paul's "large letters" are an ancient style of our "boldfacing" or "italicizing." This latter view has commended itself to a large number of scholars today. Already J. B. Lightfoot said that Paul wrote with large letters "to arrest the eye and rivet the mind."[6] It might be wise for publishers of New Testament translations to italicize verses 11–18.

Paul's Concluding Summary of the Situation (vv. 12–17)

ONE FINAL TIME Paul gets in a few more swats at the Judaizers by evaluating the situation. There are two sections here: Paul's critique of the Judaizers (vv. 12–13) and his evaluation of himself (vv. 14–17).

Paul finds four problems with the Judaizers: (1) Their method is force (v. 12a); (2) their motive is fear (v. 12b); (3) their consistency is flawed (v. 13a); and (4) their goal is to flaunt (v. 13b). He then evaluates himself by (1) revealing his goal (v. 14), (2) reiterating his perspective on nationalism (vv. 15–16), (3) and declaring his justification for being right: he has been persecuted (v. 17).

---

6. So J. B. Lightfoot, *Galatians*, 221; H. D. Betz, *Galatians*, 314; F. F. Bruce, *Galatians*, 268; R. N. Longenecker, *Galatians*, 290. It ought to be observed that at this time in history writers used all capital letters, did not separate words by a space, and did not make sure that a line ended with the end of a word.

The problems of the Judaizers (vv. 12–13). (1) The first problem is that the method of the Judaizers was *force* (v. 12a). While the leaders at Jerusalem did not "compel" Titus to be circumcised (2:3), these Judaizers were clearly trying to force the Galatians to accept circumcision to demonstrate their commitment to the law of Moses. To be sure, we are not to imagine here that the Judaizers were invading homes at the threat of death, stealing the males, and taking them to the edge of the city where a kosher knife was waiting. Instead, this force is both psychological and physical. They were demanding ("To be accepted by God you *must* do this!") this act as the completion of their conversion. They did this in the same way as Peter had been forcing others to eat according to Jewish food laws (2:14). But, as F. F. Bruce has said, "This was mere scalp-hunting."[7]

I have seen this kind of pressure exerted even today with the rite of adult immersion, where pastors and leaders and "significant others" have put considerable pressure on people to get them to admit their infant baptism was inadequate. At times, I have seen such people surrender to this force solely to avoid social shame—disrespecting their own conscience in the matter.

(2) Their motive was *fear* (v. 12b)—a fear of persecution. These Judaizers, coming as they did from Jerusalem, were getting pressured themselves from the Jews and conservative Jewish Christian parties in Jerusalem and Palestine over the kind of life the converts of Paul were actually living. They had been sent out (or rather pressured to go out) to get the converts of Paul in line with the basics of Judaism. Here is where Paul stepped in: their motive in all of this was "to avoid being persecuted for the cross of Christ." To fear persecution at the hands of the Jewish leaders in Jerusalem was nothing, as far as Paul was concerned. It was far more important to fear God and serve the Christ of the cross. Accordingly, Paul saw in their succumbing to the pressure of the Jerusalem Jews a denial of the gospel, and that is the heart of his letter: the Judaizing wing did not see what the cross of Christ did to nationalism and to the era of the law. They had come to their end in Christ, and now God's people was much larger than the Jewish nation.

(3) Their consistency was *flawed* (v. 13). As an aside, Paul contends that those who pushed circumcision as the ultimate sign of commitment to the law did not even keep the law themselves. It is not clear here whether the "circumcisers" and the "Judaizers" are the same group. At 2:12–13 I argued that the "circumcisers" were not the same as the "men from James," and it may be that the "circumcisers" here were not Christians at all. They may have been some zealous Jews who accompanied the Judaizers to make sure that the job

---

7. F. F. Bruce, *Galatians*, 270.

got done. In this case, they would represent Jerusalem and would be the ones who were actually putting the pressure on the Judaizing Christians. But we cannot be sure here; perhaps the circumcisers and Judaizers were the same group. Paul, however, treats them in a unified way because they ultimately were teaching the same thing: the law of Moses was God's means of acceptance. To argue against the people who were putting pressure on the Galatians or who were pressuring the Judaizers (who were, in turn, pressuring the Galatians) amounts to the same thing. Behind it all is a consistency that is flawed by sin.

This argument is called an *ad hominem argument*, an argument made by arguing against the people making the case. Thus, the issue becomes personal, not logical. By itself the argument that circumcision is wrong because those who embrace it do not keep the law themselves is inadequate; but as corroborating persuasion, it is most effective. Dr. Johnson, that British wit who wrote a dictionary, once blasted a woman's judgment about London when she complained that, after being in London, she always had dirty fingernails— against which Johnson retorted: "Perhaps, Madam, you scratch yourself."[8] She, of course, would have been humiliated and Johnson would have laughed (not to include those who heard him say this), but it says nothing about whether London is a good place to visit or not.

To return to our point, Paul says that the circumcisers were not good examples to follow because they could not even confirm the law of Moses in real life: they were hypocrites.

(4) Their goal was to *flaunt* (v. 13b): "that they may boast about your flesh."[9] Here Paul digs the knife even deeper: their goal in it all was to be able to return to Jerusalem and claim a prize, to claim that they had been successful and so gain the praise of the Jewish nationalists. They gloried in their statistics—statistics carefully kept about the number of converts they could count as their own, statistics on their ability to persuade Gentiles to go the whole way. All of this breathes the thick air of nationalism, which the cross of Christ ended when Jesus Christ absorbed the curse of the law (3:13).

Paul's self-evaluation (vv. 14–17). "But as for me . . ." Paul seems to be saying. He counters the approach of the Judaizers with his own by (1) revealing his goal (v. 14), (2) declaring his perspective on nationalism (vv. 15–16), and (3) declaring his justification for being right: his being persecuted (v. 17).

First, Paul *reveals his goal* (v. 14). The Judaizers may glory in the flesh, he says, but I glory exclusively in the cross of Christ. Paul knew that he had died

8. I take this story from D. H. Fischer, *Historians' Fallacies* (San Francisco: Harper and Row, 1970), 292.

9. The excised flesh of circumcision is surely in mind as well.

to the world and that the world had died to him through the cross. The world was connected to the law of Moses, and therefore the entire enterprise was done with. All that remains is Christ and glorying in the instrument that sets one free: the cross. Paul's entire goal was to glory in the cross of Christ, and so he would gladly accept persecution.

Second, Paul *declares his perspective on nationalism* (vv. 15–16). Once again, neither belonging to the Jewish nation (being circumcised) nor being a Gentile (not being circumcised) mattered: what mattered was that God had formed a new people, the church, and that this new people was an entirely "new creation." This new creation includes both Jews and Gentiles, slaves and free people, males and females (3:28); social and sexual distinctions no longer matter. God's work is the new creation principle, radically different from the nationalistic-cultural impulse that characterized Judaism. The new creation comes through faith in the crucified Christ (2:15–21), it is accompanied by the gifts of the Spirit (5:16–26), and it ends the curse of the law (3:13, 19-25) as well as the life in the flesh (5:19–21).

This new creation principle is frequently understood in the Western world in exclusively individualistic terms. Thus, verse 15 is paralleled to the individualistic comments of Paul elsewhere (e.g., Rom. 12:2; 2 Cor. 3:18; 4:16; 5:17). While it is certainly wrong to exclude the individual from this principle, narrowing it to an individual is inaccurate. What Paul is doing here is contrasting two systems, the circumcision system of Moses and the uncircumcision system of the Gentile world. He insists it does not matter whether you are Jew or Gentile; what matters now is that there is no national circle into which one must enter to join the people of God. What matters is that you are part of God's new people, God's new creation, God's new humanity. I add that determining meaning here is crucial for application; for if the idea is purely individual, then the application concerns personal relationship to God and conversion, but if the idea is the new people of God, then the application should address both personal conversion and cultural imperialism.

As Paul had cursed those who preached a different gospel (the gospel of nationalism) at the beginning of his letter (1:6–9), so now he blesses with peace those who embrace this view: "peace and mercy to all who follow this rule." What "rule"? What "standard of measurement"? The rule of universalism, the standard of measurement that does not take into consideration a person's nationality. The ones who consider a person in light of Christ and his cross are the "Israel of God."[10]

But who is this "Israel of God"? Is Paul repeating himself (so that "all who follow this rule" and "Israel of God" are identical), or is he adding a new group

---

10. The addition of "of God" to "Israel" indicates a true and false Israel. The true Israel is the Israel of God; the false Israel is simply Israel.

(so that "Israel of God" is something different from "all who follow this rule")? The Greek sentence reads literally: "And whoever follows this rule, peace on them and mercy, and on the Israel of God." This statement can be taken as a chiasm:

A. Whoever follows this rule
   B. Peace
   B.´ Mercy
A.´ Israel of God

In this case, the "whoever" and the "Israel of God" are identical, just as "peace" and "mercy" are put together into a synthesis. In this view, the church is now the "Israel of God" (emphasizing the continuity of the covenant with Abraham). After all, all the church can be called "children of Abraham" and the "true circumcision" (3:29; Phil. 3:3).[11] Alternatively, "Israel of God" may refer only to "Jewish Christians." But this latter view goes against the grain of Paul's argument, which is clearly a debunking of any kind of social barriers and nationalism. There is a way out: translate the "and" before "Israel of God" as "especially" and see it as a special blessing for the Jewish Christian who have learned to see God's people in a much broader sense. This would have been difficult for Jews. Thus, Paul's message may be: "May God's peace and mercy come to all who live according to the new creation principle, especially on the Jews who can see their way through to the freedom of the Spirit and freedom from the law." Accordingly, "Israel of God" refers to the church, whether to the church as a whole or to the whole church, including Jewish Christians.

Another view of this verse contends that it is Paul's wish. As he longed for the day when "all Israel" would be saved (Rom. 11:26), so here he wishes peace on the true Israel, which will someday turn to faith in Christ. I am of the view, however, that this view is asking for too much from the words. Paul is making a comment on the new creation principle of verse 15, and he blesses those who live by this.

Yet another view has been proposed. Since Paul never describes the church as Israel, it is unlikely that he is doing so here. Accordingly, this expression must describe Jews as Jews, and Paul is wishing a blessing on his nation. The biggest problem with this view is that Paul sees no blessing, certainly not the blessing of God, on anyone outside of Christ.

Thus, I believe it is best to see here a blessing on the church, that is on all who live according to the new creation principle. A special blessing

---

11. So R. N. Longenecker, *Galatians*, 297–99, whose discussion of the expression is extensive.

belongs to those Jews ("the Israel of God") who have had to fight hard to break down those barriers that governed their lives for so long. In coming to Christ, they have become the true people of God.

Finally, Paul *presents a case for being right: he is being persecuted* (v. 17)—an argument he has used before (3:4; 4:21–31). That this theme is important to Paul is seen by its inclusion in this final summary. He claims that he bears on his body "the marks of Jesus." While some have guessed that early Christians adopted some sort of ritual sign of membership, a tattoo or a branding of slavery to Christ, it is more likely that Paul uses this expression for the many scars on his body as evidence for his persecution for following Christ (see 2 Cor 6:4–6; 11:23–30). The account of Acts 14:19 may be what Paul is referring to precisely. If the Judaizers had a "fleshly" sign, Paul had an even better one: signs of persecution. It is unlikely that the "marks of Jesus" on Paul have anything to do with the hundreds of cases of "stigmatization" that have occurred in the history of the church, most notably with Saint Francis of Assisi.[12]

Paul's grace benediction (6:18). Paul ends with a prayer, a prayer that is a wish of grace. Having said all he wanted and having spilled out his emotions, Paul's benediction is noticeably calm and positive. He prays that God's "grace" may be with "their spirit." And he calls them "brothers" once again. While "grace" is a typical "good-bye" in the ancient world, and though we need to be careful not to read too much theology into every appearance of "grace," we are somehow unable to resist here. Having spent his entire letter spelling out the universalistic implications of faith in Christ, the ending of the law in the death of Christ, and acceptance by God on the basis of surrendering to Christ, there is no wonder that we see here more in "grace" than a simple "good-bye."

Bridging Contexts

WHAT PAUL ARGUES for here is "the new creation principle." What does this mean? Paul believes that one is accepted by God if one surrenders to Christ in faith and so lives in the Spirit of God. This acceptance is granted to whoever believes, regardless of sex, race, or culture. His emphasis in Galatians, because of the cultural imperialism of the Judaizers, is on the "whoever" rather than the "believes," though he does emphasize faith at times.

---

12. For this, see *The Little Flowers of St. Francis*, trans. R. Brown (Garden City, N.Y.: Doubleday/Image Books, 1958). The original account of Brother Ugolino can be found at pp. 171–216, and an assessment by R. Brown is found at pp. 322–24. The vast majority of Protestants have explained these spontaneous bleedings of the hands, feet, and head as the result of autosuggestion.

This is the message of Galatians, and we have seen it over and over in the letter. Repetition, Paul shows, is the mother of all learning. This concluding summary ties it all together; thus, it is appropriate for the reader to take stock of what has been said, tie it all together, and once again think in general terms about Galatians. What we need to do here is once again to explore the essential message of Galatians and see how it "fits" in our world. To do this we need to summarize its message and the message of the Judaizers, and to examine once again the mainlines of application and relevance.

What we find, then, is the message of Paul banging heads with the gospel of the Judaizers. Their message was essentially a nationalism or a cultural imperialism tacked onto the gospel, that is, the necessity of joining the Jewish nation in order to become acceptable to God. To join the Jewish nation meant to adopt the law of Moses as the moral guideline and as the means of God's acceptance. Paul, on the contrary, argued that God accepts anyone who surrenders to his revelation in Christ, in the same way Abraham had surrendered to God's promise. What Paul was emphasizing in this statement is not faith so much as *anyone*. He contended that God had brought in a new era when Christ came, one that eclipsed the era of the law; the people of God have been anointed by the Holy Spirit, and everything has changed. There is no distinction of race, of culture, or of sex. There is a "new creation."

Is the message of Galatians relevant to our age? Indeed it is; it is as fresh today as it was then. Even if we at times have to strip a passage to its essentials, we end up with a message that is highly relevant. After understanding Paul's basic message in its context, we find plenty of material that is relevant to our age. That context is the battle in the first century between two systems of religion, one that contended acceptance was based on surrender to Christ and the other on surrender to Christ and Moses; and this battle was deeply enmeshed in cultural boundaries. It was nearly impossible for a God-fearing Jew to fathom embracing God's truth without following the law of Moses. But Paul contended vigorously that the law of Moses had come to its completion in Christ and the Spirit and that the tool of separating Jew from Gentile was now a blunted, ineffective instrument. What God counts is "faith working through love" and a new creation.

This principle of the new creation is what is relevant to our age, and we fight with this principle against all distinctions between peoples and all additions to the gospel. I stated in the introduction that there were several manifestations of these additions. (1) At times people add laws and regulations to the gospel in order to find acceptance with God or in order to maintain acceptance with God. It amounts to the same thing. (2) Others argue that certain experiences are necessary to be fully blessed by God or to experience full salvation. (3) Still others assume that one must be educated in order to be fully accepted by God. Of course, this is not in some written creed, for it is obviously wrong. But the message of the need of education comes across all the time to people in the pew who are made to feel that they cannot understand their faith unless they go to seminary or to a graduate school of theology/religion. These are three "additions" to the gospel that occur in our age as much as they did in Paul's.

(4) We also find the message of Paul highly relevant to the issues of cultural imperialism which have been a particular problem in missionary work. Not infrequently, natives sense that a missionary is trying to reconstruct a given area around the Western model, trying to turn new converts to Christ into Western Christians, and attempting to create a local church that is no different than the one that sits at a four-way stop on Main Street. Another way of looking at the relevance of Galatians concerns denominationalism, which at its root is often either racial or cultural in its bias. All this is nothing more than cultural imperialism.

To the degree that there are those around who add rules and regulations to the gospel, who suggest that either experiences or education are particularly important for full acceptance with God, or who suggest that true Christianity is white, black, Methodist, Anabaptist, Roman Catholic, or Anglican—to that same degree Galatians is relevant to our world. Inasmuch as there are people of each persuasion who are contending for their views vigorously each day, it becomes fundamentally important for those who want to be biblical and Pauline to come to grips with the message of Galatians and to make its message known and felt in our world today.

IN THIS FINAL section I want to apply the general message of Galatians to two situations in our society: a movement called Christian Reconstructionism, and the Roman Catholic Church.

Christian Reconstructionism, sometimes called the Theonomy (God's law) movement, is found today in Protestant fundamentalism and evangelicalism. Its essential impulse is the belief that the law of Moses is the divine order for the world and society.[13] Hence, these people (with variations, of course) seek to apply the law of Moses to all of life with a view of reconstructing society. Its main leaders, articulate in their presentations, have been R. J. Rushdoony, Greg Bahnsen, and Gary North. They argue that the law must be applied

---

13. A brief summary may be found by R. R. Clapp, "Reconstructionism, Christian," in *Dictionary of Christianity in America*, ed. D. G. Reid, et al. (Downers Grove, Ill.: InterVarsity Press, 1990), 977–78.

exhaustively and in detail, including a widespread use of the death penalty for those involved in sodomy, Sabbath violations, and even disobedience of parents by children.

I sat in a Sunday school class one day next to a couple who were theonomists. Their applications were straight from Old Testament law, including such issues as dress (no mixing of various cloths), sexuality, and even dietary laws (no pork, no shrimp). They remind one of the Amish who squabble over whether women's dresses should be held together with hooks or pins (buttons are too modern). Behind all of this is the quest to become like the "golden days," rather than allowing for the adventure of letting the Spirit guide us into God's will for "our days." (Personally, I like my wife to wear Levi Dockers, and I prefer buttons and zippers! Thank you very much!)

Besides the alarm that most Western people would have with anyone so bold as to suggest death for disobedient children and to suggest its applicability for the entire society, and besides the implausible viability of applying laws designed for a theocratic society of Jews to our modernized, secular society, there is a fundamental problem with this movement that is revealed in the book of Galatians.[14] To show how unsettling the book of Galatians can be to members of this movement, I want to give an illustration of an encounter I had in class with two young Christian reconstructionists. I should add at this point that I am aware that there are excesses and that these should not be seen as representative of the entire movement. But these students do function to illustrate the importance this movement gives to the law of Moses.

The class was a New Testament survey, and the class theme happened to be Jesus' view of the law. I presented a (commonly held) view that Jesus believed the law had come to its fulfillment in his person and teachings (Matt. 5:17). By this I meant that he saw the Old Testament law as pointing forward to a "better day" when God's full will would be revealed to his people. The implication of this view was obvious: in some sense, the law of Moses is no longer binding on Christians. At this point these two students "jumped on my case" for suggesting that there was something wrong with the law (which I did not suggest) and for suggesting that Christians were not obliged to keep the law of Moses (which I did then, and do now, believe).

In response to them I went to Galatians 3:19–25 and argued that the law was never given to provide life, that its purpose was to reveal sin and increase sin-consciousness, and that it was fulfilled in God's gift of the Spirit to his church. Therefore, I argued further, the Christian is bound to live in the Spirit

---

14. A thorough critique of the movement may be found in W. S. Barker and W. R. Godfrey, *Theonomy: A Reformed Critique* (Grand Rapids: Zondervan, 1990).

and not under the law of Moses as the moral guide for Christian life. These two students were visibly upset, threw the class into turmoil for nearly forty-five minutes, and, in my opinion, lost their ability to reason with me over the meaning of Scripture because they saw in the view I was teaching a total denial of what they believed. It became clear that to them, the law of Moses was for today and that I was denying the authority of Scripture. Interestingly, the next day they apologized to me for their behavior and both pledged to examine the texts more carefully. One of them presented a paper to me later on the topic that was well-thought out and carefully argued, though still not in line with what Galatians teaches.

The reason I bring this matter up is simple. Galatians teaches that *the law of Moses came to an abrupt halt for guiding God's people when Christ came to earth.* Galatians also teaches that God has appointed the Spirit of God as the sure guide to Christian morality and that the law of Moses is now to be seen as God's preliminary description of his will for his people but belonging to an era that is now passé. To use my old illustration again, obeying the law belongs to the manual typewriter era; but this is the computer age, and the response now is surrender to Christ and life in the Spirit.

In my view, the Christian reconstructionists are contemporary Judaizers. At times, they even move into heresy, though I am not sure that this is necessarily the case for this movement. There are variations among different theonomists and different applications made by those under its influence. Some have nothing but a heart after God that is slightly misdirected: what can be wrong with trying to agitate in one's society for God's will? The law of Moses is not, I repeat, contrary to the will of God. Others, however, go to the extreme, so that if one does not adopt their view of God's law, then that person is wrong or, at best, deeply inferior and out of God's blessing. While these people may preach the gospel of grace, faith, and Christ, the message that is conveyed is the gospel of Moses. And when this happens, these people become little different from a modern Judaizer.

What about *Roman Catholicism?* I have resisted this application since the introduction for two reasons: (1) Galatians is not about "works righteousness," which is the main accusation many evangelicals have about Roman Catholics, which may or may not be true; and (2) we need to focus on applications that are directly relevant to the issues Paul faced: cultural imperialism and nationalism and the demand of the Mosaic law. How do Protestant polemics against Roman Catholicism fit into all this?

First, there is genuine faith in the Roman Catholic Church (=RCC). Some may stand aghast at this statement; others may see it as trite—this point is intended for the former group. Anyone who genuinely opens his or her mind to the facts will, through discussions with RCs, realize that the RCC has within it both genuine Christians and non-Christians—just like other denominations.

Once when I was traveling to Indianapolis on a short flight from Chicago, I sat next to a nice-looking young gentleman. I needed to prepare a little for a lecture I was giving, so I took out my Greek New Testament and began to read. The man next to me asked me what I was reading. Telling people the New Testament (in Greek!) is not always the easiest entry into conversation, but I told him. He then said, "Which book?" I then said, "Matthew." "I love Matthew," he responded. We were friends because it is my favorite book as well. We talked all the way to Indianapolis, but the time I lost in preparation did not seem to matter. I learned that he was a good student of the Bible; that he trusted in Christ daily; that he based his entire life in a dependency on the Holy Spirit; that he had a disciplined prayer life; that he was regularly involved in evangelism; that he was a youth leader at his local church; that he had been to Chicago for a youth conference; and then I learned that he was a RC. His being a RC made no difference in my realization that he was a wonderful Christian man. As we departed, we blessed each other with "The peace of the Lord be with your spirit," to which I responded "And with your spirit as well." (I had heard enough liturgy to respond appropriately!) This point is clear: There are genuine believers in the RCC, and it is contrary to Galatians to think that all true believers are outside that body. Galatians teaches us to evaluate on the basis of faith in Christ and life in the Spirit.

On the other hand, however, I do want to say that I am a Protestant, and I grieve over some of the theology taught in the RCC and over the impact it seems to have on many of its parishioners. This is where the Judaizing accusation comes in. The RCC has set up, through its history, an elaborate approach to God; the one that troubles me most is the view that "outside the church there is no salvation/grace" (*extra ecclesiam nulla conceditur gratia*). While this view has been modified since the Second Vatican Council,[15] it remains an important part of Roman Catholicism to this day. Anyone who embraces this view and equates people of God with the RCC is in essence a Judaizer, for it is nothing other than cultural imperialism in religious dress. Just as the Judaizers said you had to become a Jew to be a full Christian, so some RCs claim that one must become a RC to become a full Christian.

---

15. For those who want to read the proper document here, see A. P. Flannery, *Documents of Vatican II* (Grand Rapids: Eerdmans, 1975), document #28 ("The Dogmatic Constitution of the Church"), 350–440.

What about "works"? Do RCs think one is "saved by works"? I do not want to get into any elaborate discussion of RC theology and its soteriology, but it is often enough at odds with the Protestant principles of salvation to say that there is a problem here. But more importantly, we need to look at what it takes to be accepted by God. According to Galatians, one must surrender to Christ and so live in the Spirit. Anything contrary to this, anything added to this (subtraction is not the issue), is contrary to Galatians and can be called "works" (but probably not totally in line with what "works" means in Galatians). I fear, at times, that RCs do add to this simple message. For some, one must attend weekly mass, confess his or her sins on a regular basis, donate money to the church, and/or be a RC to be a Christian and to be accepted by God. Anyone who teaches this becomes a modern Judaizer. But I should hasten to add that it is not just RCs who do this; other Christians do it as well.

The heart of the problem is probably the common perception on the part of RCs that one is saved through the sacraments, by taking communion on Sunday. This perception (whether truly RC or not) is there, and I have run into it hundreds of times in my conversations with RCs. This is contrary to the gospel *if the person thinks that the actual sacrament is necessary for acceptance with God.* There is no harm in weekly partaking in communion if that communion is seen as an expression of one's faith in the sufficiency of Christ's work on our behalf. There is harm, however, if that person thinks salvation is actually dependent on the partaking in the sacraments. So, for the RC, the additions of the sacraments (baptism, confirmation, eucharist, penance, anointing the sick, marriage, and orders) can be a snare for adding to the message of the gospel. Always? No. Sometimes? Yes.

This application to the RCC needs to be seen in perspective. Paul is no more against the abuses of Catholic theology than he is of Protestant theology. What matters is that God has acted for us in Christ, we must surrender in faith to Jesus Christ, and we must live in the Spirit. What matters is that there is a new creation principle operating on our behalf. It does not matter if we are, in origin, Jew or Gentile, Roman Catholic or Protestant, man or woman, black or white, employee or employer. These distinctions are done away with by Christ. What matters now is "faith working through love" and the "new creation."

Who, then, are the *primary targets of Galatians in our world?* This is the best question we can ask of ourselves. The answer is not a specific group, whether that group be defined religiously (Judaism, Roman Catholics, Christian Reconstructionists, Baptists, Amish), sexually (males, females), or culturally (Americans, Europeans, Africans). It does no good just to point fingers at others, for the real problem is far more subtle than that. The target of

Galatians today is *anyone who depreciates Jesus Christ as sufficient Savior and minimizes the power of the Holy Spirit as sufficient guide.* It is a disposition, often transcending or neglecting one's theological viewpoints, toward what God has done for us through Christ and in the Spirit. Whoever minimizes the sufficiency of Christ or discounts the power of the Spirit finds the finger of Paul pointing right at him or her. Whenever we are tempted to type once more on that manual typewriter for fear of what the computer might do for us, we are guilty of the Judaizing heresy. We, then, are the targets.

Paul's message is powerful and liberating. Søren Kierkegaard once said that "whereas Christ turned the water into wine, the church has succeeded in doing something more difficult; it has turned wine into water."[16] That is what Paul's message in Galatians is all about: turning the water of the flesh into the wine of the Spirit. Galatians challenges each of us to let that water be turned into wine by letting the Spirit have control of our lives—whoever we are, wherever we come from, and whatever sex we may be.

May the grace of God be with you, may the Spirit of Christ fill you, and may the universalism of the church guide you; through Christ and in the Spirit. Amen.

---

16. I borrow this quote from D. F. Watson, *I Believe in the Church* (Grand Rapids: Eerdmans, 1978), 13 (undocumented quotation of Kierkegaard).

Scripture Index

Scripture Index